Colorado's Fourteeners

From Hikes to Climbs

Second Edition

Gerry Roach

Fulcrum Publishing
Golden, Colorado

To my sister, Jan Roach.
She taught me how to climb the mountains of my mind.

Library of Congress Cataloging-in-Publication Data
  Roach, Gerry.
    Colorado's fourteeners : from hikes to climbs / Gerry Roach.—2nd ed.
      p.   cm.
    Includes index.
    ISBN 1-55591-412-8 (pbk.)
      1. Mountaineering—Colorado—Guidebooks.   2. Hiking—Colorado—Guidebooks.
    3. Backpacking—Colorado—Guidebooks.   4. Colorado—Guidebooks.   I. Title
    GV199.42.C6R63   1999
    796.52'2'09788—dc21   98–50301
                                                                   CIP

Book and map design by Bill Spahr

Printed in Thailand
0 9 8 7 6 5 4 3 2 1

Fulcrum Publishing
350 Indiana Street, Suite 350
Golden, Colorado 80401-5093
(800) 992-2908 • (303) 277-1623
website: www.fulcrum-books.com
e-mail: fulcrum@fulcrum-books.com

Contents

List of Photographs

List of Maps

Mount of the Holy Cross and Angelica couloir.

Preface

Colorado's Fourteeners: From Hikes to Climbs is a celebration of the joys that come from climbing Colorado's highest peaks. Colorado's 14,000-foot peaks offer the hiker and mountaineer one of the finest arrays of alpine challenges in the Rocky Mountains. You can be in the heart of Colorado's fourteener country in a few hours from its metropolitan areas, and the proximity of these peaks to population centers makes them even more precious. A lifetime of adventures is waiting for you in Colorado's mountains. Climbing fourteeners has become increasingly popular in recent years, and the challenge of climbing all the fourteeners captures many people. The elevation celebration continues.

This guide offers a broad view of Colorado's fourteeners. Besides the often-climbed standard routes, it describes many alternate routes on the easier fourteeners and, also, several technical routes. Most of the routes on Colorado's fourteeners are walk-ups (Class 1, Class 2, Easy Snow), but there are many wonderful scrambles (Class 3, Moderate Snow) and technical climbs (Class 4, Class 5, Steep Snow) on these peaks. For the best routes, regardless of difficulty, I use the designation *Classic*. Most climbers on Colorado's fourteeners climb the standard routes, and these routes are becoming crowded. However, you can still spend days climbing fourteeners and never see another person. If you are tired of crowded routes, try Longs' Loft Route, Democrat's North Ridge Route, Elbert's Southeast Ridge Route, Yale's East Ridge Route, the western approaches to the Crestones or El Diente's South Slopes Route. Colorado is still full of wilderness!

I grew up climbing with the following definition of difficulty: 5.7 is *hard* climbing, 5.8 is where you worry about falling off and 5.9 is where you *are* falling off. If this definition sounds familiar, this book is for you. The hardest climb in this guide is rated 5.8. Over the years, I have cherished the easy routes as much as the harder ones, and I have included a mixture of routes that will titillate the senses of almost anybody. All the routes described in this guide lead to the summit of a peak.

This is a guidebook pure and simple. It describes where to climb but not how to climb. No book can make judgments for you, but there are several good instructional books that can aid the process of learning the fundamentals. For an introduction to the sport of mountaineering, I recommend

Mountaineering: The Freedom of the Hills by Don Graydon and The Mountaineers book staff (Seattle: The Mountaineers, 1998).

The trailheads I describe are places passenger cars can reach. Sometimes these places are well-marked parking lots at the end of a road, and sometimes they are just places along a continuing road where the road becomes too rough for passenger cars. Four-wheel-drive vehicles can shorten many of the ascents in Colorado, but I have never felt like this aid was necessary. I need more mountain, not less.

Unlike most guidebooks, which are compilations of many people's route descriptions, this book is the result of one man's labor of love. I started climbing in Colorado in 1955 and have spent the last five decades climbing Colorado's fourteeners. I have not rushed through my fourteeners. I spent a leisurely 20 years climbing them all for the first time. Then I leisurely climbed them all again. I climbed many routes specifically for this guide and documented them immediately after each climb. I continue to field check this guide extensively. When the huge extent of this body of information threatened to overwhelm me, I received valuable assistance from Chris Haaland, Cory Brettman, Cleve McCarty, Dennis Brown, Alannah McTighe, Randy Rhodes, Gary Neptune and my wife, Jennifer Roach.

Because one person has climbed and reported on these routes, the descriptions are consistent. I believe climbing is a very personal activity, and I seldom give opinions that might intrude on yours. Still, my bias creeps in from time to time.

This guide is not comprehensive in its coverage of the routes on the fourteeners. I have not revealed all the secrets of these special peaks. There are many more routes that I could have included. For every route I climbed, I saw two more! Never lose your spirit of discovery. You should finish each climb and each book wanting more.

I welcome route information and constructive criticism from readers. Mail your comments to Gerry Roach, P.O. Box 3303, Boulder, CO 80303, or e-mail them to GRoachHigh@aol.com.

Anyone who climbs all the Colorado fourteeners deserves the title Dr. Colorado. Anyone who climbs every route in this guide has graduated Summit Cum Laude! Climb safely and don't forget to have fun.

–Gerry Roach
January 1999

Introduction

Safety First

Climbing is dangerous, and each individual should approach these peaks with caution. Conditions can vary tremendously depending on time of day and time of year. The route descriptions in this book assume good, summer conditions. Lightning is always a serious hazard in Colorado during the summer months. Snow conditions and cornices vary from year to year. Spring and early summer avalanches can be a function of winter storms that occurred months earlier. The previous winter's snowfall determines snow conditions in August.

Before charging forth with your city energy and competitive urges, take some time to understand the mountain environment you are about to enter. Carefully study your chosen route and don't be afraid to retreat if your condition, or the mountain's, is unfavorable. Better yet, do an easier climb nearby to become familiar with the area. When both you and the mountain are ready, come back and do your dream climb.

Lightning

Colorado is famous for apocalyptic lightning storms that threaten not just your life, but your soul as well. This section will have special meaning if you have ever been trapped by a storm that endures for more than an hour and leaves no gap between one peal of thunder and the next. The term *simultaneous flash-boom* has a very personal meaning for many Colorado climbers.

Dangers
- Lightning is dangerous!
- Lightning is the greatest external hazard to summer mountaineering in Colorado.
- Lightning kills people every year in Colorado's mountains.
- Direct hits are usually fatal.

Mount Massive from the southwest.

Precautions

- Start early! Be off summits by noon and back in the valley by early afternoon.
- Observe thunderhead buildup carefully, noting speed and direction; towering thunderheads with black bottoms are bad.
- When lightning begins nearby, count the seconds between flash and thunder, then divide by 5 to calculate the distance to the flash in miles. Repeat to determine if lightning is approaching.
- Try to determine if the lightning activity is cloud-to-cloud or ground strikes.
- Get off summits and ridges.

Protection

- You cannot outrun a storm; physics wins.
- When caught, seek a safe zone in the 45-degree cone around an object 5 to 10 times your height.
- Be aware of ground currents; the current from a ground strike disperses along the ground or cliff, especially in wet cracks.
- Wet ropes are good conductors.
- Snow is not a good conductor.
- Separate yourself from metal objects.
- Avoid sheltering in spark gaps under boulders and trees.
- Disperse the group. Survivors can revive one who is hit.
- Crouch on boot soles, ideally on dry, insulating material such as moss or grass. Dirt is better than rock. Avoid water.

- Do not put your hands down. Put elbows on knees and hands on head. This gives current a short path through your arms rather than the longer path through your vital organs.
- Do not lie down; current easily goes through your vital organs.

First Aid

- Know and give CPR. Many lightning-strike victims have been revived by CPR.
- Treat for burns.
- Evacuate.

Avalanche

Hazard Forecasting

- Avalanches are the greatest external hazard to winter mountaineering in Colorado; gravity never sleeps.
- Loose-snow avalanches start at a single point and fan out downward; the danger is highest after new snowfall.
- Slab avalanches occur when an entire slope of snow starts in motion at once.
- Consistent winds of more than 15 miles per hour can build up soft slabs.
- Consistent winds of 25 to 50 miles per hour can build up hard slabs.
- Hard slabs develop more rapidly at low temperatures and are sensitive to temperature changes.
- Most avalanches occur on slopes of 30 to 45 degrees.
- Most avalanches that trap people are triggered by the victims themselves.
- Most avalanches that trap skiers are relatively small.
- Avalanches occur on open slopes, in gullies and in open stands of trees. Ridges, outcrops and dense stands of trees (too dense to ski comfortably) are safer.
- Beware of avalanche danger during and after heavy winter storms. The danger factor decreases with time. The rate of decrease depends strongly on temperature. Near 32 degrees Fahrenheit, the danger may persist for only a few hours. Below 0 degrees Fahrenheit, it may last for many days or even weeks.
- Deep snow smooths out terrain irregularities and promotes avalanching.
- Warm snow will bond to a warm surface much better than cold snow will bond to a cold surface. Therefore, monitor the temperature at the start of a storm.
- It generally takes 10 to 12 inches of new snow to produce serious avalanche danger.
- Prolonged snowfalls of 1 inch or more per hour should always be viewed with suspicion.

- Snowfalls that begin warm and then cool off tend to be more stable than those with the opposite trend.
- Extensive sluffing after a fresh snowfall is evidence of stability.
- Sunballs rolling down a slope are indicators of rapid changes taking place in the snow. The danger is not high if the sunballs are small and penetrate only a few inches into the surface layer. If these balls grow in size during the day and eventually achieve the form of large snow wheels that penetrate deeply into the snow, wet-snow avalanching may be imminent.
- "Talking snow," a hollow drumlike sound under your footsteps or skis, or a booming sound with or without a dropping jar, is a sign of serious avalanche hazard.
- Other things being equal, convex slopes offer more slab-avalanche danger than concave slopes. However, many avalanches do start on concave profiles.

Precautions
- Never travel alone.
- Avoid avalanche areas and times of high danger. The probability of being caught in an avalanche is directly proportional to the time you spend in the danger zone.
- Carry at least one shovel and avalanche beacons if possible.

If you must cross an avalanche slope:
- Proceed through the danger zone one person at a time. If you are buried, your rescue depends on your unburied companions.
- Remove the wrist loops of your ski poles from your wrists.
- Unhitch any ski safety straps.
- Put on hat and mittens, and close your parka.
- Loosen pack straps.

If you are caught in an avalanche:
- Discard poles, skis and pack.
- Attempt to stay on the surface with a swimming motion.
- Attempt to work to the side of the avalanche.
- Grab trees.
- Close your mouth.
- As the avalanche slows, cover your face with your hands.
- Make an air space.
- Don't shout when buried. Sound goes into but not out of snow.

Rescue
- Don't panic. A buried person only has a 30 percent chance of survival after 30 minutes. Organized rescue in most backcountry situations is at least one hour from the scene. The lives of your buried companions depend largely on what *you* do.

- Assess any additional avalanche hazard and plan escape routes.
- Mark the last-seen point.
- If equipped with avalanche beacons, the *entire* unburied party must turn their beacons to receive. Search in a pattern that zeroes in on the strongest signal. Turn down the volume and pinpoint the victim's exact position, then dig.
- Do a quick search below the last-seen point. Scruff around. Look for any clues and mark their location. Search likely areas near trees, on benches and near the end of the debris.
- Start a thorough search. Search the most likely area first. Use ski poles as probes if that's all you have. Do a coarse probe, making probe holes about 2 feet apart. Have all searchers form a straight line and move uphill. A coarse probe has a 70 percent chance of finding a victim buried in the probe area. Repeat a coarse probe of the most likely area several times, then move to the next most likely area.
- Go for help. Determining when to send some of your party for additional help is a judgment call that depends on the size of your group, how far into the backcountry you are and the availability of trained rescue groups.

Leave No Trace

If you use the wilderness resource, it is your responsibility to help protect it from environmental damage. The old adage "Take nothing but pictures; leave nothing but footprints" is no longer good enough. The footprints of thousands of visitors can cause extensive damage to fragile alpine areas. The ground plants above tree line are especially vulnerable because they cling to a tenuous existence. If you destroy a patch of tundra with a careless step, it may take a hundred years for the plants to recover. In some cases, they may never recover.

The routes in this book all pass through the alpine zone. Tread lightly. Stay on the trails. Stay on the trails and where trails do not exist travel on durable surfaces like rock and snow. Walk on rocks in the tundra, not on the tundra itself. If traveling over tundra is the only option, be sure to disperse use over a wide area. Let your eyes do the walking sometimes. You do not have to explore every inch on foot. Respect the environment you are entering. If you don't show respect, you are an intruder, not a visitor.

Leave No Trace (LNT), a national nonprofit organization dedicated to educating people about responsible use of the outdoors, recommends a few simple techniques for minimum-impact travel through fragile alpine environments. Learn them. Abide by them. For more information about LNT and minimum-impact outdoor ethics, call (800) 332-4100 or visit the LNT website at www.LNT.org. The six tenets of the LNT movement are:

1. Plan Ahead and Prepare

- Know the regulations and special concerns for the area you are visiting.
- Visit the backcountry in small groups.
- Avoid popular areas during times of high use.
- Choose equipment and clothing in subdued colors.
- Repackage food into reusable containers.

2. Camp and Travel on Durable Surfaces

On the Trail

- Stay on designated trails. Walk in single file in the middle of the path.
- Do not shortcut switchbacks; this can cause severe erosion problems.
- Where multiple trails exist, choose the one that is most worn.
- Where no trails exist, spread out across the terrain.
- When traveling cross-country, choose the most durable surfaces available: rock, gravel, dry grasses or snow.
- Rest on rock or in designated sites.
- Avoid wetlands and riparian areas.
- Use a map and compass to eliminate the need for rock cairns, tree scars and ribbons.
- Step to the downhill side of the trail and talk softly when encountering pack stock.

At Camp

- Choose an established, legal site that will not be damaged by your stay.
- Camping above treeline is not recommended because of damage to tundra plants.
- Restrict activities to the area where vegetation is compacted or absent.
- Keep pollutants out of water sources by camping at least 200 feet (70 adult steps) from lakes and streams.
- Move campsites frequently.

3. Pack It In, Pack It Out

- Pack everything that you bring into wild country back out with you.
- Protect wildlife and your food by storing rations securely.
- Pick up all spilled foods.

4. Properly Dispose of What You Can't Pack Out

- Deposit human waste in catholes dug 6 to 8 inches deep at least 200 feet from water, camp or trails. Cover and disguise the cathole when finished.
- Use toilet paper or wipes sparingly. Pack them out.
- To wash yourself or your dishes, carry water 200 feet away from streams or lakes, and use small amounts of biodegradable soap. Strain and scatter dish water; pack out remaining particles.

Early morning light on Ellingwood Point.

- Inspect your campsite for trash and evidence of your stay. Pack out all trash: yours and others'.

5. Leave What You Find
- Treat our national heritage with respect. Leave plants, rocks and historical artifacts as you find them for others to discover and enjoy.
- Good campsites are found, not made. Altering a site should not be necessary.
- Observe wildlife quietly from a distance; never feed wild animals.
- Let nature's sounds prevail. Keep loud voices and noises to a minimum.
- Control pets at all times. Remove dog feces.
- Do not build structures or furniture or dig trenches.

6. Minimize Use and Impact of Fires
- Campfires can cause lasting impacts to the backcountry. Always carry a lightweight stove for cooking. Enjoy a candle lantern instead of a fire.
- When fires are permitted, use established fire rings, fire pans or mound fires. Do not scar large rocks or overhangs.
- Gather sticks no larger than an adult's wrist.
- Do not snap branches off live, dead or downed trees.
- Put out campfires completely.
- Remove all unburned trash from the fire ring and scatter the cool ashes over a large area far from camp.

The Rating System

I have used an extended Yosemite Decimal System (YDS) to rate each route's difficulty. Each route's rating has four parts: Grade, Class, Snow Steepness and Length, which includes both the route's round-trip mileage and round-trip elevation gain. Grade rates the route's overall difficulty. Class rates the route's most difficult free-climbing rock pitch. There are no aid routes in this guide. Snow Steepness rates the route's steepest snow or ice (if any). The distance and elevation gain give additional information that is particularly pertinent for Colorado's fourteeners.

Grade

A roman numeral from I to VII, representing an ascending order of difficulty, denotes a route's overall difficulty. This number does not apply to a route's individual pitches or moves. A route's Grade expresses the route's seriousness based on the peak's elevation, the length of the approach and climb viewed in both time and distance, elevation gain, objective dangers, technical difficulty of hardest pitch, average technical difficulty, whether or not the climb is sustained, the exposure, probability of bad weather and difficulty of retreat. As used in this guide, the Grade rates a route's overall length and commitment as follows:

Grade I: A short day climb. May require up to 3,000 vertical feet of elevation gain and/or three pitches of technical climbing.

Grade II: A day climb. May require up to 6,000 vertical feet of elevation gain and/or six pitches of technical climbing.

Grade III: A long day climb. May require up to 10,000 vertical feet of elevation gain and/or 10 pitches of technical climbing and/or a considerable amount of Class 3 scrambling.

Grade IV: A very long day climb. Will require more than 10,000 vertical feet of elevation gain and/or 10 pitches of technical climbing.

There are no routes harder than Grade III in this guide, but you can combine two or more routes to produce a Grade IV climb. For example, the Prow on Kit Carson plus the Ellingwood Arête on Crestone Needle done in the same day is a Grade IV climb. The word **Grade** is usually implicit and does not appear in the ratings. Only the roman numeral appears. The term **technical climbing** refers to Class 4 or Class 5 climbing on rock, or climbing on a snow slope steeper than 45 degrees. Classes are defined below. A pitch is usually 100 to 150 feet long.

People can and have done each route in this guide in one day from the nearest trailhead. The use of a high camp can make any route easier. My Grades are based on doing the route in one day from the nearest trailhead. If you do a technically easy Grade III route with a lot of elevation gain from a high camp, it will only be Grade II or Grade I. To grade your ascent from a high camp, evaluate the vertical gain and number of technical pitches from the high camp to the summit(s). You can use these two criteria, as listed above, to grade any ascent.

Class

A route's Class is denoted by the word **Class**, followed by a number from 1 to 5.14, in ascending order of difficulty of the route's most difficult free-climbing rock pitch. Used elsewhere, a Class rating refers to a single pitch or move. Difficulties from Class 1 to Class 4 are described with a single digit only. When the difficulty reaches Class 5, the description includes decimal places. In this guide, Class 5 difficulty ranges from 5.0 to 5.8. I have made no attempt to distinguish between 5.0, 5.1 and 5.2. I indicate difficulty in this range with the rating **Class 5.0–5.2**. Occasionally, I also combine 5.3 and 5.4 with the rating **Class 5.3–5.4**.

I have not used adjectives such as **easy, difficult** or **severe** to rate the rock pitches. What is easy for one person may be difficult for another, and words like this only confuse the issue. In place of adjectives, I use examples to describe difficulty. The answer to the question "Just how hard is Class 3 anyway?" is "Climb Longs' Keyhole Route, then you will know." A list of example routes follows that includes some of the classic Front Range rock climbs for comparison. I have ordered the routes roughly from easiest to hardest within each Class.

Class 1:   Grays Peak–North Slopes
               Mount Elbert–East Ridge
               Pikes Peak–East Slopes
               Quandary Peak–East Slopes

Class 2:   Mount Massive–East Slopes
               Mount of the Holy Cross–North Ridge
               Handies Peak–Grizzly Gulch
               Mount Yale–East Ridge

Class 2+:   Windom Peak–West Ridge
               Challenger Point–North Slopes
               Mount Sneffels–South Slopes
               Mount Lindsey–North Face

Class 3:   Kit Carson Peak–West Ridge
               Longs Peak–Keyhole
               Longs Peak–Loft
               Wilson Peak–West Ridge
               Crestone Needle–South Face

Class 4:	Sunlight Peak–South Slopes (final summit block)
	Mount Wilson–North Slopes (final 150 feet)
	Second Flatiron–Freeway
	Crestone Peak to Crestone Needle traverse
	Crestone Peak–North Buttress
Class 5.0–5.2:	Little Bear to Blanca traverse
	Third Flatiron–Standard East Face
	Longs Peak–Notch Couloir
Class 5.3–5.4:	Longs Peak–Kieners
	Longs Peak–North Face
	First Flatiron–North Arête
Class 5.5:	Third Flatiron–East Face Left
	Longs Peak–Keyhole Ridge
	Boulder Canyon Dome–East Slab
	Longs Peak–Alexander's Chimney
Class 5.6:	First Flatiron–Direct East Face
	Eldorado Wind Tower–Calypso
	Mount Sneffels–North Buttress
Class 5.7:	Crestone Needle–Ellingwood Arête
	Boulder Canyon Castle Rock–Cussin' Crack
	Third Flatiron–Friday's Folly
	Longs Peak–Stettner's Ledges
Class 5.8:	Eldorado Bastille–The Bastille Crack
	Kit Carson Peak–The Prow
	Crestone Needle–North Pillar
	Eldorado Bastille–West Arête

These difficulty ratings are for good, dry conditions. High-country rock rapidly becomes more difficult as it becomes wet, and a route becomes a different climb entirely when snow-covered. For example, the difficulty of Longs' Keyhole Route can jump from Class 3 to Class 5 when it is wet or snow-covered.

I discuss descent routes only occasionally. You can descend by reversing the ascent route or by descending easier routes. When I include technical routes on a peak, I always discuss an easier route, and this is usually the logical descent route. There are often several easy routes to choose from. You must use good mountaineering judgment when selecting descent routes.

Longs Peak from the south, showing the upper part of the Kieners Route.

Because I have defined difficulty on rock by example, people unfamiliar with the YDS will have to do some climbs before they understand what the different Class ratings mean. This is particularly true for the more difficult ratings. The following descriptions can help.

Class 1 is trail hiking or any hiking across open country that is no more difficult than walking on a maintained trail. The parking lot at the trailhead is easy Class 1, groomed trails are midrange Class 1 and some of the big step-ups near the top of the Barr Trail are difficult Class 1.

Class 2 is off-trail hiking. Class 2 usually means bushwhacking or hiking on a talus slope. You are not yet using handholds for upward movement. Occasionally, I use the rating *Class 2+* for a pseudo-scrambling route where you will use your hands but do not need to search very hard for handholds. Most people are able to downclimb Class 2+ terrain facing out.

Class 3 is the easiest climbing category, and people usually call it "scrambling." You are beginning to look for and use handholds for upward movement. You are now using basic climbing, not walking, movements. Although you are using handholds, you don't have to look very hard to find them. Occasionally putting your hand down for balance while crossing a talus slope does not qualify as Class 3. That is still Class 2. Many people feel the need to face in while downclimbing Class 3.

Class 4 is in the realm of technical climbing. You are not just using handholds; you have to search for, select and test them. You are beginning to use muscle groups not involved with hiking, those of the upper

YDS	NCCS	UIAA	French	British	Australian	German
Class 1	F1	I		Easy		
Class 2	F1	I		Easy		
Class 3	F2	I, II		Easy		
Class 4	F3	I, II		Easy		
Class 5.0–5.2	F4	I, II	1	Moderate	10	I
Class 5.3	F5	II	2	Difficult	11	II
Class 5.4	F5	III	3	Very Difficult	12	III
Class 5.5	F6	IV	4	4a (Severe)	12, 13	IV
Class 5.6	F6	V-	5	4b (Severe)	13	V
Class 5.7	F7	V	5	4b, 4c (JVS)	14, 15	VI
Class 5.8	F8	V+, VI-	5+	4c, 5a (VS)	15, 16, 17	VIIa, VIIb
Class 5.9	F9	VI	6a	5a, 5b (VS)	17, 18	VIIb, VIIc
Class 5.10a	F10	VI+	6a+	5b (Hard)	19	VIIc
Class 5.10b	F10	VII-	6a+, 6b	5b, 5c	20	VIIIa
Class 5.10c	F11	VII-, VII	6b	5c	20, 21	VIIIa, VIIIb
Class 5.10d	F11	VII	6b+	5c	21, 22	VIIIb, VIIIc
Class 5.11a	F12	VII+	6c	5c, 6a	22, 23	VIIIc, IXa
Class 5.11b	F12	VII+, VIII-	6c+	6a	23	IXa
Class 5.11c	F13	VIII-	7a	6a	24	IXb
Class 5.11d	F13	VIII	7a+	6a, 6b	25	IXb, IXc
Class 5.12a	F14	VIII+	7b	6b	25, 26	IXc
Class 5.12b	F14	VIII+, IX-	7b+	6b	26	Xa
Class 5.12c	F15	IX-	7b+, 7c	6b, 6c	26, 27	Xb
Class 5.12d	F15	IX	7c	6c	27	Xb, Xc
Class 5.13a	F16	IX	7c+	6c	28	Xc
Class 5.13b	F16	IX+	8a	6c, 7a	29	Xc
Class 5.13c	F17	X-	8a, 8a+	7a	30, 31	XIa
Class 5.13d	F17	X	8b, 8b+	7a	31, 32	XIb
Class 5.14a	F18	X+	8c	7b	33	XIc

body and abdominals in particular. Your movement is more focused, thoughtful and slower. Many people prefer to rappel down a serious Class 4 pitch rather than downclimb it. Many Class 3 routes in California would be rated Class 4 in Colorado.

Class 5 is technical climbing. You are now using a variety of climbing techniques, not just cling holds. Your movement may involve stemming with your legs, cross-pressure with your arms, pressing down on handholds as you pass them, edging on small holds, smearing, chimneying, jamming and heel hooks. A lack of flexibility will be noticeable and can hinder your movement. Your movement usually totally occupies your mind. You have come a long way from walking across the parking lot and entertaining a million thoughts. Most people choose to rappel down Class 5 pitches.

Class ratings of individual moves and pitches are solidified by the consensus of the climbing community at large and the local climbing community who are most familiar with the area. Only when there is considerable consensus for a rating can it be used as an example of that difficulty.

The Class ratings do not make any statement about how exposed a move or pitch is. Exposure is a subjective fear that varies widely from person to person. Exposure usually increases with difficulty, but there are some noticeable exceptions to this rule. Some Class 2 passages are very exposed. A good example of this is the Catwalk on Eolus' northeast ridge. The upper part of this route is Class 3, but the Catwalk is only Class 2. If exposure bothers you to the point where it impairs your movement, increase my ratings accordingly.

I do not define difficulty in terms of equipment that you might or might not use. Historically, Class 3 meant unroped climbing and Class 4 was roped climbing. Unfortunately, there is a lot of historical momentum behind those old definitions. Under the old definition, when people tell me that they "third-classed" a pitch, all I know is that they climbed it unroped. I do not know how hard it is. After all, the Diamond on Longs Peak (5.10) has been "third-classed." I know how hard a pitch I am willing to do unroped, but I do not know how hard a pitch *you* are willing to do unroped. There are many people who can free solo up and down every route in this guide, and many more who cannot do any of the routes, with or without a rope. The decision of when to rope up must always be the individual's.

Snow Steepness

The third part of the rating system used in this guide refers to the route's *steepest* snow or ice. The Snow Steepness rating is not part of the YDS, but I have added it to provide more information about a route. If there is no snow or ice on a route, this designation is absent. Because a

At the top of the Lost Rat couloir on Grays Peak.

slope's steepness can be measured, this part of the rating is easier to define. The following adjectives refer to a snow slope's angle:

Easy:	0 to 30 degrees
Moderate:	30 to 45 degrees
Steep:	45 to 60 degrees
Very Steep:	60 to 80 degrees
Vertical:	80 to 90 degrees

Climbers seldom measure a slope angle accurately. They usually estimate the angle by the slope's feel, and these feelings vary widely. Even experienced climbers are notorious for guessing a slope angle to be steeper than it is. I have kept this in mind when determining the slope angles used in this guide. When a slope angle is hovering around the critical junction between Moderate and Steep, I apply the Steep rating.

Length

For the fourth part of a route's rating, I have given the route's round-trip mileage and elevation gain. The elevation gain includes any extra upward gains, both on the ascent and descent. This typically happens when you must traverse over false summits. If you ascend one route and descend another, your round-trip mileage may be different from the mileage listed in this guide. This is most likely to be the case when you ascend a difficult route and descend an easier route.

Other Rating Systems

The Yosemite Decimal System (YDS) is widely used in the United States and has evolved as the national standard. The National Climbing Classification System (NCCS) was intended to be the standard, but it has not gained wide acceptance. The difference between the YDS and NCCS numbers is confusing. The table on page xx lists the correspondence between these two U.S. systems and several of the popular international systems. Note that the British system started with adjectives. It became confusing with Just Very Severe (JVS), Very Severe (VS) and Hard. These adjectives have been replaced with numbers.

Goals

Goals on Colorado's fourteeners are as numerous as the people who climb them. Some people are content just to look at the fourteeners. Some people are excited if they manage to climb one. Many are content to climb the Class 1 and Class 2 routes and just look at the harder fourteeners. These people can climb two-thirds of the fourteeners. The standard goal is to climb all the fourteeners on some list. Choose your list. The number of people who have climbed all the fourteeners is approaching 1,000.

Purists accept the goal of not only climbing all the fourteeners, but gaining 3,000 feet on each one. This is a much harder goal, one that I did not achieve until recently. This goal can be harder than climbing all the fourteeners twice. For example, consider Lincoln, Democrat and Bross. Even if you are careful to start 1,000 feet below 12,000-foot Kite Lake on your initial climb of all three, you have only gained 3,000 feet on one of the three peaks. To gain 3,000 feet on all three, you will have to do this standard climb three times, or do alternate routes to the other two peaks on two more occasions. Then, if you want to gain 3,000 feet on low-power summits such as Cameron, you will have to make a fourth trip to the same area.

At least one group climbed all the fourteeners and used human-powered transport between each group of peaks. Hard-core mountaineers climb all the fourteeners in winter. This is a difficult goal for a single individual. Extreme skiers ski from the summit of all the fourteeners. Lou Dawson was the first to do this, finishing in spring 1991. The record for the most times one person has climbed all the fourteeners is now more than 10. There is a youngest and an oldest person to complete all the fourteeners. Tyle Smith finished climbing all the fourteeners in 1968 at age eight. His long-standing record was broken by seven-year-old Megan Emmons in 1997. In recent years, it has become popular to organize events that place someone on top of each fourteener on the same day. Ham radio enthusiasts have attempted broadcasting from all the summits simultaneously. Dogs have climbed all the fourteeners.

There is, of course, a speed record for climbing all the fourteeners. In 1960 Cleve McCarty climbed the then recognized 52 fourteeners in 52 days. This stately record receives my vote as the most elegant. Then the mania began. In 1974 the Climbing Smiths climbed Colorado's fourteeners in 33 days. They went on to California and Washington and completed the then recognized 68 fourteeners of the contiguous 48 states in 48 days. In 1976 Steve Boyer climbed Colorado's fourteeners in a 22-day tour de force. In 1980 Dick Walters smashed the 20-day mark and climbed them all in 18 days, 15 hours, 40 minutes. This impressive record stood for a decade.

In 1990 the quest for speed intensified. With detailed knowledge of the routes, Quade and Tyle Smith ascended and descended 54 Colorado fourteeners in an astonishing 16 days, 21 hours, 25 minutes. They were careful to ascend at least 3,000 feet on foot to the first peak of a series. After that, traverses were allowed. Then they would descend at least 3,000 feet back to their vehicle. Ah, competition. In 1992 the superbly conditioned ultramarathoner Adrian Crane took more than a day off the Smiths' time, setting the record at 15 days, 17 hours, 19 minutes. The Smiths hiked fast, but Adrian ran on the trails. Adrian was careful to observe the 3,000-foot rule set as a standard by the Smiths in 1974. In 1993 Jeff Wagoner summited 55 Colorado fourteeners in 14 days, 3 hours, but he did not observe the 3,000-foot rule.

In 1995 a powerful pair of Colorado mountain runners, Rick Trujillo of Ouray, a five-time winner of the Pikes Peak Marathon, and Ricky Denesik of Telluride, climbed the traditional 54 Colorado fourteeners in 15 days, 9 hours, 55 minutes, taking more than 7 hours off Adrian's 1992 record. The two Ricks, or "Rick squared" as they were called during the event, were careful to observe the 3,000-foot rule. They gained a total of 156,130 feet and covered 337 miles.

Applying their experience, Rick squared went at it again in August 1997. Bad, El-Niño–related weather hampered their effort on most days. Rick Trujillo dropped out of the record attempt on day nine but remained in support. Ricky Denesik continued and was on track to finish in 13 days, 16 hours when a heinous storm drove him back from the Keyhole on Longs—his last peak. A silver moon and I accompanied Ricky on his second attempt. After moonset and an icy homestretch, we reached Longs' silent summit at 1 A.M. Ricky logged a time of 14 days, 16 minutes; a gain of 153,215 feet; and a distance of 314.2 miles.

In 1998 Ricky took more than 30 minutes off Trujillo's record in the Hard Rock 100—Colorado's most difficult mountain footrace. Empowered and powerful, Ricky has announced plans to run the fourteeners again in 1999. To make life interesting, Teddy Kaiser of Coos Bay, Oregon, has also announced plans to try for the record in 1999.

When setting your goals, remember one thing: Records can be broken, but a victory is yours to keep forever. In pursuit of your goals, you might choose to rely on the standard 10 essentials.

1. Map
2. Compass
3. Sunglasses and sunscreen
4. Extra food
5. Extra clothing
6. Headlamp/flashlight
7. First-aid supplies
8. Firestarter
9. Matches
10. Knife

I choose to rely on my Classic Commandments of Mountaineering:

1. Never get separated from your lunch.
2. Never get separated from your sleeping bag.
3. Never get separated from your primal urges.
4. Carefully consider where your primal urges are leading you.
5. Expect to go the wrong way some of the time.
6. First aid above 26,000 feet consists of getting below 26,000 feet.
7. Never step on the rope.
8. Never bivouac.
9. Surfer Girl is not in the mountains.
10. Never pass up a chance to pee.
11. Don't eat yellow snow.
12. Have fun and don't forget why you started.

Vaya con Dios.

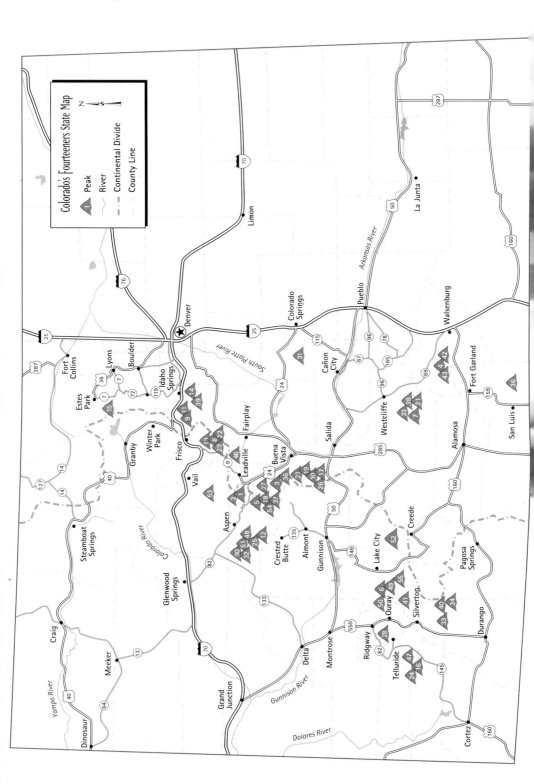

Colorado's Fourteeners

Peak Index

1	14,433	Elbert, Mt	29	14,148	Democrat, Mt
2	14,421	Massive, Mt	30	14,130	Capitol Pk
3	14,420	Harvard, Mt	31	14,110	Pikes Pk
4	14,345	Blanca Pk	32	14,092	Snowmass Mtn
5	14,336	La Plata Pk	33	14,083	Eolus, Mt
6	14,309	Uncompahgre Pk	34	14,082	Windom Pk
7	14,294	Crestone Pk	35	14,081	Challenger Point
8	14,286	Lincoln, Mt	36	14,073	Columbia, Mt
9	14,270	Grays Pk	37	14,067	Missouri Mtn
10	14,269	Antero, Mt	38	14,064	Humboldt Pk
11	14,267	Torreys Pk	39	14,060	Bierstadt, Mt
12	14,265	Castle Pk	40	14,059	Sunlight Pk
13	14,265	Quandary Pk	41	14,048	Handies Pk
14	14,264	Evans, Mt	42	14,047	Culebra Pk
15	14,255	Longs Pk	43	14,042	Ellingwood Point
16	14,246	Wilson, Mt	44	14,042	Lindsey, Mt
17	14,229	Shavano, Mt	45	14,037	Little Bear Pk
18	14,197	Belford, Mt	46	14,036	Sherman, Mt
19	14,197	Crestone Needle	47	14,034	Redcloud Pk
20	14,197	Princeton, Mt	48	14,018	Pyramid Pk
21	14,196	Yale, Mt	49	14,017	Wilson Pk
22	14,172	Bross, Mt	50	14,015	Wetterhorn Pk
23	14,165	Kit Carson Pk	51	14,014	North Maroon Pk
24	14,159	El Diente Pk	52	14,014	San Luis Pk
25	14,156	Maroon Pk	53	14,005	Mt of the Holy Cross
26	14,155	Tabeguache Pk	54	14,003	Huron Pk
27	14,153	Oxford, Mt	55	14,001	Sunshine Pk
28	14,150	Sneffels, Mt			

_NT

_NT

Chapter One

Front Range

Introduction

Colorado's Front Range extends from the Wyoming border southward for 175 miles to the Arkansas River Valley west of Pueblo. It is Colorado's longest range. When you approach the Rocky Mountains from the east, the Front Range provides an abrupt scenery change. The land is flat, then roars up like crazy!

The Front Range contains six fourteeners. Because most of Colorado's population lives in the urban corridor east of the Front Range, these peaks are easily reached. Any of these fourteeners can be climbed in one day from most Front Range cities. People climb Front Range fourteeners more often than any of the other fourteeners scattered across the state.

1. Longs Peak   14,255 feet

See Map 1 on page 5

Longs Peak is unquestionably the monarch of the Front Range and northern Colorado. It dominates all within sight of it. Longs is the highest peak in Rocky Mountain National Park and Boulder County. It is also the northernmost fourteener in Colorado and the Rocky Mountains. Its summit attracts thousands of people each year, and it is one of the most popular peaks in the western United States. The reason for its popularity is obvious. Longs enraptures all but the most heartless soul. Somehow, Longs' popularity makes people feel safer, but the opposite is the case. Many people believe the greatest climbing hazard today is being below other people. Any route on Longs is a serious undertaking.

Longs has a tremendous east face, and its great sweep has struck emotion into many hearts. Emotions range from awe to terror. Longs' closest neighbor, Mount Meeker, has a huge, sweeping north face, and these two faces combine to form Colorado's greatest mountain cirque. Beautiful Chasm Lake nestles at the base of Longs' east face. Ships Prow, a large promontory, separates Longs' east face and Meeker's north face. Ships Prow rises directly above Chasm Lake's south side to the Loft, which is the broad, 13,450-foot saddle between Longs and Meeker.

Longs' slabby north face rises above the Boulder Field, which is reached by the popular East Longs Peak Trail. Longs' northwest ridge contains the famous Keyhole, which allows easy access between the peak's east and west sides. Longs' large west face sweeps above Glacier Gorge with the well-named Keyboard of the Winds on its south edge. Longs' broken south side rises above Wild Basin and contains the Palisades' west-facing cliffs. The Notch is prominent on the ridge above the Palisades and is easily seen above Longs' east face. Longs has more than 100 routes, but most are serious technical climbs on the great east face. This guide only includes a handful of Longs' easier routes.

Maps

Required: Longs Peak, Roosevelt National Forest
Optional: McHenrys Peak, Isolation Peak, Allens Park

Trailheads

Longs Peak Trailhead

This trailhead is at 9,400 feet and provides access to the East Longs Peak Trail. This major trail serves all sides of Longs Peak. The trailhead is west of Colorado 7 and can be reached from either the north or south.

For the northern approach, measure from the junction of U.S. 36 and Colorado 7 east of Estes Park. Go south from this junction for 9.2 miles on Colorado 7 to the turnoff for the Longs Peak Ranger Station. For the southern approach, measure from the junction of Colorado 7 and Colorado 72 on the Peak to Peak Highway. Go north from this junction for 10.5 miles on Colorado 7 to the turnoff for the Longs Peak Ranger Station. Turn west (left) onto a dirt road and go 1.0 mile to the trailhead. This trailhead is accessible in winter.

Glacier Gorge Trailhead

This trailhead is at 9,240 feet and provides access to Longs' north and west sides. From Rocky Mountain National Park Headquarters on U.S. 36, go west for 1.2 miles to the Beaver Meadows Entrance Station into the park. Continue west on U.S. 36 for an additional 0.2 mile to the Bear Lake Road. Turn south (left) onto the Bear Lake Road (paved) and go 8.6 miles to the trailhead. This trailhead is accessible in winter.

There is only a small parking lot at this major trailhead, and it is full by 8 A.M. on a summer Sunday. There is a small overflow parking lot 0.5 mile east of the trailhead, but this is often full as well. Another alternative is to park at Bear Lake and follow a trail southeast for 0.4 mile from Bear Lake to the Glacier Gorge Trailhead. A final alternative is to take the shuttle bus to the trailhead. Inquire about the bus at park headquarters (or at the entrance station).

Copeland Lake Trailhead

This trailhead is at 8,320 feet and provides access to Longs' south side. The trailhead is west of Colorado 7 and can be reached from either the north or south.

For the northern approach, measure from the junction of U.S. 36 and Colorado 7 east of Estes Park. Go south from this junction for 13.1 miles on Colorado 7 to the Wild Basin Road. For the southern approach, measure from the junction of Colorado 7 and Colorado 72 on the Peak to Peak Highway. Go north from this junction for 6.6 miles on Colorado 7 to the Wild Basin Road.

From the junction of the Wild Basin Road and Colorado 7, go west for 0.4 mile on the old highway to another turnoff to Wild Basin and Copeland Lake. Turn west (right) and pass through the Rocky Mountain National Park entrance gate. The trailhead is immediately north of the gate. This trailhead is accessible in winter.

Routes

1.1 Keyhole II, Class 3, Moderate Snow (Seasonal) *Classic*

From Longs Peak Trailhead: 15.0 miles, 5,000 feet

This is the easiest route on Longs. People climb it more than any other route in this guide. Climbing the Keyhole Route on a late summer weekend is like walking on a crowded city sidewalk through a construction zone. Queues form on the Homestretch, one going up and the other going down. At midday, there can be more than 100 people on the summit. The Keyhole Route attracts several thousand people each summer.

This is a long, arduous ascent on a high, real mountain. The route's difficulty increases dramatically when conditions are bad, and many people have died here. Sudden summer storms can turn the Homestretch into a bobsled run. The Trough usually contains snow until mid-July, and an ice ax is useful until then. The Keyhole Route spirals almost completely around the mountain, and any escape from the route takes you down into Wild Basin or Glacier Gorge. Your return to the Longs Peak Trailhead from these drainages can assume epic proportions. Even when conditions are good, the route is crowded, which does not make *your* ascent safer. Understand current conditions before attempting an ascent. Don't be misled by someone else's energy. Stay true to yourself and mountaineering's fundamentals.

From the Longs Peak Trailhead, follow the well-marked East Longs Peak Trail to the Boulder Field. En route, stay left at the Eugenia Mine–Storm Pass junction at 0.5 mile, left at the Jims Grove junction at 2.5 miles and right at the Chasm Lake junction after 3.5 miles. Do not go to Chasm Lake, but take a moment to marvel at Longs' east face. From the Chasm Lake junction, the trail climbs to Granite Pass on Mount Lady Washington's north side, where you can look north to many peaks. Stay left at the North Longs Peak Trail junction in Granite Pass at 4.2 miles and continue southwest up into the expansive Boulder Field, 5.9 miles from the trailhead. The Boulder Field, at 12,750 feet, is below Longs' slabby north face.

From the Boulder Field, continue southwest to the Keyhole, which is visible on Longs' northwest ridge. The Keyhole is at 13,150 feet and consists of a large, overhanging rock jutting out to the north. The Keyhole allows easy access between Longs' east and west sides. There is a small stone building east of the Keyhole. After you scramble up the rocks into the Keyhole, you will have a great view of Glacier Gorge. The route beyond the Keyhole is more serious, and if conditions warrant a retreat, this is a good place to turn around.

Scramble through the Keyhole to the ridge's west side and traverse south on a series of ledges. The route is marked with painted bull's-eyes on the rock, so it is hard to become lost. The route climbs above west-facing, boilerplate slabs, and there is a nifty V-slot in this section. After traversing above the boilerplate slabs, the route descends south of the slabs. The route then climbs gently and reaches the large couloir called the "Trough," which is 0.3 mile south of the Keyhole. The route gains very little elevation between the Keyhole and the Trough. This section of the route is exposed to the west wind, but the views of Glacier Gorge are excellent.

The Trough is a long couloir extending all the way from Glacier Gorge to a point high on Longs' west side. Climb the Trough from 13,300 feet to the top of the couloir on Longs' west ridge at 13,850 feet. When the Trough has snow in it, try to avoid it by staying on the rocks north of the couloir. Just below the ridge at 13,850 feet, you must pass a chockstone; this may be the route's hardest move. You can climb around either side of the chockstone.

On the platform at the top of the Trough, you are close to the summit, but steep cliffs rise above you on both the west and south faces of the peak. A new vista appears to the south; this is a dramatic place. Cross to Longs' south side and traverse east across Longs' south face along a convenient, exposed ledge called the "Narrows."

Beyond the Narrows, continue east up ledges to the base of the Homestretch. It is 250 yards from the top of the Trough to the bottom of the Homestretch. The Homestretch is the weakness in the summit cliffs that

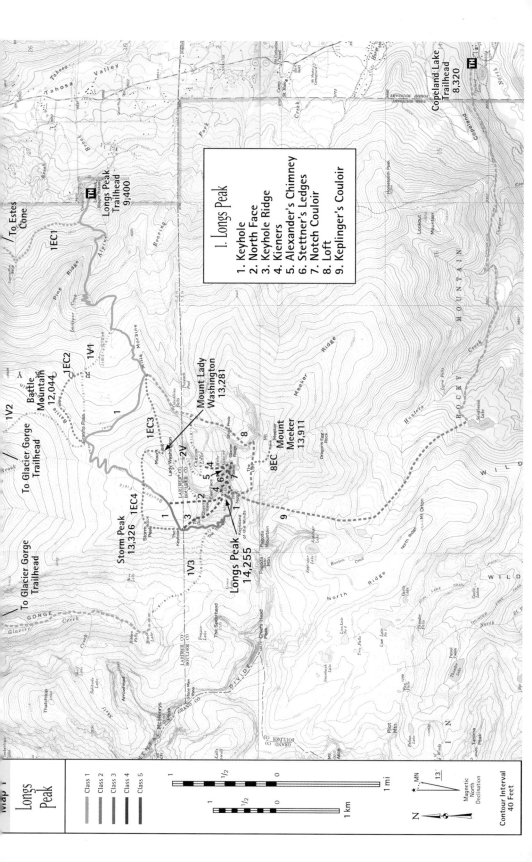

Map 1

Longs Peak

1. Longs Peak

1. Keyhole
2. North Face
3. Keyhole Ridge
4. Kieners
5. Alexander's Chimney
6. Stettner's Ledges
7. Notch Couloir
8. Loft
9. Keplinger's Couloir

Longs Peak Trailhead 9,400

Copeland Lake Trailhead 8,320

To Estes Cone

Battle Mountain 12,044

Mount Lady Washington 13,281

Mount Meeker 13,911

Storm Peak 13,326

Longs Peak 14,255

To Glacier Gorge Trailhead

To Glacier Gorge Trailhead

Class 1
Class 2
Class 3
Class 4
Class 5

1 mi
1 km
1/2
1/2
0
0

MN
13°
Magnetic North Declination

N

Contour Interval 40 Feet

the route has circled all the way around the peak to find. It consists of some parallel cracks angling up to the northeast across low-angled slabs. The Homestretch is Class 3 when it is dry, but more difficult rock lurks nearby. People have encountered trouble on the smooth slabs near the cracks. After the Homestretch, the flat summit appears abruptly, and the highest point is 100 feet north. The monarch is yours!

Variations
1.1V1 Jims Grove Trail
From Longs Peak Trailhead: 14.5 miles, 5,000 feet

At 10,960 feet, 2.5 miles above the Longs Peak Trailhead, you have a choice of two trails. The East Longs Peak Trail climbs southwest to Mills Moraine, then takes a long tack northwest to reach Granite Pass. The Jims Grove Trail goes north from the junction, climbs west past the Jims Grove campsites nestled in the trees, then switchbacks north around an enduring snowfield in a small basin west of Jims Grove. The trail then climbs steeply west to rejoin the East Longs P eak Trail at 11,920 feet, just below Granite Pass.

The Jims Grove Trail is 0.25 mile shorter one way and provides different scenery. You miss the spectacular view of Longs' east face from Mills Moraine, but you will pass through wind-twisted trees and can enjoy the little basin above Jims Grove. Perhaps you can go up one trail and down the other.

1.1V2 North Longs Peak Trail
From Glacier Gorge Trailhead: 19.3 miles, 5,160 feet

From the Glacier Gorge Trailhead, follow the North Longs Peak Trail for 6.35 miles to Granite Pass and join the East Longs Peak Trail and the Keyhole Route there. This approach to Longs is significantly longer but provides expansive views to the north and allows the possibility of a circle tour.

1.1V3 The Trough
From Glacier Gorge Trailhead: 14.0 miles, 5,000 feet
With descent of North Longs Peak Trail: 16.7 miles, 5,070 feet

From the Glacier Gorge Trailhead, follow the Glacier Gorge Trail for 5.0 miles to Black Lake. Hike east then south above the lake; proceed into the bottom of the Trough, then ascend it to the west ridge at 13,850 feet. Follow the Keyhole Route to the summit. This good, early summer snow climb can provide more than 2,000 vertical feet of moderate snow.

When it is in good condition, this is one of Colorado's longest snow climbs. As summer progresses, so does the probability of rockfall from the large number of people climbing in or near the upper part of the Trough. By August this is an undesirable route. Going up this way and down the North Longs Peak Trail makes a long but wonderful Tour de Longs.

Extra Credit
1.1EC1 Estes Cone 11,006 feet, Class 2
From East Longs Peak Trail: 5.4 miles, 1,550 feet
From Longs Peak Trailhead: 6.4 miles, 1,750 feet

Estes Cone is the symmetrical, craggy-topped peak 1.7 miles northwest of the Longs Peak Trailhead. You can see it from the trailhead above the road. From Estes Cone's summit, you have a sweeping view of Meeker, Longs, Lady Washington and Storm Peak.

From the Eugenia Mine–East Longs Peak Trail junction, 0.5 mile northwest of the Longs Peak Trailhead, go north for 0.9 mile to Eugenia Mine. Descending slightly, go east for 0.6 mile to a signed trail junction just east of Moore Park. Climb north for 0.5 mile to Storm Pass at 10,260 feet. Climb east on the trail for 0.7 mile to the west side of the rocky summit. Scramble up a break in the cliff (Class 2) and continue to the highest point 100 feet farther east.

1.1EC2 Battle Mountain 12,044 feet, Class 2
From East Longs Peak Trail: 1.0 mile, 300 feet
From Longs Peak Trailhead: 9.8 miles, 2,650 feet

Battle Mountain is a minor high point on the ridge northeast of Granite Pass and the East Longs Peak Trail. As you walk up the trail on a warm summer morning, you may wonder why such an innocuous area received this contentious name. Come back in winter. This ridge catches winds the Continental Divide couldn't handle. Never mind Longs Peak; Battle Mountain provides a tough test on occasion.

If you are descending from the Boulder Field, leave the East Longs Peak Trail at Granite Pass and scramble northeast over two other high points for 0.5 mile to reach Battle Mountain's summit. If you are ascending from the Longs Peak Trailhead, take the Jims Grove Trail above the signed trail junction at 10,960 feet. Switchback above Jims Grove, then leave the trail and climb northwest up talus for 0.5 mile to the summit.

1.1EC3 Mount Lady Washington 13,281 feet, Class 2
From Boulder Field: 1.0 mile, 530 feet
From Mills Moraine: 1.6 miles, 1,740 feet
From Longs Peak Trailhead: 10.2 miles, 3,880 feet

One of Longs' major buttress peaks, Mount Lady Washington is 0.8 mile northeast of Longs. Lady Washington's rounded mass interferes with your

Longs Peak
14,255

Longs Peak from the northwest.

view of Longs' east face from many viewpoints, including Battle Mountain and Estes Cone. To eliminate this obstacle, climb it. The view from Lady Washington is impeccable.

If you are in the Boulder Field, hike east for 0.3 mile, then north up blocky talus for 0.15 mile to the summit, which is the eastern of two high points. By swinging to the east, you avoid some troublesome talus on Lady Washington's northwest face directly above the Boulder Field. If you are at the Mills Moraine trail junction, climb 0.8 mile west up talus directly to the summit. This is a tedious slope, but you will never tire of the view from Lady Washington's summit.

1.1EC4 Storm Peak 13,326 feet, Class 2

From Keyhole: 0.7 mile, 180 feet
From Boulder Field: 0.6 mile, 580 feet
From Longs Peak Trailhead: 12.4 miles, 3,930 feet

Another of Longs' major buttress peaks, Storm Peak is 0.8 mile northwest of Longs. Storm Peak provides a superlative view of Longs' north face and the Glacier Gorge sanctuary.

From the Keyhole, scramble north over large blocky talus on the east side of the ridge. Don't cut up for the summit too soon, because Storm's high point is the farthest point to the north. From the Boulder Field, go west up blocky, sometimes loose talus directly to the summit. In early season, this slope holds a snow slope that has been packed rock-hard by the winds of winter. You can avoid this slope by climbing northwest from the Boulder Field onto Storm's north ridge.

1.2 North Face II, Class 5.4

From Longs Peak Trailhead: 13.6 miles, 4,850 feet

This is the old Cables Route that used to be the standard route up Longs. In 1973 the National Park Service removed the cables, and this route reverted to its original difficulty. The eyebolts for some cables remain and provide solid belay or rappel anchors. The route is most often used as a descent route. One 140-foot or two 70-foot rappels overcome the difficulties.

Follow the Keyhole Route to the Boulder Field. From the Boulder Field, hike south up to Chasm View, which is the small 13,500-foot notch just below the north face's northeast edge. This vantage offers an awesome view of the Diamond on the east face. From Chasm View, the route ascends a series of small, west-facing corners and slabs for one long or two short Class 5.4 pitches to reach easier ground. This is where the old cables used to be. Once you are above the slabs, climb broken ledges on the upper part of the north face to reach the summit.

Variation

1.2V The Camel, Class 2+

The Camel is a hidden gully that provides easy passage from the basin west of Chasm Lake to the Boulder Field. It lets you enjoy an excursion into the sanctuary below Longs' great east face before escaping from it at the last moment. It offers a sporting start to your ascent of Longs' North Face Route. The Camel is often used as a descent route after a technical ascent on Longs.

Hike up the East Longs Peak Trail to the Mills Moraine trail junction, 3.5 miles from the trailhead. Instead of hiking north up to Granite Pass, hike west for 0.6 mile to Chasm Meadows and scramble 0.1 mile west up to the east end of Chasm Lake. The west-facing Camel Couloir is hidden from here. Don't despair. Hike around Chasm Lake's north side and look northwest to spot the namesake Camel Rock high on Lady Washington's southwest ridge. Camel Rock is a miniature keyhole overhanging to the west. To some it appears as a kneeling camel. It is distinctive in any case. Camel Rock is visible from Chasm Lake and the Boulder Field, and is the landmark that guides you to the hidden passage.

From Chasm Lake's west end, hike west for 0.15 mile to 12,000 feet, turn around and look up Camel Couloir, now east of you. Scramble east up the couloir on steep grass and talus (Class 2+) to 12,400 feet. The already overpowering view only improves as you make your escape from the basin. In winter the couloir holds hard-packed snow. As you approach the top of the couloir, stay north (left) and swing west for 100 feet to dodge a higher cliff band. Camel Rock will be visible above you. Climb directly northwest up talus to Camel Rock at 13,060 feet. Your escape is complete.

From Camel Rock, hike 0.1 mile down to the southwest to the 12,980-foot saddle between Longs and Lady Washington. Continue southwest up talus for 0.25 mile to Chasm View and join the North Face Route.

1.3 Keyhole Ridge II, Class 5.5

From Longs Peak Trailhead: 14.0 miles, 4,850 feet

This is an excellent technical route in a spectacular setting. The exposed route ascends Longs' northwest ridge. Follow the Keyhole Route to the Keyhole. Stay on the east side of the northwest ridge and ascend a Class 3 ramp for 200 yards to a higher notch in the ridge, known as the "False Keyhole." This takes you past the first tower on the ridge.

Continue up the ridge to the steep part of the second tower (Class 4), then follow a ramp east of the ridge (Class 4). At the end of the ramp, climb to the top of the second tower (Class 5.4). Descend west for 10 feet to a ledge and follow it south to the notch south of the second tower. Scramble up yet another ramp to a belay below and east of a steep face. Angle up to the left onto this face for 75 feet, then climb up on excellent rock to regain the ridge (Class 5.5). This face is the route's crux. You can pass any further difficulties by staying just off the ridge crest; near the summit, stay on the ridge. This route provides a unique approach to Longs' huge summit plateau.

1.4 Kieners III, Class 5.3–5.4, Moderate Snow/Ice *Classic*

From Longs Peak Trailhead: 12.2 miles, 4,850 feet

This is the finest mountaineering route on Longs Peak and, perhaps, the finest mountaineering route in Colorado. First climbed in 1924, it is the easiest route on Longs' east face and is a mixed climb involving both snow and rock climbing. Kieners is a serious undertaking, and you should not tackle it lightly. It is a difficult route to escape from. Above Broadway, the best retreat is a forward one over Longs' summit. This can be very difficult in bad weather. An ice ax, crampons and helmet are recommended for this route.

From the Longs Peak Trailhead, follow the East Longs Peak Trail for 4.5 miles to the ranger cabin at Chasm Meadows, below Chasm Lake. Scramble up a small gully directly west of the cabin to Chasm Lake at 11,800 feet. The view of the east face from here is world renowned.

You can see the upper part of the route from Chasm Lake. Study it carefully. Broadway is the large ledge traversing completely across the face at half height. The vertical Diamond forms the upper, northern part of the face. The Notch is on the skyline south of the summit. The Notch Couloir ascends from Broadway to the Notch. The upper part of Kieners ascends the broken face between the Notch Couloir and the Diamond. The Kieners Route is sometimes called the "Mountaineers Route."

Go west around Chasm Lake's north side and continue west for an additional 0.25 mile toward the base of the great face. Mills Glacier is a permanent snowfield at the base of the lower face. Lambs Slide is a north-facing couloir connected to Mills Glacier, which ascends along the south side of the lower east face. You cannot see Lambs Slide until you reach the bottom of the face. There is permanent snow in Lambs Slide. It is prone to avalanching in early June; as August progresses, the snow turns to ice.

The route ascends Lambs Slide to 13,000 feet, where Broadway's multiple ledges intersect Lambs Slide. Leave Lambs Slide, climb to the highest ledge and traverse north (right) along Broadway for 250 yards. The scrambling is easy initially, but the exposure increases rapidly as you traverse out over the lower face. Just as the exposure reaches a maximum, Broadway narrows and you must make a delicate, Class 5.0–5.2 traverse around a block. Many parties rope up at this point.

The bottom of the Notch Couloir is a short distance north of the block. You must reach the rock north of the couloir, and this usually requires crossing snow or ice in the Notch Couloir. The Notch Couloir begins at Broadway above 800 feet of nearly vertical rock. The prospect of being flushed out of the couloir is something to consider carefully and avoid. This is an exciting place.

Do not go too high into the Notch Couloir before climbing onto the rocks north of the couloir. The easiest line is 50 feet above Broadway. The rock is steep here but not as difficult as it looks. Climb two Class 5.3–5.4 pitches to the broken upper part of Kieners. There are several ways to do this, but the easiest line goes up for 30 feet, then back right. Once you are on the broken, upper slopes of Kieners, scramble northwest, angling right, up gullies and open slopes for several hundred feet. When the rock is dry, the difficulty does not exceed Class 4.

There are several steep cliffs above this broken section that bar easy access to the summit. The route climbs the Staircase, a series of steep steps, then traverses north (right) below the summit cliffs to reach a spectacular point above the Diamond. From here, climb west up steep talus to the summit. The flat summit provides an abrupt scenery change.

1.5 Alexander's Chimney II, Class 5.5

From Longs Peak Trailhead: 12.2 miles, 4,850 feet

First climbed in 1922 by J. Alexander, this is a time-tested rock route on the south side of the lower east face. It is one of the easiest rock routes on the east face. Alexander's Chimney ends on Broadway and, by itself, is not a summit route, but it is often used as a more technical start to Kieners. This option avoids the snow and ice in Lambs Slide. When combined with upper Kieners, the climb becomes Grade III. To descend from the top of Alexander's Chimney, traverse south on Broadway and descend Lambs

The east face of Longs Peak.

Slide. This option usually requires crampons and an ice ax. The bottom of Alexander's Chimney is often wet in early summer. Also, beware rockfall from climbers traversing Broadway above you. Leave early.

Start at the Longs Peak Trailhead and follow the Kieners Route to the base of Lambs Slide. Alexander's Chimney is the first major break in the lower face north of Lambs Slide. When you are standing at the bottom of Lambs Slide, the route is above and to the south (left). Go up Lambs Slide for 200 feet, then climb onto the rock and do an ascending traverse back right across a Class 4 slab to reach the bottom of the chimney. To avoid as much snow as possible, cross the bottom of Lambs Slide and do a longer ascending traverse left across the Class 4 slab to reach the chimney.

The route can be done in four long pitches. Pitch 1 (150 feet): From the highest ledge below the chimney, climb an often-wet wall to the left (Class 5.0), or a crack to the right (Class 5.6), to a sloping ledge. Stem up the chimney above, then angle up to the right (Class 5.5). Belay 20 feet below a huge chockstone. Pitch 2 (150 feet): Move right to escape the chockstone, then do an ascending traverse to the right on a convenient ledge system called "Alexander's Traverse" (Class 4). Belay behind the northernmost of several flakes called the "Dog Ear Flakes." Pitch 3 (130 feet): Climb a right-facing dihedral for 40 feet (Class 5.5), then angle up to the left for 80 feet (Class 5.5) to a large ledge. This is very enjoyable climbing on clean rock. Pitch 4 (160 feet): Traverse left for 75 feet into a recessed area known as the "Yellow Bowl" (Class 4) and climb the left side of the bowl (Class 5.4) to Broadway.

1.6 Stettner's Ledges III, Class 5.7+ *Classic*

From Longs Peak Trailhead: 12.2 miles, 4,850 feet

First climbed in 1927 by Paul and Joe Stettner, this remained the hardest climb in Colorado for 20 years. It remains a classic climb today. The route ascends a small buttress flanked by right-facing dihedrals on the south part of the lower east face. The bottom of Stettner's Ledges is 300 feet north of the bottom of Alexander's Chimney. When looking at the east face from a distance, Stettner's Ledges is below and south (left) of the bottom of the Notch Couloir. The climb is normally done in six pitches. As with Alexander's Chimney, you can continue on Kieners or traverse south on Broadway to Lambs Slide.

Follow the Kieners Route to Mills Glacier. Climb the south tongue of Mills Glacier and scramble up broken rock to the highest ledge below some right-facing dihedrals. Pitch 1 (150 feet): Climb a corner (Class 5.4), move right and climb a right-facing dihedral (Class 5.6) to a ledge. Pitch 2 (90 feet): Go around the right side of a flake, then climb another right-facing dihedral (Class 5.4) to a large ledge. Pitch 3 (140 feet): From an alcove formed by a flake, climb a steep corner with fixed pins (Class 5.7+). This corner is called the "Piton Ladder" and is often wet. Continue up a shallow dihedral (Class 5.6) to a large ledge called "Lunch Ledge."

Pitch 4: From the south end of Lunch Ledge, climb a corner (Class 5.5) and continue up and left (Class 5.4) to another ledge. Pitch 5: Climb up and left to a ledge system (Class 5.4). Traverse left on the ledges, then climb up and left to join the Alexander's Chimney Route and its last pitch. Pitch 6 (160 feet): Traverse left for 75 feet into the Yellow Bowl (Class 4) and climb the left side of the bowl (Class 5.4) to Broadway.

Variation
1.6V Hornsby's Direct, Class 5.8

This direct finish replaces the last two pitches with steeper, harder climbing. Pitch 5 (120 feet): From the top of pitch 4, climb shallow dihedrals (Class 5.6) to a ledge below a steep section. Pitch 6 (140 feet): Climb a right-facing dihedral and pass a roof (Class 5.8) to reach Broadway.

1.7 Notch Couloir III, Class 5.0–5.2, Steep Snow/Ice *Classic*

From Longs Peak Trailhead: 12.2 miles, 4,850 feet

When it is in good condition, this is the most spectacular snow climb in the park. The Notch Couloir ascends from Broadway to the Notch on Longs' east face. It is in the best condition from mid-June to mid-July. By August the snow melts and the couloir no longer provides a snow climb. Conditions vary greatly in this couloir, so you should study it carefully before undertaking an ascent.

Follow the Kieners Route to the bottom of the Notch Couloir. Ascend the couloir as it twists up the face to the Notch. The couloir is not consistent in its steepness, and there are short, steep sections along the way. There are several places where you can escape north (right) onto the upper part of the Kieners Route. The angle in the couloir eases as you approach the Notch, and it is best to continue all the way into the Notch.

From the Notch, climb north (right) up Class 3 ledges for 150 feet, then ascend an east-facing chimney to a ridge. This Class 5.0–5.2 chimney is 100 feet high. Once you are on the ridge, the difficulty eases considerably. Scramble north along the ridge for 100 yards to the summit. This is a dramatic approach to Longs' flat summit.

1.8 Loft II, Class 3, Moderate Snow (Seasonal) *Classic*
From Longs Peak Trailhead: 12.6 miles, 5,000 feet

In August, when the snow slopes have melted, this route is only slightly harder than the Keyhole Route. It is also shorter than the Keyhole Route and much less traveled. This route allows you to climb both Longs and Meeker. The Loft Route ascends the broad trough between Ships Prow and Meeker to the Loft, then skirts below the west side of the Palisades to the Homestretch. This route is dangerous when snow covers the ledges below the Loft. By August the route becomes a Class 3 scramble.

From the Longs Peak Trailhead, follow the East Longs Peak Trail for 4.5 miles to Chasm Meadows, below Chasm Lake. There is an old stone cabin here, but it is locked unless a ranger is in residence. From Chasm Meadows, don't go to Chasm Lake but hike straight south toward Meeker's huge, sweeping north face. Once you are past the bottom of Ships Prow, turn southwest (right) and ascend the wide slope between Ships Prow and Meeker's north face. A moderate snow slope fills this trough in June and part of July. The slope narrows, and a large, sweeping cliff band blocks simple passage to the Loft.

Scramble up 100 feet of broken, Class 3 rock to the base of the cliff band. Turn south (left) and climb onto a 10-foot-wide ledge angling up to the south across the cliff band. This ledge must be found if an easy ascent is to take place. Follow the ledge for 150 yards until it merges into the broken, upper part of the cliff band (Class 3). Switchback north on a 2-foot-wide, grass-covered ledge for 100 feet and scramble up to the talus below the Loft (Class 3). From the switchback point, you can climb straight up, but this is more difficult.

Cross the Loft's large expanse to its northwest edge. Contour northwest and look sharp for some cairns. Descend slightly and find the top of a gully leading down to the scree-filled couloirs on Longs' south side. Traverse into the gully and scramble down for 100 feet to Clark's Arrow (Class 3). Clark's Arrow is an old painted arrow pointing south. It is on a smooth, west-facing slab just north of the bottom of the gully. It is visible for a long distance when descending from Longs to the Loft. It is not visible until you come immediately upon it when using this route to ascend Longs.

From Clark's Arrow, scramble north and descend slightly to a position below the Palisades, which are the beautiful, west-facing slabs soaring above you. The total elevation loss from the Loft to the low point below the Palisades is 150 vertical feet.

From the low point below the Palisades, the route becomes simpler. Scramble north up the scree-filled couloir below the Palisades. There is some loose rock in this couloir, so you should be careful if there are other people on the route. At 13,600 feet, the couloir broadens and Longs' upper south face directly above you blocks easy ascent. The Notch is prominent up to the east.

Do an ascending traverse northwest (left) on some Class 3 ledges for 200 yards to join the Keyhole Route at 13,900 feet, just below the Home-stretch, and follow that route to the summit. On the ascending traverse from 13,600 feet to 13,900 feet, you are below the Homestretch and should be on the lookout for falling objects.

Variation 1.8V

At 13,600 feet, turn east (right) instead of west (left) and climb into the Notch. This requires 30 feet of Class 5.0–5.2 climbing just below the Notch. Once you are into the Notch, finish the climb by following the upper part of the Notch Couloir Route (Class 5.0–5.2). This variation provides a technical finish to the already interesting Loft Route and avoids the crowds on the Homestretch.

Extra Credit 1.8EC

From the Loft, hike and scramble 0.3 mile southeast to Mount Meeker's dramatic summit block. Climb the summit block's northwest side (Class 3) to reach Meeker's 13,911-foot summit.

1.9 Keplinger's Couloir II, Class 3, Moderate Snow (Seasonal)

From Copeland Lake Trailhead: 16.0 miles, 5,940 feet

This is an easy route up Longs' south side, but it is not usually climbed in one day because of its long approach and elevation gain of 5,900 vertical feet. This route is best done with a camp at Sandbeach Lake or in cross-country zone 1G. With a high camp, the route provides a quiet alternative to the crowded Keyhole Route.

From the Copeland Lake Trailhead, follow the Sandbeach Lake Trail to Sandbeach Lake at 10,283 feet. From the north end of the lake, head north then west into upper Hunter Creek and find a small unnamed lake at

11,200 feet. Head north from the unnamed lake into the high basin formed by Meeker, Longs and Pagoda.

There are many couloirs and gullies on Longs' south side. All these couloirs reach the west side of the Palisades and, ultimately, the Notch. The Palisades are west-facing cliffs high on Longs' southeast side. The Notch separates the Palisades from Longs' summit. Keplinger's Couloir is the westernmost, large couloir heading toward the west side of the Notch. It has snow in it through June.

Follow the couloir to its end at 13,600 feet, below the final summit cliffs on Longs' south face. From this area, the Notch is prominent up to the east, and the Loft Route joins this route. Do not climb into the Notch, but turn west (left) and angle northwest up ledges to join the Keyhole Route at 13,900 feet. This section of the route is below the Homestretch, and rockfall is a possibility. Once you are on the Keyhole Route, continue up the Homestretch to the summit.

1.10 The Grand Slam III, Class 3, Moderate Snow (Seasonal) *Classic*

From Longs Peak Trailhead: 16.0 miles, 7,300 feet

Climbing Longs and its four buttress peaks in one day is a project that will stir sturdy souls. Follow the Loft Route to the Loft. Hike and scramble 0.3 mile southeast to Mount Meeker's dramatic summit block. Climb the summit block's northwest side (Class 3) to reach Meeker's 13,911-foot summit. Return to the Loft and continue on the Loft Route to Longs' summit. Descend the Homestretch and proceed toward the Narrows. Before climbing to reach the Narrows, descend toward Pagoda. Easy progress is blocked by a pesky cliff band. Descend a steep gully through the upper part of the cliffs (Class 3), then traverse west on a broad ledge until you are west of the lower cliffs. Descend on talus to the Longs–Pagoda Saddle. Climb Pagoda's north ridge to Pagoda's 13,497-foot summit and return to the Longs–Pagoda Saddle. Take a deep breath. There's more.

Climb northeast on the east side of the Keyboard of the Winds to a notch at 13,400 feet between two keys. Go through the notch and descend a steep, northwest-facing gully (Class 3) until you are below the keys. Do an ascending traverse northeast to rejoin the Keyhole Route where it enters the Trough (Class 3). Follow the Keyhole Route to the Keyhole. Go through the Keyhole and climb north on the east side of Storm Peak's south ridge to Storm's 13,326-foot summit. Descend east to the Boulder Field. Continue southeast to Mount Lady Washington's 13,281-foot summit. Descend Lady Washington's east slope to the Mills Moraine trail junction and follow the East Longs Peak Trail back to your starting point.

Extra Credit
1.10EC The Radical Slam
From Longs Peak Trailhead: 18.4 miles, 8,200 feet

For the handful of souls still standing, there's more. Do the Grand Slam to Mount Lady Washington. Descend 0.8 mile north to Granite Pass. Scramble northeast over Battle Mountain's 12,044-foot summit and descend northeast 1.6 miles to Storm Pass. Follow the trail east up to Estes Cone's 11,006-foot summit. Return to Storm Pass and follow the Eugenia Mine Trail back to the Longs Peak Trailhead. Do 50 push-ups. Collapse.

2. Grays Group

Grays Peak	14,270 feet
Torreys Peak	14,267 feet

See Map 2 on page 20

These fourteeners are just a few miles south of Interstate 70. Because of their proximity to the Denver metropolitan area, they are very popular. People usually climb the two peaks together. Surprisingly, Grays and Torreys are the only Colorado fourteeners on the Continental Divide. These distinct summits are visible from many Front Range and Summit County vantage points.

Maps
Required: Grays Peak, Arapaho National Forest
Optional: Montezuma

Trailheads
Stevens Gulch Trailhead

This trailhead is at 11,230 feet and provides access to Torreys and the north side of Grays. Take Exit 221 off Interstate 70 at Bakerville. This exit is 6.3 miles west of Georgetown. Cross to the south side of Interstate 70 and find a sign for Grays Peak. Switchback south up through the trees on Forest Service 189 (dirt) for 1.0 mile to a marked junction where the Stevens Gulch and Grizzly Gulch roads split. Stay east (left) on Forest Service 189.1 and continue for 2.0 miles to the parking lot at the well-marked trailhead. This road is steep but passable for most passenger cars.

In winter Forest Service 189 is closed. Winter access to Stevens Gulch is from the south side of the Bakerville exit at 9,780 feet. For winter climbs above the Stevens Gulch Trailhead, add 6.0 miles and 1,460 feet.

Grizzly Gulch Trailhead

This trailhead is at 10,320 feet and provides access to Torreys' north side. Take Exit 221 off Interstate 70 at Bakerville, 6.3 miles west of Georgetown. Cross to the south side of Interstate 70 and proceed onto Forest Service 189, switchbacking south up through the trees. Follow this dirt road south for 1.0 mile to a marked junction between the Stevens Gulch and Grizzly Gulch roads. Turn west (right) and continue on Forest Service 189.1C for an additional 0.3 mile to the trailhead. Park passenger cars below some old buildings just before the road crosses to the west side of Quayle Creek and becomes a four-wheel-drive road. For winter climbs above the Grizzly Gulch Trailhead, add 2.6 miles and 540 feet.

Four-wheel-drive vehicles can cross to the north side of Quayle Creek and continue up the rough road, crossing back to the south side of the creek after 0.9 mile. A little beyond this point, old avalanche debris flanks the road and is an impressive reminder of the power that lives here in winter. The road reaches a meadow 1.1 miles past the two-wheel-drive trailhead, at 10,740 feet; this is a good place to park four-wheel-drive vehicles. Driving enthusiasts can cross back to the north side of the creek and continue up the now very rough road for an additional 0.7 mile to 11,000 feet, where the road is blocked to vehicles.

Loveland Pass Trailhead

Loveland Pass on U.S. 6 is at 11,990 feet and provides easy access to the surrounding high country. When approaching from the east, take Exit 216 off Interstate 70 and follow U.S. 6 west for 4.2 miles to the pass. When approaching from the west, take Exit 205 off Interstate 70 near Dillon and follow U.S. 6 east for 16.2 miles to the pass. This trailhead is accessible in winter.

Chihuahua Gulch Trailhead

This trailhead is at 10,460 feet and provides access to the southwest sides of Grays and Torreys. Follow U.S. 6 to the Keystone North Peak Ski Area Road. This road is 8.6 miles west of Loveland Pass and 7.8 miles east of Interstate 70 Exit 205 in Dillon. Leave U.S. 6, follow the ski area road south for 0.1 mile, then turn east (left) onto Montezuma Road (paved). Go 4.7 miles east on Montezuma Road, then turn left onto the Peru Creek road (dirt, unmarked). Follow the Peru Creek road east for 2.2 miles to a small parking area across from the Chihuahua Gulch four-wheel-road road (unmarked). The Chihuahua Gulch four-wheel-drive road is 0.1 mile east of the Warden Gulch road (marked). In winter the Peru Creek road is closed at the Montezuma–Peru Creek junction.

Horseshoe Basin Trailhead

This trailhead is at 11,280 feet and provides access to the east side of Grays. Drive on U.S. 6 to the Keystone North Peak Ski Area Road. This road is 8.6 miles west of Loveland Pass and 7.8 miles east of Interstate 70 Exit 205 in Dillon. Leave U.S. 6, follow the ski area road south for 0.1 mile, then turn east (left) onto Montezuma Road (paved). Go 4.7 miles east on Montezuma Road, then turn left onto the Peru Creek road (dirt, unmarked). Follow the Peru Creek road east for 4.6 miles to the Shoe Basin Mine at 11,100 feet. Either park here or continue for an additional 0.3 mile to the start of the Argentine Trail at 11,280 feet. The Peru Creek road is passable for passenger cars up to the Shoe Basin Mine but becomes progressively rougher above the mine. In winter the Peru Creek road is closed at the Montezuma–Peru Creek junction.

2. Grays Peak   14,270 feet

See Map 2 on page 20

Grays Peak is 4 miles south of Exit 221 on Interstate 70. Grays is the highest peak in both Clear Creek and Summit Counties. Grays is the highest peak on the Continental Divide in Colorado. In fact, Grays is the highest peak on the Continental Divide between the origin of the Pacific–Atlantic divide on Snow Dome in the Canadian Rockies, and the Mexican border.

Routes

2.1 North Slopes II, Class 1
From Stevens Gulch Trailhead: 8.0 miles, 3,040 feet

Grays' lofty summit is easy to reach, and many people climb this peak each summer. In August the greatest hazard on this route may be being nuzzled by a dog! Start at the Stevens Gulch Trailhead and cross to the west side of the creek on a large footbridge. Simply follow the Grays Peak Trail for 4.0 miles to the summit. Climb southwest below the east face of Kelso Mountain, then west into the small basin below Torreys' east face and Grays' north slopes. Switchback up Grays' broad northern slopes on the well-constructed trail that goes all the way to the summit.

2.2 Lost Rat Couloir II, Class 2, Moderate Snow (Seasonal)
From Stevens Gulch Trailhead: 7.0 miles, 3,040 feet

This surprising snow climb is just a short distance east of the Grays Peak Trail on Grays' small northeast face. Its steepness punctuates Grays' otherwise genial slopes. It provides a nice snow climb in late spring and early summer.

Start at the Stevens Gulch Trailhead and follow the Grays Peak Trail for 1.5 miles to 12,070 feet. The couloir is visible from here to the east of Grays. Leave the Grays Peak Trail before it climbs west into the basin

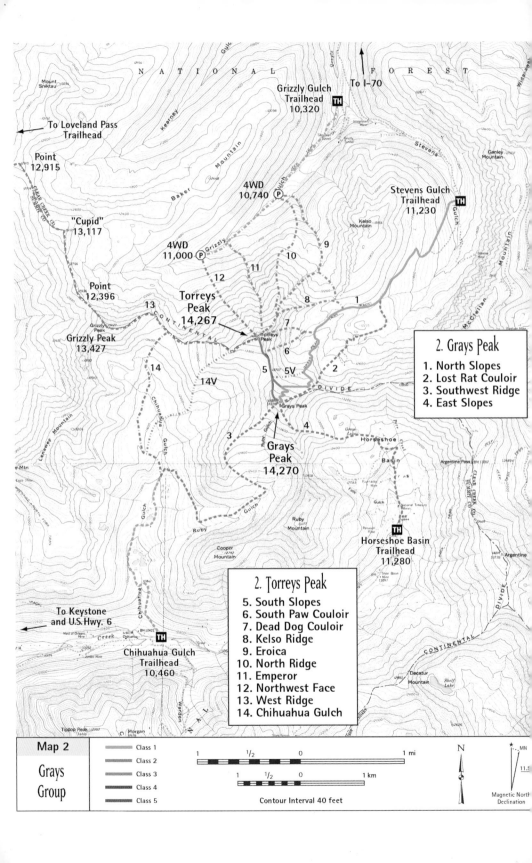

Grizzly Gulch Trailhead 10,320

To I-70

N A T I O N A L   F O R E S T

Mount Shiktau

To Loveland Pass Trailhead

Stevens Gulch Trailhead 11,230

Ganley Mountain

Point 12,915

Kelso Mountain

4WD 10,740 Ⓟ

"Cupid" 13,117

9

4WD 11,000 Ⓟ

10

Point 12,396

11

12

Torreys Peak 14,267

8

Grizzly Peak 13,427

13

1

7

2. **Grays Peak**
1. North Slopes
2. Lost Rat Couloir
3. Southwest Ridge
4. East Slopes

6

5   5V

2

14

14V

C O N T I N E N T A L   D I V I D E

Grays Peak 14,270

4

3

Horseshoe Basin

Horseshoe Basin Trailhead 11,280

Ruby Mountain

Argentine Pass

Argentine

To Keystone and U.S. Hwy. 6

Cooper Mountain

2. **Torreys Peak**
5. South Slopes
6. South Paw Couloir
7. Dead Dog Couloir
8. Kelso Ridge
9. Eroica
10. North Ridge
11. Emperor
12. Northwest Face
13. West Ridge
14. Chihuahua Gulch

Chihuahua Gulch Trailhead 10,460

Decatur Mountain

C O N T I N E N T A L   D I V I D E

Tiptop Peak

Morgan

Map 2		
Grays Group		

Class 1
Class 2
Class 3
Class 4
Class 5

1   1/2   0   1 mi

1   1/2   0   1 km

Contour Interval 40 feet

N

MN

11.5

Magnetic North Declination

Grays Peak from the northeast.

below Torreys' east face. Follow an old road south and southwest for an additional 1.0 mile to the bottom of the couloir at 12,800 feet. From here you can see the lower half of the Lost Rat Couloir. It is bounded on its west side by a dramatic pinnacle called the "Rascal."

Climb the couloir for 400 feet to a dogleg just below the embracing Rascal. At the dogleg, turn slightly east (left) and continue for an additional 400 feet as the now narrower couloir steepens slightly. The steepness reaches 40 degrees as you approach the ridge. Forged by winter's winds, the snow just below the ridge can be surprisingly hard-packed. The couloir ends on Grays' east ridge at 13,600 feet. Follow this easy ridge to the summit.

Extra Credit 2.2EC

If you descend the Grays Peak Trail, take a few steps east from the switchback at 13,500 feet and peer over an astonishing edge into the Lost Rat Couloir. The steepness here stands in sharp contrast to the trail. For even more excitement, descend north for 150 yards, then climb east to the Rascal's summit (Class 4). This is an airy perch.

2.3 Southwest Ridge II, Class 2
From Chihuahua Gulch Trailhead: 10.0 miles, 3,810 feet

Grays' south side is easily accessible from Summit County on the west side of the Continental Divide, and this side of the peak provides a refreshing alternative to the crowded North Slopes Route. The Southwest Ridge Route winds through two valleys and ascends a scenic ridge.

Start at the Chihuahua Gulch Trailhead and follow the four-wheel-drive road north into Chihuahua Gulch. The road starts on the east side of the creek, crosses to the creek's west side and passes a large meadow. The road then crosses back to the creek's east side and passes a second meadow. There are good views of the west side of Grays and Torreys from the meadows, but Grays' south side is hidden. From the second meadow's northern end, do *not* cross back to the creek's west side. The Chihuahua Gulch Road does cross the creek here, but the Ruby Gulch Road goes *up the creek* for 100 feet, then climbs north on the creek's west side. Follow Ruby Gulch Road.

After climbing north of the confluence of Ruby and Chihuahua Gulches, the road turns back southeast and climbs into Ruby Gulch south of Grays. Follow the road east to its end at an old mine building at 12,120 feet. You can see the rest of the route from here. Climb northwest from the old mine building and reach Grays' southwest ridge at 13,100 feet. Follow this colorful ridge northeast to 13,800 feet, where it merges into a scree slope. Climb straight up this 500-foot scree slope to the summit. This final slope's looseness is the only detraction from an otherwise charming route. Descending the East Slopes Route completes a southern Tour de Grays.

2.4 East Slopes I, Class 2
From Horseshoe Basin Trailhead: 5.0 miles, 2,990 feet

This is the shortest route on Grays. The East Slopes Route is easier than the Southwest Ridge Route and only slightly harder than the crowded North Slopes Route. There are roads, grass slopes and goat trails all the way. Start at the Horseshoe Basin Trailhead and follow the main four-wheel-drive road north for 1.0 mile into Horseshoe Basin. Leave the road at 12,060 feet before it turns back south. Climb west to tiny, captivating Grays Lake at 12,460 feet. Climb grass slopes west of Grays Lake and reach Grays' south ridge at 13,800 feet. Follow this ridge north to the summit.

2. Torreys Peak   14,267 feet

See Map 2 on page 20

Torreys is 3.5 miles southeast of Loveland Pass and 3.5 miles south of Interstate 70. You can see Torreys from Exit 221 on Interstate 70 at Bakerville. This is a dramatic view, especially in winter.

Routes
2.5 South Slopes II, Class 2
From Stevens Gulch Trailhead: 8.0 miles, 3,040 feet

This is the easiest route on Torreys. Start at the Stevens Gulch Trailhead. Follow the Grays Peak Trail to 13,800 feet, leave the trail and traverse northwest for 0.2 mile across talus to the Grays–Torreys Saddle at 13,707 feet. The snow slope east of this saddle persists through summer, and you should stay above the snow slope's south side. You can easily see and avoid the snow slope when approaching the saddle from the Grays Peak Trail. From the Grays–Torreys Saddle, ascend a trail for 0.4 mile up Torreys' south side to the summit.

Variation 2.5V

When conditions are good (yours and the snow's), you can ascend directly to the Grays–Torreys Saddle on steep snow.

2.6 South Paw Couloir II, Class 3, Steep Snow
From Stevens Gulch Trailhead: 7.0 miles, 3,040 feet

This is the steep couloir on the south side of Torreys' east face. It is shorter but steeper than the Dead Dog Couloir. The couloir reaches Torreys' south ridge at 13,900 feet, where, with a few cautious strides over to the edge, you can peer down South Paw from the South Slopes Route. This view has dissuaded many aspirants.

Start at the Stevens Gulch Trailhead and follow the Grays Peak Trail for 2.4 miles to a bench at 12,600 feet. The bottom of South Paw is southwest of here, 300 yards south of Dead Dog. Carefully consider conditions before attempting this climb. Even in summer, small snow slides can surprise you and take you down with them. The top of the couloir is guarded by a large, extensive cornice that persists into summer. It will likely force you onto the rocks south of the couloir to finish the climb. From the top of South Paw, climb north for 800 feet to Torreys' summit.

2.7 Dead Dog Couloir II, Class 3, Steep Snow
From Stevens Gulch Trailhead: 7.0 miles, 3,040 feet

This is the large couloir in the center of Torreys' east face, and it reaches Kelso Ridge just below the summit. When snow conditions are good, this is the premier mountaineering route on Torreys, but after the snow melts, you should avoid this couloir. There is decent snow through June, but it melts faster here than in couloirs farther north, so don't wait too long to climb this one.

A helmet is recommended for this route, because the rock surrounding the couloir is rotten and rockfall is a hazard. The rockfall problem is compounded because a long stretch of Kelso Ridge is above the couloir, and careless climbers on that route may send rocks down upon you. Leave early.

Start at the Stevens Gulch Trailhead and follow the Grays Peak Trail for 2.4 miles to a bench at 12,600 feet. The couloir is directly west and easily visible. Leave the trail and climb west up the broad slope below the couloir to the start of the couloir at 13,100 feet. The couloir winds up the face, and you can't see the top until you reach halfway. The angle in the center of the couloir is 45 degrees, and the angle near the top is 50 degrees. The finish is beautiful and reaches Kelso Ridge above 14,000 feet. The summit is only 100 yards away. This route can provide more than 1,000 vertical feet of snow climbing!

2.8 Kelso Ridge II, Class 3 *Classic*
From Stevens Gulch Trailhead: 7.0 miles, 3,040 feet
From Grizzly Gulch Trailhead: 7.0 miles, 3,950 feet

This is Torreys' northeast ridge, and it provides a sporting alternative to the South Slopes Route. It has become quite popular in recent years. There are only a few scrambling sections on Kelso Ridge, and it looks harder than it is. This ridge is a climb, not a hike.

From the Stevens Gulch Trailhead, follow the Grays Peak Trail 2.0 miles to a bench at 12,300 feet. Leave the trail and climb 200 yards northwest to the 12,380-foot saddle between Torreys and Kelso Mountain (13,164 feet). Kelso is 1.6 miles northeast of Torreys and 0.9 mile west of the Stevens Gulch Trailhead.

From the Torreys–Kelso Saddle, climb west along the gentle beginning to the ridge. The ridge soon steepens to meet the challenge. The Kelso Ridge sees many feet; there is a small trail in the easier sections, but there are also some false trails. If you are uncomfortable with this initial scrambling, a retreat to the Grays Peak Trail is prudent.

You must negotiate two towers between 12,800 feet and 13,200 feet. The first requires 30 feet of Class 3 scrambling up a small trough. The higher one can be passed on either side with 30 feet of exposed, Class 3 scrambling. The north side is easier. Above this second tower, move to the ridge's north side and scramble up a steep dirt slope to easier ground.

Continue up on the ridge's north side for 0.3 mile on a strong trail. Midway along this easy stretch, at 13,600 feet, Torreys' broad north ridge rising out of Grizzly Gulch joins Kelso Ridge. The upper part of Kelso Ridge heads southwest toward the summit. Above the junction with the north ridge, do not knock rocks down the southeast (left) side of the ridge. You are above Dead Dog Couloir, and there may be climbers below you.

Just as you think you are about to walk to the top, the route's crux appears. There is a solid rock buttress on the ridge 200 yards below the summit. There are at least three ways to solve this problem. The buttress can be climbed directly with 40 feet of Class 4 climbing, or it can be skirted on either side of the ridge with Class 3 scrambling.

Skirting the buttress on the north (right) side involves climbing up some loose, unpleasant rock, but you rapidly regain the ridge. Skirting the buttress on the south (left) side is easy at first, but leads into the top part of Dead Dog Couloir. In June and July, when there is steep snow here, this

Torreys Peak from the northeast.

is not a good alternative. After the snow melts, the upper couloir becomes a steep dirt slope and this is the easiest route. You also can regain the ridge crest from partway along the south-side traverse (Steep Class 3).

If you regain the ridge crest below the top of Dead Dog Couloir, there is one more interesting problem. Stay on the ridge crest and behold the notorious knife-edge of Kelso Ridge. It requires 30 feet of exposed, Class 3 scrambling on very solid rock, and many people choose to scoot across sitting down. Fortunately, the knife is dull! The top of Dead Dog Couloir is 100 feet beyond the knife-edge, and the summit is 100 steep yards beyond that. Continue to be careful with loose rocks all the way to the summit, because any rock knocked loose will fall into Dead Dog Couloir.

2.9 Eroica II, Class 3, Steep Snow (Seasonal)

From Grizzly Gulch Trailhead: 6.0 miles, 3,950 feet
With descent of Northwest Face: 6.8 miles, 3,950 feet
From Stevens Gulch Trailhead: 6.6 miles, 3,040 feet
With descent of South Slopes: 7.3 miles, 3,040 feet

Eroica is an eclectic climb for the erudite. It is yet another exciting climb on a peak with a reputation for being easy. Eroica is the central couloir of Torreys' tiny northeast face between the Kelso Ridge and North Ridge Routes. With both snow and rock pitches, this is Torreys' finest mixed climb. You can approach it from either the Grizzly Gulch or Stevens Gulch Trailhead, and this makes several circle tours possible.

From the Grizzly Gulch Trailhead, follow the four-wheel-drive road as it climbs southwest into Grizzly Gulch. After 1.1 miles, leave the road in a meadow at 10,740 feet and bushwhack southeast for 1.0 mile into the basin between Kelso and Torreys to the base of the climb at 12,000 feet. From the Stevens Gulch Trailhead, follow the Grays Peak Trail for 2.0 miles to a bench at 12,300 feet. Leave the trail and climb 200 yards northwest to the 12,380-foot saddle between Torreys and Kelso. Cross the saddle and descend northwest into the basin for 0.35 mile to the base of the climb at 12,000 feet.

Climb southwest up the inset couloir on moderate snow to 12,800 feet. Above this point, the couloir fans open into a tiny alpine paradise where you have several steep choices. Any of the finishes can make you feel heroic and elite. You can climb south (left) and reach Kelso Ridge at 13,440 feet, or you can climb southwest and reach Torreys' north ridge at 13,400 feet. For the most aesthetic exit, climb southeast directly to the junction of Kelso Ridge and Torreys' north ridge at 13,600 feet. From here, finish on the Kelso Ridge Route and its Class 3 crux.

2.10 North Ridge II, Class 3
From Grizzly Gulch Trailhead: 6.0 miles, 3,950 feet

This route provides a less crowded, albeit steeper and less classic alternative to the Kelso Ridge Route. Start at the Grizzly Gulch Trailhead and follow the four-wheel-drive road as it climbs southwest into Grizzly Gulch. After 1.1 miles, leave the road in a meadow at 10,740 feet. Bushwhack south up the hill and reach a bench just above tree line at 11,600 feet. Torreys' north ridge takes shape above this point. Climb the increasingly distinct ridge for 1.0 mile (Class 2). Any difficulties are easily passed on the west (right). Join the Kelso Ridge Route at 13,600 feet and follow the upper part of that route to the summit. The upper part of Kelso Ridge includes its Class 3 crux. Ascending the North Ridge Route and descending the Northwest Face Route provides a nice Tour de Torreys.

2.11 Emperor II, Class 3, Steep Snow (Seasonal)
From Grizzly Gulch Trailhead: 6.2 miles, 3,950 feet

Torreys has a small northeast face between the north ridge and Kelso Ridge, a very small north face immediately west of the north ridge and a larger northwest face farther west. Emperor ascends the couloirs in the center of the north face. This has been the standard tough climb on Torreys' north side for years. When it is in good condition, Emperor provides 3,000 feet of snow climbing. It is one of Colorado's longest snow climbs. You can preview Emperor's condition from Interstate 70.

From the Grizzly Gulch Trailhead, follow the four-wheel-drive road southwest into Grizzly Gulch for 1.1 miles to a meadow at 10,740 feet.

Cross back to the north side of the creek and follow the road for an additional 0.7 mile to 11,000 feet, where the road is blocked to vehicles. The route is directly above you to the south.

Leave the road, cross the creek and climb southeast into the tiny basin. Climb the steepening snow and pass through a narrow passage between black rocks at 12,100 feet. Continue up the relentless couloir to 12,800 feet, where you begin to have choices as the couloir splits. Continue up the central couloir between some more rocks to the upper basin at 13,400 feet. Do an ascending traverse to the southeast to reach Kelso Ridge near the notch at the top of the Dead Dog Couloir. Follow that ridge to the summit.

Variations
2.11V1 Steep Snow
From 12,800 feet, take the west (right) fork of the couloir, follow it to the talus at 13,400 feet and hike south to the summit. This couloir is steeper, but climbing it shortens the time you spend on snow.

2.11V2 Steep Snow
If snow conditions permit, you can finish your ascent by climbing south directly to the summit from 13,400 feet in the central couloir.

2.12 Northwest Face II, Class 2, Moderate Snow (Seasonal)
From Grizzly Gulch Trailhead: 7.0 miles, 3,950 feet

Torreys has a small northeast face between the north ridge and Kelso Ridge, a very small north face immediately west of the north ridge and a larger northwest face farther west. A long, wide snow couloir splits the center of the northwest face and goes directly to the summit. This is the route. This is a spring or early summer route; you should carefully consider avalanche conditions before committing to this couloir. When it is in good condition, this couloir provides 2,000 feet of snow climbing and is often used as a speedy descent route. Do not confuse Torreys' small, rugged north face with its larger, gentler northwest face.

Start at the Grizzly Gulch Trailhead and follow the four-wheel-drive road as it climbs southwest into Grizzly Gulch. Go up the valley for 1.8 miles to 11,000 feet, where the road is blocked to vehicles. Continue up the old road, now a trail, for an additional 0.3 mile to 11,200 feet. Torreys' northwest face and its couloirs will be above you to the south.

Leave the road, cross the creek and climb south to the couloir, which begins at 12,000 feet. The lower half of the climb is up the wide, straight couloir. At 12,700 feet, the couloir splits into two parallel couloirs. You can climb either branch, but the west (right) one is easier. The steepness approaches, but does not exceed, 40 degrees. Escape from the snow is possible at any point by moving onto the steep talus that flanks the couloirs.

Depending on the year and time of year, the snow may or may not extend all the way to Torreys' west ridge. If it does, it may be blasted hard by winter's winds; you will appreciate crampons for this condition. You can avoid this difficulty by moving east onto the talus. Once on Torreys' west ridge at 14,000 feet, stroll east for 0.1 mile to the summit.

2.13 West Ridge II, Class 2

From Loveland Pass Trailhead: 10.0 miles, 5,500 feet

Torreys can be climbed from Loveland Pass on U.S. 6. This is a longer route than those starting at the Stevens Gulch Trailhead. It is a refreshing ridge route that also allows you to bag Grizzly Peak.

From the Loveland Pass Trailhead, climb east up the well-traveled slope to Point 12,915. Hike south along the Continental Divide to the rounded summit of Point 13,117, alias "Cupid." This is one of Colorado's ranked thirteeners, and it provides a lovely view of the rugged terrain ahead. Continue south over Point 12,936 to reach noble Grizzly Peak (13,427 feet). In early June, there can be some dangerous cornices along this ridge. From Grizzly Peak, descend east to a 12,580-foot saddle and climb Torreys' long, easy west ridge.

2.14 Chihuahua Gulch II, Class 2

From Chihuahua Gulch Trailhead: 9.4 miles, 3,810 feet

This is a scenic, seldom climbed route on Torreys. Start at the Chihuahua Gulch Trailhead and follow the four-wheel-drive road north into Chihuahua Gulch. The road starts on the east side of the creek, crosses to the creek's west side and passes a large meadow. The road then crosses back to the creek's east side and passes a second meadow. From the second meadow's northern end, cross back to the creek's east side and reach the end of the four-wheel-drive road at 11,300 feet. Continue north on a trail into upper Chihuahua Gulch. From the end of the trail, climb a gentle slope to the 12,580-foot saddle between Torreys and 13,427-foot Grizzly Peak. Follow Torreys' west ridge along the Continental Divide to the summit.

Variation 2.14V

From 11,600 feet in Chihuahua Gulch, hike east, then ascend Torreys' rounded southwest ridge to join Torreys' west ridge at 13,900 feet. This shorter, steeper alternative avoids the 12,580-foot Torreys–Grizzly Saddle.

Extra Credit 2.14EC

From the Torreys–Grizzly Saddle, climb 0.8 mile west to the summit of Grizzly Peak (13,427 feet).

2. Grays and Torreys Combinations

See Map 2 on page 20

Routes

2.15 II, Class 2

From Stevens Gulch Trailhead: 9.0 miles, 3,600 feet

This combination is the easiest way to climb Grays and Torreys together. Follow the Grays Peak Trail to Grays' summit, descend north to the Grays–Torreys Saddle and ascend Torreys' south side. Return to the Grays–Torreys Saddle, then traverse southeast to return to the Grays Peak Trail. The snow slope below the saddle surprises some people when they approach it from above. You can do this combination in reverse, but most people climb Grays first.

2.16 II, Class 3

From Stevens Gulch Trailhead: 8.2 miles, 3,600 feet

This popular Tour de Grays and Torreys has a mountaineering flavor. Ascend the Kelso Ridge Route to Torreys' summit, descend south to the Grays–Torreys Saddle, then ascend south to Grays' summit. Descend the Grays Peak Trail.

2.17 II, Class 3, Steep Snow

From Stevens Gulch Trailhead: 8.2 miles, 3,600 feet

This combination is even more exciting. Ascend the Dead Dog Couloir to Torreys' summit, descend south to the Grays–Torreys Saddle, then ascend south to Grays' summit. Descend the Grays Peak Trail.

2.18 II, Class 2

From Loveland Pass Trailhead to Stevens Gulch Trailhead: 9.7 miles, 4,450 feet

This lofty combination requires a vehicle shuttle but allows you to climb three peaks. Start at Loveland Pass and follow Torreys' West Ridge Route over Grizzly Peak (13,427 feet) to Torreys' summit. Descend south to the Grays–Torreys Saddle, then ascend south to Grays' summit. Descend the Grays Peak Trail to the Stevens Gulch Trailhead.

2.19 II, Class 2

From Chihuahua Gulch Trailhead: 10.4 miles, 4,360 feet

This is a scenic way to climb both fourteeners from the south. Start at the Chihuahua Gulch Trailhead and ascend Grays' Southwest Ridge Route. Descend north to the Grays–Torreys Saddle, then ascend north to Torreys' summit. Descend Torreys' Chihuahua Gulch Route.

3. Evans Group

Mount Evans	14,264 feet
Mount Bierstadt	14,060 feet

See Map 3 on page 32

These peaks have the distinction of being the closest fourteeners to Denver. Mount Evans is a scant 36 miles west of Colorado's capitol building in downtown Denver. Evans' large massif forms the mainstay of Denver's mountain backdrop and is visible to millions of people. Evans serves as a constant reminder of why these people choose to live in Colorado. For many people, their Rocky Mountain High starts here.

Maps
Required: Mount Evans, Arapaho National Forest
Optional: Georgetown, Harris Park, Idaho Springs, Pike National Forest

Trailheads
Echo Lake Trailhead
This trailhead is at 10,580 feet and provides access to Chicago Creek and the paved road up Mount Evans. Leave Interstate 70 at Exit 240 in Idaho Springs. Signs for Mount Evans mark this exit. Follow Colorado 103 south for 13.4 miles to Echo Lake, which is on the south side of the highway. You also can reach Echo Lake by following Colorado 103 west for 18.5 miles from the junction of Colorado 103 and Colorado 74 in Bergen Park. From the northwest side of Echo Lake, turn west onto a dirt road with a sign for the Echo Lake Picnic Area. Go 0.2 mile west then south to the trailhead.

There is also a parking lot east of Echo Lake at the junction of Colorado 103 and Colorado 5 (the Mount Evans Road). The road to the Echo Lake Picnic Area is 0.6 mile west of the Colorado 103–Colorado 5 junction. This trailhead is accessible in winter.

Summit Lake Trailhead
This trailhead is at 12,850 feet and provides access to Evans' Northeast Face Route and the upper part of the Mount Evans Road. Leave Interstate 70 at Exit 240 in Idaho Springs. Follow Colorado 103 south for 13.4 miles to Echo Lake. You also can reach Echo Lake by following Colorado 103 west for 18.5 miles from the junction of Colorado 103 and Colorado 74 in Bergen Park.

From the east end of Echo Lake, follow Colorado 5 (the Mount Evans Road) for 9.1 miles as it climbs south to Summit Lake, which is on the west (right) side of the road. There are two additional parking areas on the road between Echo Lake and Summit Lake. The first is at 11,550 feet, 2.9 miles above Echo Lake. The second is at 12,150 feet, 4.8 miles above Echo Lake. Colorado 5 is closed in winter.

The Forest Service took over management of Summit Lake from the city of Denver in 1998. With that change came a $6 fee for driving up the Mount Evans Road. A seasonal pass costs $15. Rangers collect the fee on Colorado 5 at Echo Lake. The Forest Service uses the money to improve trails and other public services, and to protect natural resources.

West Chicago Creek Trailhead

This trailhead is at 9,600 feet and provides access to the West Chicago Creek Trail. Leave Interstate 70 at Exit 240 in Idaho Springs. A sign for Mount Evans marks this exit. Follow Colorado 103 south for 6.6 miles to a dirt road on the south (right) side of the highway. This junction has a sign for the West Chicago Creek Campground. Leave Colorado 103 and follow the dirt road southwest for 2.8 miles to the West Chicago Creek Campground and the trailhead. In winter the snowplow turns around at the start of a switchback 2.0 miles above Colorado 103; you can often drive beyond this point.

Guanella Pass Trailhead

This trailhead is at 11,669 feet and provides access to the west sides of Evans and Bierstadt. Take Exit 228 off Interstate 70 at Georgetown and follow Guanella Pass Road south for 10.0 miles, or leave U.S. 285 at Grant and follow Guanella Pass Road north for 12.2 miles. Guanella Pass Road is mostly dirt but is passable for passenger cars. Guanella Pass Road is open in winter but is the last priority for the snowplow crew. You can see Bierstadt's rounded mass east of Guanella Pass.

Scott Gomer Creek Trailhead

This trailhead is at 9,620 feet and provides access to the Abyss Lake Trail and the south sides of Evans and Bierstadt. Leave U.S. 285 at Grant and follow Guanella Pass Road north for 5.0 miles. You can reach the trailhead by taking Exit 228 off Interstate 70 at Georgetown, following Guanella Pass Road south for 10.0 miles to Guanella Pass and continuing south for an additional 7.2 miles to the trailhead, which is adjacent to Burning Bear Campground. This trailhead is accessible in winter.

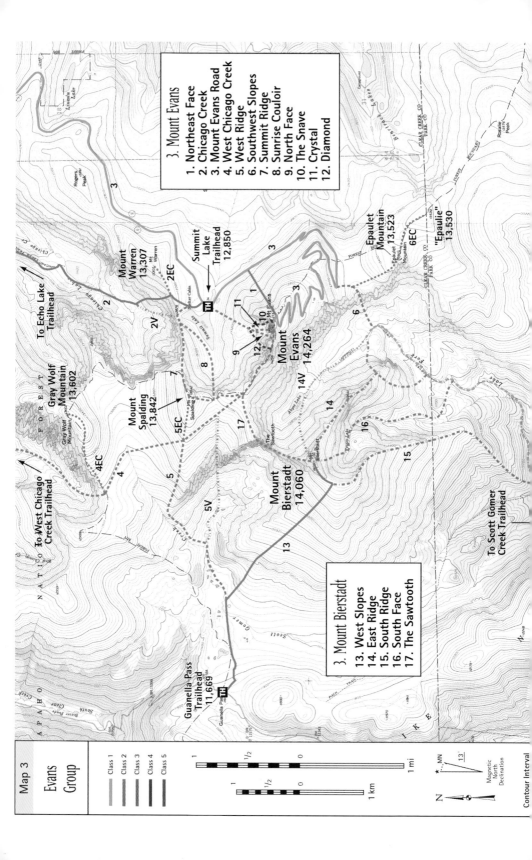

Map 3

Evans Group

3. Mount Evans
1. Northeast Face
2. Chicago Creek
3. Mount Evans Road
4. West Chicago Creek
5. West Ridge
6. Southwest Slopes
7. Summit Ridge
8. Sunrise Couloir
9. North Face
10. The Snave
11. Crystal
12. Diamond

3. Mount Bierstadt
13. West Slopes
14. East Ridge
15. South Ridge
16. South Face
17. The Sawtooth

Class 1
Class 2
Class 3
Class 4
Class 5

Magnetic North
Declination

Contour Interval

Mount Warren
13,307

Summit Lake
Trailhead
12,850

Mount Evans
14,264

Epaulet Mountain
13,523

"Epaulie"
13,530

Mount Spalding
13,842

Gray Wolf Mountain
13,602

Mount Bierstadt
14,060

Guanella Pass Trailhead
11,669

To Echo Lake Trailhead

To West Chicago Creek Trailhead

To Scott Gomer Creek Trailhead

3. Mount Evans   14,264 feet

See Map 3 on page 32

Mount Evans' proximity to Denver, plus a paved road to the summit, makes Evans exceedingly popular. Serious cliff bands interrupt Evans' gentle slopes, and there are many adventures available on this large, complex peak.

Routes

3.1 Northeast Face I, Class 2
From Summit Lake Trailhead: 2.0 miles, 1,420 feet

This is a short, popular route. If you are more interested in an outing than a climb, this may be it. Start at the Summit Lake Trailhead. From the east side of Summit Lake, hike south and a little east to Evans' talus-covered northeast face. Climb south up the northeast face for 0.6 mile to the summit.

Do not confuse Evans' gentle northeast face with the steep northwest face. Many people have been involved in accidents on the northwest face when trying to descend to Summit Lake on foot after driving to the summit.

3.2 Chicago Creek II, Class 2
From Echo Lake Trailhead: 14.0 miles, 4,600 feet

This route avoids most of the Mount Evans Road and is the normal route for mountaineers. From the Echo Lake Trailhead, walk south into the open woods near the southwest corner of the lake. You also can reach this point from the east end of Echo Lake by following a trail on the lake's south side.

Find the Chicago Lakes Trail near the slight ridge southwest of Echo Lake. Look for old blazes on the trees. Follow the Chicago Lakes Trail, cross to the west side of the ridge southwest of Echo Lake, descend southwest and switchback down to reach Chicago Creek at 10,300 feet. This point is south of the private property at Camp Shwayder.

Cross to the west side of Chicago Creek on a three-log bridge and walk southwest up the valley on an old dirt road to the Chicago Creek Reservoir at 10,600 feet. Continue on the road around the west side of the reservoir and enter the Mount Evans Wilderness south of the reservoir. Hike southwest on a trail to southernmost Chicago Lake at 11,750 feet. From the southern end of this lake, climb south up a broken slope for 0.6 mile to Mount Warren's west ridge at 13,060 feet. Descend 0.2 mile south to Summit Lake at 12,850 feet. The Mount Evans Road passes Summit Lake, and this is a popular place in summer. Continue up the Northeast Face Route to the summit.

Variation 3.2V

From the southernmost Chicago Lake at 11,750 feet, ascend the slope directly into the 12,876-foot saddle between Mount Warren and Mount Spalding. This requires a little Class 3 scrambling. Do not stray onto the slope west of the saddle, because the difficulty increases rapidly in that direction.

Extra Credit 3.2EC

From Summit Lake, climb northeast for 0.5 mile to the 13,307-foot summit of Mount Warren.

3.3 Mount Evans Road II, Class 1

From Echo Lake Trailhead: 29.2 miles, 3,700 feet
Via Northeast Face Route: 20.0 miles, 3,700 feet

This is the easiest route up Evans, but it is long and high. Start at the Echo Lake Trailhead and walk, run, ski or bike up the Mount Evans Road. A significant shortcut for hikers uses the Northeast Face Route above Summit Lake instead of following the road. People who have driven a car up Evans have told me, with evident pride, that they climbed the peak! Ahem. If you drive up, your *vehicle* has climbed the peak. *You* are awarded a nice view but no mountaineering credit at all.

There has been a sporadic Mount Evans Trophy Run up the Mount Evans Road. It is billed as the world's highest road race. The race starts at the gate just beyond the parking lot at the junction of Colorado 103 and Mount Evans Road, and finishes in the summit parking lot. The distance is 14.6 miles. The men's record is 1 hour, 41 minutes, 35 seconds, and the women's record is 2 hours, 7 minutes, 14 seconds. Any male finisher under 2 hours, 40 minutes, and any female finisher under 3 hours receives a special trophy, usually a rock mounted on a plaque. Runners reveal a mountaineering appetite if they continue 300 feet past and above the summit parking lot to reach Evans' highest point.

3.4 West Chicago Creek II, Class 2

From West Chicago Creek Trailhead: 16.0 miles, 4,900 feet

This long, arduous ascent ends with a traverse of Evans' high west ridge. The route is above tree line for 4 miles! Don't confuse West Chicago Creek with Chicago Creek.

From the West Chicago Creek Trailhead, follow the West Chicago Creek Trail south 3.8 miles to its end at 11,200 feet in Hells Hole. Continue southeast then south for an additional 1.5 miles up the narrow, rocky basin under the impressive northwest face of Gray Wolf Mountain (13,602 feet). There is a huge split boulder at the top of the basin. Climb south to the 12,740-foot saddle between Gray Wolf Mountain and Point 12,988. The introduction is over.

Contour east for 0.5 mile, then climb south for 0.6 mile to Mount Spalding's broad west ridge at 13,400 feet. Continue southeast for 0.75 mile to the west end of Evans' west ridge at 13,900 feet. This route joins the West Ridge Route here. Scramble 0.7 mile east along the west ridge to Evans' summit. Most of this airy, fun traverse is above 14,000 feet.

Extra Credit 3.4EC

Gray Wolf Mountain is a "Bi," one of Colorado's 200 highest peaks. It is 0.5 mile east of this route, and you can reach its 13,602-foot summit by hiking up grass and talus.

3.5 West Ridge II, Class 2

From Guanella Pass Trailhead: 9.0 miles, 3,100 feet

You can climb Evans by itself from Guanella Pass. From Guanella Pass, hike 2.0 miles northeast across the shallow basin at the head of Scott Gomer Creek. Skirt north of all the cliffs that extend for 1 mile northwest of the Sawtooth and reach the gentle, open slopes on the northwest side of Mount Spalding (13,842 feet). Cross to the south side of Spalding's broad west ridge, skirt south of Spalding's summit and reach the west end of Evans' west ridge at 13,900 feet. Scramble east along this ridge for 0.7 mile to Evans' summit (Class 2). Most of this airy, fun traverse is on solid, sculpted rock. The traverse stays above 14,000 feet as it crosses two false summits. The eastern false summit reaches 14,256 feet.

Variation 3.5V

From Guanella Pass Trailhead: 8.0 miles, 3,100 feet

This significant and frequently used shortcut provides the shortest route up Evans that does not use the Mount Evans Road. Instead of climbing around the north end of all the cliffs extending northwest from the Sawtooth, continue straight east at 11,600 feet and ascend a scree gully through the center of the cliffs (Class 2). Rejoin the route on the slope above. You can easily see the shortcut gully from Guanella Pass. It rarely holds snow in winter.

Extra Credit 3.5EC

From the open slopes between Mount Spalding and the west end of Evans' west ridge, climb north for 0.5 mile to the summit of Mount Spalding (13,842 feet), one of Colorado's 100 highest peaks.

3.6 Southwest Slopes II, Class 2

From Scott Gomer Creek Trailhead: 16.0 miles, 4,650 feet

This route is noteworthy because it is seldom climbed. Scott Gomer Creek offers an alternative approach to Evans' crowded northern slopes. The route is long, but easy for the most part. Start at the Scott Gomer

Creek Trailhead and follow the Abyss Lake Trail northeast for 3.8 miles to a trail junction at 10,600 feet. Stay on the Abyss Lake Trail as it climbs east then north past tree line into the basin between Evans and Bierstadt.

Look for a keyhole-shaped pinnacle guarding the southern entrance to a steep scree gully on the east side of the valley. Leave the trail at 12,200 feet, climb east and ascend the scree gully north of the pinnacle. This gully reaches the low point of the broad saddle between Evans and Epaulet Mountain (13,523 feet). From this saddle, hike northwest for 1.0 mile to reach Evans' summit. Use or avoid the road as you desire.

Extra Credit 3.6EC

From the Evans–Epaulet Saddle, hike south for 0.5 mile to Epaulet Mountain (13,523 feet). For even more credit, continue southeast for an additional 0.7 mile to Point 13,530. This unnamed summit is higher than Epaulet, and purists debate whether it is really Epaulet's summit. My opinion is that these are two separate summits, one named but unranked, and one ranked but unnamed. If you climb both summits, you have certainly climbed Epaulet and can add your voice to the debate. Because Point 13,530 is between Epaulet and 13,575-foot Rosalie, which is higher still, the silly name "Epaulie" has been suggested for Point 13,530.

3.7 Summit Ridge I, Class 2

From Summit Lake Trailhead: 5.0 miles, 2,260 feet

With descent of Northeast Face: 3.5 miles, 1,840 feet

This circular ridge walk with impressive views keeps you high and provides a unique approach to Evans' summit. Start at Summit Lake and walk north along the east side of the lake for 0.25 mile to the 12,876-foot saddle between Mount Warren and Mount Spalding. Climb west for 1.0 mile up Spalding's east ridge to Spalding's 13,842-foot summit. The view of Evans' north face is spectacular from this ridge. Descend 0.25 mile south to the 13,580-foot Evans–Spalding Saddle. Climb south for an additional 0.3 mile and join Evans' West Ridge Route. Follow that route east along the famous ridge to Evans' summit. For solitude, return the same way. To complete a circle tour and considerably shorten your return, descend the Northeast Face Route.

Variation 3.7V

From Echo Lake Trailhead: 17.0 miles, 5,460 feet

With descent of Northeast Face: 15.5 miles, 5,040 feet

Summit Ridge provides a roadless, alpine finish to the Chicago Creek Route. Follow the Chicago Creek Route to 13,060 feet on Mount Warren's west ridge. Descend west to the Warren–Spalding Saddle and continue on the Summit Ridge Route to Evans' summit.

The north face of Mount Evans.

3.8 Sunrise Couloir I, Class 3, Steep Snow

From Summit Lake Trailhead: 4.7 miles, 1,740 feet

With descent of Northeast Face: 3.2 miles, 1,580 feet

Sunrise Couloir rises 700 feet above the west end of Summit Lake to the Evans–Spalding Saddle. The route is easily visible from Summit Lake, where you can preview conditions from the comfort of your car. This route will gratify those looking for a technical snow challenge with a minimal approach.

To avoid trampling tundra, walk around the north side of Summit Lake and walk west to the bottom of the couloir. Although the couloir itself is a straightforward climb, it is almost always capped by a pesky cornice, even in late summer. Climb the steepening couloir and find a way to overcome the cornice. In most years, you can execute a clever climb by sneaking between the rock and snow on the north (right) side of the cornice (Class 3). Mortals will appreciate crampons and an ice ax. From the Evans–Spalding Saddle, continue on the Summit Ridge and West Ridge Routes to Evans' summit.

3.9 North Face I, Class 3, Moderate Snow (Seasonal)

From Summit Lake Trailhead: 2.0 miles, 1,420 feet

Evans has a sweeping, mile-wide north face that extends west below the summit. The cliffs below the summit are the most serious, and difficulties moderate to the west. Although much of the face is broken, there are many technical treasures hidden here. Expert enthusiasts ski and snowboard the many available couloirs. The easiest route, described here, is a sweeping snowfield near the center of the face. This is a route for May or June. By August the upper part of this slope is odious rubble.

Climb southwest from the east end of Summit Lake into the Summit Lake Bowl, below the face. From a bench at 13,300 feet, the route is directly above you to the south. Ascend the steepening and narrowing snowfield to Evans' west ridge. The steepness reaches 40 degrees and the views halfway up the slope are distinctly alpine. The snow does not always reach the ridge. Depending on the year, you may have to steer around exposed rocks or scramble up talus as you approach the ridge. The route reaches Evans' west ridge in the 14,140-foot saddle midway between Point 14,256 and Evans' summit. Hike east along the west ridge for 0.2 mile to the tippy top.

3.10 The Snave II, Class 4, Steep Snow (Seasonal)
From Summit Lake Trailhead: 1.8 miles, 1,420 feet

The name *Snave* is *Evans* spelled backward, and it fits this serpentine tour. Climb southwest from the east end of Summit Lake into the Summit Lake Bowl, below Evans' rugged northwest face. This face has a lower cliff band and the summit cliffs. Bypass the lower cliff band on its north end. Do an ascending traverse south on the ramp between the lower and upper cliffs. This ramp holds good snow into June. Reach the inset couloir in the middle of the face and ascend it. The snow steepens in the couloir and ends in rocks below the summit. Climb a Class 4 pitch up the upper couloir to reach a small notch and the tourist trail just north of the summit. Your arrival here is bound to attract attention.

Tourists trundling rocks from the summit could pelt this route with deadly missiles. Although this has not been a problem in recent years, leave early to beat rush hour on the summit.

3.11 Crystal II, Class 3, Steep Snow (Seasonal)
From Summit Lake Trailhead: 1.8 miles, 1,420 feet

This steep route is on the south side of Evans' northwest face. It is a test piece for skiers and a nifty climb. You may be able to identify the climbing route by spotting ski tracks. Climb southwest from the east end of Summit Lake into the Summit Lake Bowl, below Evans' northwest face. Crystal is a narrowing couloir south (right) of the cliffs below the summit. Start below the summit and climb south along the south side of the lower cliff band until you reach the summit cliffs on the upper end of the ramp that splits this face. This is the ramp used by the Snave Route. Escape the summit cliff by climbing south along the narrow, steep-sloped ramp and reach a small saddle and the tourist trail 100 yards south of the summit.

3.12 Diamond II, Class 4, Steep Snow (Seasonal)
From Summit Lake Trailhead: 2.0 miles, 1,420 feet

This mixed tour provides a sensuous snow slope capped by a rock challenge. Climb southwest from the east end of Summit Lake into the Summit Lake Bowl, below Evans' northwest face. Diamond ascends the snow slope west of the first large rock buttress 0.2 mile west of the summit. The route is west of the North Face Route and you may spot ski tracks on it in June. Climb the sweet, steepening snow until it ends below cliffs. Stay east (left) of some steep rock and climb two Class 4 pitches to reach Evans' west ridge just east of Point 14,256.

3. Mount Bierstadt   14,060 feet

See Map 3 on page 32

This peak is 2.4 miles east of Guanella Pass and 1.4 miles west of the more famous Mount Evans. Bierstadt is important because it is one of Colorado's easiest fourteeners. People often climb it in winter, and it is a good test piece for winter mountaineers.

Routes
3.13 West Slopes I, Class 2
From Guanella Pass Trailhead: 6.0 miles, 2,770 feet

This is the easiest route on Bierstadt. Start at the Guanella Pass Trailhead and descend gently southeast from the pass for 1.0 mile to the flats near Scott Gomer Creek at 11,400 feet. Engage the famous Bierstadt Willows. You must cross this sea of willows to reach Bierstadt, and they are no joke. A trail now winds through the north end of the willows and makes life easy.

Before the trail appeared, hardened mountaineers took the direct line toward the summit and bashed through the heart of the willows. Clever mountaineers attempted to find a lost trail through the south end of the willows and spent even more time thrashing around. People wearing shorts went way around the south end of the willows and spent a long time climbing Bierstadt. People without a mission went a little way into the willows and returned to the pass!

The willows are even bad in winter. Snow appears to cover them, but it is generally not consolidated and sets you up for a big letdown. Snowshoes help, but they do not solve the problem and often lead to some hysterical tableaux. Remember, it is poor etiquette to laugh at the leader—your turn is next!

Once you are past the willows, continue on the trail as it winds up Bierstadt's broad western slope for 1.5 miles to a shoulder south of the

Mount Bierstadt from the northeast.

summit at 13,780 feet. From the shoulder, climb 0.25 mile northeast along the ridge to the summit.

On winter climbs, keep the following facts in mind. Winter's strong west winds blow freely across Guanella Pass. The wind is at your back on the ascent, but you must face it on the return. Many cold parties turn to discover that the return trip into the wind is much worse than the climb. Many parties become disoriented in whiteouts when returning across the flats near Scott Gomer Creek. Some parties have even turned south and descended into the depths of the Scott Gomer Creek drainage. This is a bad mistake, because it leaves you many miles from Guanella Pass. It is prudent to use a compass to protect your retreat. Finally, remember that the last mile back to the pass is uphill!

3.14 East Ridge II, Class 3 *Classic*

From Scott Gomer Creek Trailhead: 16.0 miles, 4,600 feet

With descent of Northeast Face: 16.5 miles, 4,600 feet

This is the most interesting route on Bierstadt, but it is seldom climbed. The ridge is surprisingly rugged as it crosses Point 13,641. The rock is beautiful and solid. This ridge can be climbed via Scott Gomer Creek or on a blitz from the Mount Evans Road. This description assumes the Scott Gomer Creek approach. See Combination 3.19 for the approach from the Mount Evans Road.

Start at the Scott Gomer Creek Trailhead and follow the Abyss Lake Trail for 5.8 miles to 11,800 feet. From here you can see an impressive buttress forming the bottom of Bierstadt's east ridge. Leave the trail, hike north up an open slope and reach Bierstadt's east ridge at 13,000 feet, above the initial buttress.

Head northwest up the ridge, scrambling over and around some large blocks to reach Point 13,420. From here you can see the rest of the challenge, which is an improbable ridge rising up to Point 13,641. Scramble to the bottom of more difficult climbing and traverse northwest on an exposed ledge on the northeast (right) side of the ridge (Class 3). When difficulties above you relent, climb to the ridge crest (Class 3). Continue on or near the now broader ridge crest and ascend a beautiful slab with two parallel cracks in it to reach Point 13,641 (Class 3). Scramble west over Point 13,641 and do a Class 3 descent to reach easier ground. Follow the east ridge's easier, upper portion for 0.6 mile to the summit.

Variation 3.14V
From Scott Gomer Creek Trailhead: 17.0 miles, 4,600 feet

If the east ridge is not to your liking, continue on the trail all the way to Abyss Lake at 12,650 feet and climb Bierstadt's northeast face (Class 2). This route provides a nice descent after an ascent of the East Ridge Route.

3.15 South Ridge II, Class 2
From Scott Gomer Creek Trailhead: 13.6 miles, 4,450 feet

This ridge provides another salubrious sojourn on Bierstadt's backside. Start at the Scott Gomer Creek Trailhead and follow the Abyss Lake Trail northeast for 3.8 miles to a trail junction at 10,600 feet. This point is at the base of Bierstadt's 3-mile-long south ridge. Stay on the Abyss Lake Trail for another 0.25 mile, then bushwhack straight north for 300 yards to reach the rounded ridge. Bushwhack northeast on the ridge for 0.6 mile to tree line at 11,800 feet. From here the route is clear. Follow the now distinct ridge north for 1.4 miles to Bierstadt's south shoulder at 13,780 feet. As you approach the shoulder, you have some unique views of Frozen Lake in the basin to the north. The West Slopes Route also reaches the south shoulder, and you are likely to meet other people here. From the shoulder, climb 0.25 mile northeast along the ridge to the summit.

3.16 South Face II, Class 2, Steep Snow (Seasonal)

From Scott Gomer Creek Trailhead: 14.5 miles, 4,450 feet

This route offers industrious mountaineers a chance to visit Frozen Lake and enjoy more than 1,000 feet of fanciful snow climbing. This south face is best climbed in May or early June after a heavy-snow winter.

Start at the Scott Gomer Creek Trailhead and follow the Abyss Lake Trail northeast for 3.8 miles to a trail junction at 10,600 feet. Continue on the Abyss Lake Trail for an additional 1.8 miles to 11,600 feet. Leave the trail and hike west for 0.25 mile to a heart-shaped lake at 11,730 feet. Continue west over a small ridge and proceed into the drainage below Frozen Lake. Climb north up this drainage for 0.8 mile, then climb west through broken cliffs to reach Frozen Lake at 12,940 feet. This well-named lake is seldom visited by climbers. From the lake's north side, climb north for 1,100 feet up the consistent slope directly to Bierstadt's summit.

If snow conditions are favorable, glissade back to Frozen Lake and return as you came. If you prefer, a descent of the South Ridge Route completes a rotund Tour de Bierstadt.

3. Evans and Bierstadt Combinations

See Map 3 on page 32

3.17 The Sawtooth II, Class 3 *Classic*

From Guanella Pass Trailhead: 9.7 miles, 3,840 feet

Bierstadt is 1.4 miles west of Evans; you can climb these two peaks together by starting at Guanella Pass. The ridge connecting Evans with Bierstadt contains a step called the "Sawtooth." The Sawtooth and Evans' west ridge look more difficult than they are. This high, wonderful ridge traverse is fun when it is dry.

Start by ascending Bierstadt's West Slopes Route. From Bierstadt's summit, descend north for 0.4 mile to 13,200 feet on the east side of the 13,340-foot saddle between Bierstadt and the Sawtooth. Bypass some initial gendarmes on the ridge's east side. From a point below a second saddle, scramble up, do a rolling traverse on the ridge's east side, then scramble up to the ridge crest (Class 3). This portion of the route is well cairned. Cross to the ridge's west side, traverse on a large ledge below the ridge crest, cross a scree gully and ascend a large, exposed diagonal ledge through the Sawtooth's cliff band to reach easier ground (Class 3). Several cairns mark the top of the diagonal ledge if you choose to do this traverse in the other direction.

Once you are past the Sawtooth, hike east across open slopes for 0.5 mile to the beginning of Evans' west ridge at 13,900 feet. Scramble east along this airy, fun ridge for 0.7 mile to Evans' summit (Class 2). Descend Evans' West Ridge Route to return to Guanella Pass.

3.18 II, Class 3

From Scott Gomer Creek Trailhead: 17.0 miles, 5,500 feet

This is tough. Start at the Scott Gomer Creek Trailhead and climb Bierstadt's South Ridge Route. Continue to Evans via the Sawtooth (described in Combination 3.17). Descend Evans' Southwest Slopes Route.

3.19 I, Class 3 *Classic*

From 13,300 feet on Mount Evans Road: 6.3 miles, 3,000 feet

This route maximizes excitement and minimizes walking. It traverses the best ridges Evans and Bierstadt have to offer. Start at the switchback on the Mount Evans Road at 13,300 feet in the broad saddle between Evans and Epaulet Mountain (13,523 feet). This switchback is 11.4 miles from Echo Lake, and there is parking available at the switchback.

Hike south to the low point of the Evans–Epaulet Saddle, then descend west down a scree gully to the Lake Fork of Scott Gomer Creek. Hike west across the valley near a small unnamed lake at 12,360 feet, then climb an open slope to reach Bierstadt's east ridge at 13,100 feet. Follow the upper part of Bierstadt's East Ridge Route to Bierstadt's summit. Traverse to Evans via the Sawtooth (described in Combination 3.17). From Evans' summit, descend southeast for 1.0 mile to your starting point.

4. Pikes Peak   14,110 feet

See Map 4 on page 44

Pikes Peak is the easternmost fourteener in the United States and needs little introduction. It soars west of the Colorado Springs metropolitan area and is often the first peak seen when approaching the Rocky Mountains from the east. Its colorful history has been told many times.

Pikes is the southern Front Range's monarch and the highest peak in El Paso County. Pikes has the largest elevation gain in Colorado. The peak rises a staggering 7,800 vertical feet above downtown Manitou Springs in a horizontal distance of 7.25 miles. No other Colorado peak can match that!

Each year, thousands of people reach Pikes' summit by road, rail and trail. People run, roll, ride, bike, hike, ski, camp, stamp, stomp and sell Pikes. The song "America the Beautiful" was written on the summit.

Maps

Required: Pikes Peak, Pike National Forest
Optional: Manitou Springs

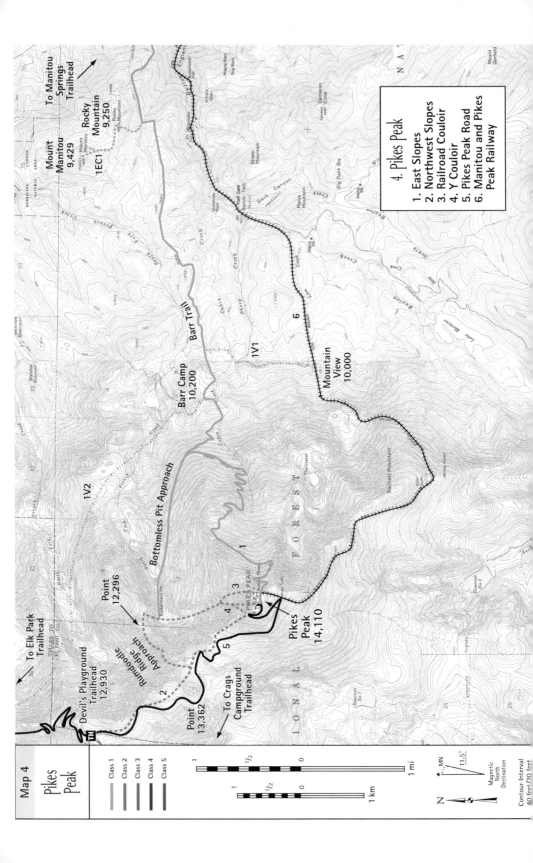

Map 4

Pikes Peak

4. Pikes Peak
1. East Slopes
2. Northwest Slopes
3. Railroad Couloir
4. Y Couloir
5. Pikes Peak Road
6. Manitou and Pikes
   Peak Railway

To Manitou
Springs
Trailhead

Mount Manitou
9,429

Rocky
Mountain
9,250

1EC1

Barr Trail

Barr Camp
10,200

Bottomless Pit Approach

Mountain
View
10,000

1V1

1V2

Point
12,296

Devil's Playground
Trailhead
12,930

To Elk Park
Trailhead

Ruthdoodle
Ridge
Approach

2

Point
13,362

To Crags
Campground Trailhead

3

4

5

PIKES PEAK

Pikes Peak
14,110

NATIONAL   FOREST

Sachet Mountain

1

Class 1
Class 2
Class 3
Class 4
Class 5

1   1/2   0   1 mi

1   1/2   0   1 km

MN

11.5°

Magnetic
North
Declination

N

Contour Interval
40 feet/20 feet

Trailheads

Manitou Springs Trailhead

This trailhead is at 6,700 feet and provides access to the Barr Trail on Pikes' east side. Go west for 0.4 mile on the U.S. 24 Business Loop from City Hall in the center of Manitou Springs. Turn west (left) onto well-marked Ruxton Avenue and follow it for 0.7 mile to the cog railway depot. Continue west for an additional 0.1 mile past the depot, then turn north (right) onto Hydro Street (paved). Go north on Hydro Street for 100 yards to the large parking lot at the well-marked trailhead. Although large, this parking lot fills up early on summer weekends. Arrive earlier. This trailhead is accessible in winter.

Crags Campground Trailhead

This trailhead is at 10,100 feet and provides access to Pikes' northwest side. Take Exit 141 off Interstate 25 and go west on U.S. 24 for 18.4 miles to the junction of Colorado 67 and U.S. 24 in Woodland Park. Continue west on the combined Colorado 67 and U.S. 24 for an additional 6.8 miles to the next junction of Colorado 67 and U.S. 24 in the small community of Divide. Leave U.S. 24, turn south (left) onto Colorado 67 and go 4.3 miles to Teller County 62 (dirt). This poorly marked junction has two small signs, one for the Rocky Mountain Camp and the other for the Crags Campground. Turn east (left) onto Teller County 62 and go 1.6 miles to the Rocky Mountain Camp. Turn south (right) onto the main road and continue for an additional 1.6 miles to the entrance to the Crags Campground. Turn east (left) into the campground and go 0.3 mile to the well-marked trailhead on the campground's east side. Winter road closure is near the Rocky Mountain Camp.

Elk Park Trailhead

This trailhead is on the Pikes Peak Road at 11,900 feet and provides access to the Elk Park Trail and Barr Camp. Take Exit 141 off Interstate 25 and go west on U.S. 24 for 10.0 miles to Cascade. Follow good signs and turn onto the Pikes Peak Road. Follow the toll road for 13.0 miles to Glen Cove. Continue for an additional 1.0 mile to the trailhead at mile 14. The trailhead is on the road's east side, midway through a sweeping north-to-south turn. The winter road closure is at Glen Cove at 11,500 feet.

Devil's Playground Trailhead

This trailhead is on the Pikes Peak Road at 12,930 feet and provides access to Pikes' north side, including Bottomless Pit. Take Exit 141 off Interstate 25 and go west on U.S. 24 for 10.0 miles to Cascade. Follow good signs and turn onto the Pikes Peak Road. Follow the toll road for

16.0 miles past Glen Cove to the Devil's Playground in the 12,930-foot saddle between Point 13,070 and Pikes' long, ambling northwest ridge. There is ample off-road parking here.

There are several constraints to using this trailhead. The road is not open to Devil's Playground in winter. The winter road closure is at Glen Cove at 11,500 feet. The road above Glen Cove opens just before Memorial Day each year. Even when open, the road is closed at night and no overnight parking is allowed along the road. The road opens at 9:30 A.M. each day, which negates early morning starts from this trailhead. The evening closing time varies but is never later than 10 P.M.; it may be much earlier in bad weather. Walking on the road or its shoulder and hitchhiking are illegal. You must walk at least 50 feet from the road; 100 feet is better. Frequent road patrols enforce these restrictions.

Approaches

4.A1 Bottomless Pit Trail Approach II, Class 1
From Manitou Springs Trailhead: 17.2 miles, 4,940 feet
From Barr Camp: 6.0 miles, 1,480 feet

You can use this approach to reach the technical routes on Pikes' north face. Bottomless Pit, the dramatic bowl below the north face, can be reached by a long trail hike. Start at the Manitou Springs Trailhead and follow the Barr Trail for 5.6 miles to Barr Camp at 10,200 feet. Continue on the Barr Trail for an additional 1.0 mile to the prominent switchback at 10,830 feet. Leave the Barr Trail and climb gently around Pikes' broad northeast slopes on the Bottomless Pit Trail for 2.0 miles into the Pit at 11,640 feet.

4.A2 Rumdoodle Ridge Approach I, Class 3
From Devil's Playground Trailhead: 5.0 miles, 1,700 feet
From 13,100 feet on Pikes Peak Road: 2.4 miles, 1,500 feet

Rumdoodle Ridge is a shorter but much more difficult approach route to Bottomless Pit. Start at the Devil's Playground Trailhead and walk south above the road, skirting Points 13,190 and 13,250 on their west sides. Leave the road and skirt Point 13,363 on its east side to reach the 13,110-foot saddle between Point 13,363 and the small Point 13,230 to the east.

You can also park or be dropped off at 13,100 feet on the road just after it traverses around to the southeast side of Point 13,363. This point is 1.8 miles beyond Devil's Playground and just south of the 13,110-foot saddle. Remember, there is no overnight parking allowed on the Pikes Peak Road.

From the 13,110-foot saddle, go northeast, skirt Point 13,230 on its west side and find the top of Rumdoodle Ridge just beyond. Scramble northeast down the rocky ridge (Class 3) for 0.5 mile to the very small Point 12,296. This ridge requires careful route finding to keep the difficulty at Class 3. Harder climbing lurks in the many small cliffs. From the south side of Point 12,296, descend east for an additional 0.2 mile to a 12,070-foot saddle, then descend straight south for 0.2 mile to the bottom of Bottomless Pit at 11,640 feet. Now you are set to climb to the sky.

Routes

4.1 East Slopes III, Class 1 *Classic*

From Manitou Springs Trailhead: 25.8 miles, 7,400 feet

This is the easiest hiking route on Pikes' east side. From the Manitou Springs Trailhead at 6,700 feet, follow the Barr Trail as it winds up Pikes' eastern slopes for 12.9 miles to the summit. The elevation gain is a brutal 7,400 vertical feet, Colorado's greatest vertical rise. The excellent trail breaks naturally into four segments, each with its own personality and challenges.

The first trail segment takes you up the east slopes of Rocky Mountain and Mount Manitou. You meet their challenge immediately above the trailhead as the trail switchbacks steeply up these east slopes. The trail distance and elevation are marked with large metal signs with holes for the letters. The first sign reads "Peak 12 MI, Elev. 7,200." These signs were placed a long time ago and you should only use the information as a general guide, because both distance and elevation are often wrong. The first sign is no exception, especially when compared with the sign at the trailhead.

After the first set of switchbacks, the trail flattens out and passes through a natural rock arch. Beyond the arch you will learn the law of the Barr Trail: Every flat section is quickly followed by a steep section. Beyond the arch, climb steeply through two switchbacks and continue straight at the junction with the trail leading north to the top of the old Mount Manitou incline cog railway. The trail descends briefly, then climbs to cross No Name Creek at 8,720 feet. A sign here reads "Pikes Peak Summit 9.5, Barr Camp 3.5."

The second trail segment takes you to Barr Camp. After a set of switchbacks, the trail flattens and occasionally descends as it rolls along through a Hansel and Grettle forest toward your still distant goal. This is the easiest stretch of the Barr Trail. Enjoy it. Pass a sign that reads "Pikes Peak Summit 7.5, Top of Incline 2.5" and continue to another sign that reads "Barr Trail Elev. 9,800', Barr Camp .5, Pikes Peak Summit 6.5, Manitou Springs 6.5." Continue straight at the trail junction near this sign. The trail heading south goes 1.5 miles to the Mountain View Station on the Manitou and Pikes Peak Cog Railway. See Variation 4.1V1 for details on this trail.

Pikes Peak
14,110

Pikes Peak from the east.

Halfway into your ascent in both distance and elevation gain, the trail reaches Barr Camp at 10,200 feet. It is hidden in the trees just north of the trail and is operated under permit from the Forest Service. Constructed in 1921 by Fred Barr, the designer and builder of the Barr Trail, Barr Camp offers many amenities for weary hikers. There are two cabins, an A-frame and two lean-to shelters for overnight stays. You might consider spending a night at Barr Camp to cut Pikes Peak down to size.

A bunk in the main cabin costs $10 per night, and the upper cabin, which sleeps 10, costs $75 per night. The A-frame, which sleeps 4, costs $10 per night. Tent camping is free. The cabins have propane cookstoves, mattresses, a fireplace, picnic tables and even a well-stocked library. There is filtered drinking water here, which any hiker can access. You can buy an all-you-can-eat breakfast for $5 and dinner for $7. Bring your own lunch. You can buy T-shirts, sodas and candy. Donations are appreciated. If Pikes Peak is not providing enough exercise, you can play horseshoes, badminton and volleyball. You can reserve the A-frame, lean-to shelters and upper cabin by calling (719) 630-3934. The 20 bunks in the main cabin are rented on a first-come, first-served basis. Groups of 5 or more should always notify Barr Camp in advance. Refreshed by your stop at Barr Camp, you can return to the task of climbing Pikes Peak.

The third trail segment takes you to tree line. Immediately beyond Barr Camp, continue straight at the junction with the Elk Park Trail, which goes north and west for 4.5 miles to the Elk Park Trailhead at mile 14 on the toll road. See Variation 4.1V2 for details on this trail. Pass a helicopter landing pad 200 yards beyond Barr Camp, east of the trail. Above Barr

Camp, the trail finally climbs in earnest again and passes close to Cabin Creek before climbing northwest to the junction with the Bottomless Pit Trail at 10,840 feet. The sign here reads "Pikes Peak Summit 4.8, Bottomless Pit 2.4." Do not continue straight here but switchback to the south before the rock in front of the sign.

From the switchback, climb steadily southwest for 0.6 mile, then negotiate 15 switchbacks up to the A-frame shelter near tree line at 11,900 feet. Look for a sign that reads "Timberline shelter, Pike National Forest." From this sign, the A-frame shelter is down to your left. The sturdy shelter can provide a welcome respite, especially in bad weather.

The fourth trail segment takes you to the summit. Two short switchbacks above the A-frame is a sign that reads "Barr Trail Elev 11,500', Pikes Peak Summit 3." The elevation is wrong on this sign. It is closer to 11,950 feet. As you approach tree line, you go through a grotesque dead forest that burned in 1910. Above the trees, Pikes' upper east face, and your final challenge, sweeps up in a singular slope.

A mind-numbing 23 switchbacks above the A-frame shelter near tree line is a sign that reads "Barr Trail Elev 12,700', Pikes Peak Summit 2." These are encouraging numbers, but you may be too tired to appreciate them. A 0.7-mile ascending traverse takes you from the north edge of the east face to some teethlike notches on the south edge, where you can peer south into Pikes' southern cirque. The trail switchbacks near the cirque's edge, past a sign that reads "Peak 1 Mi, Elev 13,300." You must be close; the sign writers no longer felt the need to remind you that the peak you are climbing is Pikes.

The trail has some rough spots as it strains for the summit, where you can see tourists watching you. Your final challenge is the 16 Golden Stairs. A Golden Stair is a switchback pair, so you have 32 switchbacks to go. Six switchbacks below the summit is a memorial plaque to Fred Barr, who constructed this amazing trail between 1914 and 1918.

At the summit, you enter another universe. You will join many people who reached this point by road or rail. As you explore the summit and, perhaps, buy refreshments in the cafeteria, you can rest with the knowledge that you have *climbed* Pikes Peak. Purists will seek out the mountain's high point, which is a lump west of the summit house. Remember that, from this ubiquitous summit, you can see from sea to shining sea. All you have to do is ignore the crowds and look beyond the horizon.

Variations
4.1V1

Buy a halfway ticket on the Manitou and Pikes Peak Cog Railway for $7 and get off at the Mountain View Station at 10,000 feet. Follow a trail north for 1.5 miles and join the Barr Trail at 9,820 feet. Barr Camp is 0.6 mile west of this junction. This approach greatly reduces the effort needed to reach Barr Camp, but be aware that you cannot reboard the train at Mountain View or at the summit.

4.1V2

This variation provides you with some interesting options. Start at the Elk Park Trailhead and descend southeast on the Elk Park Trail for 1.3 miles to a trail junction at 11,150 feet. Turn east (left) at this junction, cross French Creek's North Fork and continue east then southeast on a long contour at 10,700 feet. Descend to cross French Creek's South Fork at 10,200 feet and contour south to join the Barr Trail just west of Barr Camp. It is 4.5 miles from the Elk Park Trailhead to Barr Camp.

Extra Credit
4.1EC1

If climbing Pikes Peak is not enough for you, leave the Barr Trail at No Name Creek at 8,720 feet and hike north for 0.3 mile on a trail to Rocky Mountain's 9,250-foot summit. To complete your day, continue northwest for an additional 0.6 mile to Mount Manitou's 9,429-foot summit.

4.1EC2

If hiking up the Barr Trail leaves you fresh, run the Pikes Peak Marathon. The famous race is one of America's premier mountain runs. The race, held in mid-August each year, starts and finishes in Manitou Springs, which increases the mileage to 26.2 miles and the elevation gain to 7,800 feet. To reduce congestion on the trail, there are now two races. The ascent is held on Saturday and the round-trip marathon on Sunday. In recent years, more than 2,000 people have been finishing the two races, with the ascent being more than twice as popular as the grueling marathon. A few souls do the two races on successive days.

The male ascent record is 2 hours, 1 minute, 6 seconds, set by 29-year-old Matt Carpenter in 1993. He set this astonishing time en route to his round-trip marathon record of 3 hours, 16 minutes, 39 seconds. The female ascent record is 2 hours, 33 minutes, 31 seconds, set by 24-year-old Lynn Bjorklund in 1981 en route to her round-trip marathon record of 4 hours, 15 minutes, 18 seconds. There are records for each 5-year age group for ages 16 to 89. For more information on the Pikes Peak Marathon, visit the website at www.skyrunner.com.

4.2 Northwest Slopes II, Class 2

From Crags Campground Trailhead: 11.4 miles, 4,100 feet
From Devil's Playground Trailhead: 5.0 miles, 1,200 feet

This alternative to the popular Barr Trail requires far less effort. This is also a good route to use when the Pikes Peak Road is closed for the season.

Start at the Crags Campground Trailhead and go east on the Crags Trail for almost 200 yards. It is difficult to see the terrain in the trees, and critical route finding is imminent. If you continue on the Crags Trail, you will end up in the wrong drainage. Look for three metal water tubes with different diameters on the north (left) side of the trail. Go east on the Crags Trail for 100 feet past the tubes. Two converging creeks are only a few feet south of the trail at this point, and the two creeks come from different drainages. You want to proceed into the southern drainage. Leave the comfort of the Crags Trail and go south (right) across the northern creek. Find an old rocky road between the two creeks and follow it east along the northern side of the southern creek. Finding this old road is the key to this route.

Follow the old road east for 1.0 mile. In this mile, the road crosses to the south side of the southern creek, then back to the north side at 10,900 feet under a soaring block of rock to the north. The drainage east of this point opens into a sweeping basin. Follow the now ancient road as it climbs the slope to the east. At 11,200 feet, leave the northeast-angling road and climb east on a strong climber's trail. Switchback twice, angle southeast and climb steeply to the highest trees at 11,800 feet.

The strong trail continues for a few hundred yards into the tundra, then slowly fades but remains discernible. To avoid trampling tundra, try to follow the trail up the lush tundra slope as you angle slightly south (right) to reach the broad, 12,730-foot saddle at the top of the slope. From here, Pikes pops into view and you can see Pikes Peak Road and the upper part of the route.

From the 12,730-foot saddle, walk northeast then east on an old spur road (closed to vehicles) for 0.7 mile to the Devil's Playground Trailhead, which is in a 12,930-foot saddle on Pikes Peak Road. This saddle is east of Point 13,070 on Pikes' long northwest ridge. You could start this route at the Devil's Playground Trailhead, but because of the road restrictions, that is not recommended.

Cross to the east side of Pikes Peak Road and walk south above the road. Walking along the popular road or its shoulder and hitchhiking are illegal. You must walk at least 50 feet from the road; 100 feet is better. Frequent road patrols stop offenders. Stay above the road as you skirt Points 13,190 and 13,250 on their west sides. Then skirt Point 13,363 on its east side; this is a good shortcut that provides brief relief from the road. At 13,400 feet, leave the road and climb talus (Class 2) on Pikes' upper northwest slope to the broad summit.

Extra Credit 4.2EC

From Devil's Playground, climb west to the summit of Point 13,070. This unnamed summit has the distinction of being the highest point in Teller County, and you might as well bag it while you are so close.

4.3 Railroad Couloir II, Class 3, Steep Snow/Ice (Seasonal)

From Bottomless Pit: 2.0 miles, 2,470 feet
From Barr Camp: 8.0 miles, 3,950 feet
From Devil's Playground Trailhead: 7.0 miles, 4,170 feet
From Manitou Springs Trailhead: 19.2 miles, 7,400 feet

Many people are surprised to learn that Pikes has exciting technical routes. Not surprisingly, they are on Pikes' north face. The Railroad Couloir, in spite of its name, provides a titillating, sky-reaching snow climb in a rugged setting. It is the easiest route on Pikes' north face. Snow conditions are best in May and June, and the couloir is bare in August. Preview conditions from a distance before committing to this climb.

Use either the Bottomless Pit Trail Approach or the Rumdoodle Ridge Approach to reach Bottomless Pit at 11,640 feet. The Railroad Couloir is the easternmost couloir on the north face. Angling slightly to the east (left), climb south into the snow bowl in the center of the face at 12,600 feet. Stay to the east (left) and climb the now distinct couloir as it steepens and narrows. Pass a large rock buttress, then angle west (right) at 13,700 feet. Continue straight up for the steepest, most classic finish, or angle east (left) for an easier finish. Your climb and solitude end abruptly a few feet from the end of the cog railway line on the east side of the summit.

An unusual hazard on this climb is tourists on the summit who try to fill up Bottomless Pit by tossing rocks down your route. To minimize this risk, consider being dropped off and climbing early from a bivouac in Bottomless Pit. A very early start from Barr Camp is another good alternative. In any case, wear a helmet.

4.4 Y Couloir II, Class 3, Steep Snow/Ice (Seasonal) *Classic*

From Bottomless Pit: 2.0 miles, 2,470 feet
From Barr Camp: 8.0 miles, 3,950 feet
From Devil's Playground Trailhead: 7.0 miles, 4,170 feet
From Manitou Springs Trailhead: 19.2 miles, 7,400 feet

The Y Couloir is the premier mountaineering route on Pikes' north face. It is centrally located on the north face and is slightly steeper and harder than the Railroad Couloir. The Y Couloir offers two branches near the summit. Snow conditions are best in May and June. You can sometimes find alpine ice here in July. Preview conditions from a distance before committing to this climb.

Use either the Bottomless Pit Trail Approach or the Rumdoodle Ridge Approach to reach Bottomless Pit at 11,640 feet. Angling slightly to the east (left), climb south into the snow bowl in the center of the face at 12,600 feet. Curve to the west (right) and climb the well-defined couloir to 13,400 feet, where the two branches of the couloir diverge.

The west (right) branch of the Y Couloir is the easier choice. The last 600 feet provide vintage Colorado couloir climbing. The angle remains a consistent 45 degrees. You top out abruptly at 14,000 feet at the road's last switchback, on the west end of the summit plateau. Use caution: You may surprise a motorist.

The east (left) branch of the Y Couloir is steeper, exceeding 50 degrees in places. It also has rock bands that can add considerable difficulty. A large rock band is almost always present at 13,500 feet, just above the junction of the two branches. Smaller rock bands will appear in the last 500 feet as the couloir melts out. When in good condition, this is a scintillating finish. The east branch ends with some Class 3 scrambling and tops out just west of the large Olympic Memorial, where many motorists mill in summer.

Summit tourists who try to fill up Bottomless Pit by tossing rocks down your route are usually unaware that there may be climbers below them. Nevertheless, the rocks are a huge hazard for climbers. Tourists are most likely to trundle from near the Olympic Memorial; the Y Couloir will catch more of these rocks than the Railroad Couloir. Consider being dropped off and climbing early from a bivouac in Bottomless Pit. A very early start from Barr Camp is another good alternative. In any case, wear a helmet.

Leave No Trace!

Camp and Travel on Durable Surfaces

- Stay on designated trails; do not shortcut switchbacks.
- Where multiple trails exist, choose the one that is most worn.
- Where no trails exist, spread out across the terrain.
- When traveling cross-country, choose the most durable surfaces available.
- Rest on rock or in designated sites.
- Avoid wetlands and riparian areas.
- Choose an established, legal campsite that will not be damaged by your stay.
- Keep pollutants out of water sources.
- Camp at least 200 feet (70 adult steps) from lakes and streams.
- Move campsites frequently.

Chapter Two

Tenmile–Mosquito Range

Introduction

This range carries the distinction and confusion of two names. The two named ranges are geographically continuous. The Continental Divide sneaks through this north–south range on an east–west line as if impatient to be elsewhere. The Tenmile Range is north of the divide, and the Mosquito Range is south of the divide.

The Tenmile Range's northern end is near Frisco on Interstate 70. The Tenmile Range has 10 numbered peaks and several imaginatively named peaks close to the Continental Divide, including one fourteener. The Mosquito Range has four fourteeners close to the divide and runs south over several lower peaks. The Mosquito Range's practical southern boundary is Trout Creek Pass on U.S. 285. Colorado 9 and U.S. 285 mark the range's east edge. Interstate 70, Colorado 91 and U.S. 24 mark the range's west edge.

Access to these gentle peaks is usually from the east, and the trailheads are high. All the fourteeners in the Tenmile–Mosquito Range can be ascended with Class 1 or easy Class 2 hiking. These are some of Colorado's easiest fourteeners, but the range does hide a few technical challenges. Also, remember that easy peaks do not ensure good weather!

5. Quandary Peak   14,265 feet

See Map 5 on page 56

Quandary is 6 miles southwest of Breckenridge and 3 miles northwest of Hoosier Pass on Colorado 9. It is the Tenmile Range's unquestioned monarch. The Tenmile Range's lesser peaks rise in concert, each higher than the last, toward Quandary. Quandary is justifiably popular because of its proximity to Denver and a major highway. It is a celebrated winter ascent, and people often ski the gentle east slopes. Quandary is also a good spring training climb. The west and northeast ridges offer a more technical challenge. Quandary has something for everyone.

Maps
Required: Breckenridge, Arapaho National Forest
Optional: Copper Mountain

Trailheads
If approaching from the north, go 7.9 miles south on Colorado 9 from the junction of Ski Hill Road and Lincoln and Main Streets in the center of Breckenridge. If approaching from the south, go 2.2 miles north on Colorado 9 from the summit of Hoosier Pass. Turn west onto Summit County 850. Three trailheads can be reached from here.

Monte Cristo Trailhead
This trailhead is at 10,900 feet and provides access to Quandary's east side. Go west on Summit County 850 for 0.4 mile to a small parking lot on the north side of the road. This is the trailhead. It is accessible in winter.

Blue Lake Trailhead
This trailhead is at 11,700 feet and provides access to Quandary's south and west sides. Go west on Summit County 850 for 2.2 miles to the dam at upper Blue Lake on Monte Cristo Creek. There is ample parking below the dam. The winter road closure is at the Monte Cristo Trailhead.

McCullough Gulch Trailhead
This trailhead is at 11,100 feet and provides access to Quandary's north and west sides. Go west on Summit County 850 for 0.1 mile. Turn north (right) onto Summit County 851 and follow it as it curves around Quandary's east end and enters McCullough Gulch on the peak's north side. Stay south (left) at 1.6 miles and park below a locked gate after 2.2 miles. Summit County 851 is closed in winter.

Routes
5.1 East Slopes II, Class 1 *Classic*
From Monte Cristo Trailhead: 5.4 miles, 3,370 feet
This is the popular normal route on Quandary. There is a good climber's trail all the way. Start at the Monte Cristo Trailhead and climb north up the hillside. At the outset, there are several old mining roads that can be confusing. Persevere north up the slope past some old mines and take care to avoid the posted private property. The trail is clear above the mines. The trail reaches Quandary's east ridge near tree line at 11,700 feet. From tree line, follow the trail and easy slopes west for 2.0 miles to the summit.

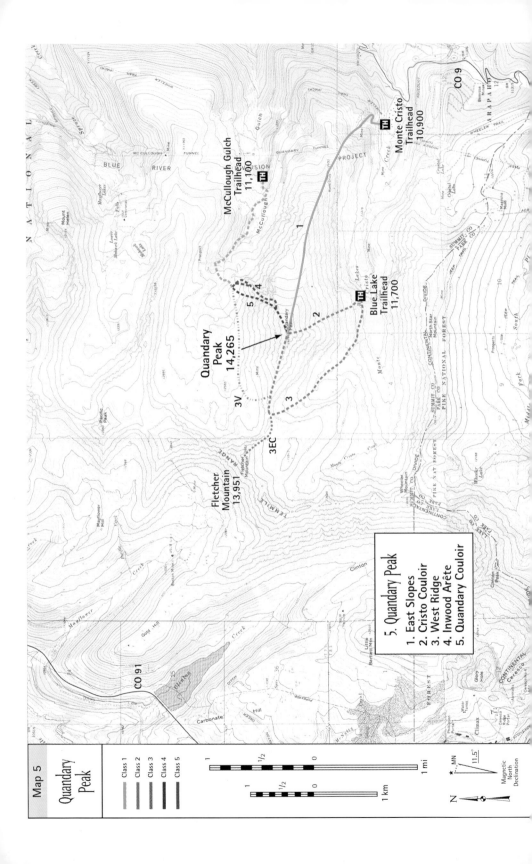

Map 5

Quandary Peak

Class 1
Class 2
Class 3
Class 4
Class 5

1 mi
1/2
0
1 km
1/2
0

MN
11.5°
Magnetic
North
Declination

N

5. Quandary Peak

1. East Slopes
2. Cristo Couloir
3. West Ridge
4. Inwood Arête
5. Quandary Couloir

Quandary Peak
14,265

McCullough Gulch
Trailhead
11,100

Monte Cristo
Trailhead
10,900

Blue Lake
Trailhead
11,700

Fletcher
Mountain
13,951

CO 9

CO 91

Quandary Peak from the southeast.

5.2 Cristo Couloir I, Class 2, Moderate Snow (Seasonal)

From Blue Lake Trailhead: 2.0 miles, 2,600 feet

This route is notable because of its brevity. The Cristo Couloir is the shallow, south-facing couloir on Quandary's south face; it holds snow into June. You can use it as an early season snow climb and speedy descent route in spring. Start at the Blue Lake Trailhead and climb north up the steep slope for 1.0 mile to the summit. There is a climber's trail on the couloir's west side, but it is eroding badly and should be avoided.

5.3 West Ridge I, Class 3 *Classic*

From Blue Lake Trailhead: 5.6 miles, 2,600 feet

This route provides a scenic approach and a sporty scramble to the summit. Ascending this route and descending either the Cristo Couloir or East Slopes Route makes an excellent climb.

Start at the Blue Lake Trailhead and hike north up the slope just west of the dam at upper Blue Lake. After 200 yards, cut west and find an old mining trail through the bushes. Beyond the bushes, follow the now clear trail northwest as it climbs into the hanging valley on Quandary's southwest side. This idyllic valley will embrace you. Quandary's rugged southwest face is above you, and you can see the west ridge in profile. It looks harder than it is.

Climb northwest up the valley to reach Quandary's west ridge at 13,400 feet on the Fletcher Mountain side of the Fletcher–Quandary Col. Fletcher

Mountain is the 13,951-foot peak west of Quandary. Turn east, start toward Quandary and pass some initial small towers on the ridge's south (right) side (Class 2). Beyond these towers, the ridge becomes a talus slope between another 13,400-foot saddle and 14,000 feet. Stay on or north of the ridge crest in this section. There is an old mining trail on the ridge's north side.

At 14,000 feet, the summit is only a few hundred yards away, but the fun has just begun. The route from here is harder than it looks. You must negotiate several towers and notches. The route finding is interesting as you pass some towers on the north, pass some on the south and climb some directly. The exposure can be startling. The route never drops more than 100 feet below the ridge. If you take care to find the easiest way, the difficulty will not exceed Class 3. Treat this ridge with respect.

The difficulties finally relent about 100 yards from the summit. You can share your adventure with the other people you are likely to find on the summit. You cannot see the west ridge's difficulties from the summit, so your acquaintances might not understand. Descend the Cristo Couloir or East Slopes Route.

Variation 5.3V
From McCullough Gulch Trailhead: 6.6 miles, 3,200 feet
You can approach the west ridge from McCullough Gulch on Quandary's north side. Start at the McCullough Gulch Trailhead and hike west up McCullough Gulch to 12,900 feet. Climb south up steep talus to reach the west ridge near the 13,400-foot saddle just east of the initial towers.

Extra Credit 5.3EC
From the beginning of the west ridge at 13,400 feet, climb northwest for 0.5 mile to 13,951-foot Fletcher Mountain, one of Colorado's 100 highest peaks.

5.4 Inwood Arête II, Class 5.4
From McCullough Gulch Trailhead: 5.0 miles, 3,170 feet
This is Quandary's finest rock route. The Inwood Arête is Quandary's rugged northeast ridge. You see it in profile when approaching the McCullough Gulch Trailhead. The ridge is named in memory of Julie Inwood, who died tragically while starting a climbing trip in Peru.

From the McCullough Gulch Trailhead, hike west up McCullough Gulch for 1.0 mile to a lake at 11,900 feet. The Inwood Arête rises directly south of this lake and offers 1,500 vertical feet of climbing and scrambling. From the lake's east end, hike south up to the base of the buttress. There is a lot of rock above you at this point, and the easiest start may not be immediately obvious. A direct start up the buttress is harder than Class 5.4. To find the easiest start, drop down to the east to a slabby face reminiscent of the Flatirons above Boulder, Colorado.

Step left to climb onto the slab (Class 5.4). This opening move will remind you that this is a climb, not a hike. Climb the solid slab above for two Class 5.3 pitches to a small northeast-facing ridge. These pitches are alpine slab mongering at its best. Stay below the crest on the north side of the small knife-edge above you and climb toward some towers on the crest of the now well-formed Inwood Arête (Class 5.0–5.2). Avoid these towers on the arête's east (left) side (Class 5.4) and climb to the crest of the Inwood Arête above the towers. The major difficulties are below you at this point, but you are only halfway. As you gaze at the rock above, you may gain new respect for Quandary Peak.

The arête's upper half requires several hundred feet of fun-filled but exposed Class 3 scrambling. The difficulties end at 13,600 feet. Hike west up Class 2 talus for 0.4 mile to the summit. Descend the East Slopes Route to tree line, then descend north back to the McCullough Gulch Road.

5.5 Quandary Couloir II, Class 4, Steep Snow
From McCullough Gulch Trailhead: 5.0 miles, 3,170 feet

Quandary's finest snow climb is just to the west of the Inwood Arête on the west end of Quandary's northeast face. The Inwood blocks your view and you cannot see the Quandary Couloir from the highway or when approaching the McCullough Gulch Trailhead. This couloir's secrets are reserved for those who make an effort.

From the McCullough Gulch Trailhead, hike west up McCullough Gulch for 1.0 mile to an unnamed lake at 11,900 feet. Hike southwest above the lake's east end until the couloir is in full view directly to the south. As always, check conditions carefully before committing to your climb. A stable late spring snowpack is ideal.

Hike south from the lake and start up steeper slopes at 12,200 feet. Rising like an arrow, the 1,600-foot high couloir averages 38 degrees and exceeds 45 degrees in places. Be prepared for ice and rock pitches. After the difficulties relent at 14,000 feet, stroll east for 0.2 mile to Quandary's summit.

6. Lincoln Group

Mount Lincoln	14,286 feet
Mount Cameron	14,238 feet
Mount Bross	14,172 feet
Mount Democrat	14,148 feet

See Map 6 on page 60

These friendly peaks are 4 miles west of Hoosier Pass on Colorado 9 between Breckenridge and Fairplay. They are gentle, forgiving and high.

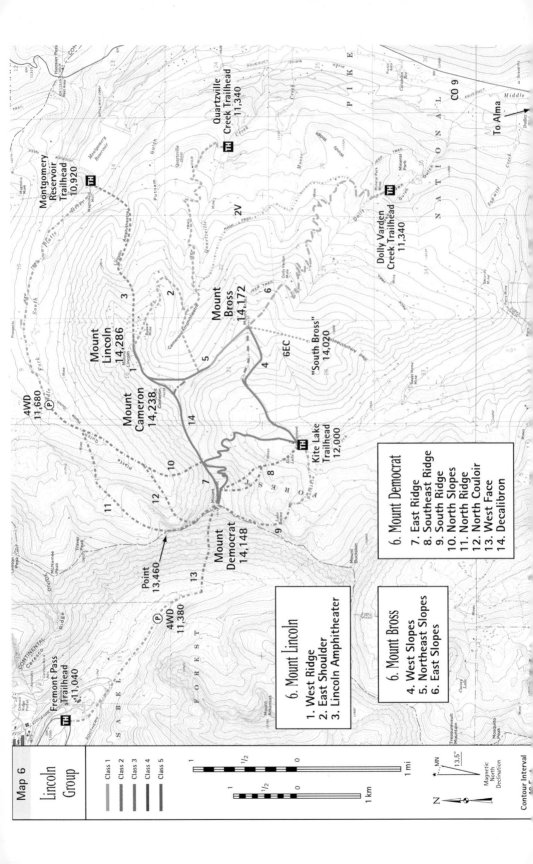

Map 6

Lincoln Group

Class 1
Class 2
Class 3
Class 4
Class 5

Contour Interval

Magnetic North Declination

13.5°

MN

N

1 mi
½   0   1

1 km
½   0   1

Fremont Pass Trailhead 11,040

Point 13,460

Mount Democrat 14,148

4WD 11,380

Kite Lake Trailhead 12,000

Mount Democrat 14,286

Mount Cameron 14,238

Mount Lincoln 14,286

Mount Bross 14,172

"South Bross" 14,020

4WD 11,680

Montgomery Reservoir Trailhead 10,920

Quartzville Creek Trailhead 11,340

Dolly Varden Creek Trailhead 11,340

To Alma

PIKE

NATIONAL

FOREST

ISABELL

CO 9

6EC

2V

6. Mount Lincoln
1. West Ridge
2. East Shoulder
3. Lincoln Amphitheater

6. Mount Bross
4. West Slopes
5. Northeast Slopes
6. East Slopes

6. Mount Democrat
7. East Ridge
8. Southeast Ridge
9. South Ridge
10. North Slopes
11. North Ridge
12. North Couloir
13. West Face
14. Decalibron

These peaks are popular as training climbs, and people usually climb them together. They are a peak bagger's delight. Nowhere else can you get so much for so little!

Maps
Required: Alma, Climax, Pike National Forest

Trailheads
Kite Lake Trailhead
This trailhead is at 12,000 feet and provides access to the south sides of Democrat, Cameron and Lincoln, and to the west side of Bross. If approaching from the south, go 6.0 miles north on Colorado 9 from the U.S. 285–Colorado 9 junction in Fairplay. If approaching from the north, go 5.8 miles south on Colorado 9 from the summit of Hoosier Pass.

Turn west onto Kite Lake Road (dirt) in the center of Alma. Park County 10 is not Kite Lake Road. The unmarked Kite Lake Road is Park County 8, and it starts across the highway from a store. Follow the Kite Lake Road for 6.0 miles northwest up Buckskin Gulch to Kite Lake at 12,000 feet. There is ample parking east of Kite Lake. Kite Lake Road is good most of the way, but the last mile to the lake is difficult for passenger cars. Many people choose to park their passenger cars near a switchback 0.6 mile below the lake. In winter the road is closed 4.0 miles above Alma, and snowmobiles make heavy use of the road above this point.

Dolly Varden Creek Trailhead
This trailhead is at 11,340 feet and provides access to Bross' east side. If approaching from the south, go 6.0 miles north on Colorado 9 from the U.S. 285–Colorado 9 junction in Fairplay. If approaching from the north, go 5.8 miles south on Colorado 9 from the summit of Hoosier Pass.

Turn west onto Kite Lake Road (dirt) in the center of Alma. Park County 10 is not Kite Lake Road. The unmarked Kite Lake Road is Park County 8, and it starts across the highway from a store. Go 2.8 miles west on Kite Lake Road, turn north (right) onto Windy Ridge Road (Forest Service 415) and go 2.9 miles to a parking area near the Mineral Park Mine. The road is good to this point. Forest Service 415 is closed in winter.

Quartzville Creek Trailhead
This trailhead is at 11,340 feet and provides access to the east sides of Lincoln, Cameron and Bross. If approaching from the south, go 8.1 miles north on Colorado 9 from the U.S. 285–Colorado 9 junction in Fairplay. If approaching from the north, go 3.7 miles south on Colorado 9 from the summit of Hoosier Pass.

Turn west onto Park County 4. This is the southern of two Colorado 9–Park County 4 junctions. There is a housing subdivision west of here, and more than one route may be used to reach the trailhead. The following is the most direct. Measuring from the south Colorado 9–Park County 4 junction, go west (left) at 0.1 mile, south (left) at 0.3 mile, hard right at 0.4 mile and follow the main road northwest as it switchbacks up the hill. Stay right at 2.7 miles, and turn left onto Forest Service 437 after 3.3 miles. This point is on Quartzville Creek's north side. There is a small parking area on the west side of Forest Service 437, just north of the subdivision road. This is the trailhead. Snowplow activity on these roads varies in the winter. The road is often plowed to the trailhead, but don't count on it, especially right after a storm.

Montgomery Reservoir Trailhead

This trailhead is at 10,920 feet and provides access to the north sides of Lincoln, Cameron and Democrat. If approaching from the south, go 10.7 miles north on Colorado 9 from the U.S. 285–Colorado 9 junction in Fairplay. If approaching from the north, go 1.1 miles south on Colorado 9 from the summit of Hoosier Pass.

Turn west onto Park County 4. This is the northern of two Colorado 9–Park County 4 junctions. Measuring from this junction, go down the hill to the west, stay right at 0.8 mile, stay right at 1.0 mile, go around Montgomery Reservoir's north side and park on the reservoir's west side after 1.9 miles. The road is passable for passenger cars to this point, but it rapidly becomes a rough four-wheel-drive road at the Magnolia Mine, just west of the reservoir. Four-wheel-drive vehicles can continue west for another 2.4 miles to 11,680 feet under Lincoln's north slopes. In winter the road is plowed to the spillway road east of the reservoir.

Fremont Pass Trailhead

This trailhead is at 11,040 feet and provides access to Democrat's west face. If approaching from the south, go 12.0 miles north on Colorado 91 from Leadville. If approaching from the north, go 9.0 miles south on Colorado 91 from Interstate 70. The trailhead is not on top of Fremont Pass but at the lower end of the sweeping switchback 0.7 mile southeast of the pass. Park on the south side of the highway in a large pullout west of some mine buildings. This trailhead is accessible in winter.

High-clearance vehicles can go 1.4 miles southeast into the valley on a decent dirt road to a closure gate at 11,380 feet. The road ends 200 yards beyond at a mine.

6. Mount Lincoln   14,286 feet

See Map 6 on page 60

Mount Lincoln is the highest peak in the Tenmile–Mosquito Range and is higher than any peak in the Front Range. Lincoln is the highest peak in Park County and the eighth highest peak in Colorado.

Routes
6.1 West Ridge I, Class 2
From Kite Lake Trailhead: 5.4 miles, 2,600 feet

This is the regular route up Lincoln. It has seen many feet. From Kite Lake Trailhead, follow the trail north to the Democrat–Cameron Saddle at 13,400 feet. Turn east and follow the ridge to Cameron's rounded summit. If Cameron is beneath your dignity, you can skirt it on its north side. Lincoln is a gentle 0.5 mile northeast of Cameron. A well-worn trail climbs through the summit rocks.

6.2 East Shoulder I, Class 1
From Quartzville Creek Trailhead: 6.4 miles, 2,950 feet
From Dolly Varden Creek Trailhead: 8.4 miles, 3,100 feet

This is a pleasant, gentle approach to Lincoln's summit that avoids the crowds ascending from Kite Lake. From the Quartzville Creek Trailhead, follow Forest Service 437 west as it climbs along Quartzville Creek's north side. Hike into the east end of Cameron Amphitheater between Mount Lincoln to the north and Mount Bross to the south. At 13,000 feet, follow the road as it switchbacks hard east and climb onto Lincoln's east shoulder at 13,200 feet. As an alternative, you can save some distance by leaving the road and cutting straight north up the slope to reach Lincoln's east shoulder at 13,500 feet.

Once on the east shoulder, hike west on the road past several old mines. Some rusty pipes laid out across the slope mark the 14,000-foot contour line (just kidding). Leave the road before it traverses to the peak's north side and continue west on a climber's trail up the final 300-foot slope to the summit. This is a good running route.

Variation 6.2V
You can approach this route from the Dolly Varden Creek Trailhead. This makes your climb of Lincoln longer but allows you to also climb Bross and make a circle tour by descending Bross' East Slopes Route. Start at the Dolly Varden Creek Trailhead, hike north onto Windy Ridge, then follow a four-wheel-drive road north and northwest into Cameron Amphitheater to join the road climbing up from the Quartzville Creek Trailhead.

Mount Lincoln and Mount Cameron from the east.

6.3 Lincoln Amphitheater II, Class 2+

From Montgomery Reservoir Trailhead: 4.0 miles, 3,370 feet

This is the shortest route on Lincoln. The Lincoln Amphitheater separates Lincoln's two east ridges and provides a much less traveled route up this popular peak. Start at the Montgomery Reservoir Trailhead. The crux of this route is a 400-foot headwall that bars easy access to Lincoln Amphitheater. Study it from the trailhead. Angle south up the scruffy slope and find a way through this maze of small cliffs by traversing on ledges until you find easy upward egress. In summer you may have to battle bushes as well as the route finding. In winter this is the popular Lincoln Falls ice-climbing area. Either way, be prepared for some adventure.

Leave the bushes behind and enter the Lincoln Amphitheater at 11,600 feet. Turn west and follow the curves of this gentle giant to 13,000 feet. In winter this basin is prone to avalanches; beware the giant's roar. The terrain relaxes above 13,000 feet as you hike west for 0.6 mile to the summit.

6. Mount Cameron   14,238 feet

See Map 6 on page 60

Cameron is centrally located between Democrat, Lincoln and Bross. Cameron is named on the Alma Quadrangle but does not pass muster as an official peak. It rises no more than 157 feet from its connecting saddle with Lincoln. People have pooh-poohed Cameron for years. It is the official unofficial peak! If Cameron were just 50 feet higher, it would reign supreme. Nevertheless, it sits there named and waiting.

Cameron is not lonely. Everybody climbs it anyway while coming from and going to the other more important peaks. It is almost always climbed with Democrat, Lincoln or Bross. Thus, specific routes on Cameron are not included here.

6. Mount Bross 14,172 feet

See Map 6 on page 60

This rotund peak challenges photographers to make it look dramatic, and people intent on checking peaks off a list love the return on investment Bross gives them. Bross' flat summit is a perfect place for lounging on a clear day. Bross is sometimes jokingly called the "Aiguille du Bross."

Routes

6.4 West Slopes I, Class 2
From Kite Lake Trailhead: 2.8 miles, 2,170 feet

This is the shortest route up Bross, and well-worn climber's trails mark the way. From the Kite Lake Trailhead, hike northeast up gentle slopes for 0.7 mile to the base of Bross. From here there are two choices. Either ascend the shallow basin or the ridge just south of the basin for 0.7 mile east to the summit. The ridge provides the best footing for the ascent and is the "greener" choice. Thousands of feet speeding down the basin have sent the scree elsewhere and the basin no longer provides pleasant footing.

6.5 Northeast Slopes I, Class 1
From Quartzville Creek Trailhead: 6.4 miles, 2,830 feet

This is a longer, gentler approach to Bross' summit. From the Quartzville Creek Trailhead, follow Forest Service 437 west as it climbs along Quartzville Creek's north side. At 13,000 feet, the road switchbacks hard east to climb onto Lincoln's east shoulder. Leave the road at this switchback and continue hiking west into Cameron Amphitheater. Hike southwest up gentle, grassy slopes to the Cameron–Bross Saddle at 13,850 feet. From the saddle, hike southeast on roads and gentle scree for a final 0.6 mile to the summit. This is a good running route.

6.6 East Slopes I, Class 1
From Dolly Varden Creek Trailhead: 7.0 miles, 2,830 feet

This is the easiest route up Bross and one of the easiest routes anywhere. As an added attraction, the route goes past the Windy Ridge Bristlecone Pine Scenic Area. Start at the Dolly Varden Creek Trailhead and follow the road west for 0.2 mile, turn north (right) onto Forest Service 415 and switchback up to Windy Ridge. A short side trip takes you to the Bristlecone Pines.

Bross' east slopes above Windy Ridge are gentle and grass-covered. A four-wheel-drive road switchbacks up these slopes to the Dolly Varden Mine at 13,300 feet. Either follow the road or hike straight up the gentle slopes. The distance given for this route assumes you follow the road to the mine. Above the Dolly Varden Mine, leave the road and hike straight up to Bross' flat summit. This is a good running route.

Extra Credit 6.6EC

From the summit of Bross, hike 0.6 mile south to Point 14,020, alias "South Bross." This summit does not have a lot of power, but it is a summit above 14,000 feet. It provides a good view of Democrat.

6. Mount Democrat   14,148 feet

See Map 6 on page 60

Mount Democrat is 1.5 miles west of the collective massif of Lincoln, Cameron and Bross. Democrat is a singular mountain and has its own unique personality. Although lower than Lincoln, Cameron and Bross, Democrat provides the most interesting mountaineering routes on these peaks.

Routes

6.7 East Ridge I, Class 2

From Kite Lake Trailhead: 3.6 miles, 2,150 feet

This is the easiest route on Democrat. Start at the Kite Lake Trailhead and follow the well-worn trail north to the Kentucky Belle Mine's ruins. Continue north on the trail as it climbs above the old gold mine and switchbacks up to the 13,380-foot saddle between Democrat and Cameron. There are old trail remnants west of this saddle, but it is just as easy to ascend Democrat's east ridge for 0.5 mile to the summit. There are building ruins in a flat area at 14,000 feet, just east of Democrat's summit. Have you ever wondered how many miners were hit by lightning?

6.8 Southeast Face I, Class 2, Moderate Snow (Seasonal)

From Kite Lake Trailhead: 2.4 miles, 2,150 feet

In May and June, this face provides a simple snow climb. Later in the summer, this is still the shortest route on Democrat. The southeast face is the face directly north of Kite Lake. Do not confuse the southeast face with the steeper south face above Lake Emma. You can preview snow conditions on the southeast face from U.S. 285 south of Fairplay.

Start at the Kite Lake Trailhead and angle northwest up the slope on the lake's west side. Stay west of the cliffs north of Kite Lake and reach the base of the southeast face at 12,800 feet. When snow conditions are favorable, climb directly up the face to 13,900 feet on the shoulder 0.2 mile east of the summit. After the snow melts, climb the small ridge on the southeast face's west edge. This ridge separates the southeast face from the south face.

6.9 South Ridge I, Class 3
From Kite Lake Trailhead: 4.0 miles, 2,150 feet

The miners a hundred years ago knew more about the secrets of this ridge than today's climbers. It is seldom climbed because of its loose rock and crumbling towers. It is not a good route for a large group. Climb it if you feel compelled and are good on "junk."

Start at the Kite Lake Trailhead and follow a trail west then north for 0.8 mile to Lake Emma. This is a worthwhile hike by itself. Lake Emma, at 12,620 feet, nestles below Democrat's south face in a surprisingly dramatic bowl. From the south side of the lake, climb west then northwest up steepening slopes to reach Democrat's south ridge at 13,400 feet. The last 400 feet to the ridge require judicious Class 3 scrambling on loose rock. The redeeming feature of this approach to the south ridge is that it avoids most of the crumbling towers that are lower on the ridge. Once on the south ridge, scramble north (Class 3) for 0.5 mile to the summit. The difficulties end at 13,800 feet.

6.10 North Slopes II, Class 2
From Montgomery Reservoir Trailhead: 9.2 miles, 3,230 feet
From 4WD parking: 4.4 miles, 2,470 feet

This is the easiest way to climb Democrat from the north. Start at the Montgomery Reservoir Trailhead and follow the four-wheel-drive road west for 2.4 miles along the Middle Fork of the South Platte. Leave this road at 11,680 feet before it crosses the creek descending from Wheeler Lake and starts the steep climb to this lake. Hike southwest on another, fainter four-wheel-drive road through the bushes. Continue south up the main valley and climb south up scree to the 13,380-foot saddle between Democrat and Cameron. Climb west for 0.5 mile to Democrat's summit.

6.11 North Ridge II, Class 3 *Classic*
From Montgomery Reservoir Trailhead: 9.8 miles, 3,230 feet
From 4WD parking: 5.0 miles, 2,470 feet

This is the best mountaineering route on Democrat. This ridge is similar to the west ridge on Quandary. Some fierce-looking notches distinguish the lower part of Democrat's north ridge, but the rock is surprisingly good and the ridge is easier than it looks.

Start at the Montgomery Reservoir Trailhead and follow the four-wheel-drive road west for 2.4 miles along the Middle Fork of the South Platte. Leave this road at 11,680 feet before it crosses the creek descending from Wheeler Lake and starts the steep climb to this lake. Hike southwest on another, fainter four-wheel-drive road through the bushes. When beyond the bushes, angle southwest up into the small basin southeast of Traver Peak (13,852 feet). Traver Peak is 1.4 miles north of Democrat. There are some old mines in this basin. From the basin, climb north to Point 13,460 on Democrat's north ridge.

Scramble south across Point 13,460 and engage the initial and most difficult notches on the ridge. There are two prominent notches separated by a shark-fin tower. Descend on the ridge's west side to reach the vicinity of the first notch (Class 3). Scramble around the shark-fin tower on its west (right) side just below the level of the notch (Class 3). Climb into the second notch, which is graced with a conspicuous chockstone. Climb south up the ridge above the second chockstone notch (Class 3). The ridge's main difficulties are now behind you.

The ridge from here to the summit is fun. It is mostly Class 2 hiking punctuated with some Class 3 scrambling. There is more Class 3 scrambling if you adhere to the ridge crest, or, if you choose, most of the remaining towers can be skirted on the ridge's west side. There is an antique mine at 13,700 feet at the top of the north couloir. There is an old trail above the mine on the ridge's west side, but it is more entertaining to continue scrambling on the ridge crest all the way to the summit. The rock becomes increasingly rotten as you approach the summit. Descend the North Slopes Route.

6.12 North Couloir II, Class 3, Moderate Snow (Seasonal)

From Montgomery Reservoir Trailhead: 9.6 miles, 3,230 feet

From 4WD parking: 4.8 miles, 2,470 feet

Miners dumped tailings down this couloir a hundred years ago, but today it is seldom seen or climbed. Because the couloir is inset and protected, it can retain snow into August. Crampons are useful after June.

Start at the Montgomery Reservoir Trailhead and follow the four-wheel-drive road west for 2.4 miles along the Middle Fork of the South Platte. Leave this road at 11,680 feet before it crosses the creek descending from Wheeler Lake and starts the steep climb to this lake. Hike southwest on another, fainter four-wheel-drive road through the bushes and continue south up the main valley. The north couloir is the westernmost and most pronounced couloir on Democrat's north face. The north couloir is immediately east of the lower part of the north ridge and is subject to rockfall from the steep wall above it, especially if there are climbers on the North Ridge Route.

From the head of the valley, climb southwest toward the north ridge and enter the couloir at 13,000 feet. Ascend the couloir for 700 exciting feet to reach the antique mine on the north ridge at 13,700 feet. The couloir averages 40 degrees and approaches 45 degrees at the steepest point. Once on the north ridge, continue up that route to the summit. Descend the North Slopes Route.

6.13 West Face II, Class 2, Moderate Snow (Seasonal)
From Fremont Pass Trailhead: 6.2 miles, 3,110 feet
From 4WD parking: 3.4 miles, 2,770 feet

When snow conditions are favorable in spring and early summer, Democrat's west face provides a long snow climb. Avoid this face when it is free of snow. You can easily see this face from Colorado 91 and you should check conditions when going to and coming from other adventures. Be patient; then, when snow conditions are perfect, climb it.

Start at the Fremont Pass Trailhead and go southeast for 1.5 miles on a dirt road along the west (right) side of the valley to a mine at 11,400 feet. Continue beyond the mine on a trail for another 0.4 mile to 11,500 feet. Democrat's 2,500-foot-high west face soars above you to the east. Cross the valley, ascend the lower slopes and do an ascending traverse to the south (right) to climb into the narrow gully that descends from near the summit. Ascend the gully on the perfect snow you have waited for and reach the top of Democrat's north ridge in a small saddle. Follow the upper north ridge to the summit. The snow steepness in the gully does not exceed 45 degrees.

6. Lincoln, Cameron, Bross and Democrat Combinations

See Map 6 on page 60

6.14 The Decalibron II, Class 2
From Kite Lake Trailhead: 7.0 miles, 3,600 feet

This is the easiest and most traveled way to climb all four peaks. Except for a short out-and-back to Lincoln, it is a perfect ring around the cirque. Start at Kite Lake Trailhead and ascend Democrat's East Ridge

Route. Descend east to the 13,380-foot saddle between Democrat and Cameron. Continue east on Lincoln's West Ridge Route over Cameron and northeast to Lincoln. Return to the broad, 14,100-foot saddle between Lincoln and Cameron. Either reascend Cameron or stay below Cameron's summit on the east side. Descend southeast to the 13,860-foot saddle between Cameron and Bross, then continue southeast up gentle slopes to Bross' summit. Descend Bross' West Slopes Route.

Before committing to this long, high traverse, consider that Cameron's south slopes are cliffy, and that there is no easy escape back to Kite Lake between the Democrat–Cameron Saddle and the Cameron–Bross Saddle. This combination works in the opposite direction, but people seldom do it that way. The ease of reaching the Democrat–Cameron Saddle on a trail and the quick descent down Bross' West Slopes Route at day's end prescribe the order given above.

6.15 II, Class 2
From Quartzville Creek Trailhead: 8.4 miles, 3,360 feet

This combination is a quick way to collect Lincoln, Cameron and Bross. Start at the Quartzville Creek Trailhead and ascend Lincoln's East Shoulder Route. Descend southwest to the broad, 14,100-foot saddle between Lincoln and Cameron and continue southwest to Cameron's broad summit. Descend southeast to the 13,860-foot saddle between Cameron and Bross, then continue southeast up gentle slopes to Bross' summit. Descend Bross' Northeast Slopes Route.

6.16 II, Class 2
From Quartzville Creek Trailhead: 11.4 miles, 5,000 feet

The Quartzville Creek Trailhead is more accessible in the winter than the Kite Lake Trailhead, and people use this combination for winter ascents of all four peaks. Start at the Quartzville Creek Trailhead, follow Combination 6.15 to Cameron's summit, do the long trek over to Democrat, return to Cameron's summit and continue to Bross. Adding Democrat to Combination 6.15 significantly increases the mileage and elevation gain.

7. Mount Sherman   14,036 feet

See Map 7 on page 72

Mount Sherman is 9 miles west of Fairplay and 8 miles east of Leadville. You can see the mountain from U.S. 285 in South Park, but the flat summit does not stand out. It is even less distinguished from the west side. Sherman's summit is on private property.

Some people malign Sherman because it is so easy to climb; others cherish Sherman because it is so easy to climb. It all depends on your outlook. Sherman is popular as an early season training climb, and sometimes people sleep on the summit before departing on high-altitude adventures in earth's elevated ranges. Thus does Sherman touch greatness.

Maps
Required: Mount Sherman, Pike National Forest
Optional: San Isabel National Forest

Trailheads
Fourmile Creek Trailhead
This trailhead is at 11,240 feet and provides access to Sherman's southeast side. From the U.S. 285–Colorado 9 junction on Fairplay's south side, go south on U.S. 285 for 1.0 mile to Park County 18. Turn west onto Park County 18 and measure from this point. Go west on Park County 18 and enter the Fourmile Creek Valley and Pike National Forest after 4.0 miles. Pass Fourmile Campground after 8.0 miles and park at the old Leavick townsite after 10.5 miles. Leavick is not marked, but there are some old mine buildings on the road's north side; this is the trailhead for passenger cars. Four-wheel-drive vehicles can continue west for an additional 2.5 miles to 12,520 feet. In winter the road is often plowed as far as Leavick, and this is a popular place for snowmobilers.

Thompson Park Trailhead
This trailhead is at 10,640 feet and provides access to Sherman's east side. From the U.S. 285–Colorado 9 junction on Fairplay's south side, go south on U.S. 285 for 1.0 mile to Park County 18. Turn west onto Park County 18 and measure from this point. Go west on Park County 18 and enter the Fourmile Creek Valley and Pike National Forest after 4.0 miles. Reach the Horseshoe Campground after 7.1 miles. Turn north, leave the Fourmile Creek Valley and climb east to a broad shoulder at 8.1 miles. Follow the road as it descends to the north and park at 8.5 miles, where the road turns east and descends into Thompson Park.

Little Sacramento Trailhead
This trailhead is at 11,140 feet and provides access to Sherman's east side. From the U.S. 285–Colorado 9 junction on Fairplay's south side, go north on Colorado 9 through downtown Fairplay for 2.1 miles to Park County 14. Turn west onto Park County 14 and measure from this point. Go west on Park County 14 for 4.5 miles and turn down to the west (left) onto a secondary road. Cross Sacramento Creek at 5.1 miles, climb back

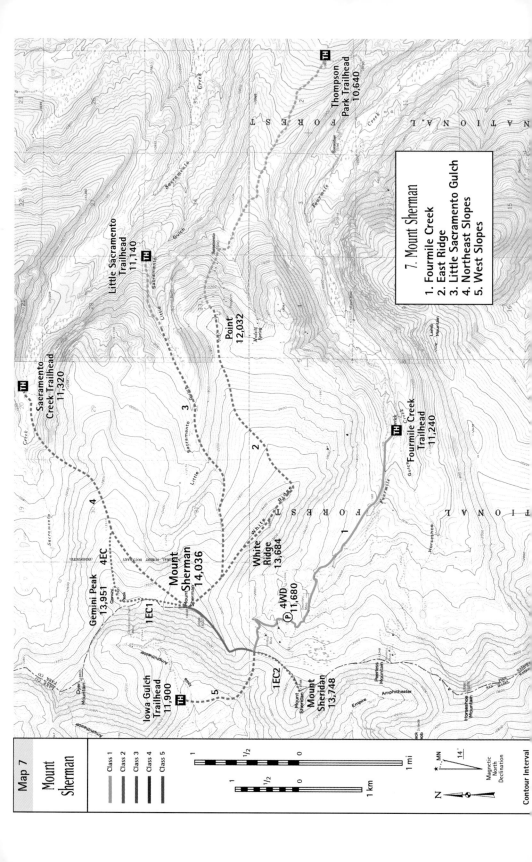

Mount Sherman from the east.

east to the ridge north of Little Sacramento Gulch and reach the trailhead at 5.6 miles.

Sacramento Creek Trailhead

This trailhead is at 11,320 feet and provides access to Sherman's north side. From the U.S. 285–Colorado 9 junction on Fairplay's south side, go north on Colorado 9 through downtown Fairplay for 2.1 miles to Park County 14. Turn west onto Park County 14 and measure from this point. Go west on Park County 14 up Sacramento Creek for 6.7 miles to the trailhead at the end of the road.

Iowa Gulch Trailhead

This trailhead is at 11,900 feet and provides access to Sherman's west side. Measure from the junction of U.S. 24 (Harrison Avenue) and East Third Street in downtown Leadville. Go east on East Third Street for 0.3 mile to South Toledo Street. Turn south (right) onto South Toledo Street, pass East Monroe Street after 0.4 mile and continue south then east on Lake County 2 (paved). Stay north (left) after 4.0 miles on a dirt road that passes north of the active ASARCO Mine. Continue east on Iowa Gulch's north side, go under some large power lines and park after 6.4 miles at 11,900 feet. The road is passable for passenger cars to this point. Lake County 2 is open to the ASARCO Mine in the winter, but not beyond.

Routes

7.1 Fourmile Creek I, Class 2

From Fourmile Creek Trailhead: 8.0 miles, 2,800 feet

This is the most popular route up Sherman. Start at the Fourmile Creek Trailhead and climb northwest up the four-wheel-drive road into the upper basin of Fourmile Creek. Pass the old Dauntless and Hilltop Mines, then climb to the 13,140-foot saddle between Sherman and Mount Sheridan (13,748 feet). Sheridan is 1.4 miles southwest of Sherman. From the saddle, climb northeast up Sherman's southwest ridge on a good trail for 0.9 mile to the long, gentle summit.

Extra Credit

7.1EC1 II, Class 2

From Fourmile Creek Trailhead: 9.4 miles, 3,300 feet

From Sherman's summit, hike north for 0.7 mile to twin-summited Gemini Peak (13,951 feet). The northeast summit is the higher of the two summits. Return over Sherman's summit.

7.1EC2 II, Class 2

From Fourmile Creek Trailhead: 9.2 miles, 3,400 feet

From the 13,140-foot saddle between Sherman and Sheridan, climb southwest up a broad ridge for 0.6 mile to Mount Sheridan's 13,748-foot summit.

7.1EC3 II, Class 2

From Fourmile Creek Trailhead: 10.6 miles, 3,900 feet

This is the big one. Besides Sherman, bag both Gemini Peak and Sheridan. This tour will augment your opinion of Sherman.

7.2 East Ridge II, Class 2

From Thompson Park Trailhead: 12.5 miles, 3,970 feet

This route, although longer than the Fourmile Creek Route, allows you to walk high and free above that route's crowds. Start at the Thompson Park Trailhead and follow a four-wheel-drive road northwest for 2.3 miles to the antique Sacramento townsite at 11,420 feet. Continue west for an additional 0.7 mile to Point 12,032 and consider your future. For once, it's easy.

Descend west, then climb west and southwest up gentle slopes for 2.0 miles to White Ridge's 13,684-foot summit. From here you can look down on the Fourmile Creek Route near the Dauntless and Hilltop Mines. Hike northwest over a false summit, descend slightly and continue northwest for 1.2 miles up to Sherman's summit.

7.3 Little Sacramento Gulch I, Class 2
From Little Sacramento Trailhead: 7.6 miles, 2,900 feet

This reciprocal route overcomes Sherman's east side directly. Start at the Little Sacramento Trailhead, drop south and proceed onto an old road leading west into Little Sacramento Gulch. After 0.6 mile the road climbs north to some old mines. Leave the road before it crosses Little Sacramento Creek and continue up the gulch for an additional 1.1 miles to 11,700 feet. From here you can look a mile west into the small cirque northeast of Sherman's summit. For the easiest ascent, don't go into the cirque. Leave Little Sacramento Gulch and climb southwest up a small drainage for 0.5 mile to 12,400 feet. Continue west up the vague drainage for 1.0 mile and join the East Ridge Route. Hike northwest for 0.4 mile to Sherman's summit.

7.4 Northeast Slopes I, Class 2
From Sacramento Creek Trailhead: 5.6 miles, 2,720 feet

This short route has been overlooked for years. Start at the Sacramento Creek Trailhead and walk west up the south side of Sacramento Creek for 0.4 mile. Leave the creek and climb southwest for 1.0 mile up a shallow gulch to 13,000 feet on Gemini Peak's east ridge. Climb west up the broad, gentle ridge for 0.4 mile to 13,300 feet. Leave the ridge and climb southwest below Gemini Peak for 1.0 mile to Sherman's summit.

Extra Credit 7.4EC

From 13,300 feet on Gemini Peak's east ridge, continue west up the ridge for 0.6 mile to Gemini Peak's 13,951-foot main summit. Don't stop here. Go southwest for 0.15 mile to Gemini Peak's 13,940-foot false summit, then hike 0.7 mile south to Sherman's summit.

7.5 West Slopes I, Class 2
From Iowa Gulch Trailhead: 4.2 miles, 2,140 feet

This is a very short climb in the summer, and Sherman's west side is often used as a winter route. From the Iowa Gulch Trailhead (summer) or ASARCO Mine (winter), hike up the road until you are beyond the willows in the valley to the south. Leave the road, descend a little and hike south across open ground toward the bottom of the shallow gully below the 13,140-foot saddle between Sherman and Sheridan (13,748 feet). Find the good trail that is visible from the trailhead and follow it east as it switchbacks to the Sherman–Sheridan Saddle, where this route joins the Fourmile Creek Route. Climb northeast up Sherman's southwest ridge on a good trail for 0.9 mile to Sherman's summit.

Chapter Three
Sawatch Range

Introduction

The Sawatch Range runs through the heartland of the Colorado Rockies. The range has 15 fourteeners—more than California, and more than any other Colorado range. Four of Colorado's five highest peaks are in the Sawatch.

Like most Colorado ranges, the Sawatch is a linear range that runs north and south. The northern boundary is Interstate 70 west of Vail. The practical southern boundary is U.S. 50 at Monarch Pass. Between are 80 miles of mountains. Only one paved road—Colorado 82 over Independence Pass—crosses the range. There are four wilderness areas in the Sawatch Range. All the Sawatch fourteeners can be climbed with Class 2 talus hiking. There are only a few technical routes tucked away on these gentle peaks.

A subgrouping of Sawatch peaks has more to do with naming conventions than geography. Five of the fourteeners in the southern half of the range carry the names of great universities, so these peaks are known as the "Collegiate Peaks." Students from schools with higher namesake peaks are quick to point that out. Students from schools with lower namesake peaks have jokingly schemed the building of large summit cairns to outdo their rivals.

8. Mount of the Holy Cross   14,005 feet

See Map 8 on page 77

Mount of the Holy Cross is one of Colorado's most beautiful fourteeners. The view of Holy Cross from Notch Mountain is breathtaking. A long, deep couloir on the east face and a ledge about two-thirds of the way up fill with snow and form the namesake cross. Because of the snow cross, people have accorded religious significance to Holy Cross throughout the past century. Even without snow in the Cross Couloir, Holy Cross is a spectacular peak. It is the most rugged of the Sawatch fourteeners and could well be Colorado's most famous fourteener.

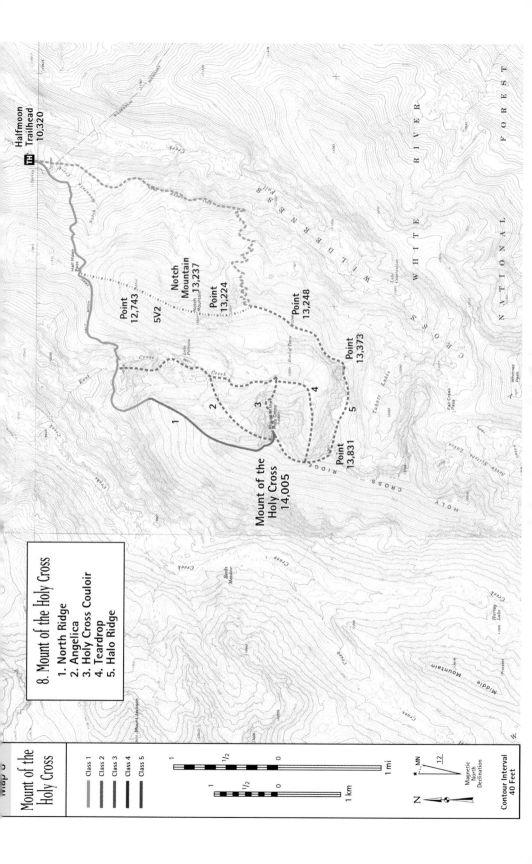

Map 8

Mount of the Holy Cross

8. Mount of the Holy Cross

1. North Ridge
2. Angelica
3. Holy Cross Couloir
4. Teardrop
5. Halo Ridge

Class 1
Class 2
Class 3
Class 4
Class 5

1 mi
1 km

MN
12

Magnetic
North
Declination

Contour Interval
40 Feet

N

Halfmoon
Trailhead
10,320

Point
12,743

5V2

Notch
Mountain
13,237

Point
13,224

Point
13,248

Point
13,373

Point
13,831

Mount of the
Holy Cross
14,005

WHITE RIVER

WILDERNESS

NATIONAL FOREST

HOLY CROSS RIDGE

Middle Mountain

Holy Cross is also a shy peak. It is only 14 miles southwest of Vail, but Notch Mountain blocks the view and you can rarely see the cross from the surrounding valleys. Distant views are afforded from the peaks of the Tenmile–Mosquito Range. Perhaps the best distant view is from the top of the Vail ski area. The spectacular, close-up view from Notch Mountain is reserved for people willing to hike.

Holy Cross is the Sawatch Range's northernmost fourteener and the highest peak in Eagle County. The Sawatch Range's southernmost four-teener, Mount Shavano, has the Angel of Shavano on its east face. It is interesting that both the Sawatch Range's northernmost and southern-most fourteeners have snow features with religious significance. Such are the Sawatch Range boundaries.

Maps

Required: Mount of the Holy Cross, White River National Forest
Optional: Minturn, Mount Jackson

Trailhead

Halfmoon Trailhead

This trailhead is at 10,320 feet and provides access to the north, east and south sides of Holy Cross. Don't confuse this trailhead with the North and South Halfmoon Creek Trailheads described with Elbert and Massive. A few miles west of Vail, take Exit 171 off Interstate 70. From the U.S. 24–Interstate 70 junction, go south on U.S. 24 for 2.0 miles to the White River National Forest Ranger Station at Main and Harrison Streets in the town of Minturn.

From the White River Ranger Station, continue south on U.S. 24 for 2.8 miles and turn west onto Tigiwon Road (Forest Service 707). This turn is on the north side of a bridge over the Eagle River. Tigiwon Road (dirt) climbs steadily in long-sweeping switchbacks, passes the Tigiwon Camp-ground after 6.1 miles and reaches the Halfmoon Trailhead after 8.4 miles. Tigiwon Road is rough but passable in passenger cars. Two trails start at this trailhead. Make sure you follow the one you want. The Halfmoon Campground is just below the trailhead. The Tigiwon road is closed   in win-ter and usually opens in mid-June.

Routes

8.1 North Ridge II, Class 2

From Halfmoon Trailhead: 12.0 miles, 5,625 feet

This is the easiest route on Holy Cross. Unfortunately, it does not provide a good view of the Cross Couloir. It is also a tough one-day climb. The route crosses Halfmoon Pass and requires 970 feet of gain on your return trip. Many people choose to ameliorate this by packing in over the pass and camping near East Cross Creek. By climbing Holy Cross in one day, you will minimize your impact on this beautiful area, but you will maximize impact on yourself. Get in shape for this one!

Start at the Halfmoon Trailhead and follow the Halfmoon Trail west for 1.7 miles to Halfmoon Pass at 11,640 feet. Continue over the pass and descend to East Cross Creek at 10,670 feet. There is a nice view of Holy Cross' north face and the Angelica Couloir on this descent, but you cannot see the Cross Couloir. Cross over East Cross Creek on a spindly log bridge. The trail continues west from East Cross Creek and climbs north of some cliffs to reach Holy Cross' north ridge. The trail then switchbacks up on the west side of the ridge to reach the highest trees at 11,600 feet. This is the end of the maintained trail.

From the end of the trail, climb south up the long north ridge. The ridge is mostly talus interspersed with short sections of climber's trail. Stay on or west of the ridge crest. There are good views of Holy Cross' north face from the ridge. With a few extra steps, you can peer down the Angelica Couloir, but you still cannot see the Cross Couloir. Do not knock any rocks down Angelica. There may be climbers below you.

The north ridge merges with the upper part of the peak at 13,400 feet. From here, climb southeast up steepening talus to a small notch at 13,700 feet. This is the top of Angelica. From here, climb a steep, west-facing talus slope to the summit. The highest point is an angular talus block that just clears 14,000 feet. The top of the Cross Couloir is 100 feet south of the highest point and, with a few cautious steps, you can peer down the entire length of the couloir. Do not knock any rocks down the couloir. There may be climbers below you.

8.2 Angelica II, Class 3, Steep Snow (Seasonal)

From Halfmoon Trailhead: 11.8 miles, 5,625 feet

With descent of North Ridge: 12.0 miles, 5,625 feet

Angelica is the couloir on the west side of Holy Cross' north face. You can easily preview it when descending from Halfmoon Pass to East Cross Creek. Angelica is beautiful to look at and scintillating to climb. It is not as famous as the Cross Couloir but provides a shorter, simpler climb. Because of its north aspect, Angelica often holds good snow well into summer.

Start at the Halfmoon Trailhead and follow the Halfmoon Trail west for 1.7 miles to Halfmoon Pass at 11,640 feet. Continue over the pass, descend to East Cross Creek at 10,670 feet and cross the creek on a spindly log bridge. Leave the main trail 60 feet west of East Cross Creek and follow a strong side trail south to some campsites. Persevere past the camp-sites and find a climber's trail in the forest. This trail is worth finding. Follow the climber's trail south for 1.0 mile as it winds through rock

Mount of the Holy Cross from the northeast.

outcrops west of East Cross Creek to reach the bench west of beautiful Lake Patricia.

From Lake Patricia's south side, continue south for 0.2 mile, then climb southwest for 0.3 mile and proceed into the tiny basin below Holy Cross' north face. From 12,000 feet, climb southwest up this basin for 0.4 mile toward your angelic objective. At 12,700 feet, the seraph steepens and embraces you.

Climb the steepening snow to 12,900 feet, where the couloir splits. A menacing cornice often threatens the northern branch. Take the southern (left) branch. Climb south up the inset, undulating couloir for 800 fanciful feet to reach the North Ridge Route at 13,700 feet. The top of Angelica does not form a cornice, and the snow rolls placidly into the talus. Some small snow gargoyles cling under the north ridge and do threaten Angelica. Don't camp in the couloir. From 13,700 feet, hike east up talus on the last part of the North Ridge Route to the summit.

8.3 Holy Cross Couloir III, Class 3, Steep Snow (Seasonal) *Classic*

From Halfmoon Trailhead: 12.0 miles, 5,625 feet

With descent of North Ridge: 12.0 miles, 5,625 feet

This couloir's fame has attracted many climbers over the years. When snow conditions are good, it is a classic climb. When the climber's condition or snow conditions are unfavorable, the experience can rapidly turn

Holy Cross couloir.

into a nightmare. Like most east-facing Colorado snow couloirs, the snow conditions are usually best from mid-June through mid-July. Before mid-June you should carefully consider the avalanche potential. By September the rubble-filled gully is no longer appealing for climbing. An ice ax *and* crampons are useful for this climb. This couloir is deeply inset and has a cliff at the bottom.

Start at the Halfmoon Trailhead and follow the Halfmoon Trail west for 1.7 miles to Halfmoon Pass at 11,640 feet. Continue over the pass, descend to East Cross Creek at 10,670 feet and cross the creek on a spindly log bridge. Leave the main trail 60 feet west of East Cross Creek and follow a strong side trail south to some campsites. Persevere past the campsites and find a climber's trail in the forest. This trail is worth finding. Follow the climber's trail south for 1.0 mile as it winds through rock outcrops west of East Cross Creek to reach the bench west of beautiful Lake Patricia.

From Lake Patricia, continue south for 1.0 mile into the rugged, boulder-strewn basin below the Cross Couloir. The couloir only becomes visible as you approach it. The bottom of the couloir is an ugly cliff that you can avoid. Continue south up the valley, pass below the bottom of the couloir and go to the northwest end of the large Bowl of Tears Lake at 12,001 feet. From here, climb west up the slope well south of the couloir and angle over to the couloir's southern edge at 12,800 feet. The entry point into the couloir is above the cliff at the bottom of the couloir and below the steeper cliffs along the couloir's southern edge.

Test the snow conditions before committing to the couloir! This is the last good place to turn around if a retreat is indicated. As soon as you enter the couloir, the possibility of falling over the cliff at the bottom of the couloir will pull at your heels.

If both you and the couloir are in good condition, enter and ascend it for 1,200 feet to the summit. The climbing is consistent and continuous. The only good place to take a sit-down rest is on the Cross Ledge two-thirds of the way up. If the ledge is snow-covered, even this can be a dicey proposition. The steepest part of the couloir is between the Cross Ledge and the summit. The angle can exceed 45 degrees in this section. The couloir ends abruptly 100 feet south of the highest point. This is one of Colorado's most dramatic finishes! Descend the North Ridge Route.

8.4 Teardrop II, Class 3, Steep Snow (Seasonal)

From Halfmoon Trailhead: 14.5 miles, 5,625 feet
With descent of North Ridge: 13.25 miles, 5,625 feet

This long route provides a good alternative to the Holy Cross Couloir and allows you to visit one of Colorado's reclusive alpine cirques. Teardrop is only a viable route with good snow conditions, and this slope tends to melt out early in the summer. Don't wait too long for this one.

Follow the Holy Cross Couloir Route to Bowl of Tears Lake at 12,001 feet. Continue south for 0.4 mile and hike west into the narrow basin under the south face of Holy Cross. This is a special, seldom visited place. Continue west up steepening snow to the 13,500-foot saddle southwest of Holy Cross. The last 300 feet of this slope are steep and the exit may be guarded by a cornice. The easiest exit is north of the cornice. From the 13,500-foot saddle, climb northeast for 0.4 mile to the summit.

8.5 Halo Ridge II, Class 2

From Halfmoon Trailhead: 18.0 miles, 5,200 feet
With descent of North Ridge: 15.0 miles, 5,410 feet

This route circles the Bowl of Tears Basin and provides excellent views of the Cross Couloir. It is a long route, but the distance can be broken into stages by sleeping in the Notch Mountain Shelter Cabin. This shelter is not locked, but check with the Forest Service office in Minturn for current conditions. The phone number is (303) 827-5715.

From the Halfmoon Trailhead, follow the Fall Creek Trail south for 2.5 miles to the bottom of the Notch Mountain Trail at 11,160 feet. Hike west up the Notch Mountain Trail for an additional 2.8 miles to the Notch Mountain Shelter at 13,080 feet. Holy Cross pops into view as you crest the ridge.

At the shelter, Holy Cross' summit is less than 1,000 feet above you, but the Bowl of Tears Basin intervenes. The long Halo Ridge around the south end of the basin crosses three progressively higher summits. From the shelter, go south to Point 13,248, a ranked thirteener, and continue south to Point 13,373. Turn the corner and go west to a wide, flat portion of the ridge, where you can rest suspended between the summits. Continue west to Point 13,831, which is the summit of Holy Cross Ridge and one of Colorado's 100 highest peaks. Climb 0.7 mile north to the remaining summit—Holy Cross.

Variations
8.5V1 II, Class 2
From Halfmoon Trailhead: 15.0 miles, 5,410 feet

Instead of returning to the Notch Mountain Shelter, descend the North Ridge Route. This descent shortens the distance and increases the total elevation gain. This tour is best done as a long day hike, because you do not retrace any steps.

8.5V2 II, Class 3
From Halfmoon Trailhead: 13.4 miles, 6,040 feet
With descent of North Ridge: 12.7 miles, 6,250 feet
With descent of Notch Mountain Trail: 15.7 miles, 5,610 feet

This long, scenic tour is the big one. Modify the beginning of the Halo Ridge Route to include a traverse of Notch Mountain. Start at the Halfmoon Trailhead and follow the Halfmoon Trail to Halfmoon Pass. Leave the trail, hike south up talus to Point 12,743 and continue south on the ridge over blocky talus to the 13,237-foot summit of Notch Mountain. The view of Holy Cross from Notch Mountain's summit is even better than the view from the shelter cabin.

The traverse across the notch between Notch Mountain's two summits requires careful route finding and some Class 3 scrambling. The north face of Point 13,224—Notch Mountain's lower, southern summit—rises above the notch in a smooth sweep of rock. Navigating around this cliff is the crux of the route.

From Notch Mountain's 13,237-foot main summit, scramble down to the south on the ridge's east side. Descend a series of broken ledges leading down to the couloir on the east side of the notch. Cross the couloir below the notch. An ice ax is useful if there is snow in the couloir. Climb to a narrow ledge that cuts through the barrier cliff on the ridge's east side (Class 3). You can easily see this ledge while you are descending from the main summit. Follow the narrow ledge around a corner, then scramble up broken rock to Point 13,224 (Class 3). From here, hike south down talus to the Notch Mountain Shelter Cabin and continue on the Halo Ridge Route to Holy Cross' summit. Descend the North Ridge Route or return to the Notch Mountain Trail.

9. Mount Massive   14,421 feet

See Map 9 on page 85

Mount Massive is 11 miles southwest of Leadville and its east slopes dominate the view. Massive is massive. The mountain's name captures its essence. Massive has five summits above 14,000 feet on a 3-mile-long summit ridge. Massive is not just a peak; it is a region. No other single fourteener carries with it such a large area above tree line. If Massive were truncated at 14,000 feet, the area of the resulting plateau would be nearly half a square mile! No other peak in the 48 contiguous states has a greater area above 14,000 feet. By this measure, Massive reigns supreme.

Maps
Required: Mount Massive, San Isabel National Forest

Trailheads
Mount Massive Trailhead
This trailhead is at 10,050 feet and provides access to Massive's east side. From Third Street and U.S. 24 (Harrison Avenue) in downtown Leadville, go 3.6 miles southwest on U.S. 24 to Colorado 300. Turn west onto Colorado 300 and measure from this point. Go west on Colorado 300 (paved) and turn south (left) onto Lake County 11 (dirt) at 0.7 mile. Turn southwest (right) at 1.8 miles onto another dirt road marked with signs for Halfmoon Creek. Pass the San Isabel National Forest boundary at 3.9 miles, Halfmoon Campground at 5.6 miles and Elbert Creek Campground at 6.7 miles, and reach the well-marked Mount Massive Trailhead at 7.0 miles. The road is good to this point, and there is a parking lot on the road's north side. Winter road closure varies from the start of the Halfmoon Creek Road 1.8 miles from U.S. 24 to the Halfmoon Campground at mile 5.6.

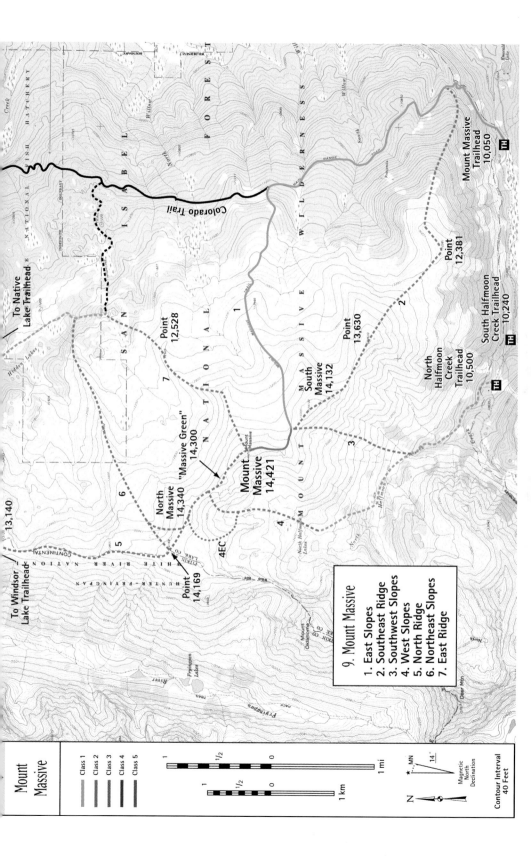

Mount
Massive

Class 1
Class 2
Class 3
Class 4
Class 5

1 mi
1/2
0
1 mi

1 km
1/2
0
1 km

N

MN
14°
Magnetic
North
Declination

Contour Interval
40 Feet

9. Mount Massive

1. East Slopes
2. Southeast Ridge
3. Southwest Slopes
4. West Slopes
5. North Ridge
6. Northeast Slopes
7. East Ridge

Mount Massive Trailhead 10,050

South Halfmoon Creek Trailhead 10,240

North Halfmoon Creek Trailhead 10,500

Point 12,381

Point 13,630

South Massive 14,132

Mount Massive 14,421

"Massive Green" 14,300

North Massive 14,340

Point 12,528

4EC

Point 14,169

To Windsor Lake Trailhead

13,140

To Native Lake Trailhead

Colorado Trail

WILDERNESS

ISABEL

FOREST

NATIONAL

SAN

MOUNT MASSIVE

HUNTER-FRYINGPAN

WHITE RIVER NATIONAL

CONTINENTAL

North Halfmoon Creek Trailhead

This trailhead is at 10,500 feet and provides access to Massive's south and west sides. Don't confuse this trailhead with the Halfmoon Trailhead described with Mount of the Holy Cross. From the Mount Massive Trailhead (mile 7.0), continue west; pass the Forest Service 110–1103A junction at 9.0 miles, continuing straight on Forest Service 110; and reach the trailhead at 9.5 miles. The road beyond the Forest Service 110–1103A junction is four-wheel-drive, and most people park passenger cars at this junction.

Native Lake Trailhead

This trailhead is at 10,760 feet and provides access to Massive's northeast side. From Sixth Street and U.S. 24 in downtown Leadville, go 4.4 miles west to the south edge of Turquoise Lake on Lake County 4. Cross the dam, go along the south side of Turquoise Lake and continue west on Lake County 4 (the Hagerman Pass Road) for an additional 6.8 miles. The marked trailhead is on the south side of the road, just before the road curves back to the northeast and starts climbing to the pass. There is a small parking lot at the trailhead.

Windsor Lake Trailhead

This trailhead is at 10,780 feet and provides access to Massive's north side. From the Native Lake Trailhead, continue west for an additional 200 yards to the Windsor Lake Trailhead. There is ample parking on the north side of the road, just before the road curves back to the northeast and starts climbing to Hagerman Pass.

To find the start of the Windsor Lake Trail, cross to the south side of the torrent of water coming out of the Carlton diversion tunnel; use a plank bridge to cross the concrete channel. Cross a second, small stream and find the trail sign just beyond.

Routes

9.1 East Slopes II, Class 2

From Mount Massive Trailhead: 13.6 miles, 4,450 feet

This long hike is mostly on a good trail, and this is the easiest way to climb Massive. Start at the Mount Massive Trailhead and follow the Colorado Trail northeast then north through the forest. Cross South Willow Creek at mile 2.4, cross Willow Creek at mile 3.0 and, at mile 3.3, reach the junction with the Mount Massive Trail at 11,260 feet. Go west on the Mount Massive Trail up Massive's vast east slopes. The trail becomes less distinct above tree line, but you do not need a trail on these gentle slopes. Climb to the 13,900-foot saddle between South Massive (14,132 feet) and Massive. From this saddle, climb west then north on a climber's trail along

Massive's south ridge to the summit (Class 2). The size of this peak will become apparent long before you reach the summit.

Extra Credit 9.1EC

From the 13,900-foot saddle, climb southeast for 0.3 mile to South Massive's 14,132-foot summit. The high point is a spectacular block perched above the others.

9.2 Southeast Ridge II, Class 2

From Mount Massive Trailhead: 11.4 miles, 5,820 feet

With descent of East Slopes: 12.5 miles, 5,130 feet

This laconic tour collects Massive's three southern summits. If you are fit and like to wend your way above the trail and its attendant crowds, this route is for you. Start at the Mount Massive Trailhead and follow the Colorado Trail northeast for 1.0 mile to 10,600 feet, where the trail turns northwest. The introduction is over.

Leave the comfortable trail and climb west through open trees for 1.1 miles to tree line at 11,800 feet. You've paid your dues. More than 3 miles of unfettered ridge now lie ahead of you. Continue west to 12,200 feet and discover a hidden alcove. Wend your way southwest through this petite parlor to Point 12,381. If you are lucky, you may see goats here. Point 12,381 is one of Massive's least-visited summits, and it will reward you with an unobstructed view of Mount Elbert.

From Point 12,381, descend northwest to a 12,180-foot saddle, then climb northwest for 0.8 mile up a grassy slope to Point 13,630, alias "South South Massive." This is another of Massive's seldom visited summits and, no matter what your mood is, you will be isolated here. Descend northwest to a 13,380-foot saddle, then climb northwest for 0.5 mile up the now rougher ridge to 14,132-foot South Massive. The highest point of this significant summit is a spectacular block perched above its neighbors.

From South Massive, descend northwest to the 13,900-foot saddle at the top of the Mount Massive Trail. Your isolation ends here. Continue northwest up the ridge on the top part of the East Slopes Route to the summit. Descending the East Slopes Route will put your ascent into perspective.

9.3 Southwest Slopes II, Class 2

From North Halfmoon Creek Trailhead: 6.2 miles, 3,960 feet

This is the shortest route up Massive, but it is much steeper than the East Slopes Route. Start at the North Halfmoon Creek Trailhead and follow the North Halfmoon Creek Trail northwest into the Mount Massive Wilderness for 1.3 miles to a large meadow just beyond a small creek crossing. Massive's large southwest slopes and its southern subpeaks are now directly northeast of the trail. At the northwest (upper) end of the

Mount Massive from the east.

meadow, leave the North Halfmoon Creek Trail and turn north (right) onto a climber's trail leading directly up Massive's steep southwest slopes. Only a cairn marks this turn, and many people miss it.

Skirt some initial cliffs on their northwest end and climb the shallow, grass-filled basin between South Massive (14,132 feet) and Massive. The climber's trail up this basin is sometimes strong and sometimes nonexistent. Climb north into the 13,900-foot saddle between South Massive and Massive. The relentless ascent from the valley to this high saddle requires 2,750 feet of gain. Compensations are the wonderful wildflowers near tree line and the expansive views. From the saddle, climb west then north on a climber's trail along Massive's south ridge to the summit.

9.4 West Slopes II, Class 2

From North Halfmoon Creek Trailhead: 8.6 miles, 4,200 feet

With descent of Southwest Slopes: 7.4 miles, 4,100 feet

This route allows you to touch the heart of the Mount Massive Wilderness. It also offers you the opportunity to traverse Massive's long summit ridge. Start at the North Halfmoon Creek Trailhead and follow the North Halfmoon Creek Trail northwest into the Mount Massive Wilderness as the trail climbs on the east side of North Halfmoon Creek. Pass the meadow where the Southwest Slopes Route leaves the valley. Continue northwest then north on the North Halfmoon Creek Trail into the large basin under Massive's west slopes. The trail does not go to North Halfmoon Lakes but climbs up grassy, flower-laden benches east of the lakes. The trail becomes less distinct as it climbs north into the basin and finally disappears.

Massive's summit is on the basin's east side, and North Massive (14,340 feet) is at the basin's north end. There is an impressive tower at the south end of a subsidiary ridge running southwest from North Massive. Several routes are possible from the basin to Massive's summit. They all involve climbing up tedious talus and scree slopes. The route described here minimizes time spent on steep scree slopes.

Climb northeast into the upper basin between the ridge with the impressive tower on it and the north ridge of Massive. This basin is under North Massive's south face. Stay north of some cliffs and climb steep scree to Massive's north ridge at the 14,060-foot saddle between North Massive and Massive. This saddle is just south of some pesky rock towers on Massive's north ridge. Stay south of these towers when approaching the ridge. From the 14,060-foot saddle, climb southeast on the gentle ridge over the rounded 14,300-foot summit of "Massive Green" and continue on the still gentle ridge to Massive's 14,421-foot main summit. Descend the Southwest Slopes Route.

Extra Credit 9.4EC
From North Halfmoon Creek Trailhead: 8.7 miles, 4,630 feet

This lofty Tour de Massive collects most of Massive's summits. From the upper basin of the West Slopes Route, climb northeast up a scree slope to reach the south ridge of North Massive (14,340 feet). This is the ridge with the impressive tower on its south end. Climb north up the now easy ridge to the gentle slopes west of North Massive's summit. This is a special, seldom visited place. Climb east to North Massive's surprising summit. The western of two summits is the highest. This summit is Colorado's fifth highest summit, and it very nearly qualifies for official fourteener status.

Scramble east, visit North Massive's spectacular east summit, then descend southeast to a 14,100-foot saddle southeast of North Massive. This lively descent requires careful route finding and some minor Class 3 scrambling. There are several ways to accomplish this descent and, with very careful route finding, you can keep the difficulty at Class 2. From the 14,100-foot saddle, scramble southeast on or below the rough ridge. This stretch of ridge also requires careful route finding and some minor Class 3 scrambling to pass some rock towers on their west sides. The difficulties end abruptly as you reach the 14,060-foot saddle south of these towers and rejoin the West Slopes Route. From the 14,060-foot saddle, continue on the now gentle ridge to the broad 14,300-foot "Massive Green." Continue on the still gentle ridge to Massive's 14,421-foot main summit.

Descend southeast on the upper part of the East Slopes Route to the 13,900-foot saddle between Massive and South Massive. Climb southeast to South Massive's 14,132-foot summit, return to the 13,900-foot saddle and descend the Southwest Slopes Route.

9.5 North Ridge II, Class 3

From Windsor Lake Trailhead: 11.8 miles, 4,660 feet
With descent of East Ridge: 11.8 miles, 4,900 feet

For aficionados of the high and wild, this is it. You can spend the day above the trees walking along one of the highest stretches of the Continental Divide in North America. Start at the Windsor Lake Trailhead and follow a steep trail southwest for 1.0 mile to Windsor Lake at 11,620 feet. When dawn light glances across snow slopes above the lake, this is one of Colorado's most beautiful places.

Climb southwest above the lake up a lush basin dotted with marsh marigolds. Angle southwest, cross a small drainage, then climb a steep slope to the 12,660-foot saddle on the Continental Divide, just south of the rocky ramparts of Point 12,740. From the saddle, you are treated to a unique view of upper Fryingpan River Valley. The introduction is over and, from just beyond the saddle, you can peer south toward Massive's main summit, almost 4 miles away.

Hike south along the divide and contour below Points 13,020 and 13,140 on their west sides. These gentle slopes harbor fleets of alpine wildflowers. On Massive's north ridge, you are suspended between the Mount Massive Wilderness and the Hunter–Fryingpan Wilderness. Hike high and free for an additional 1.5 miles to Point 14,169. This seldom visited summit commands a massive view. The Continental Divide continues south from here and avoids Massive's main summit. Going where the divide dares not, hike southeast to 14,340-foot North Massive and continue on the Northeast Slopes Route to Massive's main summit. If the day is long and electricity-free, you may choose to return along the divide. Descending the East Ridge Route completes a comprehensive Tour de Massive.

Extra Credit 9.5EC

Go to the summits of Points 13,020 and 13,140 along the way.

9.6 Northeast Slopes II, Class 3, Moderate Snow

From Native Lake Trailhead: 14.2 miles, 5,950 feet
With descent of East Ridge: 13.0 miles, 5,530 feet

Removed from the crowds in Halfmoon Creek, this long route is suitable for a backpacking adventure and it allows you to ascend the permanent snowfield on North Massive's northeast flank. This snowfield is prominent from Leadville and it graces Massive long after other snowfields melt.

Start at the Native Lake Trailhead and follow the Highline Trail south for 1.3 miles to a broad saddle at 11,860 feet. Descend a sweeping switchback and continue south for an additional 2.3 miles to 11,400 feet, where the trail climbs out of the Hidden Lakes Basin. If you begin descending to the east along the trail, you have gone too far. Leave the trail and hike west to the bottom of North Massive's east ridge. Proceed onto this distinct ridge and follow it west for 1.0 mile to the basin you have worked so hard to reach. Choose your line on the snowfield and climb it. From the top of the snowfield, it is easy to climb Point 14,169, Massive's northernmost 14,000-foot summit. Hike east to North Massive's 14,340-foot summit and continue southeast for 0.9 mile along the lively high traverse to Massive's 14,421-foot summit (Class 3). Ascending the Northeast Slopes Route and descending the East Ridge Route makes a pithy Tour de Massive.

9.7 East Ridge II, Class 2

From Native Lake Trailhead: 11.7 miles, 5,040 feet

This route retains the wilderness flavor of the Northeast Slopes Route but eliminates its extra summits and difficulties. Start at the Native Lake Trailhead and follow the Highline Trail south for 1.3 miles to a broad saddle at 11,860 feet. Descend a sweeping switchback and continue south for another 2.3 miles to 11,400 feet, where the trail climbs out of the Hidden Lakes Basin. This is the cutoff point for the Northeast Slopes Route. Continue south on the trail for another 0.25 mile to 11,580 feet, where the trail turns east just north of two small lakes.

Leave the trail and hike southwest 0.4 mile past tree line to the base of a northeast-facing slope. Climb this slope for 0.4 mile to tiny Point 12,528 on the ridge above, where you can rest for a moment apart. Follow the now well defined ridge as it curves gracefully southwest toward Massive's heights. The ridge levels briefly at 13,500 feet before turning west and merging with Massive's final face. Climb west directly to the summit.

9.8 Massive Mania II, Class 3

From Windsor Lake Trailhead: 11.6 miles, 5,000 feet

This is the big one. You have looked at it from Leadville for years. Now climb it. Start at the Windsor Lake Trailhead and ascend the North Ridge Route. Descend the Southeast Ridge Route to the Mount Massive Trailhead and a prearranged vehicle shuttle. Along the way, you can climb all nine of Massive's summits, five of which are above 14,000 feet. At the end of this expedition, you will appreciate firsthand that Massive is massive.

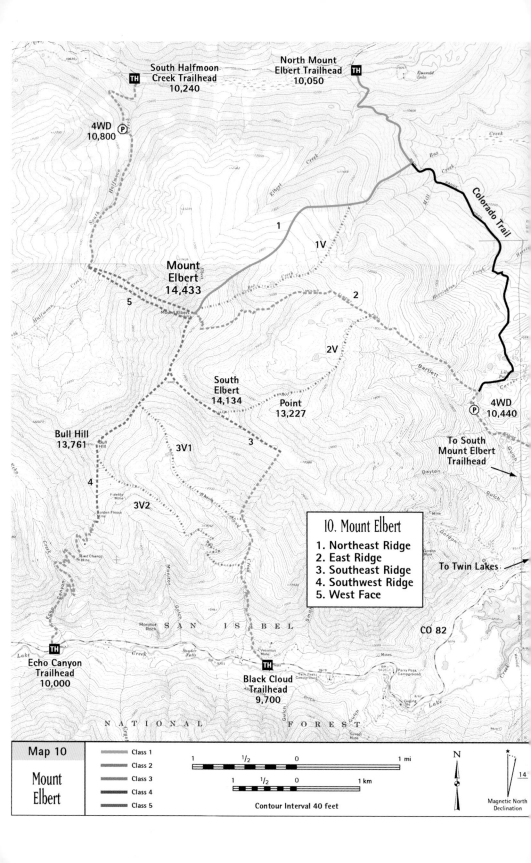

South Halfmoon Creek Trailhead 10,240

North Mount Elbert Trailhead 10,050

4WD 10,800 (P)

Colorado Trail

1

1V

Mount Elbert 14,433

2

5

2V

South Elbert 14,134

Point 13,227

Bull Hill 13,761

3V1

3

4

3V2

4WD 10,440 (P)

To South Mount Elbert Trailhead

10. Mount Elbert
1. Northeast Ridge
2. East Ridge
3. Southeast Ridge
4. Southwest Ridge
5. West Face

To Twin Lakes

CO 82

SAN   ISABEL

Echo Canyon Trailhead 10,000

Black Cloud Trailhead 9,700

NATIONAL   FOREST

Map 10	Class 1
	Class 2
Mount Elbert	Class 3
	Class 4
	Class 5

1   1/2   0   1 mi

1   1/2   0   1 km

Contour Interval 40 feet

N

Magnetic North Declination

14

10. Mount Elbert   14,433 feet

See Map 10 on page 92

All rise. This mighty lump has received many accolades. Mount Elbert is the highest peak in Lake County, in Colorado and in the Rocky Mountains. Elbert is in plain view 12 miles southwest of Leadville, but many people mistake Colorado's highest peak for a thirteener. With a more intense inspection, you can see Elbert for the monarch it is. Elbert's size, not its height, fools people. Elbert is one of Colorado's most enjoyable fourteener hikes. Occasionally, football fans call Colorado's highest peak "Mount Elway."

Maps

Required: Mount Elbert, Mount Massive, San Isabel National Forest
Optional: Granite

Trailheads

North Mount Elbert Trailhead

This trailhead is at 10,050 feet and provides access to Elbert's northeast side. From Leadville, follow the directions to the Mount Massive Trailhead (see Mount Massive). The North Mount Elbert Trailhead is 0.1 mile east of the Mount Massive Trailhead on the south side of the road at mile 6.9.

South Halfmoon Creek Trailhead

This trailhead is at 10,240 feet and provides access to Elbert's west face. Don't confuse this trailhead with the Halfmoon Trailhead described with Mount of the Holy Cross. From the North Mount Elbert Trailhead (mile 6.9), continue west and reach the South Halfmoon Creek Trailhead at the Forest Service 110–1103A junction at mile 9.0. The road is good to this point.

South Mount Elbert Trailhead

This trailhead is at 9,560 feet. It provides access to Elbert's east side and the Mount Elbert Trail. Turn north from Colorado 82 onto Lake County 24. This turn is 4.0 miles west of the U.S. 24–Colorado 82 junction and 2.3 miles east of the town of Twin Lakes on Colorado 82. Measure from the Colorado 82–Lake County 24 junction, and go west on Lake County 24 (paved) for 1.0 mile to the Lakeview Campground. The trailhead is at the northwest end of the campground. This area is accessible in winter.

High-clearance vehicles can go farther. Continue past the campground to the "Sure Pretty" overlook. Just west of the overlook, follow a four-wheel-drive road west for 1.8 miles to its end near a creek crossing at 10,440 feet.

Black Cloud Trailhead

This trailhead is at 9,700 feet and provides access to Elbert's south side. The trailhead is just north of Colorado 82. The easily missed turn is 10.5 miles west of the U.S. 24–Colorado 82 junction, 4.2 miles west of the town of Twin Lakes and 4.0 miles east of the Colorado 82–South Fork Lake Creek Road junction. The trailhead is marked with a small sign for the Black Cloud Trail, and there is room for several vehicles to park 100 feet north of Colorado 82. The trail starts east of the parking spaces.

Echo Canyon Trailhead

This trailhead is at 10,000 feet and provides access to Elbert's southwest side. This trailhead is not far north of Colorado 82, but the turn is easily missed. The turn is 12.5 miles west of the U.S. 24–Colorado 82 junction, 6.2 miles west of the town of Twin Lakes and 2.0 miles east of the Colorado 82–South Fork Lake Creek Road junction. The trailhead is marked with a small sign for the Echo Canyon Trail. Turn north off Colorado 82 onto a dirt road in front of a cabin and go west for 100 feet. There is room for one or two vehicles to park here, and passenger cars should stop here. A rough four-wheel-drive road climbs north from this spot, and this road is the start of the Echo Canyon Trail.

Routes

10.1 Northeast Ridge II, Class 1

From North Mount Elbert Trailhead: 9.0 miles, 4,400 feet

This is the most popular route up Elbert. There is a good trail all the way to the summit. You will appreciate Elbert's size long before you reach the summit. Start at the North Mount Elbert Trailhead and climb southeast on a trail for 0.3 mile to Elbert Creek. Cross the creek and continue south on the Colorado Trail for an additional 0.5 mile as it climbs to 10,600 feet on the lower part of Elbert's northeast ridge. Continue south on the trail for an additional 0.5 mile as it levels out then drops a little. Before the Colorado Trail crosses Box Creek, leave it at 10,560 feet and turn west onto a recently constructed trail. Switchback up on this good trail for 1.0 mile to tree line at nearly 12,000 feet. The trail continues above tree line to the crest of Elbert's northeast ridge. Follow the ridge to the summit.

Variation 10.1V

Instead of climbing to Elbert's northeast ridge on the trail, continue up into the tiny cirque at the head of Box Creek. In June there are several shallow, snow-filled couloirs in the cirque's headwall. Any of them pro-vides a moderate snow climb. Choose your couloir and climb it. The tops of the couloirs are at 13,800 feet, 0.5 mile east of the summit.

10.2 East Ridge II, Class 1 *Classic*

From South Mount Elbert Trailhead: 11.2 miles, 4,850 feet
From 4WD parking at 10,440 feet: 7.6 miles, 4,000 feet

This is the easiest route on Elbert. It follows the excellent Mount Elbert Trail all the way to the summit. From the South Mount Elbert Trailhead at the Lakeview Campground, this route is longer than the Northeast Ridge Route, but from the road's end at 10,440 feet, it is shorter.

Start at the South Mount Elbert Trailhead and follow the Colorado Trail west along the dirt road for 1.8 miles to the road's end at 10,440 feet. Cross the creek on a log bridge and continue on the Colorado Trail for 200 yards to a well-marked junction with the Mount Elbert Trail. Leave the comfortable Colorado Trail and climb steeply west on the Mount Elbert Trail as it climbs past tree line then angles northwest to reach the crest of Elbert's broad east ridge at 12,380 feet. The view to the north opens at this point. Follow the trail up the east ridge to 13,700 feet. The trail takes a surprising turn to the south and reaches the summit by switchbacking up southeast-facing slopes. The Mount Elbert Trail joins the Northeast Ridge Route 100 yards east of the summit. On a busy summer day, Colorado's highest summit will hold many people.

Variation 10.2V

Leave the Mount Elbert Trail at 12,000 feet and contour west for 0.2 mile. Cross a branch of Bartlett Creek and contour south for 0.4 mile to the main branch of Bartlett Creek. Cross this creek and climb south to the crest of South Elbert's east ridge. Climb west up this ridge for 0.7 mile to Point 13,227. From this lofty perch, you can look northwest to the upper part of the Mount Elbert Trail and Elbert's main summit. If you are out of shape, you may wonder why you chose this circuitous route. If you are in shape, you may enjoy your solitary position.

Continue west for an additional 0.6 mile up steep talus to South Elbert's 14,134-foot summit. This significant summit is 1.0 mile from Elbert's main summit and rises 234 feet above the connecting saddle. South Elbert is well worth climbing, and no matter what shape you are in, you should feel better here. Hike northwest 0.5 mile down a gentle, grassy slope to the broad 13,900-foot saddle between Elbert and South Elbert. Climb north for 0.7 mile to Elbert's main summit. Ascending this variation and descend-ing the East Ridge Route on the Mount Elbert Trail makes a nifty Tour de Elbert.

Mount Elbert from the southwest (photo by Steve Hoffmeyer).

10.3 Southeast Ridge II, Class 2

From Black Cloud Trailhead: 10.0 miles, 5,250 feet

This is a scenic alternative to the crowded trails on Elbert's east side. Surprisingly, there is a trail most of the way up this route. However, this is a tougher climb than the east-side routes. Your reward is the opportunity to climb two 14,000-foot summits. Start at the Black Cloud Trailhead and follow the excellent Black Cloud Trail as it switchbacks steeply up on the east side of Black Cloud Creek. Cross to the west side of the creek at 10,860 feet and continue up along the west side of the creek. Do not follow another trail that angles west at 11,020 feet. Higher, at 11,200 feet, cross back to the east side of Black Cloud Creek and climb to an old cabin at 11,600 feet. There are good views of La Plata Peak from Black Cloud Gulch.

Continue on the unmarked but good trail above the cabin as it climbs past a tailings pile, then switchbacks up large, southwest-facing slopes to reach Elbert's long, southeast ridge at a level stretch at 13,540 feet. At this point, you may feel like you have already climbed a mountain, and the view of Elbert's summit, still 2.0 miles distant, may be discouraging. There is no trail along the ridge, but none is needed. Climb northwest for 0.8 mile to the summit of 14,134-foot South Elbert. Descend southwest to the broad, 13,900-foot saddle between South Elbert and Elbert's main summit, then climb north over talus for 0.6 mile to the summit.

Variations
10.3V1 II, Class 2
From Black Cloud Trailhead: 9.6 miles, 4,800 feet

From the old cabin at 11,600 feet, leave the trail and hike northwest into upper Black Cloud Gulch. Climb to the 13,340-foot saddle between 13,761-foot Bull Hill and Elbert, then climb northeast to rejoin the route at the 13,900-foot saddle between South Elbert and Elbert. This variation avoids the climb over South Elbert's summit. Ascending via South Elbert's summit and descending this variation saves some effort and makes a scenic circle tour.

10.3V2 II, Class 2
From Black Cloud Trailhead: 10.0 miles, 5,640 feet

Leave the Black Cloud Trail at 11,020 feet and follow another trail west toward Fidelity Mine. Leave this trail at 12,000 feet and climb onto Bull Hill's southeast ridge. Follow this ridge 1.5 miles up to Bull Hill's 13,761-foot summit. Descend northeast from Bull Hill to the 13,340-foot saddle between Bull Hill and Elbert. From this saddle, climb northeast into the broad, 13,900-foot saddle between 14,134-foot South Elbert and Elbert. Climb north along a gentle ridge for 0.6 mile to Elbert's main summit. Ascending the Southeast Ridge Route and descending this variation makes an interesting Tour de Elbert that allows you to collect three summits.

10.4 Southwest Ridge II, Class 2
From Echo Canyon Trailhead: 10.6 miles, 5,250 feet

This interesting alternative route is far removed from the crowds on Elbert's eastern slopes. This route is rougher and longer than the eastern routes, and it requires you to cross or skirt mighty Bull Hill twice. You will spend a long time on ridges above 13,000 feet.

Start at the Echo Canyon Trailhead and go north up the four-wheel-drive road for 0.3 mile to an old concrete foundation at 10,200 feet. Cross to the east side of Echo Creek below the concrete foundation and follow an old road along the creek for 0.8 mile to a trail junction. Turn east (right), leave Echo Creek and follow the trail that switchbacks steeply up the southwest slopes of 13,761-foot Bull Hill. The road ends at the Golden Fleece Mine at 12,700 feet. Climb above the mine and reach Bull Hill's gentle, upper south ridge at 12,800 feet. Climb north along this grassy ridge to 13,400 feet and either continue to Bull Hill's summit or skirt it on its south side. Bull Hill has the distinction of being Colorado's highest named hill.

Descend northeast from Bull Hill to the 13,340-foot saddle between Bull Hill and Elbert. From this saddle, climb northeast into the broad,

13,900-foot saddle between 14,134-foot South Elbert and Elbert. South Elbert is 1 mile south of Elbert. Climb north along a gentle ridge for a final 0.6 mile to Elbert's main summit. Ascending this route and descending the Southeast Ridge Route makes an arduous Tour de Elbert that allows you to collect three summits. On Colorado 82, Black Cloud Trailhead is 2.0 miles from Echo Canyon Trailhead.

10.5 West Face II, Class 2, Moderate Snow (Seasonal)

From South Halfmoon Creek Trailhead: 8.0 miles, 4,200 feet

This route provides a workout. From the South Halfmoon Creek Trailhead, cross to the south side of Halfmoon Creek on a broken bridge. Follow the four-wheel-drive road south as it switchbacks steeply up the hill. After 1.0 mile, cross to the east side of South Halfmoon Creek on another broken bridge at 10,800 feet. Continue south on the four-wheel-drive road for an additional 1.5 miles to a clearing at 11,400 feet, under the center of Elbert's steep west face. The introduction is over.

Elbert's summit is only 1.3 miles away but an astonishing 3,000 feet above you. There is a shallow couloir in the center of Elbert's west face that leads directly to the summit. When this couloir is full of stable snow, this is the best alternative. After the snow melts, the rounded shoulder just south of the couloir provides the best footing. Leave the road, hike east and choose your workout.

11. La Plata Peak   14,336 feet

See Map 11 on page 100

La Plata, Colorado's fifth highest peak, is 3 miles south of Colorado 82, about halfway between Twin Lakes and Independence Pass. The proud peak is clearly visible from Colorado 82 east of Independence Pass. *La Plata* means "silver" in Spanish. La Plata's elegant ridges and embracing cirques command a degree of respect that other Sawatch fourteeners lack. In simple language, La Plata is steeper than its neighbors. La Plata's standard routes are easy, but it is not surprising that La Plata also offers one of the more interesting technical routes on a Sawatch fourteener.

The 1979 photoinspection of the Mount Elbert Quadrangle designates La Plata's altitude as 14,361 feet instead of its long-standing altitude of 14,336 feet. I called the USGS, which verified that 14,361 feet is *incorrect*. There was an editing error during the preparation of the new map. The original altitude of 14,336 feet is still correct and will be reinstated on a future printing. Unfortunately, the U.S. Forest Service and other agencies are using the incorrect altitude on their maps. It will be decades before the error is fully corrected.

Maps

Required: Mount Elbert, San Isabel National Forest
Optional: Winfield, Independence Pass

Trailheads

Lake Creek Trailhead

This trailhead is at 10,160 feet and provides access to La Plata's north and west sides. Park at the Colorado 82–South Fork Lake Creek Road junction. This junction is 14.5 miles west of the U.S. 24–Colorado 82 junction. Do not park on the South Fork Lake Creek Road, because the first quarter mile south of Colorado 82 is on private property. This trailhead is accessible in winter.

West Winfield Trailhead

This trailhead is at 10,380 feet and provides access to La Plata's south side. Turn west from U.S. 24 onto Chaffee County 390 (dirt). This junction is 14.9 miles north of the stoplight in the center of Buena Vista, 4.3 miles south of the U.S. 24–Colorado 82 junction and 19.3 miles south of the West Sixth–U.S. 24 junction in the center of Leadville. Go west on Chaffee County 390 for 11.8 miles to Winfield. There are many informal camping areas along this road. From the center of Winfield, go north (right) for 60 yards, then go west (left) on the rough but passable road for an additional 0.4 mile to the Winfield Cemetery. Continue west for an additional 0.2 mile; here the road becomes rougher. Park on the south (left) side of the road in an open area.

Routes

11.1 Northwest Ridge II, Class 2

From Lake Creek Trailhead: 9.0 miles, 4,300 feet

This is the most popular route on La Plata, but it is not the easiest route on La Plata. Start at the Lake Creek Trailhead and go south on the South Fork Lake Creek Road. Cross the vehicle bridge over Lake Creek and continue south on the South Fork Road for 0.3 mile past all the no-trespassing signs. When the road angles southwest up a hill, leave it and hike straight east through the trees for 200 yards to the South Fork of Lake Creek. Find and cross the South Fork on an exposed but solid, multi-log bridge over a small gorge. Finding this bridge is important, because the South Fork is difficult to cross on foot and there is private property just north of the bridge. The bridge is complete with a handrail and is in the rocks just southeast of an old cabin. By following the directions given here, you can avoid the private property north of the log bridge.

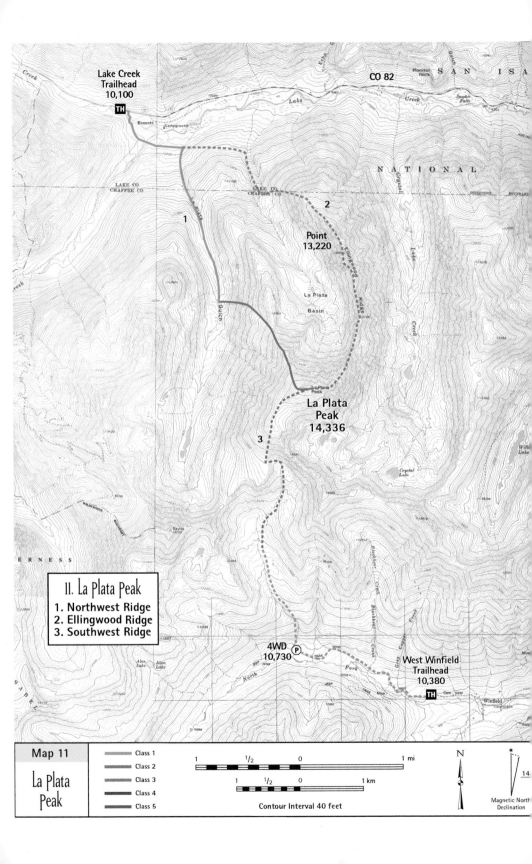

Lake Creek
Trailhead
10,100
TH

CO 82

SAN ISA

N A T I O N A L

LAKE CO
CHAFFEE CO

LAKE CO
CHAFFEE CO

1

2

Point
13,220

La Plata
Basin

La Plata
Peak

La Plata
Peak
14,336

3

II. La Plata Peak
1. Northwest Ridge
2. Ellingwood Ridge
3. Southwest Ridge

4WD
10,730 **P**

West Winfield
Trailhead
10,380
TH

Winfield

Map 11	Class 1
	Class 2
La Plata	Class 3
Peak	Class 4
	Class 5

1   1/2   0   1 mi

1   1/2   0   1 km

Contour Interval 40 feet

N

14

Magnetic North
Declination

La Plata Peak from the north (photo by Steve Hoffmeyer).

After crossing the bridge, go north (left) on a good trail along the South Fork's east side, then east along Lake Creek's south side for 0.4 mile to La Plata Gulch. Cross La Plata Gulch Creek and follow the good trail south (right) along the east side of the creek for 1.8 miles up La Plata Gulch to 11,200 feet, near tree line.

Turn east (left), leave the comfort of the valley and angle southeast up the Colorado Fourteener Initiative trail on the steep slope above you for 1,500 feet to reach La Plata's northwest ridge at 12,760 feet. From the ridge, the view of the long, jagged Ellingwood Ridge across La Plata Basin to the east is startling and spectacular. From your airy aerie, turn south (right) and ascend La Plata's easy northwest ridge for 1.0 mile to the summit.

11.2 Ellingwood Ridge III, Class 3 *Classic*

From Lake Creek Trailhead: 10.0 miles, 5,000 feet

The Ellingwood Ridge is La Plata's *long*, jagged northeast ridge. Do not confuse La Plata's famous Ellingwood Ridge with the even more famous Ellingwood Arête on Crestone Needle. La Plata's Ellingwood Ridge is long and complex, but it is not as hard as its reputation implies. If you take care to find the easiest passage when faced with a problem, the difficulty will not exceed Class 3. Nevertheless, take care on this long, tiring route. This route has been rated Grade III for a reason.

Start at the Lake Creek Trailhead and follow the Northwest Ridge Route to La Plata Gulch. Cross La Plata Gulch Creek, go north (left) for 100 feet and continue east along Lake Creek's south side on a faint trail to La Plata Basin Gulch. Do not confuse La Plata Gulch with La Plata Basin

Gulch. La Plata Gulch is west of the northwest ridge. You want to go to La Plata Basin Gulch, which is between the northwest ridge and the Ellingwood Ridge to the east.

There is a faint trail up the west side of La Plata Basin Gulch Creek. Even if you find it, it won't aid your approach much. Cross to the east side of La Plata Basin Creek and bushwhack south up the rugged gulch. Find and follow a small, sharp ridge east of the creek. The crest of this hidden ridge provides good passage. From the top of the ridge at 11,200 feet, you will break out of the trees and see the Ellingwood Ridge's northern ramparts. From 11,200 feet, leave La Plata Basin Gulch and climb east up a long, steep, loose, tiring talus slope to reach Ellingwood Ridge's northern end at 12,600 feet. The introduction is over. A 2-mile stretch of rugged ridge separates you from the summit.

Climb south along the famous ridge and bypass an initial series of small summits. When faced with a difficult section, you will always find the easiest passage on the ridge's east side. You will usually have to drop down below the cliffs to keep the difficulty at Class 3, and you will spend very little time on the ridge crest. Climb to near the summit of Point 13,206. The view from here is discouraging. Dozens of towers and ramparts still separate you from the summit. Descend and contour on the ridge's east side, then climb to a small, grassy 13,140-foot summit. The view from here is discouraging. Dozens of towers and ramparts still separate you from the summit, and they are closer and look more difficult. It is also clear that you will have to give up a lot of your hard-earned elevation.

Angle down from Point 13,140, then descend east down one of several available grassy gullies until you can contour south to a small but distinct dirt bench on a rib. From the bench, climb to another small but distinct dirt bench on a rib. Continue this technique. You will climb up and down a lot as you slowly solve the ridge's problems.

At 13,000 feet, contour below a flat section of ridge and engage the upper part of the peak. Climb a talus slope, then continue to use the up-and-over technique (you should be good at it by now) and bypass the next buttress on its east side. Reach a large, long, east-facing talus slope and climb it to 14,000 feet. Cross above a snow-filled gully, traverse across broken, east-facing slabs and climb to the summit of Point 14,180. From here you have a good view of the summit and (as you doubtless expect) several more towers. Descend west and bypass these towers on their south (left) sides. Struggle back up to the ridge one more time, then walk triumphantly to the summit, which is 100 yards west.

Variation 11.2V

Climbing along Ellingwood Ridge is not an exact science. The closer you stay to the ridge crest, the greater the difficulty will be. Staying directly on the ridge crest all the way is an endeavor that requires several rappels, much Class 4 climbing, some Class 5 climbing and, possibly, more than one day to complete.

11.3 Southwest Ridge II, Class 2

From West Winfield Trailhead: 9.4 miles, 3,960 feet

From 4WD parking: 7.0 miles, 3,610 feet

This is the easiest route on La Plata. It is a gentler, scenic alternative to the more popular Northwest Ridge Route. Start at the West Winfield Trailhead and go west on the four-wheel-drive road for 1.2 miles. In an open meadow at 10,730 feet, follow another four-wheel-drive road north (right) for 300 yards to a gate at the end of the road. Climb north then northwest on a trail for 1.0 mile into a beautiful valley. Hike north across the valley and climb to La Plata's southwest ridge via a steep slope. Once on the broad ridge at 13,200 feet, continue northeast for 1.0 mile on a rolling stretch to the summit.

12. Huron Peak   14,003 feet

See Map 12 on page 104

Huron is a shapely, shy peak hidden in the heart of the Sawatch about halfway between Buena Vista and Independence Pass. Huron just barely rises above 14,000 feet but compensates by being the Sawatch fourteener that is farthest from a paved road. The view from Huron's summit is one of the best in the Sawatch. A good dirt road provides easy access to Huron, and Huron's routes are simple climbs. Huron is one of the few Sawatch fourteeners with an elevation gain of less than 4,000 feet.

Maps

Required: Winfield, San Isabel National Forest

Trailheads

Rockdale Trailhead

This trailhead is at 9,940 feet and provides access to Huron's east side and Missouri's west side. Turn west from U.S. 24 onto Chaffee County 390 (dirt). This junction is 14.9 miles north of the stoplight in the center of Buena Vista, 4.3 miles south of the U.S. 24–Colorado 82 junction and 19.3 miles south of the West Sixth–U.S. 24 junction in the center of Leadville. Go west on Chaffee County 390 for 9.8 miles to Rockdale, which is at an unmarked turn on the south side of the road. Turn south (left), go past Rockdale's four cabins and curve down to a parking area on the north side

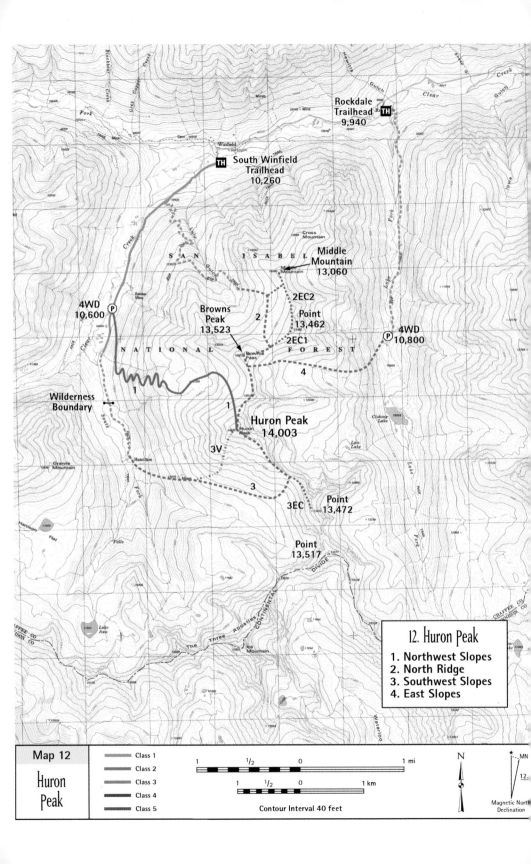

Rockdale
Trailhead
9,940

South Winfield
Trailhead
10,260

Middle
Mountain
13,060

2EC2

4WD
10,600

Browns
Peak
13,523

2

Point
13,462

2EC1

4WD
10,800

4

1

1

Wilderness
Boundary

Huron Peak
14,003

3V

3

3EC

Point
13,472

Point
13,517

12. Huron Peak

1. Northwest Slopes
2. North Ridge
3. Southwest Slopes
4. East Slopes

Map 12

Huron
Peak

Class 1
Class 2
Class 3
Class 4
Class 5

1   ½   0   1 mi

1   ½   0   1 km

Contour Interval 40 feet

N

MN

12.

Magnetic North
Declination

Huron Peak from the southwest.

of Clear Creek. Passenger cars should park here at 9,950 feet. Four-wheel-drive vehicles can ford Clear Creek and continue south for an additional 2.4 miles toward Clohesy Lake to a signed parking area at 10,800 feet. The ford of Clear Creek is difficult in high water.

South Winfield Trailhead

This trailhead is at 10,260 feet and provides access to Huron's north and west sides. From the turn to the Rockdale Trailhead at mile 9.8, continue west on Chaffee County 390 to Winfield at mile 11.8. There are many informal camping areas along Chaffee County 390. From the center of Winfield, turn south and cross to the south side of Clear Creek on a bridge. Turn west (right) and follow the road for an additional 0.3 mile; here the road becomes dramatically rougher. There are parking spaces on both sides of the road; this is the trailhead. Four-wheel-drive vehicles can continue south for an additional 2.0 miles to a Forest Service closure gate at 10,600 feet.

Routes

12.1 Northwest Slopes II, Class 2

From South Winfield Trailhead: 8.0 miles, 3,740 feet

From 4WD parking: 4.0 miles, 3,400 feet

This is the shortest and standard route up Huron. Start at the South Winfield Trailhead and follow the four-wheel-drive road southwest for 0.4 mile to another four-wheel-drive road that climbs the hill south (left) of you. Do not take this road. Continue on the main four-wheel-drive road up the valley and, after an additional 1.0 mile, pass the turn up to the old

Banker Mine. Do not go to the Banker Mine. Continue south (straight) on the main road up the valley for an additional 0.6 mile to a Forest Service closure gate at 10,600 feet. Continue south on the old road for an additional 100 yards to 10,620 feet. From here, leave the valley trail and climb steeply southeast on the Colorado Fourteener Initiative (CFI) trail as it switchbacks into the charming basin at 12,300 feet, west of 13,523-foot Browns Peak and Huron. From the basin, continue southeast on the CFI trail as it winds up a long, northwest-facing slope to Huron's summit.

12.2 North Ridge II, Class 2

From South Winfield Trailhead: 8.4 miles, 4,180 feet

With descent of Northwest Slopes: 8.1 miles, 3,960 feet

This scenic alternative to the Northwest Slopes Route allows you to bag two peaks. Start at the South Winfield Trailhead and follow the four-wheel-drive road southwest for 0.4 mile to another four-wheel-drive road that climbs the hill south of you. Turn south (left) onto this road and follow it as it switchbacks up the lower , northwest shoulder of 13,523-foot Browns Peak. When the road reaches a junction at 11,400 feet, take the east (left) fork and go east then southeast into Lulu Gulch, which is northwest of Browns Peak and 13,060-foot Middle Mountain. Stay on the deteriorating road as it crosses Lulu Gulch, then climbs southeast up the gulch.

When the road turns sharply back to the north, leave it and continue southeast up the slope at the head of Lulu Gulch. Climb to the 13,140-foot saddle between Browns Peak and Point 13,462, which is 0.5 mile northeast of Browns Peak, between Browns Peak and Middle Mountain. All these summits are on Huron's long north ridge. From the 13,140-foot saddle, climb west to the summit of Browns Peak, then follow the ridge south for 0.75 mile to Huron's summit. En route, you can skirt Point 13,518 on its west side. Ascending this route and descending the Northwest Slopes Route makes a good Tour de Huron.

Extra Credit
12.2EC1 II, Class 2

For a third peak, climb northeast for 0.3 mile from the 13,140-foot saddle to the summit of Point 13,462, a ranked thirteener.

12.2EC2 II, Class 2

For a fourth peak, leave the route at 12,600 feet and climb northeast for 0.25 mile to the 12,940-foot saddle between Middle Mountain and Point 13,462. Climb northwest for 0.15 mile to Middle Mountain's 13,060-foot summit and return to the saddle. Climb south for 0.5 mile to the summit of Point 13,462 and descend southwest for 0.3 mile to rejoin the route in the 13,140-foot saddle.

12.3 Southwest Slopes II, Class 2

From South Winfield Trailhead: 10.6 miles, 3,740 feet

From 4WD parking: 6.6 miles, 3,400 feet

This route is longer but gentler than the Northwest Slopes Route. Start at the South Winfield Trailhead and follow the four-wheel-drive road southwest for 0.4 mile to another four-wheel-drive road that climbs the hill south (left) of you. Do not take this road. Continue on the main four-wheel-drive road up the valley and, after an additional 1.0 mile, pass the turn up to the old Banker Mine. Do not go to the Banker Mine. Continue south (straight) on the main road up the valley for an additional 0.6 mile to a Forest Service closure gate at 10,600 feet. Continue south on the old road for an additional 1.4 miles, entering the Collegiate Peaks Wilderness en route, to the Hamilton Townsite at 10,820 feet.

Hike east above Hamilton on a good trail to tree line at 12,000 feet. From here, contour southeast for 0.6 mile, then climb northeast for 0.4 mile to the 13,060-foot saddle between Huron and Point 13,472. From the saddle, climb 0.7 mile northwest along a scenic ridge to Huron's summit.

Variation 12.3V

From 12,000 feet, climb east then southeast directly up the steep slope for 0.7 mile to Huron's summit.

Extra Credit 12.3EC

From the 13,060-foot saddle, climb southeast for 0.4 mile along a rugged ridge to the summit of Point 13,472, a ranked thirteener.

12.4 East Slopes II, Class 2

From Rockdale Trailhead: 9.4 miles, 4,100 feet

From Clohesy Lake 4WD parking: 4.6 miles, 3,200 feet

This is a rugged alternative to the routes starting at the South Winfield Trailhead. Start at the Rockdale Trailhead and ford Clear Creek, which can be difficult in high water. Go 2.4 miles south up the four-wheel-drive road to a signed parking area at 10,800 feet. There is a trail sign for Huron 100 feet south of this parking area. It is not necessary to go all the way to Clohesy Lake. From the Huron trail sign, follow the trail southwest and cross to the west side of Clear Creek's Lake Fork.

Find and follow a faint trail to tree line in the small basin east of Browns Peak and Point 13,518. This is *not* the basin directly above Clohesy Lake and directly below Huron. From tree line, hike west over large boulders and climb to the 13,340-foot saddle between Browns Peak and Huron. Turn south (left) and follow Huron's north ridge for 0.7 mile to Huron's summit. You can skirt Point 13,518 on its west side.

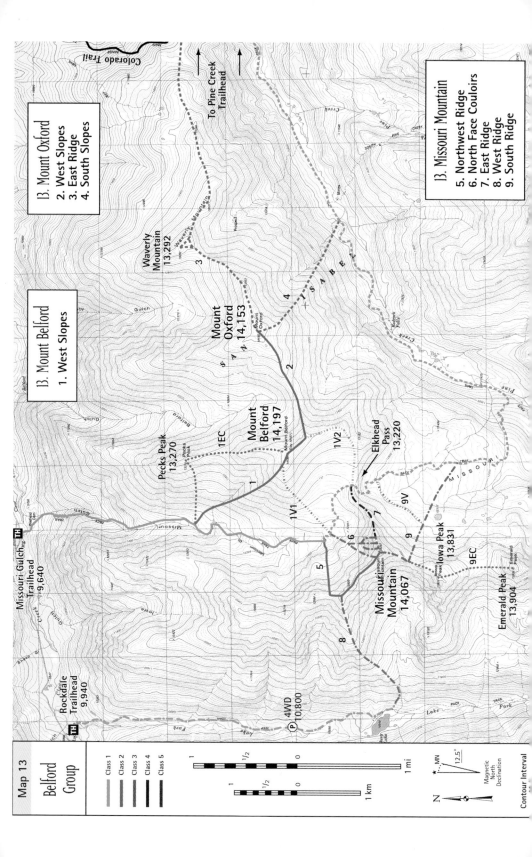

Map 13

Belford
Group

Class 1
Class 2
Class 3
Class 4
Class 5

1 mi

1 km

Magnetic
North
Declination

12.5°

MN

N

Contour Interval

13. Mount Belford

1. West Slopes

13. Mount Oxford

2. West Slopes
3. East Ridge
4. South Slopes

13. Missouri Mountain

5. Northwest Ridge
6. North Face Couloirs
7. East Ridge
8. West Ridge
9. South Ridge

Colorado Trail

To Pine Creek
Trailhead

Waverly
Mountain
13,292

Mount
Oxford
14,153

Mount Oxford

Mount
Belford
14,197

Pecks Peak
13,270

Mount Belford

1EC

1

2

3

4

ISABEL

Creek

Pine

Elkhead
Pass
13,220

1V2

1V1

9V

7

6

5

9

8

MISSOURI

Missouri
Mountain
14,067

Iowa Peak
13,831

Iowa Peak

9EC

Emerald Peak
13,904

Missouri Gulch
Trailhead
9,640

Rockdale
Trailhead
9,940

4WD
10,800

P

Belford
Gulch

Missouri
Gulch

Iowa
Gulch

13. Belford Group

Mount Belford	14,197 feet
Mount Oxford	14,153 feet
Missouri Mountain	14,067 feet

See Map 13 on page 108

Nestled in the heart of the Sawatch, these fourteeners are 8 miles west of U.S. 24, about one-third of the way from Buena Vista to Leadville. These peaks are not easily visible from roads, but good trails approach the peaks, and they are very popular summer hikes. The high, gentle mass of Belford and Oxford requires little more than a sturdy pair of legs, while the more rugged Missouri offers a choice of technical routes.

Maps

Required: Mount Harvard, Winfield, San Isabel National Forest
Optional: Harvard Lakes

Trailheads

Missouri Gulch Trailhead

This trailhead is at 9,640 feet and provides access to the north sides of Missouri and Belford, and to the west ridge of Oxford. Turn west from U.S. 24 onto Chaffee County 390 (dirt). This junction is 14.9 miles north of the stoplight in the center of Buena Vista, 4.3 miles south of the U.S. 24–Colorado 82 junction and 19.3 miles south of the West Sixth–U.S. 24 junction in the center of Leadville. Go west on Chaffee County 390 for 7.7 miles to

Missouri Mountain 14,067

Mount Belford 14,197

Mount Oxford 14,153

The Belford Group from the northwest.

Vicksburg. There are many informal camping areas along this road. The trailhead is across from Vicksburg on the south side of the road.

Pine Creek Trailhead

This trailhead is at 8,800 feet and provides access to Oxford's south side and Harvard's north side. Turn west from U.S. 24 onto Chaffee County 388 (dirt). This junction is 13.2 miles north of the stoplight in the center of Buena Vista, 6.0 miles south of the U.S. 24–Colorado 82 junction and 21.0 miles south of the West Sixth–U.S. 24 junction in the center of Leadville. Measure from the U.S. 24–Chaffee County 388 junction. Go west on Chaffee County 388 and continue straight at 0.3 mile on the less traveled road. At 0.6 mile, the road makes a sharp turn up the hill to the right and becomes rougher. Park here. A gate to the private Pine Creek Ranch is 100 yards west. Respect the private property here and, via an honor system, pay a small fee for crossing the ranchland.

13. Mount Belford   14,197 feet

See Map 13 on page 108

Belford's lofty, rounded mass sits stately between its lower companions Oxford and Missouri. There is a trail most of the way up Belford, and the peak is one of Colorado's easiest fourteeners. Like most Sawatch fourteeners, Belford requires more than 4,000 feet of elevation gain, but it's a manageable workout.

Route

13.1 West Slopes II, Class 2 *Classic*
From Missouri Gulch Trailhead: 7.0 miles, 4,560 feet

This delightful hike is the easiest route up Belford. The direct ascent is beautiful in its simplicity. Start at the Missouri Gulch Trailhead and cross Clear Creek on a good bridge. You will meet Belford's challenge immediately beyond the bridge as the excellent Missouri Gulch Trail climbs steeply via a series of memorable switchbacks to enter Missouri Gulch. After the switchbacks, cross to the creek's east side on a multi-log bridge, then pass an old cabin just below tree line at 11,300 feet. When you break out of the trees, you will see the rest of the route up Belford's rounded northwest shoulder. As you approach, you can see the Colorado Fourteener Initiative (CFI) trail on the shoulder.

Continue on the Missouri Gulch Trail to 11,660 feet. Before the trail crosses back to the creek's west side, look sharp for the CFI trail leading southeast. The CFI trail is the route up Belford. Follow it as it switchbacks up the relentless, rounded, grassy shoulder to 14,000 feet, then walk southeast up a gentle ridge to the highest point. Beautiful Belford is yours.

Variations
13.1V1 II, Class 2
From Missouri Gulch Trailhead: 8.0 miles, 4,560 feet

For a longer, gentler hike, continue on the Missouri Gulch Trail for an additional 1.2 miles into grassy upper Missouri Gulch. Leave the trail at 12,700 feet when it begins the final climb to Elkhead Pass, and climb Belford's rounded, grassy west shoulder to the summit.

13.1V2 II, Class 1
From Missouri Gulch Trailhead: 9.4 miles, 4,560 feet

For an even longer, even gentler hike, continue on the Missouri Gulch Trail all the way to Elkhead Pass at 13,220 feet. From the pass, climb east then south on gentle slopes to the summit. Ascending the northwest shoulder and descending either of these variations allows you to see beautiful upper Missouri Gulch.

Extra Credit 13.1EC

From Belford's summit, descend north along Belford's north ridge for 1.0 mile to the gentle summit of 13,270-foot Pecks Peak. The detour to this humble summit will take you off the busy fourteener circuit for a while. If you are lucky, you may see some goats grazing. From Pecks' summit, descend west down steep grass to the Missouri Gulch Trail.

13. Mount Oxford 14,153 feet

See Map 13 on page 108

Mount Oxford is 1.2 miles east of Belford, and people usually climb Oxford together with Belford. Few people take the time to enjoy Oxford by itself, as it should be enjoyed. Oxford offers a choice of routes and provides more solitude than the peaks closer to popular Elkhead Pass.

Routes
13.2 West Ridge II, Class 2
From Missouri Gulch Trailhead: 11.0 miles, 5,900 feet

This is the traditional and, arguably, the easiest route on Oxford. Start at the Missouri Gulch Trailhead and climb Belford's West Slopes Route to Belford's summit. Descend southeast then east along the ridge to the 13,500-foot Belford–Oxford Saddle. From the saddle, hike up the gentle slopes of Oxford's west ridge to Oxford's summit. There is a good climber's trail along this ridge. To complete this long workout, return over Belford.

Mount Oxford from the west (photo by Steve Hoffmeyer).

13.3 East Ridge II, Class 2

From Pine Creek Trailhead: 20.0 miles, 5,850 feet

This alternative to the standard route over Belford allows you to enjoy Oxford by itself. It is a long but enjoyable hike. Start at the Pine Creek Trailhead and go west up the four-wheel-drive road for 2.2 miles to 9,200 feet, where the Pine Creek Trail starts. Follow the Pine Creek Trail west up the valley for 2.5 miles to 10,400 feet, where the Colorado Trail crosses the Pine Creek Trail. Follow the Colorado Trail north as it climbs to 11,650 feet, near tree line on Oxford's long east ridge.

Leave the Colorado Trail and hike west through open trees, then ascend the broad, gentle ridge to Waverly Mountain's multiple summits. You can easily bypass the eastern, 13,007-foot summit, but you will have to climb most of the way to the higher, 13,292-foot summit. You may as well take the few extra steps required to touch Waverly's highest point. From Waverly, follow the remaining 1.2 miles of Oxford's now better defined east ridge to the summit.

13.4 South Slopes II, Class 2

From Pine Creek Trailhead: 18.0 miles, 5,350 feet

This is another Oxford alternative that can be used on a backpacking trip into upper Pine Creek. Start at the Pine Creek Trailhead and go west up the four-wheel-drive road for 2.2 miles to 9,200 feet, where the Pine Creek Trail starts. Follow the Pine Creek Trail west up the valley for 5.0 miles to Little Johns Cabin at 10,700 feet. Just west of the cabin, cross the side stream coming from the north, leave the Pine Creek Trail and start climbing northwest through the trees. Ascend the small ridge just west of the side stream. The terrain is rugged until you reach tree line at 11,800 feet. Above tree line, continue up the small but relentless ridge to Oxford's summit.

13. Missouri Mountain   14,067 feet

See Map 13 on page 108

Missouri Mountain is 1.3 miles southwest of Belford and 0.7 mile west of Elkhead Pass. The peak forms the southern end of Missouri Gulch, and Missouri Mountain is more of a ridge than a mountain. Missouri is harder to climb than either Belford or Oxford, and this strange peak offers some of the few technical routes on Sawatch fourteeners.

Routes

13.5 Northwest Ridge II, Class 2
From Missouri Gulch Trailhead: 10.0 miles, 4,450 feet

This is the traditional route up Missouri. Start at the Missouri Gulch Trailhead, cross the bridge over Clear Creek and ascend several memorable switchbacks into Missouri Gulch. Continue on the excellent Missouri Gulch Trail to 12,600 feet. When the trail turns east toward Elkhead Pass, leave the trail and climb west up grassy slopes to a 13,700-foot saddle on Missouri's northwest ridge. Climb south over Point 13,930 and continue southeast for 0.5 mile to the summit. Near the summit, there are some rock towers on the ridge that you can bypass on the west.

13.6 North Face Couloirs II, Class 3, Moderate Snow (Seasonal)
From Missouri Gulch Trailhead: 9.0 miles, 4,450 feet

Missouri's craggy north face offers a choice of four couloirs that make good early summer snow climbs. Follow the Northwest Ridge Route to 12,700 feet, into Missouri Gulch, and choose your couloir. The westernmost couloir, called the "C Couloir," is the easiest, and it curves gracefully up to the summit. The two central couloirs climb straight to Missouri's upper east ridge. The easternmost and most difficult couloir is not visible until you reach 12,800 feet on the Missouri Gulch Trail. This narrow couloir cuts through Missouri's steeper northeast face and is a more serious climb.

13.7 East Ridge II, Class 4
From Missouri Gulch Trailhead: 9.6 miles, 4,450 feet

This route's Class 4 rating disguises a serious and dangerous climb. What should be Missouri's premier mountaineering route is so rotten that it is relegated to this author's nightmares. This is unfortunate, because there are few technical climbs on Sawatch fourteeners.

Start at the Missouri Gulch Trailhead and follow the Missouri Gulch Trail all the way to Elkhead Pass. As you approach the pass, you can inspect the route. The east ridge's salient feature is a band of white rock that cuts across the center of the ridge. There is a steep buttress below the band and a multi-faced, flatiron-like buttress above the band. These two buttresses and the white band are the ridge's cruxes. They require four Class 4 pitches.

From Elkhead Pass, hike and scramble west along the ridge to a small saddle below the first buttress. There is a significant pinnacle north of the ridge that will attract your attention, and you may see black ravens perching like a portent on the pinnacle's summit. Climb straight up the ridge to 100 feet below the top of the first steep buttress (Class 3). Traverse under the buttress on the ridge's north side on a solid ledge (Class 3). Climb a steep wall at the end of the ledge to reach the rubble-filled gully of the white band (Class 4). Climb the gully or the broken wall right of the gully to a small ridge (Class 4). These pitches are precarious because of the rubble on every hold. Climb into the large, north-facing dihedral of the upper buttress (Class 4). Ascend the dihedral's east face for 100 feet on the route's only solid rock (Class 4). Above these difficulties, scramble up Missouri's upper east ridge for 400 yards to the summit (Class 3). Descend another route.

13.8 West Ridge II, Class 2

From Rockdale Trailhead: 12.0 miles, 4,200 feet
From Clohesy Lake 4WD parking: 5.0 miles, 3,100 feet

This alternative route up Missouri avoids the crowds at Missouri Gulch. Start at the Rockdale Trailhead (see Huron Peak), ford Clear Creek and go 2.5 miles south up the four-wheel-drive road to a trail sign for Missouri at 10,880 feet. From the Missouri trail sign, follow the trail on the east side of Clohesy Lake. When you can see the lake, climb southeast on a smaller trail to tree line and continue east into the basin below Missouri's steep, scree-covered west face. Avoid this unpleasant face by climbing northeast onto Missouri's broad, grassy west ridge. Ascend this ridge to Point 13,930 and follow the Northwest Ridge Route from there.

13.9 South Ridge II, Class 2

From Pine Creek Trailhead: 26.0 miles, 5,300 feet
From Missouri Gulch Trailhead: 11.6 miles, 5,270 feet

This remote ridge can be used on a backpacking trip into upper Pine Creek or Missouri Gulch. With its vertical mile, it makes a great workout for the superfit. Mortals will enjoy the pleasures of Colorado camping.

Start at the Pine Creek Trailhead and go west up the four-wheel-drive road for 2.2 miles to 9,200 feet, where the Pine Creek Trail starts. Follow the Pine Creek Trail west up the valley for 5.0 miles to Little Johns Cabin at 10,700 feet. Continue west on the trail for an additional 3.0 miles to the junction of the Elkhead Pass and Silver King Lake Trails at 11,500 feet. Hike west then north on the Elkhead Pass Trail for 1.3 miles to 12,400 feet. Leave the trail and climb west for 1.2 miles to the 13,540-foot saddle between Missouri and Iowa Peak (13,831 feet). Your 12.7-mile approach is over. Now for the climb! Hike north for 0.3 mile to the summit.

Variation 13.9V

This climb is much shorter from the Missouri Gulch Trailhead, and you can use this route when coming and going on peak-bagging extravaganzas. From Missouri Gulch Trailhead, follow the Missouri Gulch Trail for 4.0 miles to Elkhead Pass at 13,220 feet. Continue over the pass and descend south for 0.4 mile to 12,800 feet. Leave the trail, contour southwest for 0.8 mile under Missouri's south face, then climb west for 0.3 mile to the Missouri–Iowa Peak Saddle. Hike north for 0.3 mile to Missouri's summit.

Extra Credit 13.9EC

From the 13,540-foot Missouri–Iowa Peak Saddle, climb 0.3 mile south to 13,831-foot Iowa Peak, one of Colorado's 100 highest peaks. For even more credit, continue south for 0.8 mile to 13,904-foot Emerald Peak, another centennial peak.

13. Belford, Oxford and Missouri Combinations

See Map 13 on page 108

13.10 II, Class 2

From Missouri Gulch Trailhead: 11.0 miles, 5,900 feet

This is the standard way of climbing Belford and Oxford together. Start at the Missouri Gulch Trailhead and climb Belford's West Slopes Route to Belford's summit. Descend southeast then east along the ridge to the 13,500-foot Belford–Oxford Saddle. From the saddle, hike up the gentle slopes of Oxford's west ridge to Oxford's summit. Return over Belford and descend Missouri Gulch.

13.11 III, Class 2

From Missouri Gulch Trailhead: 14.5 miles, 7,400 feet

This is the easiest way to climb Belford, Oxford and Missouri together, but it is a tough day. Start at the Missouri Gulch Trailhead and climb Missouri's Northwest Ridge Route. Descend that route to 12,600 feet, into upper Missouri Gulch, and ascend Belford's west shoulder. Traverse to Oxford as in Combination 13.10 and return over Belford to Missouri Gulch.

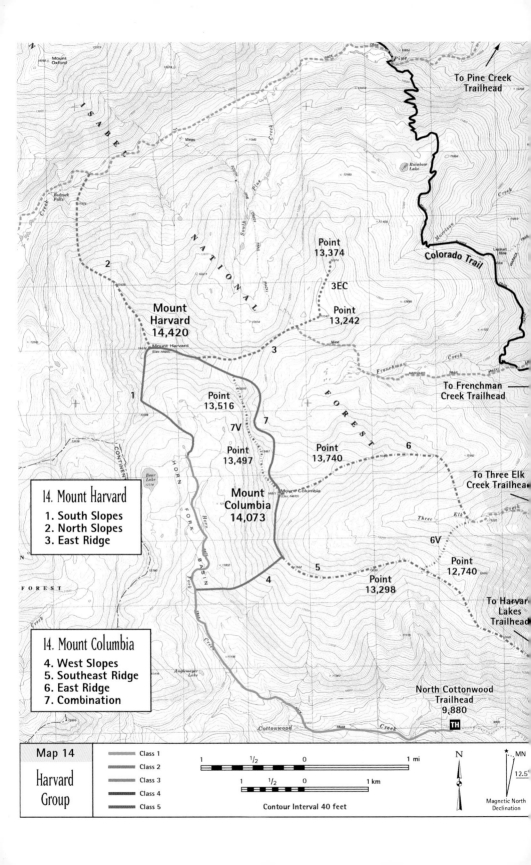

To Pine Creek
Trailhead

Colorado Trail

To Frenchman
Creek Trailhead

To Three Elk
Creek Trailhead

To Harvard
Lakes
Trailhead

Point
13,374

3EC

Point
13,242

Mount
Harvard
14,420

Point
13,516

7V

Point
13,497

Mount
Columbia
14,073

Point
13,740

Point
13,298

Point
12,740

6V

North Cottonwood
Trailhead
9,880

TH

14. Mount Harvard

1. South Slopes
2. North Slopes
3. East Ridge

14. Mount Columbia

4. West Slopes
5. Southeast Ridge
6. East Ridge
7. Combination

Map 14		Class 1
Harvard		Class 2
Group		Class 3
		Class 4
		Class 5

N

MN

12.5°

Magnetic North
Declination

Contour Interval 40 feet

1   ½   0   1 mi

1   ½   0   1 km

14. Harvard Group

Mount Harvard   14,420 feet
Mount Columbia   14,073 feet

See Map 14 on page 116

  Mount Harvard, together with its companion Mount Columbia, forms a large, high massif 11 miles northwest of Buena Vista. Harvard is Colorado's third highest peak, but unlike the first and second highest peaks, Elbert and Massive, which are obvious from Leadville, Harvard does not reveal itself so easily. When viewed from neighboring peaks to the north or south, however, Harvard's bulk, height and shape are unmistakable.

Maps

Required: Mount Harvard, Mount Yale, San Isabel National Forest
Optional: Harvard Lakes, Buena Vista West

Trailheads

Harvard Lakes Trailhead

  This trailhead is at 9,420 feet and provides access to the east sides of Harvard and Columbia. From the Chaffee County 306–U.S. 24 junction in the center of Buena Vista (stoplight), go north on U.S. 24 for 0.4 mile. Turn west onto Chaffee County 350 (Crossman Avenue) and measure from this point. Go west on Chaffee County 350 for 2.1 miles to a T-junction and turn north (right) onto Chaffee County 361. Chaffee County 361 turns to dirt at mile 2.4, then angles northwest. At mile 3.0, turn sharply south (left) onto Chaffee County 365, which soon turns west and enters the San Isabel National Forest at mile 5.4. Reach the Harvard Lakes Trailhead on the north side of the road at mile 6.6. The trailhead is marked with signs for the Colorado Trail and Harvard Lakes.

North Cottonwood Trailhead

  This trailhead is at 9,880 feet and provides access to the south sides of Harvard and Columbia. From the Harvard Lakes Trailhead (mile 6.6), continue west, pass the Silver Creek Trailhead (see Mount Yale) on the south side of the road at mile 6.7 and reach the North Cottonwood Trailhead at the end of the road at mile 8.2.

Three Elk Creek Trailhead

  This trailhead is at 9,260 feet and provides access to Columbia's east side. From the Chaffee County 306–U.S. 24 junction in the center of Buena

Vista (stoplight), go north on U.S. 24 for 0.4 mile. Turn west onto Chaffee County 350 (Crossman Avenue) and measure from this point. Go west on Chaffee County 350 for 2.1 miles to a T-junction. Turn north (right) onto Chaffee County 361 and go 3.8 miles to Chaffee County 368 at mile 5.9. Turn west (left) onto Chaffee County 368 and go 1.2 miles to Chaffee County 368A at mile 7.1. Turn southwest onto Chaffee County 368A and go 0.1 mile to Forest Service 368 at mile 7.2. Turn west (right) onto Forest Service 368 and go 0.8 mile to the signed trailhead at mile 8.0. The Three Elk Creek Trail heads south from here.

Frenchman Creek Trailhead

This trailhead is at 9,300 feet and provides access to Harvard's east side. Turn west from U.S. 24 onto Chaffee County 386 at the tiny community of Riverside. This junction is 7.5 miles north of the stoplight in the center of Buena Vista, 12.0 miles south of the U.S. 24–Colorado 82 junction and 27.0 miles south of the West Sixth–U.S. 24 junction in the center of Leadville. Go west on Chaffee County 386 for 0.3 mile to Forest Service 386. Turn west (right) onto Forest Service 386 and go 1.4 miles to the trailhead at a fork in the road. Park two-wheel-drive vehicles here. Four-wheel-drive vehicles can continue on the south (left) road for an additional 2.2 miles to the Collegiate Peaks Wilderness boundary at 10,800 feet.

14. Mount Harvard   14,420 feet

See Map 14 on page 116

Mount Harvard is one of only three Colorado peaks to rise above 14,400 feet. Harvard is also the highest peak in Chaffee County. Like most Sawatch fourteeners, Harvard is easy to climb, but requires more effort than most. Many parties choose to pack in when climbing Harvard. Harvard will both test and reward you.

Routes

14.1 South Slopes II, Class 2

From North Cottonwood Trailhead: 12.6 miles, 4,550 feet

This is the traditional and easiest route on Harvard. Start at the North Cottonwood Trailhead and cross to the south side of North Cottonwood Creek on a good bridge. Follow the North Cottonwood Trail west for 1.5 miles to a junction just after the trail returns to the creek's north side. Turn north (right) onto the trail to Horn Fork Basin and Bear Lake. Follow this trail north into Horn Fork Basin and reach tree line at 11,600 feet. There are several good campsites just below tree line. You can see Harvard to the north at the head of the basin, and Columbia's steep west slopes are above you to the east.

Continue north on the trail up into the beautiful basin. It is not necessary to go all the way to Bear Lake, but the side trip to this amazing lake is worth the effort if you have time. Leave the trail east of Bear Lake and climb into the upper basin under Harvard's gentle south slopes. Climb grassy benches on the western edge of these slopes to Harvard's boulder-strewn summit.

14.2 North Slopes II, Class 2

From Pine Creek Trailhead: 19.6 miles, 5,650 feet

This alternative route avoids the crowds at Horn Fork Basin and allows you to combine Harvard with Belford and Oxford to the north. This long route is best done with a backpack into Pine Creek. Start at the Pine Creek Trailhead (see Belford Group) and go west up the four-wheel-drive road for 2.2 miles to 9,200 feet, where the Pine Creek Trail starts. Follow the Pine Creek Trail west up the valley for 5.0 miles to Little Johns Cabin at 10,700 feet. Continue west on the trail for an additional 1.0 mile to 11,000 feet, then leave the trail, cross to the south side of Pine Creek and begin climbing Harvard's huge north slopes. Climb these long, grassy slopes until they become a ridge at 13,400 feet. Follow this gentle ridge south for 1.0 mile to the summit.

14.3 East Ridge II, Class 2

From Frenchman Creek Trailhead: 13.6 miles, 5,120 feet

This route has gained in popularity in recent years. Its simplicity is its charm. Start at the Frenchman Creek Trailhead and go west up the four-wheel-drive road for 2.2 miles to the Collegiate Peaks Wilderness boundary at 10,800 feet. Continue west up the closed road for an additional 1.8 miles to tree line at 11,800 feet and bask in the beautiful basin. The road becomes the Mount Harvard Trail; follow it north then west for 1.2 miles to a 12,980-foot saddle on Harvard's east ridge. Climb west on the rocky ridge for 1.6 miles to the summit.

Extra Credit 14.3EC

From the 12,980-foot saddle, climb east for 0.4 mile to Point 13,242 and continue north for an additional 0.6 mile to Point 13,374, one of Colorado's ranked thirteeners.

14. Mount Columbia   14,073 feet

See Map 14 on page 116

Columbia, 1.9 miles southeast of Harvard, is best known as Harvard's lower companion peak, but it is a fine peak by itself. Columbia's east slopes sweep up from the Arkansas River Valley, and Columbia towers over Horn Fork Basin to its west. Columbia is most often climbed with Harvard, but the traverse between the two peaks is long; some people find Columbia alone a sufficient challenge.

Routes

14.4 West Slopes II, Class 2
From North Cottonwood Trailhead: 10.0 miles, 4,200 feet

This is the easiest route on Columbia. Start at the North Cottonwood Trailhead and cross to the south side of North Cottonwood Creek on a good bridge. Follow the North Cottonwood Trail west for 1.5 miles to a junction just after the trail returns to the creek's north side. Turn north (right) onto the trail to Horn Fork Basin and Bear Lake. Follow this trail north into Horn Fork Basin and reach tree line at 11,600 feet. You can see Harvard to the north at the head of the basin, and Columbia's steep west slopes are above you to the east.

Leave the trail just below tree line and climb east onto Columbia's west slopes. The slopes directly below the summit are steep and unpleasant. The easiest terrain is 1.0 mile south of the summit, so don't go too far into Horn Fork Basin before beginning your ascent. Climb the long, tedious slope and reach Columbia's gentle south ridge at 13,700 feet. Walk north along this ridge for 0.6 mile to the summit.

14.5 Southeast Ridge II, Class 2
From Harvard Lakes Trailhead: 12.0 miles, 4,800 feet

This is a longer, more challenging alternative to the standard West Slopes Route. Start at the Harvard Lakes Trailhead and follow the Colorado Trail north up the first steep switchbacks for 0.5 mile to a ridge. This is Columbia's southeast ridge. Follow the trail west along the ridge for another 0.2 mile. When the trail levels out and turns north at 10,000 feet, leave the trail and hike northwest up the ridge through open trees. Climb steadily along the ridge for 2.0 miles to Point 12,740. From this tiny summit, follow the rocky ridge west for 0.8 mile to Point 13,298. Continue west then north along the easy ridge for an additional 1.6 miles to the summit.

Mount Harvard and Mount Columbia from the northwest.

14.6 East Ridge II, Class 2
From Three Elk Creek Trailhead: 10.0 miles, 4,810 feet

This is the cardinal Colorado climb. Nestled in the heart of the state's central range, it offers route finding that leads you to wilderness and, if you are lucky, wildlife. This route somehow seems to further the fantasy that every dirt road in Colorado leads to a fourteener. The fantasy is especially rich when newly fallen aspen leaves dot the road.

Start at the Three Elk Creek Trailhead and go south on a logging road for 300 yards. Leave the logging road when it turns west and continue south on a marked trail. Cross several other logging roads and reach Three Elk Creek in a small gorge. Cross the creek and climb south for 100 yards to an abandoned road that is now the Three Elk Creek Trail. Go west on this trail for 1.0 mile to the Colorado Trail, just north of Harvard Lakes at 10,260 feet.

Cross the Colorado Trail and continue west on the Three Elk Creek Trail for an additional 1.5 miles to tree line at 11,300 feet. Leave the trail, climb northwest for 1.0 mile and reach Columbia's east ridge near 12,600 feet. Climb west along the gentle ridge for 1.8 miles to the summit. There are three false summits along the way.

Variation 14.6V

To complete a beautiful circle tour, descend the Southeast Ridge Route to 12,640 feet, then descend steeply northeast through an incredible stand of bristlecone pine for 1.0 mile to the Three Elk Creek Trail.

14. Harvard and Columbia Combination

See Map 14 on page 116

14.7 II, Class 2

From North Cottonwood Trailhead: 13.5 miles, 5,900 feet

This is the easiest way to climb Harvard and Columbia together. Start at the North Cottonwood Trailhead and climb Harvard's South Slopes Route. The 2.2-mile traverse to Columbia is arduous. Descend east and a little south for 1.0 mile from Harvard's summit to the vicinity of Point 13,516. Stay north of Point 13,516 and descend east into the Frenchman Creek Drainage to 12,800 feet. Contour south below the connecting ridge's difficulties and climb Columbia's gentle, grassy north slopes to Columbia's summit. Descend Columbia's West Slopes Route.

Variation 14.7V

You can stay closer to the ridge crest and save a few hundred feet of elevation loss, but this rocky ridge is much more difficult. From Point 13,516, descend south along the ridge to the 13,180-foot Harvard–Columbia Saddle and continue south on or near the ridge toward Columbia. Avoid several pinnacles known as the "Rabbits" by doing exposed Class 4 traverses on the east side of the ridge. Rappel or downclimb (Class 5.7) into a notch, then climb or skirt Point 13,497 (Class 5.0–5.2). Continue south for an additional 0.5 mile to Columbia's summit.

If you do the first part of the traverse on the ridge but then change your mind about the Rabbits, you can descend a steep scree gully to the west and finish the traverse well below the ridge on its west side.

15. Mount Yale   14,196 feet

See Map 15 on page 124

Mount Yale is 9 miles directly west of Buena Vista. Yale is 1 foot lower than neighboring Mount Princeton, and is not easily seen from the Arkansas River Valley. These trivial differences with the stately Princeton only thinly disguise a great peak. Unlike Princeton, Yale is in the Collegiate Peaks Wilderness and offers a choice of several routes. Yale, like most Sawatch fourteeners, rises abruptly from its surrounding valleys. No matter how you tackle Yale, the peak will test your legs. From Yale's summit, you are rewarded with a view of 30 of Colorado's fourteeners.

Maps
Required: Mount Yale, San Isabel National Forest
Optional: Buena Vista West

Trailheads
Denny Creek Trailhead
This trailhead is at 9,900 feet and provides access to Yale's southwest side. From a stoplight on U.S. 24 in the center of Buena Vista, go west on Chaffee County 306 (paved) for 11.0 miles to the Collegiate Peaks Campground. Continue west for an additional 1.0 mile to the well-marked trailhead on the north side of the road. Do not confuse Denny Creek with Denny Gulch farther east. This trailhead is accessible in winter.

Avalanche Gulch Trailhead
This trailhead is at 9,300 feet and provides access to Yale's east side. From a stoplight on U.S. 24 in the center of Buena Vista, go west on Chaffee County 306 (paved) for 9.1 miles to the signed trailhead on the north side of the road. There is a large, paved parking lot here. This trailhead is accessible in winter.

Silver Creek Trailhead
This trailhead is at 9,400 feet and provides access to Yale's east side. Follow the directions for the Harvard Lakes Trailhead (see Harvard Group). From the Harvard Lakes Trailhead on the north side of the road at mile 6.6, continue west and reach the Silver Creek Trailhead on the south side of the road at mile 6.7. The trailhead is marked with signs for the Colorado Trail.

Routes
15.1 Southwest Slopes II, Class 2
From Denny Creek Trailhead: 7.0 miles, 4,300 feet
This has become the standard route on Yale. It has replaced the historic route up Denny Gulch farther east. For environmental reasons, the brutally steep route up Denny Gulch is no longer used. Do not confuse Denny Creek and Denny Gulch.

Start at the Denny Creek Trailhead and walk north for 0.9 mile up the Denny Creek Trail. Near the junction of Denny Creek and Delaney Creek at 10,400 feet, look sharp for a smaller trail leading up Delaney Creek. Finding this trail is the key to this route. Leave the Denny Creek Trail and

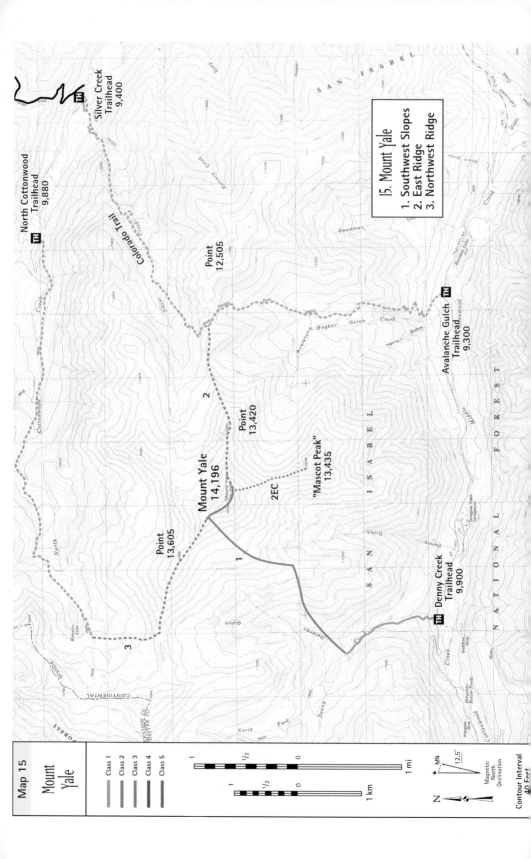

Map 15

Mount Yale

Class 1
Class 2
Class 3
Class 4
Class 5

15. Mount Yale
1. Southwest Slopes
2. East Ridge
3. Northwest Ridge

Silver Creek Trailhead 9,400

North Cottonwood Trailhead 9,880

Colorado Trail

Point 12,505

SAN ISABEL

Deadman

Avalanche Gulch Trailhead 9,300

Point 13,420

2

Mount Yale 14,196

"Mascot Peak" 13,435

2EC

Point 13,605

1

Denny Creek Trailhead 9,900

Point 13,605

3

CONTINENTAL DIVIDE

NATIONAL FOREST

SAN ISABEL

N

MN
12.5°

Magnetic North Declination

Contour Interval 40 Feet

1 mi
1/2
0

1 km
1/2
0

Mount Yale from the southwest.

follow the climber's trail up Delaney Creek for 0.5 mile, then ascend the steep slope to the east (right). Reach Yale's broad southwest shoulder at 12,200 feet. Climb north up this grassy shoulder and climb another slope to reach Yale's northwest ridge at 13,900 feet. Go southeast along this ridge for 0.3 mile to the summit. You can bypass a small buttress just below the summit on its west side.

15.2 East Ridge II, Class 2 *Classic*
From Avalanche Gulch Trailhead: 10.4 miles, 5,000 feet
From Silver Creek Trailhead: 10.8 miles, 4,900 feet

This route provides an uncrowded alternative to Yale's popular Southwest Slopes Route. The east ridge is a little longer, but the additional effort is a small price to pay for solitude. You can approach the east ridge from either the Avalanche Gulch or Silver Creek Trailhead. From the Avalanche Gulch Trailhead, climb north on the Colorado Trail for 3.2 miles to the 11,900-foot saddle between Yale and Point 12,505, which is 2.4 miles east of Yale. This trail climbs steeply at first, then wanders up through delightful forest glades. If you start at the Silver Creek Trailhead, follow the Colorado Trail southwest up Silver Creek for 3.4 miles to the 11,900-foot saddle.

From the 11,900-foot saddle, leave the Colorado Trail and hike west past tree line, then go over or around the north side of a small, 12,140-foot summit. Continue on Yale's now well defined east ridge and climb rough boulders to a pair of small, 13,420-foot summits, from which you can see Yale's summit. The remaining 0.7 mile of the ridge is less steep, and you can spy on the approaching summit long before you reach it.

Ascending the East Ridge Route from Avalanche Gulch Trailhead and descending the Southwest Slopes Route makes a comprehensive climb. On this circle, you will have to hitchhike, walk, bike or jog for 2.9 miles down the road back to the Avalanche Gulch Trailhead.

Extra Credit 15.2EC

From Yale's summit, go back down the east ridge for 200 yards, then descend south for 0.4 mile to a 13,060-foot saddle. Climb south for 0.3 mile to Point 13,435, alias "Mascot Peak." This ranked summit is a "Tri," one of Colorado's 300 highest peaks, and it provides a suspended view of Yale and Princeton. Return to the 13,060-foot saddle. From here, either climb back to Yale's east ridge at 14,040 feet or descend east down Avalanche Gulch to rejoin the Colorado Trail. Do not descend Denny Gulch to the southwest. It is no longer politically or environmentally correct to do so.

15.3 Northwest Ridge II, Class 2
From North Cottonwood Trailhead: 14.0 miles, 4,320 feet

This increasingly popular route is often done with a backpack to Kroenke Lake. Start at the North Cottonwood Trailhead (see Harvard Group) and cross to the south side of North Cottonwood Creek on a good bridge. Follow the North Cottonwood Trail west for 1.5 miles to a junction just after the trail returns to the creek's north side. Do not take the north (right) trail to Horn Fork Basin. Continue west (straight) on the North Cottonwood Trail for an additional 2.5 miles to Kroenke Lake, near tree line at 11,500 feet. This is a classic Colorado cirque surrounded by unnamed summits, with a fourteener hulking in the distance.

Continue on the trail around the south side of Kroenke Lake, hike to 11,900 feet, leave the trail and climb south for 0.7 mile to a 12,540-foot saddle on Yale's distinguished northwest ridge. Climb east on the ridge for 0.75 mile to Point 13,605 and behold the beauty. Continue southeast for 0.8 mile to Yale's summit and behold it all.

16. Mount Princeton   14,197 feet

See Map 16 on page 128

Princeton is a singular mountain. It is a true monarch because its neighbors are far lower and far away. Princeton is one of Colorado's most powerful peaks. Its summit is less than 9 miles southwest of Buena Vista, and the peak rises abruptly out of the Arkansas River Valley.

Princeton is the southernmost and most visible of the Collegiate fourteeners. As you descend west into the Arkansas River Valley on U.S. 285, Princeton stares you smack in the face for many miles. You cannot ignore its gaze. When snow graces Princeton's slopes, the view is breathtaking.

Maps

Required: Mount Antero, San Isabel National Forest
Optional: St. Elmo, Buena Vista West, Mount Yale

Trailheads

Mount Princeton Road

The Mount Princeton Road starts at 8,900 feet and ends at 12,150 feet at Bristlecone Park, on Princeton's southeast side. If approaching from the north, go south on U.S. 285 for 5.6 miles from the U.S. 24–U.S. 285 junction just west of Johnsons Village, near Buena Vista. If approaching from the south, go north on U.S. 285 for 15.4 miles from the U.S. 50–U.S. 285 junction in Poncha Springs.

Leave U.S. 285 and go west on Chaffee County 162 (paved) for 4.4 miles to Chaffee County 321, near Mount Princeton Hot Springs. Turn north (right) onto Chaffee County 321 (paved), go 1.3 miles, turn west (left) onto Chaffee County 322 (dirt) and go 0.9 mile to the start of the Mount Princeton Road. There is a large parking lot at the bottom of the Mount Princeton Road at 8,900 feet. If you value your vehicle, park here; this is the trailhead.

The Mount Princeton Road is continuously steep and narrow, but is passable for some passenger cars to 11,000 feet. It is difficult to pass vehicles going the opposite direction, difficult to turn around and difficult to park on the Mount Princeton Road. At 3.2 miles, the road reaches a ridge at 10,820 feet, near some radio towers, and there is limited parking here. The road then climbs west along the ridge, and there is limited parking after 3.5 miles at 11,000 feet. The road beyond this point is four-wheel-drive.

Grouse Canyon Trailhead

This trailhead is at 9,100 feet and provides access to Princeton's southwest side. If approaching from the north, go south on U.S. 285 for 5.6 miles from the U.S. 24–U.S. 285 junction just west of Johnsons Village, near Buena Vista. If approaching from the south, go north on U.S. 285 for 15.4 miles from the U.S. 50–U.S. 285 junction in Poncha Springs.

Leave U.S. 285 and go west on Chaffee County 162 (paved) for 4.4 miles to Mount Princeton Hot Springs, a favorite place for post-climb

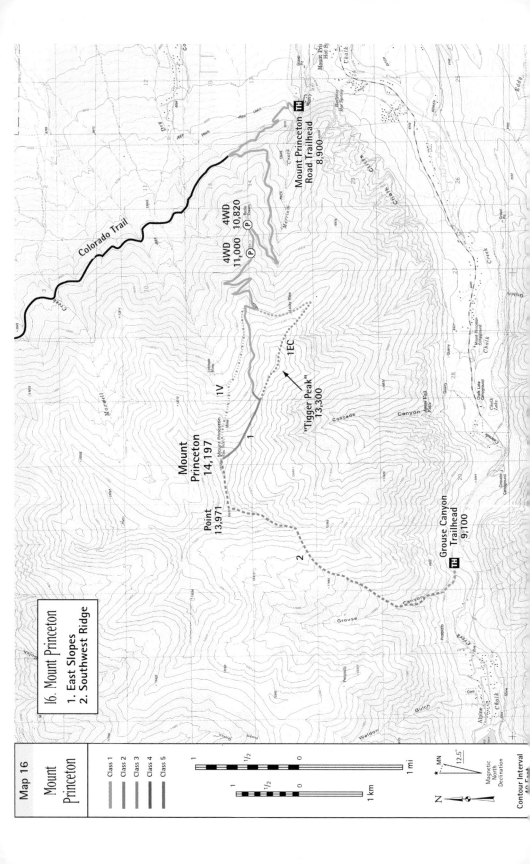

Mount Princeton from the east.

soaking. Continue west on Chaffee County 162 for an additional 5.7 miles, passing under the famous Chalk Cliffs. Turn north (right) onto Chaffee County 292 and cross Chalk Creek on a bridge. Follow Chaffee County 292 west for 0.4 mile and turn north (right) onto an unsigned dirt road. Go north for 100 yards and park. Respect private property in this area.

Routes

16.1 East Slopes II, Class 2

From Mount Princeton Road: 6.0 to 13.0 miles, 3,200 to 5,300 feet

This is the easiest and most popular route up Princeton. The length of the climb depends on how far you drive up the Mount Princeton Road. The lower numbers assume a start at 11,000 feet; the higher numbers assume a start at 8,900 feet.

Follow the Mount Princeton Road to tree line at 11,820 feet. Leave the road just as it starts to head south toward Bristlecone Park and climb north on a trail to a small ridge at 12,000 feet. The junction of trail and road is not marked and is easy to miss. You can see Princeton's upper slopes from the ridge.

Continue on the trail as it climbs west across a north-facing slope below Point 13,300. The trail is not destined for Princeton's summit but for an old mine at 13,100 feet, east of the summit. Do not follow the trail all the way to the mine, because the slope above the mine is unpleasant. Leave the trail between 12,700 feet and 12,900 feet and climb southwest up talus to Princeton's southeast ridge. The view of Mount Antero from the ridge is striking. Follow the easy southeast ridge to the summit.

Variation 16.1V

The Line Glacier was originally named as a joke, but the name endures. The Line Glacier is a narrow snow finger that sometimes exists in the basin east of Princeton's summit. Like the perfect wave, it is rarely there. When you spot it in good condition, climb it! Leave the trail on the small ridge at 12,000 feet, traverse northwest to the snow finger and ascend directly to the summit. After all, hotshots climb the *face*.

Extra Credit 16.1EC

Either going to or coming from Princeton's summit, stay on the southeast ridge and traverse over Point 13,300, alias "Tigger Peak." Tigger is a child's paraphrase of the Princeton mascot, the tiger.

16.2 Southwest Ridge II, Class 2

From Grouse Canyon Trailhead: 7.0 miles, 5,100 feet

This short, steep route provides a rough but still sanguine alternative to Princeton's crowded east side. Start at the Grouse Canyon Trailhead and follow the four-wheel-drive road for 0.25 mile to a well-defined trail. Follow the trail to Grouse Creek at 9,440 feet, at the bottom of Grouse Canyon. Your brief introduction is over—now for the climb.

Climb north on the sometimes ill defined trail up Grouse Canyon for 0.5 mile to 10,200 feet. Leave Grouse Canyon and find a good trail on the slope east of and above Grouse Creek. Follow this trail northeast up a side drainage. During the arduous, 1.3-mile ascent up the side drainage, take time to enjoy the creek's miniature, mossy mosaics. Pass tree line at 11,400 feet and reach Princeton's southwest ridge at 13,000 feet. The altruistic approach is over; now for your reward.

Climb north along the studded ridge for 0.7 mile to Point 13,971, an unranked but significant false summit. Enjoy your respite in this privileged position. The views are expansive to the north, west and south, and the civilization to the east is mercifully hidden. When ready, continue 0.5 mile east to Princeton's stately but now pedantic summit.

17. Mount Antero   14,269 feet

See Map 17 on page 132

Mount Antero is named after a Native American chief of the Unitah Nation. The peak is 3 miles south of Chalk Creek and is easily visible from U.S. 285 in the Arkansas River Valley. Antero is more famous among gem collectors than it is among mountaineers. It has produced some truly remarkable aquamarine and topaz gems, and quartz crystals.

Mountaineers should keep their eyes open while hiking up Antero, because it is still possible to find a modest prize. It is much more likely, though, that you will see only people—many people—looking for gems and views. Most of them drive up the four-wheel-drive road that goes up Baldwin Gulch and reaches 13,700 feet on a shoulder south of Antero's summit. On a busy summer weekend, you can hear the sounds of four-wheel-drive vehicles grinding up this road from Tabeguache Peak, 4 miles south of Antero. Antero does offer a choice of routes, but don't expect solitude.

Maps

Required: Mount Antero, St. Elmo, San Isabel National Forest

Trailheads

Cascade Trailhead

This trailhead is at 9,020 feet and provides access to Antero's north side. If approaching from the north, go south on U.S. 285 for 5.6 miles from the U.S. 24–U.S. 285 junction just west of Johnsons Village, near Buena Vista. If approaching from the south, go north on U.S. 285 for 15.4 miles from the U.S. 50–U.S. 285 junction in Poncha Springs. Leave U.S. 285 and go west on Chaffee County 162 (paved) for 9.6 miles to the Cascade Campground. The campground is the trailhead, and hikes start from the top of the campground loop road. This trailhead is accessible in winter.

Baldwin Gulch Trailhead

This trailhead is at 9,420 feet and provides access to Antero's west side. From the Cascade Trailhead (mile 9.6), continue west on Chaffee County 162 for an additional 2.0 miles to the Baldwin Gulch Road (dirt), which is on the south side of Chaffee County 162, 11.6 miles from U.S. 285. Park at the bottom of the Baldwin Gulch Road. Four-wheel-drive vehicles can climb southeast then south into Baldwin Gulch for 3.0 miles to a road junction at 10,840 feet. This is a good place to park four-wheel-drive vehicles.

Browns Creek Trailhead

This trailhead is at 8,920 feet. It provides access to the east and south sides of Antero, and to the north side of Shavano and Tabeguache. If approaching from the north, go south on U.S. 285 for 8.8 miles from the U.S. 24–U.S. 285 junction just west of Johnsons Village, near Buena Vista. If approaching from the south, go north on U.S. 285 for 12.2 miles from the U.S. 50–U.S. 285 junction in Poncha Springs. Leave U.S. 285 and go west on Chaffee County 270 (dirt). Measure from the U.S. 285 and Chaffee

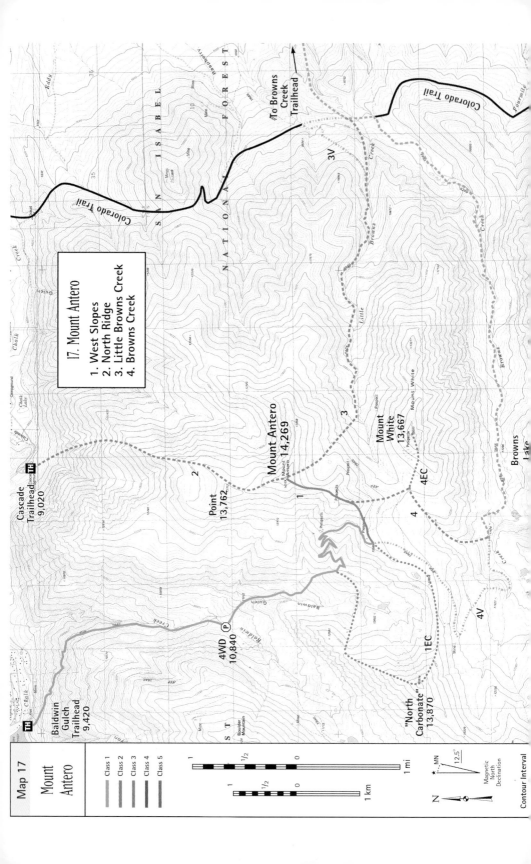

Mount Antero from the west.

County 270 junction. Go west on Chaffee County 270, continue straight on Chaffee County 272 (the Browns Creek Road) at 1.5 miles, turn south (left) at 3.5 miles and reach the Browns Creek Trailhead after 5.1 miles. The well-marked trailhead is on the west side of the road, and there is good camping nearby.

Routes

17.1 West Slopes II, Class 2

From Baldwin Gulch Trailhead: 11.2 to 16.0 miles, 4,900 feet

This is the easiest and most popular route up Antero. A four-wheel-drive road goes to 13,700 feet. Start at the Baldwin Gulch Trailhead and follow the steep four-wheel-drive road southeast then south for 3.0 miles to a road junction at 10,840 feet. Turn east (left), cross Baldwin Creek and continue south into upper Baldwin Gulch. Do not follow the four-wheel-drive road to Baldwin Lake. At 12,000 feet, the road switchbacks up Antero's west slopes, then angles south to reach Antero's south ridge at 13,089 feet. Stay on the road and avoid the temptation to head straight up the steep, loose scree; it's hard on you and the environment. Once on the south ridge, leave the road, hike north, cross Point 13,820 and continue north for 0.5 mile to the summit.

Extra Credit 17.1EC

From 13,089 feet on Antero's south ridge, descend southwest from the four-wheel-drive road on easy slopes for 1.0 mile to a 12,820-foot saddle. From the saddle, climb west on a ridge for 0.8 mile to Point 13,870, alias

"North Carbonate," one of Colorado's 100 highest peaks. For the easiest descent, reverse your ascent. For a shorter but steeper return to Baldwin Gulch, descend the north ridge of Point 13,870 to 12,600 feet, leave the ridge and descend east to Baldwin creek at 11,800. Cross the stream and contour north to reach the Baldwin Gulch Road at 12,000 feet.

17.2 North Ridge II, Class 2, Moderate Snow (Seasonal)

From Cascade Trailhead: 7.0 miles, 5,300 feet

This steep, direct route is not recommended for casual fourteener hikers. When snow conditions are favorable, it does provide some good snow climbing, but the route ascends a large avalanche chute; you should carefully consider snow conditions before ascending it. The gully contains unpleasant scree when it is snow-free.

Start at the Cascade Trailhead, angle up to the southeast and proceed into a prominent, treeless gully. This is the western of two gullies seen from the Cascade Campground entrance. Ascend the gully and reach Antero's north ridge at 12,200 feet. Ascend this ridge for a long mile, pass Point 13,762 on its east side and continue south for 0.5 mile to the summit. Do not descend the unnamed basin east of the north ridge.

17.3 Little Browns Creek II, Class 2

From Browns Creek Trailhead: 14.0 miles, 5,350 feet

This long route provides an escape from the four-wheel-drive road. Start at the Browns Creek Trailhead and follow the Browns Lake Trail west for 1.3 miles to the Colorado Trail. Follow the Browns Lake Trail south until it crosses Little Browns Creek. The Colorado Trail and the Browns Lake Trail are the same at this point. Do not confuse Little Browns Creek with Browns Creek, which is 0.4 mile farther south. The two creeks drain different valleys. Little Browns Creek is in the higher, narrower valley between Mount White and Antero.

Leave the comfort of the Browns Lake Trail and bushwhack west along the north side of Little Browns Creek. Higher up, an old trail may aid your progress. Enduring Little Browns Creek's roughness is the price of solitude. The climb up this enchanting valley is steady and long. From 12,000 feet, climb northwest for 1.0 mile to Antero's summit.

Variation 17.3V

For a longer, easier approach, start at the Browns Creek Trailhead and follow the Browns Lake Trail west for 1.3 miles to the Colorado Trail. Follow the Colorado Trail north for 0.5 mile and look sharp for a rocky old road heading up the hill to the southwest. Follow this old road southwest as it climbs toward the Little Browns Creek drainage. Reach the drainage at 10,200 feet and continue on the route described above.

17.4 Browns Creek II, Class 2
From Browns Creek Trailhead: 19.0 to 22.0 miles, 5,400 feet

This is the longest route on Antero, and it is best done as a backpacking adventure. It is an easy route that uses trails and roads most of the way. With a camp at Browns Lake, it is possible to climb Shavano, Tabeguache and Antero.

Start at the Browns Creek Trailhead down on the deck of the Arkansas River Valley. Follow the Browns Lake Trail for 6.0 miles to Browns Lake at 11,286 feet. You also can reach Browns Lake by four-wheel-drive vehicle from Baldwin Gulch, west of Antero. From Browns Lake, hike west on the four-wheel-drive road for 1.0 mile, leave the road and climb north up a small side valley for 1.0 mile to reach the broad, 12,820-foot saddle between Antero and Mount White (13,667 feet). From here, hike north for 1.5 miles to Antero's summit.

Variation 17.4V

For an even easier hike, follow the four-wheel-drive road all the way from Browns Lake to 13,700 feet.

Extra Credit 17.4EC

From the broad, 12,820-foot saddle between Antero and Mount White, climb east for 0.6 mile to Mount White (13,667 feet). The southwest summit is the highest.

18. Shavano Group

Mount Shavano	14,229 feet
Tabeguache Peak	14,155 feet

See Map 18 on page 136

These two peaks are the southernmost fourteeners in the Sawatch Range. They are 12 miles northwest of Poncha Springs, which is near the U.S. 50–U.S. 285 junction. Shavano dominates the view from U.S. 285 north of Poncha Springs, while Tabeguache hides behind its higher neighbor. *Shavano* and *Tabeguache* are Native American names from the Ute Nation.

Maps

Required: Maysville, Garfield, St. Elmo, Mount Antero,
San Isabel National Forest

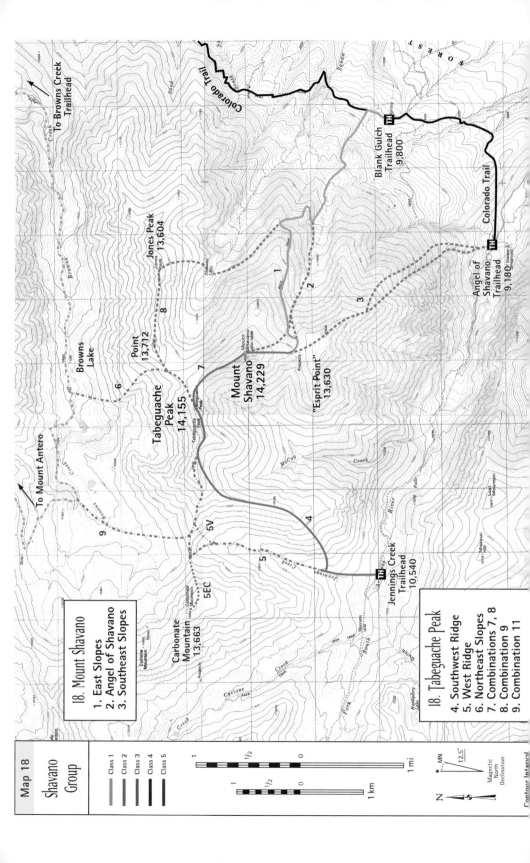

Map 18

Shavano Group

18. Mount Shavano
1. East Slopes
2. Angel of Shavano
3. Southeast Slopes

18. Tabeguache Peak
4. Southwest Ridge
5. West Ridge
6. Northeast Slopes
7. Combinations 7, 8
8. Combinations 7, 8
9. Combination 9

Class 1
Class 2
Class 3
Class 4
Class 5

1   1/2   0   1 mi

1   1/2   0   1 km

N

MN
12.5°
Magnetic North
Declination

Contour Interval

To Browns Creek Trailhead

Colorado Trail

Blank Gulch Trailhead 9,800

Angel of Shavano Trailhead 9,180

Colorado Trail

Jones Peak 13,604

Point 13,712

Browns Lake

Tabeguache Peak 14,155

Mount Shavano 14,229

"Esprit Point" 13,630

To Mount Antero

Carbonate Mountain 13,663

Jennings Creek Trailhead 10,540

Trailheads

Angel of Shavano Trailhead

This trailhead is at 9,180 feet and provides access to Shavano's south and east sides. On U.S. 50, go 6.1 miles west of the U.S. 50–U.S. 285 junction in Poncha Springs. Turn north onto Chaffee County 240 and measure from this point. Chaffee County 240 is paved initially, turns to dirt at 2.7 miles and reaches the Angel of Shavano Campground and Trailhead at 3.8 miles. The road is good to this point. The trailhead is on the north side of the road and the campground is on the south side. This trailhead is accessible in winter.

Jennings Creek Trailhead

This trailhead is at 10,540 feet and provides access to Tabeguache's southwest side. From the Angel of Shavano Campground (mile 3.8), continue west on Chaffee County 240 for an additional 3.8 miles and reach the Jennings Creek Trailhead at mile 7.6 from U.S. 50. The road beyond the Angel of Shavano Campground is rough but still passable for passenger cars. There are many campsites above the Angel of Shavano Campground, but none at the trailhead, and parking there is limited. The trailhead is on the north side of the road and marked with two signs. In winter Chaffee County 240 is plowed to the Angel of Shavano Campground but not beyond.

Blank Gulch Trailhead

This trailhead is at 9,800 feet and provides access to Shavano's east side. On U.S. 285, go 20.0 miles south of the U.S. 24–U.S. 285 junction just west of Johnsons Village, near Buena Vista. Turn west onto Chaffee County 140 (paved) and measure from this point. The U.S. 285–Chaffee County 140 junction is 1.0 mile north of the U.S. 50–U.S. 285 junction in Poncha Springs.

Follow Chaffee County 140 west for 1.7 miles, turn north (right) onto Chaffee County 250 (dirt), stay left at 5.7 miles on Chaffee County 252, cross Placer Creek at 6.5 miles (camping), go straight at 7.3 miles, go straight at 8.7 miles, go straight at 8.9 miles and reach the Blank Gulch Trailhead after 9.0 miles. The trailhead is at the old Blank Cabin site. There is no longer a Blank Cabin, but a stone memorial marks the spot. The Colorado Trail is 100 yards west of the memorial. It is best to park passenger cars below the memorial, because the continuing road becomes rough and doesn't go very far.

18. Mount Shavano   14,229 feet

See Map 18 on page 136

Mount Shavano is famous for the Angel of Shavano on its east face. The Angel is a shallow, snow-filled couloir with two diverging branches at the top. In the spring and early summer, the snow gullies resemble an angel with upstretched arms. It is interesting to note that both the northernmost and southernmost Sawatch fourteeners, Mount of the Holy Cross and Shavano, have snow features with religious significance. Shavano is also the easternmost Sawatch fourteener.

Routes

18.1 East Slopes II, Class 2
From Blank Gulch Trailhead: 9.7 miles, 4,430 feet

This is the easiest route on Shavano. There is a good trail all the way to the high saddle south of Shavano's summit. This is not the most popular route on Shavano because the Blank Gulch Trailhead has not been used much in recent years. Most people reach Shavano's summit by traversing over the top of Tabeguache. See Shavano and Tabeguache Combination 18.10 for this route.

For the East Slopes Route, start at the Blank Gulch Trailhead and go north on the Colorado Trail for 0.25 mile to the start of the Mount Shavano Trail. Turn west (left) and ascend the Mount Shavano Trail as it climbs through a beautiful forest. As it climbs past tree line, the trail is on the north side of the basin that holds the Angel of Shavano. Finally, the trail angles west to reach the 13,330-foot saddle south of the summit. From this saddle, turn north (right) and ascend 0.6 mile over talus to the summit.

Extra Credit 18.1EC

From the 13,330-foot saddle south of the summit, climb south for 0.35 mile to Point 13,630, alias "Esprit Point." This unranked but classy summit has airy views. This is a good place to set aside the cares of the lower world for a while as you look at the Angel.

18.2 Angel of Shavano II, Class 2, Easy Snow (Seasonal) *Classic*
From Blank Gulch Trailhead: 7.9 miles, 4,430 feet

This is the best route on a fourteener in the southern Sawatch Range. The route is not difficult, but it has personality. The Angel of Shavano is the snow slope with two upstretched arms in the center of Shavano's east slopes. It is in good condition for climbing in late May and June. You can easily check the condition of the Angel from U.S. 285.

The Angel of Shavano spawned the colorful legend of a Native American princess who prayed for rain at the base of Shavano during a severe drought. The princess sacrificed herself to the gods and reappears every year as the Angel of Shavano. As she melts, her tears send life-giving water to the plains below.

Start at the Blank Gulch Trailhead and go north on the Colorado Trail for 0.25 mile to the start of the Mount Shavano Trail. Turn west (left) and ascend the Mount Shavano Trail as it climbs through a beautiful forest and crosses the small drainage below the Angel. Leave the trail at 11,100 feet before it starts switchbacking north away from the drainage. Bushwhack west up the drainage and hike up the basin to the base of the Angel.

The Angel is a gentle snow slope that does not exceed 30 degrees in steepness. An ice ax is useful, because the slope is still steep enough to produce a serious fall. The body of the Angel rises from 12,000 feet to 12,800 feet. At the top of the body, you must choose an arm. The southern arm usually has better snow conditions and leads to the 13,380-foot saddle south of the summit. The northern arm is the usual choice, because it leads directly toward the summit. The northern arm melts out before the southern arm; in some years, the northern arm is not present at all. Finally, leave the Angel behind and climb talus to the summit.

18.3 Southeast Slopes II, Class 2, Moderate Snow (Seasonal)
From Angel of Shavano Trailhead: 6.4 miles, 5,570 feet

This is the shortest route up Shavano, and it can provide a good snow climb in June. The route ascends in or near a shallow couloir on Shavano's southeast slopes. This is an arduous climb up steep terrain and requires a lot of elevation gain. It is not a good choice for the casual fourteener hiker. Do not use this route after the snow melts. The steep scree is unpleasant to ascend, and ascending or descending it is environmentally incorrect.

Start at the Angel of Shavano Trailhead and bushwhack north between two drainages. Continue bushwhacking northwest along the east side of the western drainage. At tree line, either climb this drainage or the small ridge north of it. In either case, you will end up at 13,000 feet on Shavano's southeast ridge. Follow this ridge to Point 13,630, alias "Esprit Point." Descend north to the 13,380-foot saddle between "Esprit Point" and Shavano. Continue north for 0.6 mile to Shavano's summit. Remember, on the return you must reascend "Esprit Point."

Mount Shavano and Tabeguache Peak from the southwest.

18. Tabeguache Peak   14,155 feet

See Map 18 on page 136

Tabeguache is not as well known as its higher, more visible neighbor, Shavano. It is important because most people reach Shavano's summit by traversing over Tabeguache.

The ascent or descent of McCoy Gulch on the south side of Tabeguache is not recommended. The upper part of the gulch looks easy, but the lower part is a cliffy gorge. Many parties encounter trouble trying to descend McCoy Gulch. The Chaffee County Sheriff's office has placed large warning signs at both the Jennings Creek and Blank Gulch Trailheads.

Routes

18.4 Southwest Ridge II, Class 2

From Jennings Creek Trailhead: 6.0 miles, 3,700 feet

(Note: Due to environmental concerns, the U.S. Forest Service has placed a sign at the Jennings Creek Trailhead asking hikers to stay off the southwest ridge trail of Tabeguache and, instead, climb the peak from Mount Shavano and the Blank Gulch Trailhead.)

This is the standard route up Tabeguache, and Shavano as well. Tabeguache's southwest ridge is the ridge separating Jennings Creek from McCoy Creek. Start at the Jennings Creek Trailhead and follow the well-worn climber's trail through the trees as it climbs north on the east side of Jennings Creek. At 11,200 feet, the trail leaves the Jennings Creek Drainage near a small pond and climbs steeply northeast to reach Tabeguache's southwest ridge at 12,900 feet. This is a steep climb and the trail is faint in places, but you do not need a trail above tree line.

From the southwest ridge, the view opens across McCoy Gulch, and you can see Shavano's west side and Tabeguache's summit. Hike north along the ridge, pass Point 13,198 and approach Point 13,936 on Tabeguache's west ridge. It is not necessary to climb Point 13,936. A vague trail angles northeast under Point 13,936 to reach Tabeguache's west ridge in a 13,820-foot saddle. From the west ridge, the view opens to the north, and you can see Mount Antero across Browns Creek, along with the rest of the Sawatch Range stretching far to the north.

Climb east along the west ridge to a 14,060-foot false summit. There are some abrupt views down Tabeguache's ugly north face as you approach the false summit. The final 300 yards from the false summit to the summit are bumpy if you stay directly on the ridge crest. The easiest route stays below the rock points on the ridge's south side.

18.5 West Ridge II, Class 2
From Jennings Creek Trailhead: 7.2 miles, 3,900 feet

The West Ridge Route shares a common start and finish with the Southwest Ridge Route and is a little longer. Start at the Jennings Creek Trailhead and follow the well-worn climber's trail through the trees as it climbs north on the east side of Jennings Creek. At 11,200 feet, leave the climber's trail near a small pond and hike north up Jennings Creek. There is no trail up Jennings Creek and the valley is rough in spots. The easiest climbing is on a series of grassy benches on the east side of the creek. These benches support many wildflowers. Near the head of the basin, climb northwest to the 12,610-foot saddle between Tabeguache and Carbonate Mountain (13,663 feet).

Turn east (right) and climb Tabeguache's broad west ridge to Point 13,936. There is a good view of Tabeguache from here. Descend east and join the Southwest Ridge Route in a 13,820-foot saddle. Continue east on that route for 0.5 mile to the summit.

Variation 18.5V

From the upper part of the Jennings Creek Valley, climb a scree slope 0.5 mile east of the 12,610-foot saddle and reach Tabeguache's west ridge at 13,000 feet. The scree on this shortcut is unpleasant, so this variation is best taken on the descent.

Extra Credit 18.5EC

From the 12,610-foot saddle, climb west for 0.5 mile and 1,050 feet of gain to Carbonate Mountain (13,663 feet).

18.6 Northeast Slopes II, Class 2

From Browns Creek Trailhead: 17.0 miles, 5,250 feet

People seldom climb this route because of its length, but it is a good route for a backpacking excursion. Start at the Browns Creek Trailhead (see Mount Antero) and follow the Browns Creek Trail for 6.0 miles to Browns Lake at 11,286 feet. You also can reach Browns Lake by four-wheel-drive vehicle from Baldwin Gulch, west of Antero.

From the west end of Browns Lake, climb southwest then south up a slope. Climb on grass at first, then talus, to reach the 13,380-foot saddle between Tabeguache and Point 13,712. It is not necessary to climb Point 13,712. From this saddle, climb southwest to reach the 13,700-foot saddle between Shavano and Tabeguache, then continue west for 0.25 mile to Tabeguache's summit.

18. Shavano and Tabeguache Combinations

See Map 18 on page 136

18.7 II, Class 2

From Jennings Creek Trailhead: 8.0 to 9.2 miles, 4,700 to 4,900 feet

This is the most popular way of climbing Shavano and Tabeguache together. Start at the Jennings Creek Trailhead and ascend either Tabeguache's Southwest Ridge Route or its West Ridge Route to Tabeguache's summit. Descend east for 0.25 mile to the 13,700-foot saddle between Shavano and Tabeguache, then climb southeast for 0.75 mile to Shavano's summit.

Descend by returning back over the top of Tabeguache. The effort involved in doing this deters many people, and they either descend McCoy Gulch or Shavano's south slopes. Descending McCoy Gulch will entangle you in cliffs, so this is *not* recommended. Descending Shavano's south side is rough and will leave you many miles from the Jennings Creek Trailhead. Assess the weather and your capabilities carefully before committing to this traverse.

18.8 II, Class 2, Easy Snow (Seasonal and Optional)

From Blank Gulch Trailhead: 9.9 to 11.7 miles, 5,410 feet

This is the flip side of Combination 18.7. Start at the Blank Gulch Trailhead and ascend either Shavano's Angel of Shavano Route or its East Slopes Route to Shavano's summit. Descend northwest for 0.75 mile to the 13,700-foot saddle between Shavano and Tabeguache, then climb 0.25 mile west to Tabeguache's summit.

Descend by returning back over the top of Shavano. This effort again deters many people, and they try to skirt Shavano's summit on the return or, worse yet, descend McCoy Gulch. Skirting Shavano's summit on either side is unpleasant, and it is better to climb back over the top.

18.9 II, Class 3, Easy Snow (Seasonal and Optional)

From Blank Gulch Trailhead: 11.2 to 13.0 miles, 5,500 feet

This is a Shavano and Tabeguache climb for hardened peak baggers. Start at the Blank Gulch Trailhead and follow Combination 18.8 as far as the 13,700-foot saddle between Shavano and Tabeguache on the return from Tabeguache's summit. The good news is you don't have to reclimb Shavano. The bad news is you have to climb Jones Peak instead.

Descend northeast to the 13,380-foot saddle between Tabeguache and Point 13,712, then climb east to the summit of Point 13,712. This ranked summit is a "Bi," one of Colorado's 200 highest peaks. From Point 13,712, scramble east for 1.0 mile to the summit of Jones Peak (13,604 feet). This difficult ridge requires some Class 3 scrambling over and around several obnoxious, rotten towers. You are committed now!

From the summit of Jones Peak, descend south down open slopes to the east end of beautiful, seldom visited Shavano Lake. Do an ascending traverse southeast from the lake to 12,100 feet, then contour southeast through dense thickets to Shavano's east ridge. Find the Mount Shavano Trail near 11,800 feet and follow it back to the Colorado Trail and the Blank Gulch Trailhead. Finding the Mount Shavano Trail near Shavano's east ridge is not a fail-safe operation, and your route-finding skills may be tested.

18.10 II, Class 2

From Browns Creek Trailhead: 18.5 miles, 5,800 feet

This combination avoids having to reclimb the first peak on the return, but it has a long approach. Start at the Browns Creek Trailhead (see Mount Antero) and follow Tabeguache's Northeast Slopes Route to Tabe-guache's summit. Traverse to Shavano, return to the 13,700-foot saddle and descend Tabeguache's Northeast Slopes Route back to Browns Lake. This combination works just as well if you climb Shavano first.

18.11 III, Class 2

From Jennings Creek Trailhead to Baldwin Gulch Trailhead: 16.6 miles, 7,000 to 7,200 feet

This traverse allows you to climb Shavano, Tabeguache and Antero together. Start by climbing Shavano and Tabeguache, using either Combination 18.7 or Combination 18.8. From Tabeguache's summit, descend west for 1.5 miles to the 12,610-foot saddle between Tabeguache and Carbonate Mountain. Descend north into upper Browns Creek and hike 3.0 miles northeast to Antero's summit. Descend Antero's West Slopes Route to the Baldwin Gulch Trailhead and a prearranged vehicle shuttle.

Chapter Four
Sangre de Cristo Range

Introduction

Sangre de Cristo means "blood of Christ" in Spanish, and the name suits this ancient place. The Sangre de Cristo Range is a long, linear range that starts where the Sawatch Range ends. The Sangres start south of Salida and run south for 220 miles to Santa Fe, New Mexico. The Sangre de Cristo Range is longer than any other Colorado range. Indeed, Colorado cannot contain it!

The northern part of the range is flanked on the east by the Wet Mountain Valley and Huerfano Park. The large, flat San Luis Valley lies west of the range. The winds scouring this valley cannot carry their burden over the Sangres and have left behind 700-foot-high sand dunes. The range averages only 10 to 20 miles in width, and the high peaks rise abruptly with few foothills. Approaching the Sangres is always an awesome, neck-bending experience.

Crestone conglomerate.

The Sangres contain 10 named fourteeners in Colorado and all the thirteeners in New Mexico. The fourteeners are clustered in three groups—the Crestone Group, the Blanca Group and the solitary Culebra Peak. Unlike the gentle summits of the Sawatch, the Sangres contain some of Colorado's most difficult fourteeners. The Crestone Group's conglomerate rock is surprisingly good, and these peaks hold many fine technical routes.

19. Crestone Group

Crestone Peak	14,294 feet
Crestone Needle	14,197 feet
Humboldt Peak	14,064 feet
Challenger Point	14,081 feet
Kit Carson Peak	14,165 feet

See Map 19 on page 148

These peaks are the northernmost fourteeners in the Sangre de Cristo Range. They are 12 miles southwest of Westcliffe in the Wet Mountain Valley. The Crestone Group is one of Colorado's finest collections of fourteeners. There is something for everybody here. There are walk-ups, moderate scrambles and serious technical climbs. After Longs Peak, the Crestone Group has the best concentration of technical climbing on Colorado's fourteeners.

The geology of the Crestone Group is different from other Colorado ranges, and the conglomerate rock here comes as a pleasant surprise. The rock is full of imbedded knobs. An exciting part of the Colorado fourteener experience is tiptoeing up on these knobs. Occasionally a knob will pull out, but they are generally solid. Finding good protection on technical routes can be difficult, and these beautiful peaks have occasionally proven deadly.

Maps
Required: Crestone Peak, San Isabel National Forest
Optional: Crestone, Beck Mountain, Rio Grande National Forest

Trailheads
South Colony Trailhead
This trailhead is at 8,780 feet on the range's east side. It provides access to Humboldt Peak and the east sides of Crestone Peak, Crestone Needle and Kit Carson Peak. This is the only trailhead for the Crestone

Group giving reasonable access to all five peaks. From the south end of Westcliffe, go south on Colorado 69 for 4.4 miles, turn south (right) onto Colfax Lane and go south for 5.6 miles to a T-junction. Turn west (right) and proceed for 1.5 miles. Park passenger cars in a parking area on the north side of the road, just before the road becomes rougher. This is the trailhead.

Four-wheel-drive vehicles can continue west for an additional 5.0 miles to 11,060 feet, into the South Colony Creek Drainage. This road is one of Colorado's roughest, and it becomes a little rougher every year.

Willow Creek Trailhead

This trailhead is at 8,880 feet on the range's west side. It provides access to Willow Lake on the north side of Kit Carson Peak and Challenger Point. If approaching from the north, go 13.8 miles south on Colorado 17 from the Colorado 17–U.S. 285 junction. If approaching from the south, go 16.8 miles north on Colorado 17 from the Colorado 17–Colorado 112 junction in Hooper. Turn east onto a paved road 0.5 mile south of the center of Moffat. Go 12.5 miles east to the town of Crestone. The Crestones and Kit Carson loom higher and higher as you approach them.

From the center of Crestone, go east on Galena Street, enter the Rio Grande National Forest at 1.1 miles and reach the trailhead after 2.3 miles. The last 1.2 miles of this road are rough; some people choose to park passenger cars at the forest boundary.

Spanish Creek Trailhead

This trailhead is at 8,260 feet on the range's west side. It provides access to the south side of Kit Carson and the north side of Crestone Peak. This trailhead is on private property. Please protect the permission that allows you to use it. If approaching from the north, go 13.8 miles south on Colorado 17 from the Colorado 17–U.S. 285 junction. If approaching from the south, go 16.8 miles north on Colorado 17 from the Colorado 17–Colorado 112 junction in Hooper. Turn east onto a paved road 0.5 mile south of the center of Moffat. Go 11.8 miles east to the entrance of the Baca Grande Chalets Grants.

Turn south (right) and measure from this point. Follow Camino Baca Grande (paved) through the subdivision, cross Crestone Creek at 0.8 mile and cross Willow Creek at 2.2 miles, where the road turns to dirt. Continue south to reach Spanish Creek and the trailhead after 3.6 miles. Park on the north side of the creek. The Spanish Creek Trail starts on the north side of the creek.

Cottonwood Creek Trailhead

This trailhead is at 8,400 feet on the range's west side. It provides access to the south sides of Crestone Peak and Crestone Needle. This trailhead is on private property. Please protect the permission that allows you to use it. From Spanish Creek Trailhead (mile 3.6), continue south for an additional 1.8 miles to reach Cottonwood Creek and the trailhead at mile 5.4. Park on the north side of Cottonwood Creek near a water tank. The Cottonwood Creek Trail is initially a road, and it starts 100 feet north of Cottonwood Creek.

Approaches

19.A1 South Colony Lakes Approach

From South Colony Trailhead: 11.8 to 12.8 miles, 2,920 feet

This is the standard approach to the Crestone Group. Start at the South Colony Trailhead and follow the rough four-wheel-drive road west for 1.4 miles to the boundary of San Isabel National Forest. Camping is not permitted between the trailhead and the forest boundary. Continue southwest up the road, pass the rainbow trail 0.8 mile beyond the forest boundary and cross to South Colony Creek's north side 1.3 miles beyond the forest boundary. The road becomes rougher beyond this crossing. Continue southwest for an additional 2.5 miles to a parking area at 11,060 feet, 100 yards before the road crosses back to the creek's south side. From here you have a choice.

The approach continues on the road as it crosses back to South Colony Creek's south side. There is a sturdy, double-log footbridge at this crossing. There is a second parking area 100 yards beyond this crossing, and the road is gated at this point. Continue southwest for 0.7 mile on the old road. There are good views of Humboldt Peak here, and the east face of Broken Hand Peak towers over you. Turn north, pass the end of the road and continue on a good trail for 0.7 mile to the outlet stream below Lower South Colony Lake at 11,660 feet. There is good camping near the lake.

19.A2 Willow Lake Approach

From Willow Creek Trailhead: 7.4 miles, 2,700 feet

This is a beautiful hike. Start at the Willow Creek Trailhead, go 100 yards east, turn south (right) and cross South Crestone Creek. Follow the Willow Creek Trail as it climbs east and south into the Willow Creek Drainage. The trail climbs east up this valley to Willow Lake at 11,564 feet. The eastern end of the lake is ringed with cliffs and graced with a waterfall. This is a spectacular place. There are camping spots near the western end of the lake. The north sides of Challenger Point and Kit Carson are 1 mile south from the lake's eastern end.

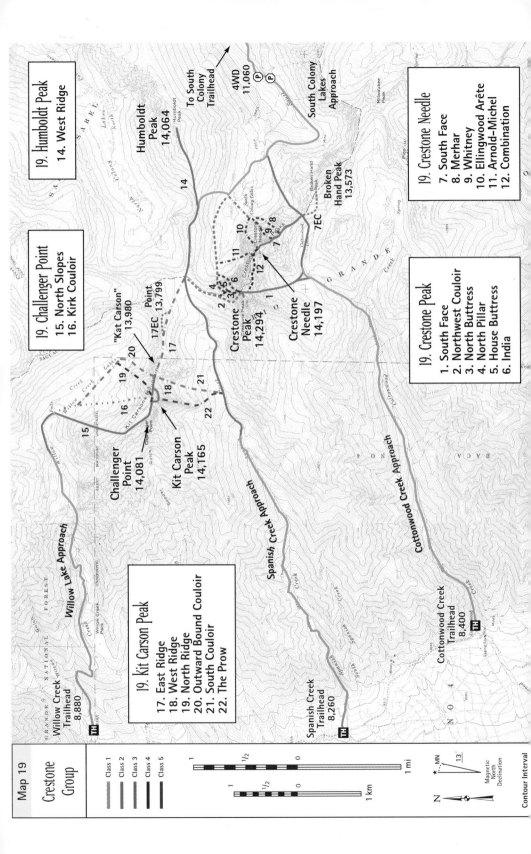

Map 19

Crestone Group

Class 1
Class 2
Class 3
Class 4
Class 5

Contour Interval

Magnetic North Declination

19. Humboldt Peak
14. West Ridge

19. Challenger Point
15. North Slopes
16. Kirk Couloir

19. Crestone Needle
7. South Face
8. Merhar
9. Whitney
10. Ellingwood Arête
11. Arnold-Michel
12. Combination

19. Crestone Peak
1. South Face
2. Northwest Couloir
3. North Buttress
4. North Pillar
5. House Buttress
6. India

19. Kit Carson Peak
17. East Ridge
18. West Ridge
19. North Ridge
20. Outward Bound Couloir
21. South Couloir
22. The Prow

Humboldt Peak
14,064

To South Colony Trailhead

4WD
11,060

South Colony Lakes Approach

Broken Hand Peak
13,573

GRANDE Creek

"Kat Carson"
13,980

17EC Point

Challenger Point
14,081

Kit Carson Peak
14,165

Crestone Peak
14,294

Crestone Needle
14,197

Willow Lake Approach

Willow Creek Trailhead
8,880

GRANDE NATIONAL FOREST

SANGRE

Spanish Creek Approach

Cottonwood Creek Approach

Cottonwood Creek Trailhead
8,400

Spanish Creek Trailhead
8,260

BACA

19.A3 Spanish Creek Approach

From Spanish Creek Trailhead: 7.0 miles, 2,750 feet

This is a difficult approach starting on the deck of the San Luis Valley, so this hike can be brutally hot. Start at the Spanish Creek Trailhead. The Spanish Creek Trail starts on the north side of Spanish Creek, passes under a solar-powered ashram and climbs east into the Spanish Creek Drainage. The little-used Spanish Creek Trail is rough and difficult to follow in spots. The trail is mostly on the north side of the creek, but it does cross to the south side twice. Between 9,600 feet and 10,600 feet, the trail climbs relentlessly through an old burn on the north side of the creek. Above 10,600 feet, the angle of the valley relents and there are good camping spots near tree line at 11,000 feet. Kit Carson's southern routes and the Northwest Couloir Route on Crestone Peak are accessible from here.

19.A4 Cottonwood Creek Approach

From Cottonwood Creek Trailhead: 9.0 miles, 3,900 feet

This arduous approach leads to beautiful Cottonwood Lake, south of the Crestones. Both Crestone Peak and Crestone Needle can be climbed from here. If you have the energy, this is a wonderful alternative to the crowded South Colony Lakes Approach. Start at the Cottonwood Creek Trailhead. The Cottonwood Creek Trail is initially a road, and it starts 100 feet north of Cottonwood Creek. The trail stays on the north side of the creek. The Cottonwood Creek Trail is easier to follow than the Spanish Creek Trail, but there is a difficult section between 10,600 feet and 11,000 feet near some boilerplate slabs.

At 11,100 feet, leave the main trail and turn north (left) into the side valley leading to Cottonwood Lake. A steep, rough trail climbs into this valley on the west side of the creek. At tree line, the trail fades into talus and meadows. Continue climbing northeast to Cottonwood Lake at 12,310 feet. The views of the Crestones will lure you on. Idyllic Cottonwood Lake is nestled under Crestone Needle's south face.

19. Crestone Peak 14,294 feet

See Map 19 on page 148

Crestone Peak is one of Colorado's finest peaks. High and wild, it was once proclaimed unclimbable. It is now simply called the "Peak" by those who know it. The Peak draws some people like a siren but rejects others. If it draws you, approach with respect and caution.

Crestone Peak's main summit is the highest point in Saguache County. Crestone Peak has two summits, and the 14,260-foot eastern summit is the highest point in Custer County. Crestone Peak is one of Colorado's hardest fourteeners—some people proclaim it *the* hardest. The Northwest Couloir Route has been the standard route on the Peak for decades, but it may not be the easiest or safest route. There are alternatives. Consider choices and conditions before launching.

Routes

19.1 South Face II, Class 3, Moderate Snow (Seasonal) *Classic*

From Cottonwood Lake: 2.0 miles, 2,000 feet
From Cottonwood Creek Trailhead: 11.0 miles, 5,900 feet
From Lower South Colony Lake: 4.6 miles, 3,850 feet
From South Colony Trailhead: 16.4 to 17.4 miles, 6,770 feet

Depending on conditions, this may be the easiest and safest route on Crestone Peak. The approach to the south face is longer and more complicated than the approach to the Northwest Couloir Route, but you can avoid the vagaries of the northwest couloir. Clean scrambling and moderate snow replace the northwest couloir's ice and rubble. Approach the south face from Cottonwood Lake. You can reach this Elysian lake from the west by following the Cottonwood Creek Approach.

You also can reach Cottonwood Lake from Lower South Colony Lake. From the trail-crossing of the outlet stream below Lower South Colony Lake, hike south on the trail for 100 yards and find a strong climber's trail heading west through the bushes. Follow this trail west into the little bowl under the north face of 13,573-foot Broken Hand Peak. This bowl is south of all the difficulties on Crestone Needle's northeast face.

Climb up the bowl and ascend a 400-foot northeast-facing couloir to 12,900-foot Broken Hand Pass between Crestone Needle and Broken Hand Peak. This shaded couloir can retain snow until mid-July, so be prepared for some moderate snow climbing until then. After the snow melts, the couloir requires a little Class 3 scrambling. From the pass, descend west to Cottonwood Lake (Class 2).

From Cottonwood Lake, contour west under the broken south face of Crestone Needle, then hike north into the basin under Crestone Peak's south face and Crestone Needle's west face. Complicated terrain is above this point. Make sure you understand it before committing to anything difficult. The entire traverse between Crestone Peak and Crestone Needle is east of you. Crestone Peak's large south face is north of you. In the center of this face, there is a long, south-facing couloir leading to the 14,180-foot red notch between Crestone Peak's main summit and the slightly lower east summit. This couloir is the key to the route.

It is possible to climb the inset, lower part of the couloir, but it's easier to avoid the lower couloir by scrambling up the rock on the couloir's east (right) side. This solid, Class 3 scrambling is fun. The terrain leads you into the couloir at 13,500 feet. Above this point, the couloir is wider and less steep. Proceed into the couloir and ascend it for 700 feet to the red notch between the two summits. The upper part of the couloir retains snow well into July. Either climb the snow or scramble up rocks on the couloir's east (right) side. Even if you try to avoid the snow, you may find some unavoidable patches. In August the upper couloir is a rubble scramble.

From the red notch at the top of the couloir, scramble west for 250 feet to the summit. This easy, Class 3 scramble is exciting, and Crestone Peak's thrilling summit hears many spontaneous yodels.

Extra Credit 19.1EC

From the 14,180-foot red notch between the twin summits, scramble east for 200 feet to Crestone Peak's 14,260-foot east summit. This entertaining, Class 3 scramble is slightly harder than the scramble to the main summit. Crestone Peak's east summit is a significant summit with dramatic views. It is also the highest point in Custer County.

It is possible to climb directly to the east summit from the upper couloir. Leave the couloir where a large ledge runs southeast from it. Climb a break in the cliffs above this ledge, reach the east summit's south ridge and finish on this ridge. This Class 4 variation involves considerable exposure.

19.2 Northwest Couloir II, Class 3, Steep Snow/Ice

From Lower South Colony Lake: 4.0 miles, 2,750 feet

From South Colony Trailhead: 15.8 to 16.8 miles, 5,670 feet

From camp at Spanish Creek: 5.0 miles, 3,300 feet

From Spanish Creek Trailhead: 12.0 miles, 6,050 feet

This route has been the standard route on Crestone Peak for decades, but it may not be the easiest or safest route. It has been popular because it is the easiest way to climb Crestone Peak from South Colony Lakes. The alternative South Face Route requires a longer approach.

The deeply inset northwest couloir retains snow and ice through the summer. As the snow melts, it leaves water on the slabs and rubble on the ledges. The northwest couloir has caused at least one fatal accident. Despite its disadvantages, this is a practicable route for experienced parties, and it is the most direct route through Crestone Peak's upper difficulties.

You can approach the Northwest Couloir Route from either South Colony Lakes or Spanish Creek. From Lower South Colony Lake, hike northwest to Upper South Colony Lake and climb a south-facing scree gully to the long ridge connecting Humboldt Peak with Crestone Peak. Scramble west on or below this ridge to the broad, 13,140-foot Crestone Peak–Kit

Carson Saddle. This open area is called the "Bear's Playground." If you are approaching from Spanish Creek, climb east to the head of Spanish Creek and reach the Bear's Playground from the west. There are spectacular profile views of the Ellingwood Arête from here.

From the Bear's Playground, climb south along the talus ridge toward Crestone Peak. Before you reach the steeper mass of the upper peak, leave the ridge and traverse southwest (right) on the west side of the ridge at 13,400 feet to reach the northwest couloir. You must cross a vague couloir before you reach the northwest couloir. The northwest couloir is in the center of Crestone Peak's northwest face. The entry point into the couloir is the highest easy access near a small elbow in the couloir. Below the elbow, the couloir faces more to the northwest, then ends above a serious cliff. When descending this route, be sure to exit the couloir before you reach the cliff.

Once in the couloir, ascend it for 800 feet to the 14,180-foot red notch between Crestone Peak's main summit and the slightly lower east summit. The exact line for climbing the couloir depends on conditions. If snow conditions are good, the ascent is a simple but steep snow climb. By mid-summer, the snow is no longer continuous and the ascent alternates between snow and broken, rubble-covered ledges on the couloir's sides. Helmets, ice axes and crampons are recommended for this couloir. Short sections of ice are often unavoidable until late August.

From the red notch at the top of the couloir, scramble west for 250 feet to the summit. This easy, Class 3 scramble is a welcome finish after the couloir's dark confines. The summit may feel quite airy.

19.3 North Buttress II, Class 4

From Lower South Colony Lake: 4.0 miles, 2,750 feet
From South Colony Trailhead: 15.8 to 16.8 miles, 5,670 feet
From camp at Spanish Creek: 5.0 miles, 3,300 feet
From Spanish Creek Trailhead: 12.0 miles, 6,050 feet

This is a rock route on the buttress to the east of the Northwest Couloir Route. The north buttress avoids the snow and ice in the northwest couloir. Do not confuse the North Buttress and North Pillar Routes. Follow the Northwest Couloir Route to 13,400 feet on the talus ridge below the steep upper portion of the peak. Instead of traversing southwest into the northwest couloir, continue up the buttress above you. Pass the tops of the east-facing North Pillar and House Buttress on the west side of the ridge.

After 800 feet of delightful, Class 3 climbing on solid, conglomerate knobs, you will reach the top of an isolated, 14,240-foot tower 200 yards northeast of Crestone Peak's east summit. The isolated tower is lower than

Crestone Peak from the north.

the east summit and separated from it by a deep notch. A direct climb from the tower to the east summit would be very difficult.

The crux of this route is climbing from the tower to the red notch at the top of the northwest couloir between the east and main summits. Do a tricky, Class 4 downclimb on the tower's west side, then do a complicated, exposed, Class 4 traverse across unprotected slabs to reach the red notch. From the notch, scramble west for 250 feet to the summit.

19.4 North Pillar III, Class 5.8 *Classic*

From Lower South Colony Lake: 3.8 miles, 2,750 feet

From South Colony Trailhead: 15.6 to 16.6 miles, 5,670 feet

The North Pillar is the northernmost buttress on Crestone Peak's northeast face. You can easily see and approach the North Pillar from Upper South Colony Lake. From the lake, the pillar forms part of the northern skyline of the northeast face. The North Pillar consists of a narrow east face and a larger north face. The edge between these two faces is usually the line created where sunlight meets shadow, and it gives the pillar its dramatic appearance.

This 900-foot, 10-pitch climb is beautiful, sustained and Dolomite in character. The route ascends the east face near the edge between the east and north faces. It involves six sustained, Class 5.7 pitches. On the seventh, crux pitch, angle south (left) to reach a weakness in a modest overhang, climb the overhang (Class 5.8) and angle back north (right) to the edge. The angle then eases, and three more pitches (Classes 5.6, 5.4, 4) take you to the top of the pillar. Belays and protection are adequate on this climb. The top of the pillar is a small, 13,700-foot summit. From the top of the pillar, continue on the North Buttress Route.

19.5 House Buttress III, Class 5.7

From Lower South Colony Lake: 3.8 miles, 2,750 feet

From South Colony Trailhead: 15.6 to 16.6 miles, 5,670 feet

The House Buttress is the large, broken buttress just south (left) of the easily identified North Pillar on the northern end of Crestone Peak's northeast face. This climb is longer and easier than the North Pillar. Approach the climb from Upper South Colony Lake.

Start south of the base of the North Pillar and do an ascending traverse south (left) on a ledge cutting across the bottom of the House Buttress. Before reaching the couloir on the south edge of the buttress, climb straight up the broken south edge of the buttress. Higher up, work left into the small basin on the south side of the buttress. Climb up this basin and join the North Buttress Route at 13,800 feet.

19.6 India III, Class 5.8

From Lower South Colony Lake: 3.8 miles, 2,750 feet

From South Colony Trailhead: 15.6 to 16.6 miles, 5,670 feet

This route winds up through the center of the complex northeast face between Crestone Peak and Crestone Needle. Approach the route from Upper South Colony Lake. Start on the south (left) side of the large broken buttress in the center of the lower face. Ascend slabs along the south edge of the buttress, then do an ascending traverse on a prominent ledge leading north across the buttress. Climb the upper part of the buttress along its north side and reach a lower-angled section above the buttress. Climb slabs to reach the south ridge of Crestone Peak's east summit, and follow that ridge north to the east summit. Scramble west to the main summit.

19. Crestone Needle   14,197 feet

See Map 19 on page 148

Crestone Needle is Crestone Peak's companion. The needle begins where the peak ends. The needle is a singular summit of distinguished beauty. It is 0.5 mile southeast of the peak, and a jagged 0.5-mile-long ridge of considerable notoriety separates the two peaks.

Crestone Needle is slightly easier to climb than Crestone Peak, but still ranks as of one of Colorado's hardest fourteeners. The standard route is on the complex south face, while the pristine northeast face holds several fine technical routes.

The northeast face of the needle and the peak combine to form one of Colorado's most glorious mountain walls. The wall is a mile long, always at least 1,000 feet high and reaches a 2,000-foot climax under Crestone Needle's summit. The most famous of the Crestone Group's technical routes is the Ellingwood Arête, which ascends the highest, steepest part of the wall directly to the needle's summit. Crestone Needle vaulted into the international spotlight when the Ellingwood Arête was included in the popular book *Fifty Classic Climbs of North America* by Steven Roper and Allen Steck (San Francisco: Sierra Club Books, 1979). Crestone Needle carries the honor well.

Routes

19.7 South Face II, Class 3, Moderate Snow (Seasonal) *Classic*

From Lower South Colony Lake: 2.6 miles, 2,550 feet

From South Colony Trailhead: 14.4 to 15.4 miles, 5,470 feet

From Cottonwood Lake: 2.0 miles, 1,900 feet

From Cottonwood Creek Trailhead: 11.0 miles, 5,800 feet

This is the easiest route on Crestone Needle. It is a sharp scramble to a spectacular summit. You can approach the route from either Lower South Colony Lake or Cottonwood Lake.

From the trail-crossing of the outlet stream below Lower South Colony Lake, hike south on the trail for 100 yards and find a strong climber's trail heading west through the bushes. Follow this trail west into the little bowl under the north face of 13,573-foot Broken Hand Peak. This bowl is south of all the difficulties on Crestone Needle's northeast face.

Climb up the bowl and ascend a 400-foot northeast-facing couloir to 12,900-foot Broken Hand Pass between Crestone Needle and Broken Hand Peak. This shaded couloir can retain snow until mid-July, so be prepared for some moderate snow climbing until then. After the snow melts, the couloir requires a little Class 3 scrambling. From Cottonwood Lake, hike east up to Broken Hand Pass. The western approach to the pass is much easier.

From Broken Hand Pass, climb northwest on the west side of Crestone Needle's southeast ridge to 13,300 feet. A good climber's trail leads you through the minor cliff bands on this section of the route. At 13,300 feet, you have neatly bypassed the difficulties of the lower part of the needle's convoluted south face. Above 13,300 feet, the upper part of the south face rears up in earnest, and you cannot avoid it.

There are two couloirs on the eastern edge of the upper south face. Either couloir can be climbed, and it is possible to traverse between the couloirs in a few places. The Class 3 climbing in the couloirs on solid, conglomerate knobs is enjoyable.

Start up the eastern (right) couloir and, when it becomes steep, angle over into the western (left) couloir. Follow the western couloir until it merges with the eastern couloir and becomes shallow near the summit. The steep part of the eastern couloir is more exposed and slightly harder than the steep part of the western couloir. From the top of the couloirs, scramble northwest to the highest point. Crestone Needle's summit will thrill all but the most dispassionate soul.

Extra Credit 19.7EC

From 12,900-foot Broken Hand Pass, descend to the west for 200 feet, traverse south below a rock buttress, then climb south and east to the summit of 13,573-foot Broken Hand Peak. If you climb to the north ridge en route, you can view the thumb. This freestanding pinnacle gives this peak its handlike appearance when viewed from the east. The thumb has been climbed but, it's hard.

19.8 Merhar II, Class 5.6
From Lower South Colony Lake: 2.0 miles, 2,550 feet
From South Colony Trailhead: 13.8 to 14.8 miles, 5,470 feet

This technical climb flirts with the difficulties of Crestone Needle's great northeast face. It is well south of the Ellingwood Arête and is the southernmost route on the face. From the western end of Lower South Colony Lake, climb west to 12,200 feet at the southern end of the face. Climb a short gully above a scree cone to avoid the lower cliffs on the face. Do an ascending traverse north on a large, sloping ledge above the lower cliffs. Climb directly up 700 feet of Class 5.6 rock on the north (right) side of a narrow couloir that is the northern of two upper extensions of the initial gully. Join the South Face Route at 13,300 feet.

19.9 Whitney III, Class 5.8, Steep Snow/Ice
From Lower South Colony Lake: 2.0 miles, 2,550 feet
From South Colony Trailhead: 13.8 to 14.8 miles, 5,470 feet

This route shares a start with the Ellingwood Arête but takes a different line on the upper part of the face. The upper part of this route is 800 feet south of the Ellingwood Arête. From the western end of Lower South Colony Lake, climb west to 12,200 feet under the center of the east-facing portion of the needle's northeast face.

Ellingwood Arête on Crestone Needle.

Climb through the lower cliff band (Class 3). Climb directly up the face above on the north (right) side of a narrow, cracklike couloir (Class 4). Follow a crack system in this section of the face. Proceed into the cracklike couloir (often snow-filled) at 13,000 feet on a lower-angled section of the face. Climb the steep, upper portion of the cracklike couloir (Class 5.8, Steep Snow/Ice). This 500-foot crux couloir requires both snow and rock climbing. The top of the couloir is in the notch between a 13,660-foot summit of some stature and the upper part of Crestone Needle. The climb to the 13,660-foot summit is optional. From the notch, descend northwest and join the South Face Route in its eastern couloir.

19.10 Ellingwood Arête III, Class 5.7 *Classic*
From Lower South Colony Lake: 2.0 miles, 2,550 feet
From South Colony Trailhead: 13.8 to 14.8 miles, 5,470 feet
This is one of the finest technical climbs on Colorado's fourteeners. It has attracted climbers since 1916, when Albert Ellingwood first spied it while descending after his first ascent of Crestone Needle. Ellingwood returned in 1925 to make the first ascent of the route that now carries his

name. Do not confuse the Ellingwood *Arête* on Crestone Needle with the Ellingwood *Ridge* on La Plata Peak.

The Ellingwood Arête ascends the rounded arête between the east-facing and north-facing portions of the needle's northeast face. The 2,000-foot route leads directly to the summit. The lower portion of the route is simple, but the upper, steeper portion looks dubious from below. The sustained nature of the crux pitches so close to the summit sets this route apart.

The excellent nature of Crestone rock also sets this route apart. The conglomerate rock thrusts forth so many pink-colored knobs that sometimes you don't know which one to grab! An occasional hole testifies that the knobs can pull out, but they are generally quite firm. Tiptoeing up the knobs on this exposed route is an ethereal experience.

The route rises directly above Upper South Colony Lake. Hike southwest from the lake to 12,200 feet at the base of the center of the east-facing portion of the face. Scramble up the lower cliff band where the angle of the initial slabs relents (Class 3). Do a long, ascending traverse north (right) on broken, grassy benches to reach the arête (Class 3). The exposure gradually increases as you gain height on this initial, easy section.

Once on the arête, ascend it on steepening, Class 4 rock. There are still plenty of ledges, but steep steps separate them. The exposure continues to increase and the place to rope up on this route is difficult to prescribe. Use *your* judgment.

After 1,500 feet of climbing, you will arrive at the base of the steep upper wall. If forward progress looked dubious from below, it probably will look even worse from here. The upper wall is full of blank faces and overhanging cul-de-sacs. In particular, there is one prominent, smooth slab and, to its south, a giant overhang. The trick is to sneak up between them.

Overcome the initial part of the upper wall by ascending a 200-foot-long chimney system just north (right) of the crest of the arête. There are several chimneys here. Climb either the central or northern one. At the top of the chimneys, climb a left-angling gully to a large ledge on the crest of the arête. Continue up and go left around a corner to another ledge at the base of the famous Head Crack.

The Head Crack pitch is the route's crux. To do it, climb the awkward crack for a few feet, then move right to some small holds (Class 5.7). Continue up and slightly right to the base of a wide crack. Stem the wide crack until you can exit right. The summit is not far above this point, and your arrival there may seem abrupt.

Variation 19.10V

Take a more direct start by climbing a north-facing open book just south of a point below the upper arête (Class 5.3–5.4). This start shortens the climb and replaces some of the Class 3 scrambling with quality, Class 5 pitches. An even harder direct start ascends the wall directly below the arête.

19.11 Arnold–Michel III, Class 5.8, Steep Snow/Ice

From Lower South Colony Lake: 2.2 miles, 2,550 feet

From South Colony Trailhead: 14.0 to 15.0 miles, 5,470 feet

This mixed climb has an alpine flavor. The route ascends the prominent couloir on the north-facing wall on the north side of the Ellingwood Arête. From Upper South Colony Lake, hike west to 12,400 feet at the base of the wall. Climb the rock on the west (right) side of the lower portion of the couloir. Proceed into the couloir near a turn in the couloir and ascend it for several hundred feet. When the couloir narrows and steepens, either climb the couloir directly (difficult) or climb the rock on the right side of the couloir (easier). Higher up, proceed back into the couloir and follow it to the deep, 13,780-foot notch between the Black Gendarme and the ridge leading to Crestone Peak. The Black Gendarme is the highest, most spectacular spire on the ridge connecting Crestone Needle and Crestone Peak. From the notch, descend on the southwest side of the ridge and join the Peak to Needle traverse route (see Combination 19.12).

19. Crestone Peak and Crestone Needle Combinations

See Map 19 on page 148

19.12 II, Class 4 *Classic*

From Lower South Colony Lake: 3.9 miles, 3,250 feet

From South Colony Trailhead: 15.7 to 16.7 miles, 6,170 feet

The traverse of the Crestones is one of Colorado's four great fourteener traverses. People usually climb Crestone Peak and Crestone Needle together from South Colony Lakes. Climbers debate about which peak should be climbed first. There are trade-offs for each direction. Consider the trade-offs, then make a decision that suits *you*.

The most difficult part of the traverse is the 500 feet on the needle's north side. If you climb the needle first, you can rappel the crux, Class 4 pitch below the needle's summit instead of climbing it. This is an advantage for some people. The traverse route is slightly easier to find when going from needle to peak. Because of these facts, some consider the traverse easier when going from needle to peak.

Weigh these advantages against some additional facts. Below the crux pitch is several hundred feet of Class 3 scrambling. It is not convenient to rappel these slabs, and some of this terrain must be downclimbed when going from needle to peak. Going from needle to peak requires you to downclimb the Northwest Couloir Route on the peak late in the day, when the probability of storms is greatest.

Crestone Peak
14,294

Crestone Needle
14,197

1
12

The traverse between Crestone Peak and Crestone Needle.

I prefer to go from peak to needle. I like to climb the peak early in the day and prefer to ascend Class 3 to Class 4 terrain. The needle's South Face Route is a friendlier late-day challenge and it leads directly to camp.

The traverse is described from peak to needle. From Lower South Colony Lake, ascend either the Northwest Couloir Route or the North Buttress Route on Crestone Peak. The traverse looks awesome from the summit of the peak. The key is to stay well below the ridge on its southwest side.

Return to the 14,180-foot red notch between Crestone Peak's main summit and east summit. Descend the south-facing couloir below the notch for 300 feet. This is the top of Crestone Peak's South Face Route. Exit the couloir and scramble southeast on broken terrain. Go around a corner and descend a ledge system under a steep buttress. Pass below the 13,740-foot saddle between Crestone Peak and Crestone Needle. There is a 13,940-foot summit between the saddle and the needle. Go well below this summit on a good ledge system on the south side of the ridge. The traverse to this point includes a lot of Class 3 scrambling.

The final, steep climb to the needle is visible during most of the traverse. Study it carefully as you approach the needle. There are three gendarmes on the needle's northwest ridge. The traverse route passes under them on the ridge's southwest side. The northernmost gendarme is an impressive tower called the "Black Gendarme."

Cross the couloir below the Black Gendarme 200 feet below the bottom of the gendarme. Scramble up broken, Class 3 rock and cross the

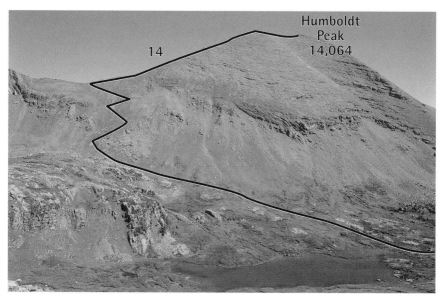

Humboldt Peak from the west.

shallow couloir below the northern end of the central gendarme. Do an ascending traverse across a knob-studded but otherwise smooth slab (Class 3). This slab takes you to the narrow gully below the notch between the central and southern gendarmes. Climb this gully to a point near the ridge crest (Class 3). Traverse around the southernmost gendarme on a ledge and climb another knobby slab leading up to the ridge crest (Class 3). This is an exposed place and the crux pitch is above you.

The Class 4 crux pitch is airy and beautiful. Climb 100 feet of steep, knobby rock directly on the ridge crest. This is Crestone knob climbing at its best. The needle's summit is just beyond the top of the crux pitch. Descend Crestone Needle's South Face Route.

19.13 II, Class 4 *Classic*

From Cottonwood Lake: 2.6 miles, 2,600 feet
From Cottonwood Creek Trailhead: 11.6 miles, 6,500 feet
From Lower South Colony Lake: 3.9 miles, 3,850 feet
From South Colony Trailhead: 15.7 to 16.7 miles, 6,770 feet

The Peak to Needle traverse can be done from Cottonwood Lake. This adds more congenial climbing to the adventure. Climb Crestone Peak's South Face Route, traverse to the needle as described in Combination 19.12 and descend Crestone Needle's South Face Route.

19. Humboldt Peak   14,064 feet

See Map 19 on page 148

Humble Humboldt sits by itself 1.0 mile northeast of South Colony Lakes and 1.8 miles east of Crestone Peak. It is the high point of a long ridge separating the South Colony Creek and North Colony Creek drainages. Humboldt's rugged north side is seldom seen; it is much better known as a shapeless hump that is easy to climb.

From Humboldt's summit and western slopes, there are superb views of the northeast face of Crestone Peak and Crestone Needle. Humboldt is a great place to either nervously preview or triumphantly review Crestone climbs. For those souls who have no intention of ever climbing Crestone Peak or Crestone Needle, Humboldt offers a safe vantage point in the heart of this exclusive place.

Route

19.14 West Ridge II, Class 2

From Lower South Colony Lake: 2.8 miles, 2,400 feet
From South Colony Trailhead: 13.8 miles, 4,560 feet

This is the easiest route on Humboldt. Use the South Colony Lakes Approach. From Lower South Colony Lake, hike northwest to the east side of Upper South Colony Lake. Follow the Colorado Fourteener Initiative trail north as it switchbacks up to Humboldt's west ridge. Reach the ridge just east of the 12,860-foot Humboldt–Crestone Peak Saddle. Climb east on the ridge for 0.7 mile to the summit. The Crestones' majesty will be obvious long before you reach the summit.

19. Challenger Point   14,081 feet

See Map 19 on page 148

Challenger Point is the west summit of Kit Carson Mountain. This summit was officially named Challenger Point in 1987 in memory of the crew of space shuttle *Challenger*. The summit rises more than 300 feet above its connecting saddle with Kit Carson's main summit, but the separation between these two summits is only 400 yards. Challenger Point qualifies as an official fourteener on some lists, but not on others. No matter how you count, Challenger Point is named, and it is above 14,000 feet. Challenger Point's summit is on private property.

Routes

19.15 North Slopes II, Class 2+

From Willow Lake: 2.8 miles, 2,520 feet

From Willow Creek Trailhead: 9.2 miles, 5,220 feet

This is the easiest route on Challenger Point. Use the Willow Lake Approach. Hike around the north side of Willow Lake and proceed onto the benches above the waterfall at the east end of the lake. Climb south for 1.0 mile up a long slope that steepens near its top and involves some Class 2+ scrambling. The slope leads to Challenger Point's northwest ridge. Follow this easy ridge to the summit.

19.16 Kirk Couloir II, Class 2, Steep Snow

From Willow Lake: 3.2 miles, 2,520 feet

From Willow Creek Trailhead: 9.6 miles, 5,220 feet

This superb, early season snow climb is an enticing way to climb Challenger Point. Use the Willow Lake Approach. Hike around the north side of Willow Lake and proceed onto the benches above the waterfall at the east end of the lake. Easily seen from here, the north-facing Kirk Couloir reaches the 13,780-foot Challenger Point–Kit Carson Peak Saddle. The slopes up to 13,000 feet are easy then moderate in steepness, while the couloir's last 800 feet reach 48 degrees. From the saddle, hike west for 0.2 mile to Challenger's summit. From the saddle, you can also continue on Kit Carson's West Ridge Route.

19. Kit Carson Peak   14,165 feet

See Map 19 on page 148

Kit Carson is on the west side of the Sangres, 1.3 miles northwest of Crestone Peak. When you view the Sangres from the San Luis Valley to the west, Kit Carson is more prominent than the Crestones. The Willow Creek drainage is north of Kit Carson, and the Spanish Creek drainage is south of the peak.

Kit Carson Mountain is a large, complex massif with two summits above 14,000 feet and another reaching 13,980 feet. The name Kit Carson *Mountain* applies to all these summits. The name Kit Carson *Peak* applies to just the highest, 14,165-foot summit. Challenger Point is the 14,081-foot west summit of Kit Carson Mountain. Before Challenger Point was officially named, some irreverent souls called this summit "Johnny Carson." Kit Carson Mountain's 13,980-foot east summit carries the nickname "Kat

Challenger Point from the east (photo by Steve Hoffmeyer).

Carson." Kit Carson is a magnificent mountain regardless of the reverence of the appellations.

Serious cliffs guard all sides of Kit Carson's summit. Kit Carson is easier to climb than either Crestone Peak or Crestone Needle, but only because the easiest routes sneak through the cliffs on surprise ledges. Kit Carson supports several fine technical routes, one of which rivals anything on the Crestones. Kit Carson's summit is on private property.

Routes

19.17 East Ridge II, Class 3

From Lower South Colony Lake: 5.8 miles, 3,400 feet
From South Colony Trailhead: 16.8 miles, 5,550 feet
From camp at Spanish Creek: 5.6 miles, 3,900 feet
From Spanish Creek Trailhead: 12.6 miles, 6,650 feet

This is the easiest way to climb Kit Carson from South Colony Lakes, but it is not the easiest route on the peak. You also can approach the East Ridge Route from Spanish Creek. Use either the South Colony Lakes or Spanish Creek Approach.

From Lower South Colony Lake, hike northwest to Upper South Colony Lake and climb a south-facing scree gully to the long ridge connecting Humboldt Peak with Crestone Peak. Scramble west on or below this ridge to the broad 13,140-foot Crestone Peak–Kit Carson Saddle. This open area is called the "Bear's Playground." If you are approaching from Spanish Creek, climb east to the head of Spanish Creek and reach the Bear's Playground from the west.

The Prow on Kit Carson.

Hike northwest across the Bear's Playground and climb to 13,500 feet. Contour west below the summit of Point 13,799 and reach the 13,460-foot saddle between Point 13,799 and Kit Carson's east peak. From this saddle, climb west up steep terrain to the easternmost of two summits that compose Kit Carson's east peak. This summit carries the nickname "Kitty Kat Carson." Continue west to the slightly higher, 13,980-foot "Kat Carson"– the true summit of Kit Carson's east peak. The introduction is over.

Descend steeply west from the summit of Kat Carson on exposed, Class 3 blocks to the 13,620-foot saddle between Kat Carson and Kit Carson's main summit. This descent is the route's crux. From this saddle, climb west on a large ledge, then scramble west up an easy, Class 3 gully to the summit. From the summit, there are spectacular views of Crestone Peak's north side, and you can preview Crestone Peak's Northwest Couloir Route.

Extra Credit 19.17EC

Either coming or going, take the time to climb Point 13,799. This is a significant summit rising 339 feet above its connecting saddle with Kit Carson. Point 13,799 is a "Bi," one of Colorado's 200 highest peaks.

19.18 West Ridge II, Class 3

From Willow Lake: 4.2 miles, 3,600 feet

From Willow Creek Trailhead: 11.6 miles, 6,300 feet

This is the easiest route on Kit Carson. This unique tour also allows you to climb Challenger Point. Use the Willow Lake Approach. Hike around the north side of Willow Lake and proceed onto the benches above the waterfall at the east end of the lake. Climb south for 1.0 mile up a long, steep slope to Challenger Point (Kit Carson's west peak). This slope steepens near its top and involves some Class 2+ scrambling.

From the summit of Challenger Point (14,081 feet), you are only 400 yards from Kit Carson's summit, but the fun has just begun. Descend east from Challenger Point to the 13,780-foot Challenger Point–Kit Carson Peak Saddle. From the saddle, do an ascending traverse south on a large ledge called "Kit Carson Avenue." Continue on the ledge, go around a corner and cross a tiny, 13,940-foot saddle between the top of the Prow (Kit Carson's south ridge) and Kit Carson's upper cliffs.

Do a descending traverse east on the continuing Kit Carson Avenue ledge (Class 2+). This large, remarkable ledge system is the key to this route. Avoid any temptation to leave Kit Carson Avenue too soon and head for the summit. Follow the ledge down until you are east of the summit, then scramble west up an easy, Class 3 gully to the summit. This is the finish used by the East Ridge Route.

19.19 North Ridge II, Class 4 *Classic*

From Willow Lake: 4.0 miles, 2,600 feet

From Willow Creek Trailhead: 11.4 miles, 5,300 feet

This remarkable climb is easier than it looks. The route ascends Kit Carson's 1,500-foot-high north ridge directly to the summit. Use the Willow Lake Approach. Go around the north side of Willow Lake and hike southeast up the valley for 1.0 mile to the bottom of the north ridge at 12,600 feet. The solid ridge averages 45 degrees. The climbing is mostly Class 3, punctuated by some Class 4 sections.

19.20 Outward Bound Couloir II, Class 3, Steep Snow/Ice

From Willow Lake: 4.2 miles, 2,600 feet

From Willow Creek Trailhead: 11.6 miles, 5,300 feet

This is an interesting mixed climb. Use the Willow Lake Approach. Go around the north side of Willow Lake and hike southeast up the valley for 1.0 mile. The Outward Bound Couloir is the deep couloir east of Kit Carson's north ridge, and it leads directly to the 13,620-foot saddle between the east summit ("Kat Carson") and Kit Carson's main summit. The couloir gradually steepens and becomes more inset as you approach the saddle.

Near the saddle, take the eastern (left) branch of the couloir. This deeply inset, north-facing couloir is often icy. Ice axes and crampons are recommended for this route. From the 13,620-foot saddle, climb west on a large ledge then scramble west up an easy, Class 3 gully to the summit. This is the finish used by both the East Ridge and West Ridge Routes.

19.21 South Couloir II, Class 3, Moderate Snow (Seasonal)

From camp at Spanish Creek: 4.0 miles, 3,150 feet

From Spanish Creek Trailhead: 11.0 miles, 5,900 feet

This is a direct way to climb Kit Carson from Spanish Creek. When snow conditions are good, this couloir can provide a speedy descent route. Use the Spanish Creek Approach, hike east to 11,800 feet in upper Spanish Creek, turn north and ascend the couloir. The south couloir is the deep couloir east of the Prow (Kit Carson's sweeping south ridge). The couloir leads directly to the 13,620-foot saddle between Kit Carson's east and main summits. From the saddle, climb west on a large ledge then scramble west up the famous Class 3 gully to the summit.

19.22 The Prow III, Class 5.8 *Classic*

From camp at Spanish Creek: 3.4 miles, 3,350 feet

From Spanish Creek Trailhead: 10.4 miles, 6,100 feet

This is the ultimate Crestone knob climb. Use the Spanish Creek Approach and hike east to 11,800 feet in upper Spanish Creek. The unmistakable Prow will have been visible to you for some time. Scramble up gentle slabs on the Prow's lower, east side and proceed onto the ridge. Consider your future, because the commitment begins abruptly.

The bottom of the Prow is a serious overhang, and the climb starts with its hardest move. Do a gymnastic, Class 5.8 move to overcome the overhang. The rest of the first pitch is Class 5.6 and it angles slightly right to dodge a bulge. The second pitch is Class 5.6 and completes the bulge dodge. The first two pitches are on the east (right) side of the edge of the Prow.

The third pitch is Class 5.5 and ends on the now well formed edge of the Prow. The nature of this climb is abundantly clear at this point. Escape and protection are difficult. There is tremendous exposure in every direction, and the commitment increases with every pitch. Climb the narrow edge as it arcs into the sky. You have no choice!

The numerous upper pitches average Class 5.3–5.4 in difficulty. Just when you think the angle might ease, the elegant edge sweeps up again and the climb continues. With each pitch, it becomes clearer that the best escape is to complete the climb. When you reach the top of the Prow—a small, 13,980-foot summit—scramble north to the "Kit Carson Avenue" ledge of West Ridge fame. Escape is possible from here, but this is not the summit. There is more. Descend north on Kit Carson Avenue

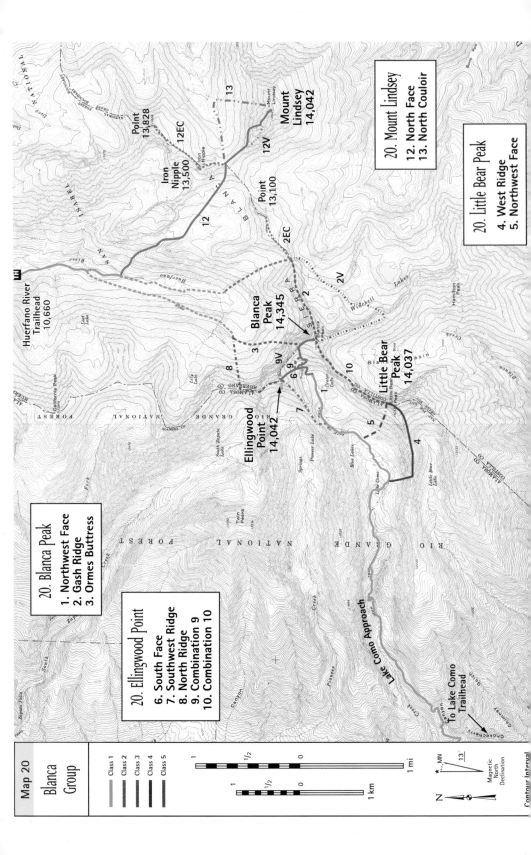

Map 20

Blanca
Group

Class 1
Class 2
Class 3
Class 4
Class 5

1 ½ 0 1 mi
1 ½ 0 1 km

N

MN
13°
Magnetic North
Declination

Contour Interval

20. Blanca Peak
1. Northwest Face
2. Gash Ridge
3. Ormes Buttress

20. Ellingwood Point
6. South Face
7. Southwest Ridge
8. North Ridge
9. Combination 9
10. Combination 10

20. Mount Lindsey
12. North Face
13. North Couloir

20. Little Bear Peak
4. West Ridge
5. Northwest Face

Huerfano River
Trailhead
10,660

Point 13,828

Iron Nipple 13,500

Mount Lindsey
14,042

Point 13,100

Blanca Peak
14,345

Ellingwood
Point
14,042

Little Bear
Peak
14,037

To Lake Como
Trailhead

Lake Como Approach

under the summit pyramid's west wall to the 13,780-foot Challenger Point–Kit Carson Saddle. Scramble up, then climb a long, Class 5.3–5.4 pitch into the center of the northwest wall of Kit Carson's summit pyramid. Finish this exercise in clairvoyance with a long, right-angling, Class 5.5 pitch on the upper wall. There is a sequence of delectable, Class 5.5 moves a few feet below the summit cairn.

Variation 19.22V

Instead of climbing the Class 5.8 overhang at the bottom of the Prow, climb easier slabs 200 yards east (right) of this direct start. Reach the edge of the Prow higher up.

20. Blanca Group

Blanca Peak	14,345 feet
Little Bear Peak	14,037 feet
Ellingwood Point	14,042 feet
Mount Lindsey	14,042 feet

See Map 20 on page 168

These magnificent peaks are 10 miles north of Fort Garland on U.S. 160. They leap from the surrounding flatness even more than the Crestone Group. The Sangre de Cristo Range takes a break south of these peaks as if to honor them. You can see these peaks for long distances while driving on U.S. 285, U.S. 160 or Colorado 159.

Maps

Required: Blanca Peak, Twin Peaks, Rio Grande National Forest
Optional: Mosca Pass, San Isabel National Forest

Trailheads

Lake Como Trailhead

This trailhead is at 8,000 feet and provides access to the west sides of Blanca Peak, Ellingwood Point and Little Bear. This is one of Colorado's lowest trailheads. From the U.S. 160–Colorado 150 junction, go north on Colorado 150 for 3.2 miles to an unmarked dirt road leading northeast. Follow this dirt road northeast straight toward the Blanca massif for 1.8 miles to 8,000 feet. Park here; the road beyond becomes exceedingly rough. It is prohibitive for passenger cars. The four-wheel-drive road to Lake Como, 5.0 miles farther at 11,740 feet, is nationally known as Colorado's toughest road.

Huerfano River Trailhead

This trailhead is at 10,660 feet and provides access to Mount Lindsey and the northeast faces of Blanca Peak and Ellingwood Point. *Huerfano* means "orphan boy" in Spanish; as you travel to this trailhead, you will appreciate this appropriate name. Take Exit 52 from Interstate 25 north of Walsenburg and go 0.3 mile south toward Walsenburg. Turn west onto Colorado 69, go 25.1 miles to Gardner and continue for an additional 0.7 mile to the far side of town. Turn west onto the Redwing spur of Colorado 69 (paved) and measure from this point. Go straight at 5.1 miles, continue on the dirt road at 6.9 miles and go straight at 7.1 miles. Do not turn left into Redwing. Turn left at a Y-junction at 12.0 miles and reach the entrance to the Singing River Ranch after 16.0 miles. The road is plowed to this point in winter.

Public access is allowed from the Singing River Ranch to the San Isabel National Forest. Do not camp on the private land you are traveling through. The road becomes rougher at the Singing River Ranch but is still passable for most passenger cars. Pass the entrance to the Aspen River Ranch after 16.9 miles, pass a distant view of Blanca Peak at 19.4 miles and reach the boundary of San Isabel National Forest after 20.4 miles. The road becomes rougher at this point but is still passable for some passenger vehicles. Reach the end of the road and the trailhead after 22.3 miles. The last mile to the trailhead is steep and may challenge low-power, low-clearance vehicles. The trailhead is at the south end of a hanging meadow above the Huerfano River; there is a good view of Blanca's northeast face from the meadow. Mount Lindsey is not visible from the trailhead.

An alternative approach to this trailhead goes 1.9 miles west of North La Veta Pass on U.S. 160, then north on Pass Creek Road (dirt) for 12.3 miles to join the route just described 2.0 miles east of the Redwing turn.

Approach

20.A1 Lake Como Approach

From Lake Como Trailhead: 10.6 miles, 3,900 feet

This is the standard approach to Blanca Peak, Little Bear and Ellingwood Point. Start at the Lake Como Trailhead. It is 5.0 tough miles from the 8,000-foot level to Lake Como. Go up the rough, four-wheel-drive road as it switchbacks toward the heights still far away. The first miles can be brutally hot in summer. The steep road climbs along Chokecherry Canyon, then angles northeast into Holbrook Creek, which it follows to Lake Como at 11,740 feet. Lake Como is on private property. Hike around the north side of the lake and continue 0.2 mile east to some camping spots on the bench above the lake at 11,900 feet. Little Bear is less than a mile east of this spot, and its imposing northwest face dominates the view.

20. Blanca Peak 14,345 feet

See Map 20 on page 168

Mighty Blanca carries many accolades. Blanca is Colorado's fourth highest peak, the highest peak in Colorado outside the Sawatch Range, the highest peak in the Sangre de Cristo Range and the highest peak in Alamosa, Costilla and Huerfano Counties. Take a fresh breath. If you traveled south from Blanca, you would have to go all the way to the high volcanoes in central Mexico to find a higher peak. Blanca is one of the Navajo's four sacred peaks. Blanca is the highest peak in Colorado with a technical route on it; its northeast face is one of Colorado's finest mountain walls. Soaring 7,000 feet above its valleys, Blanca carries its honors well. Climb it.

Routes

20.1 Northwest Face III, Class 2

From Lake Como: 4.0 miles, 2,500 feet

From Lake Como Trailhead: 14.6 miles, 6,350 feet

This is the easiest route on Blanca. Because of the low trailhead, people usually do it with a backpack and camp. Start at the Lake Como Trailhead and follow the Lake Como Approach to the camping area east of Lake Como. Still on the four-wheel-drive road, climb east up the valley for 0.5 mile to Blue Lakes. There are more camping spots near Blue Lakes at 12,100 feet. When the seemingly ceaseless road finally dies, continue up the valley on a good trail for an additional 0.5 mile to a point east of (beyond) Crater Lake at 12,900 feet. The connecting ridge between Blanca Peak and Ellingwood Point is at the top of the basin northeast (ahead) of you. Blanca is at the ridge's south end and Ellingwood Point is at the north end.

Zigzag east on trail segments up a section of broken cliffs, then ascend talus to reach Blanca's north ridge at 13,800 feet. There are spectacular views down Blanca's northeast face from the ridge, but the ridge itself is not exposed if you stay away from the edge. Follow the ridge south to Blanca's lofty summit.

20.2 Gash Ridge III, Class 5.0–5.2

From Huerfano River Trailhead: 8.6 miles, 4,000 feet

Gash Ridge is Blanca's dramatic east ridge. This ridge's classic sweep is interrupted only by its namesake gash near the bottom. This aesthetic and exciting ridge is well seen from Lindsey and the Huerfano Valley. This climb is more committing than its Class rating indicates, because retreat and escape are both difficult. This is a route on which to exercise your craft as a mountaineer, not learn it.

Blanca Peak from the north.

Start at the Huerfano River Trailhead. Walk south on the Lily Lake Trail along the west side of the Huerfano River for 1.1 miles to a trail junction at 10,720 feet, where the Lily Lake Trail heads steeply up to the west. Leave the Lily Lake Trail and continue south on the trail in the valley bottom for an additional 1.3 miles to 10,960 feet. Blanca's sweeping northeast face soars above you, and this is one of Colorado's finest places. Gash Ridge marks the east (left) boundary of this great face. Leave the comfortable valley bottom and climb steeply southeast into a small, hanging side-valley. Continue up this drainage to the 12,580-foot saddle between Blanca and Point 13,081, which is 1.3 miles northeast of Blanca. Climb west up the initially rounded ridge to Point 13,380 and gaze across the gash to the upper ridge. The introduction is over.

The difficulty increases as you descend west for 0.15 mile into the gash, and you might choose to rappel over some drops. From the 13,020-foot saddle that is the gash, start your ascent of the upper ridge. The ridge averages 30 degrees as it gains 1,325 feet in 0.45 mile. The drops on either side of the ridge are considerably steeper, and the exposure on this climb is unrelenting. The climbing is Class 4 interspersed with Class 5.0–5.2 cruxes. Take care to find the easiest route, because more difficult climbing is never far away. The summit may surprise you.

Variation 20.2V

This important variation avoids Gash Ridge and provides the easiest route on Blanca from the Huerfano Valley. It is the easiest way to combine ascents of Blanca and Lindsey. From the 12,580-foot saddle between Blanca and Point 13,081, descend south to 12,000 feet. Contour southwest, then climb to the northernmost of the two Winchell Lakes at 12,740 feet. Go around the east end of the lake, climb west and ascend a Class 4 ramp to Blanca's south ridge. Climb north on this ridge for 0.7 mile to the summit.

Extra Credit 20.2EC

If climbing Gash Ridge is not enough, climb 0.5 mile northeast from the 12,580-foot saddle between Blanca and Point 13,081 to reach Point 13,081. This rough little peak provides a great view of Gash Ridge and Blanca's northeast face, and holds other surprises. A second summit 400 feet to the northeast is a little higher and is the summit of the peak. This is really Point 13,100.

20.3 Ormes Buttress III, Class 5.6 *Classic*

From Huerfano River Trailhead: 7.6 miles, 3,700 feet

After J. Alexander made the first ascent of his namesake Alexander's Chimney on the east face of Longs Peak in 1922, and Albert Ellingwood made the first ascent of his namesake Ellingwood Arête on Crestone Needle in 1925, the hunt was on for other great Colorado rock faces. A banner year was 1927; Paul and Joe Stettner returned to Longs and climbed their namesake Stettner's Ledges while Robert Ormes made the first ascent of Blanca's more evasive northeast face. Blanca's northeast face is one of Colorado's largest mountain walls, but it is not easily seen from roads. Any view from civilization is a distant one, and this wall's majesty is reserved for those who hike up the Huerfano Valley. Ormes, a true pioneer, had a good eye for the natural line and his route remains the classic and easiest way up Blanca's nordwand.

Start at the Huerfano River Trailhead. Walk south on the Lily Lake Trail along the west side of the Huerfano River for 1.1 miles to a trail junction at 10,720 feet, where the Lily Lake Trail heads steeply up to the west. Leave the valley trail and continue on the Lily Lake Trail for an additional 1.6 miles to a switchback at 11,600 feet. This is the trail's closest approach to the face, and there are good campsites nestled in the trees nearby. Leave the trail and hike southeast and south for 0.4 mile to the base of the face at 12,400 feet. The approach is over.

The Ormes Buttress is a now easily seen buttress 700 feet northwest (right) of the center of Blanca's northeast face. It provides the only major break in this mile-wide face. Climb it! The lower part of the buttress is Class 4 climbing on loose rock. The rock becomes more solid as you climb higher. Several Class 5 pitches, including a Class 5.6 crux, take you up the great wall. Stay on or left of the crest. A helmet is highly recommended for this climb. Leaders, remember to protect your belayer.

The buttress reaches Blanca's north ridge at 13,900 feet. For a true mountaineer, the summit is never off-route. In the spirit of Ormes, hike south to Blanca's highest point.

20. Little Bear Peak   14,037 feet

See Map 20 on page 168

Little Bear is 1 mile southwest of Blanca and separated from its higher neighbor by a rough ridge. There is nothing little about Little Bear. This peak is steep on all sides and is one of Colorado's toughest fourteeners. The old approach from the south into Blanca Basin is on private property and has not been used in recent years. The Lake Como Approach is the only reliable approach.

Routes
20.4 West Ridge III, Class 4
From Lake Como: 2.2 miles, 2,150 feet
From Lake Como Trailhead: 12.8 miles, 6,050 feet

This is the most frequently climbed route on Little Bear, but it is not Little Bear's easiest route. The easiest route—from Arrowhead Ranch, to the south—is not open to the public. The West Ridge Route is short and sweet. It is also one of the most dangerous routes in this book. Loose rocks abound on the rounded ledges on the upper part of the route, and large parties can turn it into a deadly shooting gallery. I think the "Hourglass" (see below) is the most dangerous spot on any of the standard routes on Colorado's fourteeners. This route is particularly dangerous when crowds arrive on three-day holiday weekends. Climb during the week, wear a helmet and start early.

Use the Lake Como Approach. From the east side of Lake Como, Little Bear is only 1 mile away, and the challenge is obvious. Little Bear's west ridge forms the wall south of Lake Como, and the connecting ridge between Little Bear and Blanca is east of the lake. These two ridges cap a single face—Little Bear's northwest face. This face is most imposing directly under Little Bear's summit.

From the campsites at 11,900 feet east of Lake Como, look straight south to see a steep, north-facing gully leading to a distinctive notch in the lower part of Little Bear's west ridge. This gully often retains some snow through July. Climb this loose-scree or snow gully into the 12,580-

foot notch. From the notch, go east on the ridge crest to Point 12,980. You can see the rest of the route from here. Little Bear's west ridge steepens dramatically beyond Point 12,980, and the route avoids these difficulties by ascending the obvious, deep gully in the center of the small face south (right) of Little Bear's west ridge.

From Point 12,980, descend to the 12,900-foot saddle between Point 12,980 and Little Bear. From the saddle, leave the west ridge and follow a climber's trail that climbs east into the center of Little Bear's small, southwest face. The trail takes you to the base of the Hourglass—an obvious, deep gully.

After an initial 100 feet of Class 3 scrambling, ascend the steep, water-polished, Class 4 rock in the gully for 150 feet. This long pitch is the route's crux, and there is usually a sling rappel anchor at its top. If it has rained the afternoon or night before your climb, there may be water running down the center of the gully to complicate your ascent. If so, climb the rock 10 to 15 feet north (left) of the gully's center.

Above the Class 4 pitch, the angle and difficulty ease, but your responsibility increases. Any rocks knocked loose during your final climb will funnel down into the Class 4 gully. Finish the ascent with several hundred feet of Class 3 scrambling up steep sections between rubble-covered ledges. Angle slightly north (left) and arrive directly on the coveted summit.

20.5 Northwest Face III, Class 4 *Classic*

From Lake Como: 2.0 miles, 2,150 feet

From Lake Como Trailhead: 12.2 miles, 6,050 feet

This climb flirts with the major difficulties of Little Bear's imposing northwest face but avoids them at the last minute. Use the Lake Como Approach. From the campsites at 11,900 feet east of Lake Como, go straight east for 0.3 mile. Before you reach Blue Lakes, leave the road and choose your line for climbing the sweeping, ever steepening slabs of Little Bear's northwest face. Aim for the first small, rounded notch in the ridge northeast (left) of Little Bear's summit. After an initial Class 4 headwall near some black water marks, several hundred feet of enjoyable Class 3 scrambling will take you to a steeper headwall below the ridge. This headwall is north (left) of the more serious face directly under Little Bear's summit.

Choose your line carefully and continue your climb. The headwall requires 400 feet of Class 4 climbing. The steepest, most exposed and most difficult moves are just below the ridge. From the ridge, climb south up the elegant, exposed, Class 4 ridge for 300 yards to the summit. Ascending this route and descending the West Ridge Route makes a stunning Tour de Little Bear.

Little Bear Peak from Lake Como.

20. Ellingwood Point   14,042 feet

See Map 20 on page 168

Ellingwood Point is 0.5 mile northwest of Blanca, and this summit rests in the shadow of its higher neighbor's splendor. Ellingwood Point's sanctity as an official fourteener has been questioned for years, and the summit was only recently named. Ellingwood Point rises 342 feet above its connecting saddle with Blanca and has 0.5 mile of separation. Although the shapely peak does not have a lot of power, it is named, and it is above 14,000 feet. Together with Blanca, it crowns an amazing northeast face above the Huerfano Valley.

Routes
20.6 South Face III, Class 2
From Lake Como: 4.0 miles, 2,200 feet
From Lake Como Trailhead: 14.6 miles, 6,050 feet

This is the easiest route on Ellingwood Point. Use the Lake Como Approach and follow Blanca's Northwest Face Route to 13,300 feet. From here, climb northeast then northwest up steep talus for 0.5 mile to the pointed summit.

Ellingwood Point
14,042

Ellingwood Point from the north.

20.7 Southwest Ridge III, Class 3 *Classic*

From Lake Como: 3.4 miles, 2,200 feet

From Lake Como Trailhead: 14.0 miles, 6,050 feet

This is a nifty alternative to the talus on Ellingwood's southwest face. Follow the Southwest Face Route to a tiny lake at 12,540 feet. This lake is near the junction between the Twin Peaks and Blanca Peak Quadrangles but does not appear on either map. From the lake, angle up a ledge system (some Class 3) to reach Ellingwood's southwest ridge at 12,940 feet.

The ascent of this elegant ridge is pure fun. The rock is solid, the Class 3 scrambling is continuous, the motion is fluid and there are no nasty notches or other surprises on the ridge. Follow one of Colorado's finest ridges for 0.7 mile to the summit. Ascending the southwest ridge and descending the south face makes a sporting Tour de Ellingwood. Ellingwood's southwest ridge is a good tune-up for the Little Bear–Blanca traverse (see Combination 20.10).

20.8 North Ridge II, Class 5.0–5.2

From Huerfano River Trailhead: 8.0 miles, 3,400 feet

This obtuse route is only for exposure-hardened scramblers. For the initiated, it provides a wild and shorter alternative to the crowded Lake Como routes. Start at the Huerfano River Trailhead. Walk south on the Lily Lake Trail along the west side of the Huerfano River for 1.1 miles to a trail junction at 10,720 feet, where the Lily Lake Trail heads steeply up to the west. Leave the valley trail and continue on the Lily Lake Trail for an additional 1.6 miles to a switchback at 11,600 feet. This is the trail's closest approach to Ellingwood, and there are good campsites nestled in the trees nearby.

Leave the trail and hike east for 0.4 mile to 12,600 feet, below a broken rock wall 300 yards north of the base of Ellingwood's north face. Climb this 600-foot wall (Class 5.0–5.2) to the 13,220-foot saddle between Ellingwood Point and Point 13,618, which is 0.65 mile north of Ellingwood. From the saddle, climb south for 0.2 mile, then southeast for 0.25 mile to the summit (Class 5.0–5.2). This ridge is tricky. Climb on the west (right) side of the ridge to avoid difficulties. The last 150 yards to the summit is the crux section of the route. Judicious Class 5.0–5.2 climbing below the ridge crest on the exposed face to the west will take you to the highest point.

20. Blanca, Little Bear and Ellingwood Combinations

See Map 20 on page 168

20.9 III, Class 2
From Lake Como: 4.5 miles, 3,000 feet
From Lake Como Trailhead: 15.1 miles, 6,900 feet

This is the standard way of climbing Blanca and Ellingwood together. Follow Blanca's Northwest Face Route to Blanca's summit. Descend Blanca's north ridge to 13,800 feet then descend west below the ridge to 13,500 feet. Contour north on the talus below the cliffs on the connecting ridge, join Ellingwood's South Face Route and continue on that route to Ellingwood's summit. Descend Ellingwood's South Face Route.

Variation 20.9V

There is a high traverse near, but not quite on, the connecting ridge between Blanca and Ellingwood. Follow a cairned route that contours through the rocks 100 feet below the ridge crest on the ridge's west side. Some Class 3 scrambling is required.

20.10 III, Class 5.0–5.2 *Classic*
From Lake Como: 4.1 miles, 2,900 feet
From Lake Como Trailhead: 14.7 miles, 6,800 feet

The traverse between Little Bear and Blanca is one of Colorado's four great fourteener traverses. It is the most difficult of the four. Simply put, this is Colorado's most astonishing connecting ridge. Escape from this doubly exposed ridge is difficult, and this ridge is an unhappy place to be during a storm. Choose your weather carefully before attempting this traverse. Time spent on the ridge varies from two to eight hours. The traverse is best done from Little Bear to Blanca.

Use the Lake Como Approach and ascend Little Bear's West Ridge Route to Little Bear's summit. Look at Blanca 1 mile away and consider your future. If you like what you see, descend north down a solid, exposed ridge for 300 yards (Class 4). This initial stretch of ridge is a tricky downclimb and is one of the traverse's cruxes. Continue northeast along the crest of the incredibly exposed ridge. The movement is often awkward, because you must climb directly along the ridge crest—there are seldom any alternatives. There is a great deal of Class 3 scrambling, a lot of Class 4 climbing and some Class 5.0–5.2 moves. The protection offered by using a rope on this ridge is marginal, and it will slow your progress drastically.

One-quarter of the way along the ridge, you come to a square, 30-foot-high tower on the ridge that blocks easy passage. You can easily see this tower from the vicinity of Blue Lakes in the valley below, and it is a good landmark to mark your progress. Although you have stayed on the ridge crest to this point, you should pass this tower on its west (left) side via a short, exposed, Class 4 traverse. This tower has been dubbed "Captain Bivwacko Tower," because those who climb to its summit are more likely to bivouac. Beyond Captain Bivwacko Tower, scramble back to the ridge crest and continue on or very near the still very exposed ridge crest over several more rolling summits. Slowly, the difficulty relents and you can increase your speed.

Near the halfway point, you will pass the 13,660-foot Little Bear–Blanca Saddle. Beyond this saddle, the exposure eases. Two-thirds of the way across, a large gendarme (Point 13,860) blocks easy progress along the ridge crest. Bypass Point 13,860 via an easy scree slope on its south (right) side and climb into a deep notch on the ridge crest via a loose gully. The north side of this notch is a horrific chimney that you can see from Crater Lake. The only easy escape off this ridge is south from this notch, but this escape creates other problems, because it leaves you in Blanca Basin, far from your camp.

From the notch east of Point 13,860, climb along the now easier ridge crest to yet another incredibly exposed knife-edge. Creep across this scary but solid ridge, cross a final subsummit and notch, then climb an easier but still steep ridge to Blanca's summit. Descend Blanca's Northwest Face Route.

20.11 III, Class 5.0–5.2

From Lake Como: 5.0 miles, 3,400 feet

From Lake Como Trailhead: 15.6 miles, 7,300 feet

This traverse is for the insatiable peak bagger; it collects Little Bear, Blanca and Ellingwood Point in one swell foop. Do the traverse from Little

Bear to Blanca as described in Combination 20.10, then continue to Ellingwood as described in Combination 20.9.

20. Mount Lindsey 14,042 feet

See Map 20 on page 168

Overshadowed by Blanca and Ellingwood, Lindsey rests quietly by itself 2.5 miles east of Blanca. The solitary Lindsey is best seen from U.S. 160 to the south. Lindsey's southern slopes and summit are on private property, and southern approaches are not available to the public. Only the traditional routes from the San Isabel National Forest north of Lindsey are described.

Routes

20.12 North Face II, Class 2+

From Huerfano River Trailhead: 7.8 miles, 3,400 feet

This is not the easiest route on Lindsey, but it is the easiest route available to the public. It has been the standard route for many years, and it is a rewarding, scenic tour. Start at the Huerfano River Trailhead and walk south on the Lily Lake Trail on the west side of the Huerfano River for 1.1 miles to a trail junction at 10,720 feet, where the Lily Lake Trail heads steeply up to the west. Do not take the Lily Lake Trail up the hill to the west but continue south on the trail in the valley bottom for an additional 0.2 mile to a point where the trail comes close to the Huerfano River at 10,760 feet. Look for cairns that mark a developing climber's trail heading east. Leave the valley trail and cross to the east side of the Huerfano River. This crossing can be difficult in June but is easy in August. Once across the river, find a strong climber's trail in the trees. Go south on this trail along the river's east side for 0.1 mile.

Continue on the climber's trail as it leaves the Huerfano River Valley and climbs steeply along the right side of a talus field into a small side valley west of Points 12,410 and 12,915. Cross the unnamed creek in this side valley and enter a small but beautiful basin at 12,000 feet. There is a spectacular view of Blanca's northeast face from here. You can just see Lindsey's summit pyramid poking above an intermediate, west-facing ridge. Continue on the climber's trail southeast across the basin and ascend a grassy ramp to meet the west ridge at 13,000 feet. Climb 200 yards east up this ridge to reach Lindsey's northwest ridge at 13,160 feet. Lindsey's upper slopes are plainly visible from here.

Go along Lindsey's northwest ridge until the ridge steepens, then follow a strong climber's trail that angles into Lindsey's north face. Climb a steep, rubble-filled chute (Class 2+) or the rock to the north (right) of the chute (Class 3) to a tiny col, then continue doing a long, ascending traverse

Mount Lindsey from the north.

across the broken face (Class 2+). The route is steep and loose, and there is occasional exposure. Reach the crest of the northwest ridge 200 yards from the summit and follow the easy, upper ridge to the summit.

Variation 20.12V

From 13,160 feet, follow the crest of the northwest ridge all the way to the summit. The ridge crest requires some exposed, Class 3 scrambling on surprisingly solid rock. This airy alternative avoids the north face's loose rock. Comparing this ridge with the north face provides a good example of the difference between Class 2+ and Class 3 climbing. This comparison is also a good example of how a solid but harder route can be preferable to a looser, easier route.

Extra Credit 20.12EC

From 13,160 feet on Lindsey's northwest ridge, climb north for 0.2 mile to the Iron Nipple's 13,500-foot summit (Class 2+). For even more extra fun, traverse northeast for an additional 0.6 mile to Point 13,828, one of Colorado's 100 highest peaks.

20.13 North Couloir II, Class 2, Moderate Snow (Seasonal)

From Huerfano River Trailhead: 7.2 miles, 5,420 feet
With descent of North Face: 6.6 miles, 4,460 feet

This couloir provides an isolated spring snow climb. In most years, the couloir retains snow through June. It is best avoided after the snow melts. Follow the North Face Route to Lindsey's northwest ridge at 13,160 feet. Descend east for 0.7 mile to the bottom of the couloir at 12,200 feet. Climb south up the easy then moderate couloir for 0.7 mile directly to the summit. Ascending the North Couloir Route and descending the North Face Route provides a simple Tour de Lindsey.

21. Culebra Peak   14,047 feet

See Map 21 on page 184

Culebra is Colorado's southernmost fourteener. The peak hides in the southern end of the Sangres only 9 miles from the New Mexico border. *Culebra* means "harmless snake" in Spanish; perhaps the peak acquired this name because of its gentle nature and long, curving, snakelike northwest ridge. This ridge is Culebra's distinguishing feature, and you can see it from Colorado 159 near the town of San Luis.

All of Culebra is privately owned. There is no public land near Culebra, and the peak is not covered on any national forest map. As a result, the choice of routes has been limited to one in recent years. Culebra climbers should respect the landowner's wishes lest one choice become zero choices. The allowed access is through the Taylor Ranch west of the peak.

The Taylor Ranch allows climbing seven days a week during June, July and August. The ranch closes to climbers on September 1, when preparations for hunting season begin. The ranch is closed in winter. Reservations are not required, but you must call the ranch foreman at (719) 672-3580 to make arrangements. The ranch is open from 7 A.M. to 8 P.M. The ranch does not set a limit to party size, but they do like to know how many people are in each party. The charge for climbing Culebra is $40 per adult. Children under 12 are admitted for $20. Nonclimbers can stay at the campsites for free. Dogs are allowed. Unless the road is too muddy, you will be allowed to drive a four-wheel-drive vehicle above the ranch, and this can vastly reduce the length of your climb. Camping is allowed on the peak above the ranch.

Climbers who don't like to pay a fee for climbing should consider that the ranch has invested a lot of money in road improvements in recent years, something the Forest Service rarely does. If you have suffered on the South Colony or Lake Como roads, you will find the Taylor Ranch roads refreshingly smooth. Almost half of your climbing fee is used to compensate the ranch for their road improvements to Fourway and beyond. If you walk or drive on this road, you are using what you paid for. Any attempt to subvert the ranch's rules can quickly double your fee, or worse, and will only hurt the climbing community. Remember that you are a guest.

Maps
Required: Culebra Peak, El Valle Creek
Optional: Taylor Ranch

Trailhead
Taylor Ranch Trailhead
This trailhead is at 9,240 feet and provides access to Culebra's west side. From the center of San Luis on Colorado 159, go southeast on road P.6 (Fourth Street) and measure from this point. Go straight at 2.5 miles when P.6 crosses road 21. There is a stop sign at this intersection. Turn north (left) at 4.2 miles onto road L.7 at a T-junction in Chama. Turn east (right) onto road 22.3 at 4.5 miles and cross Culebra Creek. Turn north (left) onto road M.5 at 4.7 miles. Follow road M.5 as it curves east and turns to dirt, and reach the two Taylor Ranch gates at 8.8 miles. The southern gate should be open between 7 A.M. and 8 P.M. Go through the southern gate and continue south and finally east to the ranch buildings at 10.7 miles. Check in with ranch personnel, sign a waiver and pay the required fees here.

From the ranch, continue east and stay south (right) at 11.0 miles at a junction where the Whiskey Pass Road goes north. At 11.2 miles, reach a large meadow on the road's south side. This is the trailhead for passenger cars, and camping is permitted here.

The road beyond the trailhead is in good shape but is very steep. It defeats many, but not all, passenger cars. The ranch closes the road when it is muddy. From the trailhead at 9,240 feet, four-wheel-drive vehicles can continue east up the steep road for an additional 3.0 miles to a road junction called "Fourway" at 11,220 feet. Camping is permitted here, but bring your own water. From Fourway, four-wheel-drive vehicles can continue for an additional 1.0 mile to a parking area at the end of the road at 11,700 feet. Camping is permitted here near a small stream.

Route
21.1 Northwest Ridge II, Class 2
From Taylor Ranch Trailhead: 13.0 miles, 4,810 feet
From Fourway: 7.0 miles, 2,830 feet
From road's end: 5.0 miles, 2,350 feet
This is Culebra's long, distinguishing, snakelike ridge. People sometimes malign the ridge because of its length. Taking a more distant view in either time or distance, you can view the ridge curving gracefully toward its source, Culebra's summit.

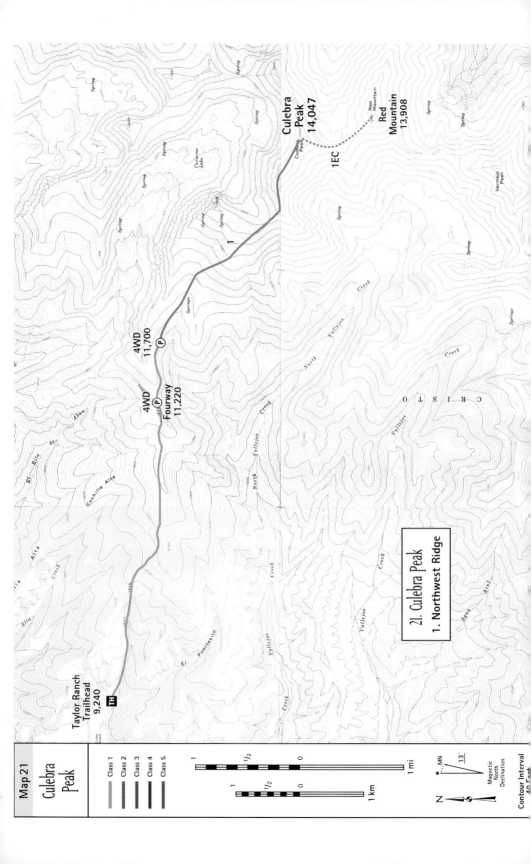

Map 21

Culebra Peak

Class 1
Class 2
Class 3
Class 4
Class 5

1   1/2   0   1 mi

1   1/2   0   1 km

MN
13°
Magnetic
North
Declination

N

Contour Interval

Taylor Ranch
Trailhead
9,240

4WD
11,700

4WD
Fourway
11,220

Culebra
Peak
14,047

1EC

Red
Mountain
13,908

Red
Mountain

Culebra
Peak

Vermejo
Peak

CRISTO

North Vallejos Creek

Vallejos Creek

Vallejos Creek

El Poentesito

Cuchilla Alta

Alta

El Rito de la Abac.

Alta Creek

Agua Azul

Carnurro
Lake

Spring

21. Culebra Peak
1. Northwest Ridge

Culebra Peak from the north.

Start at the Taylor Ranch Trailhead and climb east up the steep, straight, four-wheel-drive road for 3.0 miles to Fourway, a road junction in a saddle at 11,220 feet. From "Fourway," continue climbing east for an additional 1.0 mile to the end of the road at 11,700 feet. There is good camping near here in a tree-line meadow with a bubbling stream to serenade you.

From the end of the road, cross to the creek's south side. Climb southeast up the shallow basin for 1.0 mile to reach Culebra's northwest ridge at a 13,220-foot saddle. From the saddle, climb the curving ridge southeast and east to a 13,940-foot false summit. Continue southeast for 0.3 mile in a gentle ascent to the summit.

Extra Credit 21.1EC

From Culebra's summit, descend south for 0.5 mile to a 13,460-foot saddle, then climb south to 13,908-foot Red Mountain, one of Colorado's 100 highest peaks. There is no extra fee for climbing Red Mountain.

Leave No Trace!

Plan Ahead and Prepare

- Know the regulations and special concerns for the area you are visiting.
- Visit the backcountry in small groups.
- Avoid popular areas during times of high use.
- Choose equipment and clothing in subdued colors.
- Repackage food into reusable containers.

Chapter Five
Elk Range

Introduction

The Elk Range lies south of Glenwood Springs and Interstate 70, and west of Aspen and Colorado 82. The Elk Range receives a lot of snow, and several major ski areas near Aspen take advantage of this fact. The Maroon Bells–Snowmass Wilderness embraces the range's beauty. Except for the famous views from the Maroon Lake Road, most of the Elks' high peaks are not visible from roads or towns. The Elks' exquisite beauty is reserved for those who penetrate the wilderness.

The Elks' seven fourteeners are some of Colorado's most rugged and beautiful peaks. Often difficult and dangerous, these peaks will both inspire and challenge you. The crumbling, red sedimentary rock of the famous Maroon Bells southwest of Aspen is some of Colorado's worst rock, and it can be a nightmare to climb on for the uninitiated. The rock on Snowmass Mountain and Capitol Peak at the northwest end of the range is better, and Capitol's north face offers some fine technical routes.

22. Capitol Peak 14,130 feet

See Map 22 on page 188

Singular and stoic, Capitol stands supreme as the northernmost Elk Range fourteener. Capitol leaps from its surrounding valleys, and the extensive wilderness around the peak shields it from road-bound travelers. The U.S. Capitol building bears a faint resemblance to the stout peak, but the peak's elegant lines still challenge architects to match it.

Capitol has been called Colorado's hardest fourteener. Many dispute that claim, but Capitol is certainly one of the hardest. Capitol's fame as a difficult peak is largely because of the northeast ridge's spectacular knife-edge. Capitol's easiest route, the Northeast Ridge Route, is Class 4, and many parties use a rope on it. Capitol's 1,800-foot-high north face is one of Colorado's highest mountain faces, and this great granite wall provides several technical climbs on reasonable rock.

Maps

Required: Capitol Peak, White River National Forest

Trailhead

Capitol Creek Trailhead

This trailhead is at 9,420 feet and provides access to Capitol's north and east sides. Go south for 28.0 miles on Colorado 82 from Glenwood Springs, or go north for 13.1 miles on Colorado 82 from Maroon Creek Road on Aspen's north side, to the small town of Snowmass. Do not confuse the town of Snowmass with Snowmass Village. The town of Snowmass is on Colorado 82. In Snowmass, turn west onto Snowmass Creek Road (paved) and measure from this point. After 1.7 miles, turn right at a T-junction onto the Capitol Creek Road (paved). Stay left at 1.9 miles, straight (left) at 3.2 miles, straight (right) at 4.7 miles and right at 5.9 miles, where the road turns to dirt. Pass the Capitol Creek Guard Station at 8.0 miles and continue on the now very rough road to the trailhead at 9.5 miles. The trailhead perches on a bench above Capitol Creek, and you can see Capitol Peak 6 miles to the south. In winter the Capitol Creek Road is closed 5.9 miles from Colorado 82.

Approaches

22.A1 Capitol Creek Approach

From Capitol Creek Trailhead: 13.0 miles, 3,000 feet

This is the easiest and standard approach to Capitol. Start at the Capitol Creek Trailhead and descend 400 feet to Capitol Creek. Your return trip up this hill will compensate for your easy start. Cross Capitol Creek on a good bridge and walk up the valley on Capitol Creek's east side for 6.5 miles to scenic Capitol Lake at 11,600 feet. There are good campsites on a tree-covered knoll 200 yards north of the lake.

Variation 22.A1V

There is a slightly longer, more scenic trail on Capitol Creek's west side. From the west end of the trailhead, go west along an irrigation ditch as it contours southwest through the trees and crosses two creeks. After the second creek-crossing, the trail leaves the ditch and climbs to beautiful open benches on Capitol Creek's west side. The trail reaches and crosses Capitol Creek at 9,960 feet (no bridge) then climbs east to join the main trail at 10,000 feet.

22.A2 West Snowmass Creek Approach

From Snowmass Creek Trailhead: 11.5 miles, 3,000 feet

This is a rougher, seldom used alternative to the popular Capitol Creek Approach. You can use this approach to reach Capitol's Northeast Ridge

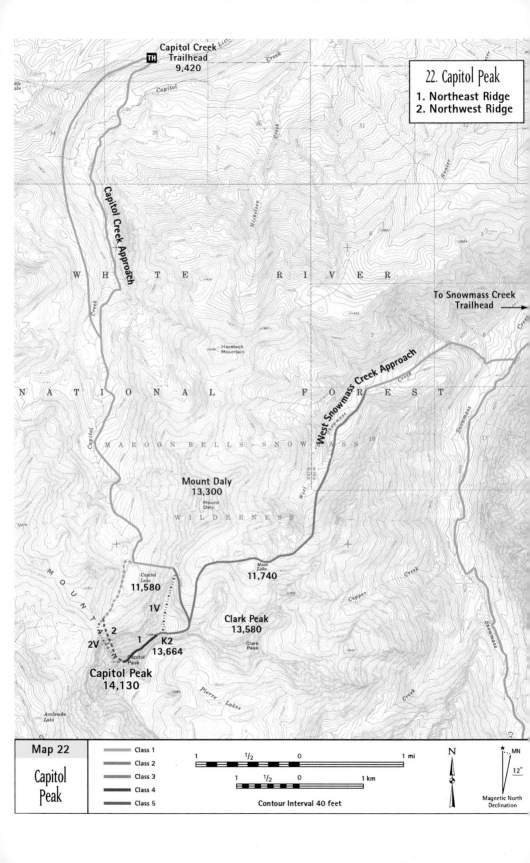

Capitol Creek
Trailhead
9,420

TH

Capitol Creek Approach

To Snowmass Creek
Trailhead →

West Snowmass Creek Approach

Haystack
Mountain

WHITE RIVER

NATIONAL FOREST

MAROON BELLS - SNOWMASS

Mount Daly
13,300

Mount
Daly

WILDERNESS

Capitol
Lake

11,580

1V

2

2V

1

K2
13,664

Capitol
Peak

Capitol Peak
14,130

Moon
Lake

11,740

Clark Peak
13,580

Clark
Peak

Copper Creek

Pierre Lakes

Avalanche
Lake

Snowmass Creek

Map 22			
	Class 1		
Capitol	Class 2		
Peak	Class 3		
	Class 4		
	Class 5		

1   1/2   0   1 mi

1   1/2   0   1 km

Contour Interval 40 feet

N

MN

12°

Magnetic North
Declination

Capitol Peak 14,130

Capitol Peak from the north.

Route. Start at the Snowmass Creek Trailhead (see Snowmass Mountain) and walk south up Snowmass Creek's east side on the Maroon–Snowmass Trail for 1.2 miles to the signed junction with the West Snowmass Trail. Leave the Maroon–Snowmass Trail and ford Snowmass Creek. During the spring and summer runoff, Snowmass Creek is a raging torrent that is difficult to cross, and this creek-crossing can easily be the crux of your adventure. The idyllic meadow on the west side of the creek will lure you on.

Once on Snowmass Creek's west side, stroll across the meadow and follow the West Snowmass Trail for 2.0 miles to another Elysian meadow at 9,800 feet. Leave the West Snowmass Trail before it starts to climb to Haystack Mountain, and continue up the west side of the valley. Cross to West Snowmass Creek's east side then find a faint trail and follow it up to a series of small lakes near tree line at 11,400 feet. There are good campsites near here. The highest and largest lake at 11,740 feet is called Moon Lake.

Routes

22.1 Northeast Ridge II, Class 4 *Classic*

From Capitol Lake: 4.0 miles, 2,800 feet

From Capitol Creek Trailhead: 17.0 miles, 5,800 feet

From West Snowmass Creek: 4.5 miles, 2,800 feet

From Snowmass Creek Trailhead: 16.0 miles, 5,800 feet

This is the easiest route on Capitol. It is most commonly approached from Capitol Creek, but you also can approach the route from West Snowmass Creek. From Capitol Lake, climb steeply east on a well-beaten path for 0.5 mile to the 12,500-foot saddle between Capitol and 13,300-foot Mount Daly, which is 1.7 miles northeast of Capitol. From the saddle, go south on a strong climber's trail that crosses some gullies as it descends slightly into the basin between Mount Daly and Clark Peak. Clark Peak is 1.2 miles east of Capitol. If you are approaching from West Snowmass Creek, you can easily reach this point from the tree-line campsites by hiking southwest up the basin. Once clear of the cliffs, climb west up the basin to Point 13,664—also known as "K2"—and consider your future. The view of Capitol from here is breathtaking.

From K2's summit, avoid the drop-offs to the south and west by climbing down K2's north side until you can proceed onto Capitol's northeast ridge. Scramble along the ridge to the notorious knife-edge. The knife-edge is a 100-foot-long, horizontal stretch of ridge. Many people scoot along the Class 4 ridge with one leg on each side. This is actually an awkward technique. It is better to grab the edge with your hands and walk your feet along underneath you. The rock here is delightfully solid. Once beyond the knife-edge, do a long, ascending traverse across the face south of the northeast ridge on looser rock. When practical, climb back to the crest of the northeast ridge and follow the ridge crest to the summit.

Variation 22.1V

From the Capitol–Daly Saddle, climb directly south along the ridge crest to K2's summit (Class 4).

22.2 Northwest Ridge III, Class 5.7, Steep Snow/Ice *Classic*

From Capitol Lake: 3.0 miles, 2,550 feet

From Capitol Creek Trailhead: 16.0 miles, 5,550 feet

Most of Colorado's great mountain faces were first climbed in the 1920s. As a testimony to its ferocity, Capitol's north face did not succumb until 1937, when a team including the pioneer Carl Blaurock climbed this route. The blunt northwest ridge is the western edge of Capitol's dramatic north face. It is the classic technical climb on this face. Use the Capitol Creek Approach. This long, deceptive climb is visible from Capitol Lake near the western skyline. The route is looser than it looks. When looking at the face from below, you cannot see the rubble that perches on hidden ledges. The ledges are welcome, but the rubble is not. Hike southwest above Capitol Lake to just below Capitol Pass, which is the 12,060-foot saddle below the northwest ridge.

Look for the Y-shaped Slingshot Couloir on the small face east (left) of the bottom of the northwest ridge. Climb the west (right) branch of the Slingshot Couloir, which contains unavoidable snow and ice. Rockfall danger in the Slingshot Couloir is extreme. Wear a helmet. Exit the couloir and climb up and slightly left over a series of ledges separated by short, steep rock faces that require Class 5.7 climbing. Above these steep steps, the angle of the face eases slightly. Climb to the crest of the now well defined northwest ridge just above a feature called the "Rotten Spire." Climb three 150-foot pitches near the ridge crest (Class 5.6–5.7). Use crack systems on the discontinuous face east (left) of the crest. Climb into a small saddle behind the "Upper Spire," which marks the top of the steep lower ridge and the beginning of the lower-angled upper ridge. Climb along the narrow ridge (Class 4), then negotiate a loose corner punctuated by a small roof (Class 5.7). Continue up the summit pyramid with another 150-foot Class 5.7 pitch. The angle eases above this pitch, and the rest of the climb is easier. Descend the Northeast Ridge Route.

Variation 22.2V

The direct start to the Northwest Ridge Route is harder but avoids the Slingshot Couloir with its attendant snow, ice and rockfall hazard. From Capitol Lake, hike all the way to Capitol Pass at 12,060 feet. Leave the trail and hike southeast up talus to the base of the rock wall. Traverse east (left) for 30 feet to the bottom of a crack system that leads to a chimney above.

Climb a 150-foot pitch up the crack system (Class 5.9). Stem up into the chimney (Class 5.8) and climb the chimney, being careful not to knock loose rock onto your belayer. Continue for 400 feet up an easy gully and Class 4 slabs. Climb steeper slabs and grooves (Class 5.7) and reach the west (right) side of "Unicorn Spire." Climb another pitch to the base of the "Rotten Spire." Look for loose blocks here. Do a loose but easy traverse around the east (left) side of the "Rotten Spire" to the small saddle beyond. Continue on the upper route as described above.

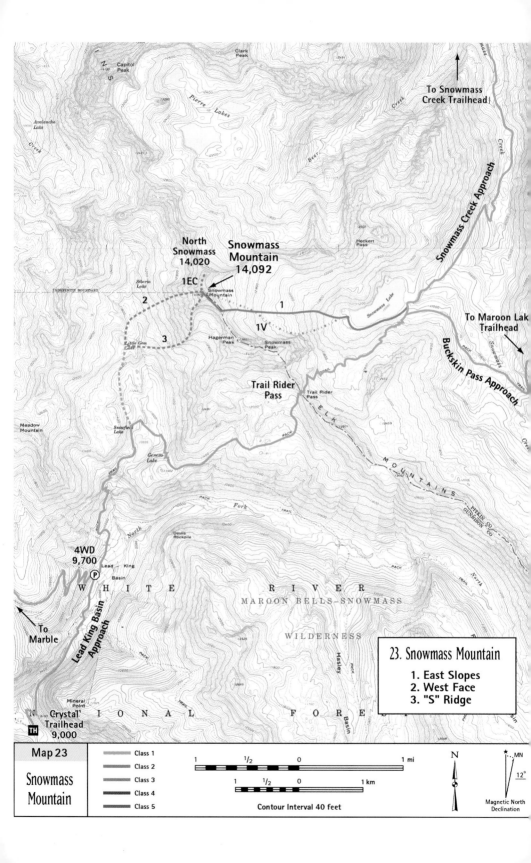

To Snowmass
Creek Trailhead

Clark
Peak

Capitol
Peak

Pierre Lakes

Snowmass Creek Approach

Avalanche
Lake

Bear Creek

Heckert
Pass

North
Snowmass
14,020

Snowmass
Mountain
14,092

1EC

Snowmass
Mountain

Siberia
Lake

INDEFINITE BOUNDARY

Snowmass Lake

To Maroon Lake
Trailhead

2

1

1V

Little Gem
Lake

Hagerman
Peak

Snowmass
Peak

3

Buckskin Pass Approach

Trail Rider
Pass

Trail Rider
Pass

ELK

Meadow
Mountain

Snowfis
Lake

Geneva
Lake

M
O
U
N
T
A
I
N
S

PITKIN CO.
GUNNISON CO.

Fork

PACK

TRAIL

North

Devils
Rockpile

4WD
9,700

P

Lead King
Basin

W H I T E   R I V E R

MAROON BELLS–SNOWMASS

To
Marble

Lead King Basin Approach

WILDERNESS

Hasley

Basin

North

23. Snowmass Mountain

1. East Slopes
2. West Face
3. "S" Ridge

Mineral
Point

Crystal
Trailhead
9,000

TH

N A L   F O R E S

Map 23	Class 1			N
	Class 2			MN
Snowmass	Class 3			
Mountain	Class 4			12°
	Class 5	Contour Interval 40 feet		Magnetic North Declination

1   1/2   0   1 mi

1   1/2   0   1 km

23. Snowmass Mountain   14,092 feet

See Map 23 on page 192

Rugged and remote, Snowmass reigns as one of Colorado's most spectacular fourteeners. Snowmass is located 15 miles west of Aspen, but you cannot see the reclusive peak from towns or highways. You can see the namesake snowfield on the peak's east side from the summits of other high peaks. Snowmass' permanent snowfield is one of Colorado's largest, and ascending it is a treat. Snowmass' white rock adds to the peak's beauty.

Maps
Required: Snowmass Mountain, White River National Forest
Optional: Capitol Peak, Maroon Bells

Trailheads
Snowmass Creek Trailhead
This trailhead is at 8,400 feet and provides access to the Snowmass Creek Approach and routes on Snowmass' east side. You can reach the trailhead via one of two roads.

For the traditional approach, go south for 28.0 miles on Colorado 82 from Glenwood Springs, or go north for 13.1 miles on Colorado 82 from Maroon Creek Road on Aspen's north side, to the small town of Snowmass. Do not confuse the town of Snowmass with Snowmass Village. The town of Snowmass is on Colorado 82. In Snowmass, turn west onto Snowmass Creek Road (paved) and measure from this point. After 1.7 miles, turn left at a T-junction. The road turns to dirt after 7.3 miles, crosses Snowmass Creek after 10.7 miles and reaches another T-junction after 10.9 miles. Turn right at the T-junction and reach the well-marked trailhead at 11.3 miles.

If starting in Aspen, the following alternative approach is shorter but rougher. From Maroon Lake Road on Aspen's north side, go 4.6 miles north on Colorado 82. Turn west onto the Snowmass Village Road (paved) and measure from this point. Go 5.1 miles to the junction of Brush Creek Road and Divide Road in Snowmass Village and turn right onto Divide Road (paved). At 6.0 miles, turn right onto a dirt road just before you reach a lodge called "The Divide" at the Snowmass Ski Area. Descend steeply on a series of switchbacks across ski runs, go straight at 7.6 miles and reach the trailhead after 8.0 miles. In winter you can usually drive to within 1.0 mile of this trailhead.

Crystal Trailhead

This trailhead is at 9,000 feet and provides access to the Lead King Basin Approach and routes on Snowmass' south and west sides. From Carbondale, go south on Colorado 133 for 22.0 miles to the northern base of McClure Pass. Leave Colorado 133 and drive east for 6.0 miles on a good paved road to the town of Marble. Continue east on a rough dirt road (Forest Service 314) for an additional 5.5 miles to the town of Crystal. This dirt road may challenge some passenger cars. Park in a flat area 0.2 mile east of Crystal just before the road switchbacks up the hill.

Four-wheel-drive vehicles can leave the Schofield Pass Road just above the trailhead and continue on the rough Lead King Basin Road (Forest Service 315) for 1.8 miles to a marked parking area at 9,700 feet. There is a longer, easier four-wheel-drive road (it, also, is Forest Service 315) to this point that leaves the Schofield Pass Road just east of Marble and goes up Lost Trail Creek. In winter the road is open to Marble.

Approaches

23.A1 Snowmass Creek Approach

From Snowmass Creek Trailhead: 16.0 miles, 2,600 feet

This is the traditional backpacking approach to Snowmass Lake and routes on Snowmass' east side. It's long but worth the effort. Start at the Snowmass Creek Trailhead and walk south up Snowmass Creek's east side on the Maroon–Snowmass Trail. Pass the junction with the West Snowmass Trail after 1.2 miles and continue south on the Maroon–Snowmass Trail. After 3.7 miles, you have an exotic view of Snowmass Mountain above Bear Creek to the west.

After 6.0 miles, you reach a lake at 10,100 feet. Continue around the lake's east side to a second lake and the approach's crux. You must cross Snowmass Creek to reach Snowmass Lake, and there is no bridge. Either cross a 100-foot-long logjam at the upper lake's northern end or wade the creek below the logjam. Either crossing can be dangerous in high water. Once on the creek's west side, continue up the trail for 2.0 miles to Snowmass Lake at 10,980 feet. This scenic lake is a popular destination in July and August. The rocky bulk of Snowmass Peak and Hagerman Peak rise directly west of the lake; beyond, you can see the gentler Snowmass Mountain. Do not confuse 13,620-foot Snowmass Peak with 14,092-foot Snowmass Mountain.

23.A2 Buckskin Pass Approach

From Maroon Lake Trailhead: 15.2 miles, 4,700 feet

With a vehicle shuttle, this route makes sense as a one-way journey. The round trip over Buckskin Pass requires more effort than the approach up Snowmass Creek, and this arduous approach is less popular than the hike up Snowmass Creek. Start at the Maroon Lake Trailhead (see Maroon Bells Group) and follow the main trail west for 1.5 miles to Crater Lake's east end. Turn right and follow the Maroon–Snowmass Trail northwest to Buckskin Pass at 12,462 feet. Descend on the trail, cross Snowmass Creek at 10,800 feet then climb northwest to Snowmass Lake.

23.A3 Lead King Basin Approach
From Crystal Trailhead: 8.4 miles, 1,950 feet

This approach is shorter and less scenic than the Snowmass Creek Approach. Start at the Crystal Trailhead and walk up the four-wheel-drive road for 0.4 mile to a junction above the first switchback. Turn north (left) and follow the rough road as it climbs on the east side of Crystal River's North Fork into Lead King Basin. Cross to the river's west side 1.4 miles above the trailhead. Reach a marked four-wheel-drive parking area 1.9 miles above the Crystal Trailhead where the road starts to switchback up the hill west of the river.

Follow the Geneva Lake Trail north into the Maroon Bells–Snowmass Wilderness. Take the west (left) fork at a junction, switchback up the steep slope at the north end of Lead King Basin and continue north to Geneva Lake's west side at 10,950 feet. There is good camping on the lake's west side, and you can see Snowmass Mountain's south and west sides rising north of the lake.

You can hike from Geneva Lake to Snowmass Lake via Trail Rider Pass. This pass allows you to visit both the east side and the west side of Snowmass. You can create a beautiful backcountry experience here.

Routes
23.1 East Slopes II, Class 3, Moderate Snow *Classic*
From Snowmass Lake: 5.0 miles, 3,100 feet

From Snowmass Creek Trailhead: 21.0 miles, 5,700 feet

From Maroon Lake Trailhead: 20.2 miles, 7,800 feet

This is the standard route up Snowmass' namesake snowfield; although it is long, it is the easiest route up Snowmass. Always interesting, it offers one of Colorado's finest fourteener tours. Use either the Snowmass Creek or Buckskin Pass Approach to reach Snowmass Lake.

From Snowmass Lake's east end, hike around the lake's south side on a small trail. A steep, unpleasant scree slope rises above Snowmass Lake's west end and bars easy access to the snowfield above it. Either climb a shallow gully on the south (left) side of the scree slope (snow-filled through June) or climb grass slopes north (right) of the scree slope.

Snowmass Mountain and Capitol Peak from the southeast.

Proceed onto the snowfield above the scree slope and walk west up its undulating surface. The steep north wall of Snowmass Peak and Hagerman Peak are south of you, and Snowmass Mountain is to the west. Aim for a rounded protrusion below Snowmass Mountain's southeast ridge about halfway between the Snowmass Mountain–Hagerman Peak Saddle and Snowmass Mountain's summit. This protrusion provides the easiest route to the summit ridge. Climb it (Class 2 or Moderate Snow) and reach Snowmass Mountain's southeast ridge at 13,700 feet. Climb northwest along the ridge for 0.2 mile to the summit. This ridge requires some Class 3 scrambling on surprisingly solid rock.

Variation 23.1V

In June of a good snow year, you can stay on the snowfield longer and climb moderate snow to reach the summit ridge closer to the summit. In early June, you can sometimes climb directly to the summit on steep snow.

Extra Credit 23.1EC

From the summit, scramble north for 0.2 mile to Snowmass Mountain's 14,020-foot north summit (Class 3). This unofficial fourteener does not have a lot of power, but it is above 14,000 feet, it is highly visible and it provides an excellent view of Pierre Lakes Basin and Capitol Peak. This airy summit is one of Colorado's more exotic 14,000-foot perches.

23.2 West Face II, Class 3

From Geneva Lake: 5.0 miles, 3,150 feet

From Crystal Trailhead: 13.4 miles, 5,100 feet

From 4WD parking: 9.8 miles, 4,400 feet

This route is a little harder than the East Slopes Route but is much shorter. It is the most expedient way to climb Snowmass. Start at the Crystal Trailhead and follow the Lead King Basin Approach to Geneva Lake. Hike around Geneva Lake's west side and continue north up the valley past Little Gem Lake to 11,700 feet.

Turn east (right) and climb steeply for 1.0 mile up Snowmass' west face. This large, broken face is full of small cliff bands, and you must do some judicious route finding to keep the difficulty at Class 3. The easiest line is just south of a rib in the center of the face. The most difficult sections are between 12,600 and 12,800 feet, and near the summit. There is a lot of loose rock on this face.

23.3 S Ridge II, Class 3

From Geneva Lake: 4.0 miles, 3,150 feet

From Crystal Trailhead: 12.4 miles, 5,100 feet

From 4WD parking: 8.8 miles, 4,400 feet

This is the shortest route on Snowmass. The S Ridge is Snowmass' southwest ridge; it received its name because of its distinctive, curving shape. Only the ridge's loose rock prevents it from being a classic climb. Start at the Crystal Trailhead and follow the Lead King Basin Approach to Geneva Lake. You can easily see the S Ridge from the lake. Hike around Geneva Lake's west side and continue north up the valley toward the base of the ridge.

Climb to 12,200 feet on the ridge's north side and angle up to the ridge crest at 12,500 feet. Scramble up the ridge crest and move to the ridge's north side to avoid any difficulties. There is more Class 3 scrambling and exposure on this ridge than on the West Face Route. Ascending the S Ridge and descending the West Face Route makes a serpentine Tour de Snowmass.

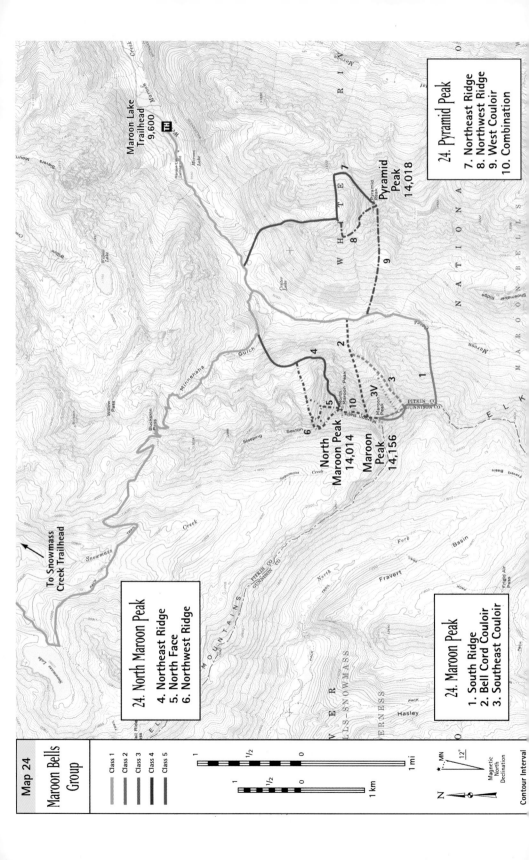

Map 24
Maroon Bells Group

Class 1
Class 2
Class 3
Class 4
Class 5

Contour Interval

N

MN

Magnetic North Declination

12°

1 mi

1/2   0   1

1 km

1/2   0   1

24. Pyramid Peak

7. Northeast Ridge
8. Northwest Ridge
9. West Couloir
10. Combination

24. North Maroon Peak

4. Northeast Ridge
5. North Face
6. Northwest Ridge

24. Maroon Peak

1. South Ridge
2. Bell Cord Couloir
3. Southeast Couloir

Maroon Lake Trailhead
9,600

Pyramid Peak
14,018

North Maroon Peak
14,014

Maroon Peak
14,156

To Snowmass Creek Trailhead

24. Maroon Bells Group

Maroon Peak   14,156 feet
North Maroon Peak   14,014 feet
Pyramid Peak   14,018 feet

See Map 24 on page 198

These three peaks are nestled in the heart of the Elk Range 10 miles west of Aspen. They are visible from many of the area's ski slopes, and millions of people have looked at these famous peaks. Maroon Peak and North Maroon Peak, together, are known as the "Maroon Bells." The Maroon Bells' beauty is world renowned. Once, on a climbing trip to Peru, I visited a small restaurant in a remote valley. On the wall above a rustic table was a picture of the Maroon Bells.

Maps
Required: Maroon Bells, White River National Forest

Trailhead
Maroon Lake Trailhead
This popular trailhead is at 9,600 feet and provides access to the Maroon Bells and Pyramid. From Aspen's north side, leave Colorado 82 and drive west on the Maroon Lake Road for 9.4 miles to the parking area east of Maroon Lake. A postcard view of the Maroon Bells greets you here.

From mid-June through September, the Maroon Lake road is closed from 8:30 A.M. to 5:00 P.M. During these hours, there is a shuttle to the lake that starts at Ruby Park in downtown Aspen. For more information, call RFTA at (970) 925-8484 or the White River National Forest at (970) 925-3445. In winter the road is gated 3.0 miles from Colorado 82 at the T-Lazy-7 Guest Ranch.

24. Maroon Peak   14,156 feet

See Map 24 on page198

This namesake peak is the highest of the Maroon Bells Group. Maroon Peak is often called "South Maroon"; you can see the peak, together with its companion summit, North Maroon, from Maroon Lake. Thousands of people have admired the postcard view of these two peaks for more than a century. On a crisp fall day, blue skies, azure lakes and brilliant aspen trees frame the Maroon Bells. Many of Colorado's best beauties are on display here.

Routes

24.1 South Ridge II, Class 3

From Maroon Lake Trailhead: 10.0 miles, 4,600 feet

This is the easiest route on Maroon Peak, but it is a long, arduous ascent on dangerously loose rock. From the Maroon Lake Trailhead, walk west for 1.5 miles to Crater Lake's east end. Turn left at a trail junction and walk south from Crater Lake along West Maroon Creek's west side for an additional 1.8 miles. During this approach hike, the Maroon Bells pass in review above you. Leave the main trail at 10,500 feet just before it crosses to the creek's east side.

Climb west for 1.0 mile up broken, Class 3 ledges to reach Maroon Peak's south ridge at 13,300 feet. The difficult, 2,800-foot ascent up this slope will test the success of your training program. The slope has several small cliff bands, but with careful route finding, the difficulty will not exceed Class 3.

Once on the south ridge, turn north (right) and follow the well-cairned route that starts on the ridge crest, then stays below the ridge on its west side. At 13,300 feet, when the ridge steepens toward dramatic Point 13,753, do a frustrating, up-and-down traverse west for 0.25 mile. Stay below the major difficulties of Point 13,753 and, at 13,400 feet, proceed into the couloir that drops southwest from the saddle between Maroon Peak and Point 13,753. Climb this gully on dangerously loose scree and, well before you reach the saddle, find an escape ledge to the northwest (left). Leave the couloir and traverse on this ledge onto Maroon Peak's southwest face. Zigzag up this face, following the path of least resistance. The exact finish to this climb is a matter of choice. You can regain the south ridge and follow it for 400 feet to the summit, or you can choose a line farther northwest.

This climb requires careful route finding to keep the difficulty at Class 3. Although the route has been well cairned in recent years, some cairns lead to bad routes. Trust your judgment, not some stranger's pile of rocks.

24.2 Bell Cord Couloir III, Class 4, Steep Snow/Ice *Classic*

From Maroon Lake Trailhead: 8.0 miles, 4,600 feet

This is the prominent couloir between Maroon Peak and North Maroon Peak. You can preview conditions in this couloir from the safety of your car at Maroon Lake. Preview carefully. In winter and early spring, the couloir is prone to avalanching, and by late summer, the snow is gone and the couloir is an undesirable scree gully speckled with rubble-infested ice. The couloir collects rockfall in all seasons, and a helmet is recommended. In most years, late June is best for a snow climb up this classic couloir.

Beware unstable snow when melting reaches its peak in early June. The couloir can present a technical ice climb in July.

From the Maroon Lake Trailhead, walk west for 1.5 miles to Crater Lake's east end. Turn left at a trail junction and walk south from Crater Lake along West Maroon Creek's west side for an additional 1.0 mile to an intermittent stream–crossing at 10,280 feet. Leave the trail and climb west into the basin between Maroon Peak and North Maroon. Enter the straight couloir at 12,000 feet and climb it to the 13,780-foot saddle between Maroon Peak and North Maroon. The 1,800-foot couloir averages 42 degrees, with the steepest portions exceeding 45 degrees. An ice ax is recommended, and crampons may be useful. From the saddle, turn south (left), climb a Class 4 cleft and then climb broken, Class 3 ledges for 0.1 mile to Maroon Peak's summit.

24.3 Southeast Couloir III, Class 3, Steep Snow/Ice
From Maroon Lake Trailhead: 8.0 miles, 4,600 feet

This couloir is on Maroon Peak's southeast side and reaches a tiny 13,660-foot saddle just south of Point 13,753 on Maroon Peak's south ridge. This couloir provides a good early summer snow climb, but after the snow melts, the couloir is a bowling alley of loose rocks.

Follow the Bell Cord Couloir Route into the basin below Maroon Peak. Climb southwest through a huge slot called the "Garbage Chute." If there is stable snow, you can climb directly up the chute. If the snow has begun melting, avoid rotting snow bridges over the stream by climbing on the north (right) side of the chute. Above the Garbage Chute, continue southwest through a small basin and enter Maroon Peak's southeast couloir at 12,200 feet.

The 1,500-foot couloir averages 40 degrees, with the steepest portions exceeding 45 degrees. This couloir is wider, shorter and gentler than the Bell Cord Couloir, but it still requires careful attention. From the 13,660-foot saddle on Maroon Peak's south ridge just south of Point 13,753, traverse on the east side of Point 13,753 to the 13,660-foot saddle just north of this summit. From here there are two choices. Either descend on the west side and finish the climb via the upper part of Maroon Peak's South Ridge Route, or do an ascending traverse from the saddle on the southwest face and finish along the upper south ridge. The southeast couloir provides a good descent after an ascent of the Bell Cord Couloir.

Variation 24.3V

There is a second couloir north of the one described above. It reaches the 13,660-foot saddle just north of Point 13,753. The northern couloir is steeper, harder and less popular than the southern one. It provides a great climb with stable snow, but avoid it if the snow is discontinuous.

North Maroon Peak and Maroon Peak from the northeast.

24. North Maroon Peak   14,014 feet

See Map 24 on page 198

When you view the Maroon Bells from Maroon Lake, North Maroon appears larger and higher than Maroon Peak. In reality, North Maroon is just a northern spur of Maroon Peak. The two summits are less than 0.4 mile apart, and North Maroon only rises 234 feet above the connecting saddle. North Maroon's status as an official fourteener has been hotly debated for decades, but its stature is never in question. This picturesque peak is one of Colorado's most famous fourteeners.

Routes

24.4 Northeast Ridge II, Class 4

From Maroon Lake Trailhead: 8.0 miles, 4,450 feet

This time-honored test piece is the standard route on North Maroon. The route is complicated, loose, exposed and dangerous. It has often rendered a fatal experience. From the Maroon Lake Trailhead, walk west for 1.5 miles to Crater Lake's east end. Turn right at a trail junction and climb west on the Maroon–Snowmass Trail for an additional 0.5 mile to a meadow at 10,700 feet. Leave the main trail at a cairn and follow a climber's trail down to Minnehaha Creek. Ford the creek and continue on the climber's trail as it climbs west to the lower end of the basin below North Maroon's north face. The introduction is over and the challenge looms overhead. The northeast ridge is the left skyline.

Hike south at 11,700 feet across a large rock glacier in the basin and aim for a point below the northeast ridge's lowest cliffs. Find a climber's trail and do an ascending, Class 2 traverse on ledges below east-facing cliffs. Near the end of the traverse, climb more steeply to a corner at 11,900 feet on the edge of a wide gully on North Maroon's east face. When descending this route, it is important to exit the gully at this corner.

From the corner, traverse south into the wide gully and climb west up it via a series of grass and dirt ledges (Class 3). The gully narrows, and a 50-foot cliff band blocks easy passage at 12,800 feet. Climb a cleft near the center of the cliff band (Class 4). Angle south (left) to a small ridge at 12,900 feet between the gully you have just ascended and another gully farther south. Traverse south into the new gully and ascend broken, Class 3 ledges to reach the crest of the northeast ridge at 13,200 feet. Climb on or near the ridge crest from this point to the summit. An occasional Class 4 move is required on the ridge's steeper portions.

24.5 North Face III, Class 4, Steep Snow/Ice *Classic*
From Maroon Lake Trailhead: 7.6 miles, 4,450 feet

This classic route is seldom in good condition for climbing. Until mid-June, the climb can be done entirely on snow, but the plentiful May snow tends to avalanche, the June snow is often rotten and the exposed rock bands of late summer are always rotten. Nevertheless, this sweeping north face has attracted many hardened mountaineers, and it is also a test piece for extreme skiers. Like the Eiger's Nordwand, this face emits a siren call for some. The 1,600-foot face averages 47 degrees and consists of a series of rock bands with steep, snow-covered ledges between them. The rock bands are the route's multiple cruxes.

Follow the Northeast Ridge Route to the basin below the north face. Climb west up the basin and inspect the face carefully as you pass below it. Climb to 12,400 feet in the basin and bypass the first rock band by climbing a wide snow slope on the west (right) side of the lower face. Angle back east (left) into the center of the face on the large snow ramp above the first rock band. Ascend the vague couloir in the center of the face through several smaller rock bands. Avoid the final rock band, which is called the "Punk Rock Band," by angling east (left) to join the northeast ridge near the summit.

Variations
24.5V1 Class 4, Steep Snow/Ice

Climb the first rock band in the center of the face via a shallow couloir. The upper part of this couloir is steep; it is best avoided by climbing 165 feet of Class 4 rock west (right) of the couloir.

24.5V2 Class 4

Climb through the center of the Punk Rock Band in a narrow, Class 4 cleft. Reach the northwest ridge 100 yards below the summit. Climbing directly through the first and last rock bands provides the most direct line on the north face.

24.6 Northwest Ridge II, Class 4, Steep Snow (Seasonal)

From Maroon Lake Trailhead: 8.0 miles, 4,450 feet

People seldom climb this straightforward ridge because of the difficulty in reaching the ridge. Follow the Northeast Ridge Route to the basin below the north face. Climb west up the basin under the north face and consider your future. The complicated, 13,460-foot massif north of North Maroon is the Sleeping Sexton. The deep, 13,020-foot saddle between Sleeping Sexton and North Maroon is called the "Gunsight." It is on North Maroon's northwest ridge above the west end of the basin below North Maroon's north face. A steep, rotten, east-facing couloir called the "Gunsight Couloir" reaches this saddle from the west end of the basin. You can see this prominent couloir from Maroon Lake.

The Gunsight Couloir is best ascended when it is snow-filled, but snow melts out rapidly in this couloir. After the snow melts, the couloir is a steep shooting gallery of loose rocks. You can avoid the couloir by climbing 200 feet of Class 4 rock south of the couloir. From the Gunsight, climb a Class 4 pitch to the south to exit the deep notch. Once above the Gunsight, follow a zigzag line just west of the northwest ridge. The actual ridge crest is not the best route. The upper ridge eases in difficulty and allows a ridge-top finish to the summit.

Variation 24.6V

There is a narrow, hidden couloir that ascends from the lower west end of the north face to a small, 13,260-foot notch on the northwest ridge above the Gunsight. When filled with stable snow, this couloir provides an excellent climb that avoids the various hazards of the Gunsight Couloir. The narrow couloir's steepness reaches 48 degrees.

24. Pyramid Peak   14,018 feet

See Map 24 on page 198

This well-named peak is 2 miles east of the Maroon Bells, and it is the first high peak you see when driving up the Maroon Lake Road. Pyramid is only 2 miles south of Maroon Lake, and the foreshortened view from the lake is neck-bending. Pyramid is at the north end of a highly convoluted,

4-mile-long ridge between West Maroon and East Maroon Creeks. Pyramid is the highest point on the ridge; it carries this distinction well.

Routes

24.7 Northeast Ridge II, Class 4

From Maroon Lake Trailhead: 6.0 miles, 4,450 feet

This is the easiest route on Pyramid. Like the Maroon Bells, steep, exposed, loose rock makes this a dangerous climb. Start at the Maroon Lake Trailhead and walk west on the main trail for 1.1 miles to a level area at 10,120 feet. Leave the main trail and follow a climber's trail southeast, then climb steeply into the hanging basin below Pyramid's north face. Hike south up the west (right) side of the basin to 11,900 feet.

Cross the upper basin and climb southeast up steep scree gullies to reach Pyramid's northeast ridge at a 12,980-foot saddle. Scramble south then southwest along the ridge crest for 0.25 mile to a forbidding notch at 13,060 feet. Climb the pale-colored, Class 4 wall beyond the notch. This is the route's technical crux, but much route finding remains. Above the crux wall, stay near the ridge crest when feasible and traverse south (left) when necessary. Most of this climbing is Class 3, but an occasional Class 4 move is required. The potential falls from this route's last 1,000 feet are almost all fatal drops. Take great care with your movement and route finding. If you find yourself faced with a Class 5 section, retreat to easier ground and try another route. When you are on or near the ridge crest, take time to peer west across Pyramid's imposing north face. Pyramid has one of Colorado's most rewarding summits.

24.8 Northwest Ridge II, Class 4

From Maroon Lake Trailhead: 6.0 miles, 4,450 feet

This ridge offers a more difficult alternative to the northeast ridge. Follow the Northeast Ridge Route into the basin below Pyramid's north face. From 12,000 feet in the basin, climb southwest up a steep, wide couloir to a 12,700-foot saddle on Pyramid's northwest ridge (Class 3).

The route from here to the summit is difficult to follow. You are rarely on the ridge crest as you link traverses and gullies on the west face. From the 12,700-foot saddle, follow the northwest ridge for 300 feet then move below the ridge on its west side to the bottom of a rubble gully. Climb the gully and stay to the right near the top. At the top of the gully's left branch is the "Keyhole," providing a spectacular view of Pyramid's north face. The terrain here is steep, loose and dangerous. It is not necessary to go into the Keyhole.

Climb the steep, Class 4 pitch above the top of the couloir's right branch. This is the route's technical crux, but tricky route finding remains.

Pyramid Peak from the north.

Beyond the crux wall, move away from the northwest ridge, traverse south on ledges, round a corner and climb short walls when necessary. Reach a small bowl at 13,700 feet on Pyramid's upper west face. You are close. Climb the shallow couloir above the bowl to just below the summit cliff. Avoid this by traversing south to a notch at 13,900 feet on Pyramid's south ridge. You are very close. Climb north along the rocky, exposed upper south ridge for 400 feet to the summit. Ascending this ridge and descending the northeast ridge makes a spectacular Tour de Pyramid.

24.9 West Couloir II, Class 4, Steep Snow (Seasonal)
From Maroon Lake Trailhead: 9.0 miles, 4,450 feet

This route is less popular than either the Northeast or Northwest Ridge Routes, probably because of its length and the couloir's loose rock. Still, this is a practicable route, especially if there is good snow in the couloir. Snow usually melts out of this couloir by mid-June.

From the Maroon Lake Trailhead, walk west for 1.5 miles to Crater Lake's east end. Turn left at a trail junction and walk south from Crater Lake along West Maroon Creek's west side for an additional 1.2 miles to 10,300 feet. Leave the trail, cross West Maroon Creek and climb east up Pyramid's enormous west face. From 10,300 feet to 12,600 feet, the climbing is straightforward but tedious.

At 12,600 feet, proceed into the more northerly of two major couloirs on the upper west face and ascend it for 1,100 feet to 13,700 feet in a small bowl below the summit. The couloir has steep sections that exceed

55 degrees; when snow-free, these bulges require Class 4 climbing. Join the Northwest Ridge Route in the small bowl at 13,700 feet and follow that route to the summit.

24. Maroon Bells and Pyramid Combinations

See Map 24 on page 198

24.10 II, Class 4 *Classic*
From Maroon Lake Trailhead: 9.4 miles, 4,850 feet

The traverse between North Maroon and Maroon Peak is one of Colorado's four great fourteener traverses. It rings both Bells. The rock is rotten and the traverse is dangerous, but it is a classic combination because of the spectacular positions achieved on these beautiful peaks. The traverse works equally well in either direction, and there are advantages for each direction. If going from north to south, you can rappel over the traverse's most difficult pitch and upclimb the tricky, north-facing slabs on Maroon Peak. If going from south to north, you can upclimb the traverse's most difficult pitch and descend the shorter route off North Maroon. The traverse described here is from north to south.

Start at the Maroon Lake Trailhead and follow North Maroon's Northeast Ridge Route to North Maroon's summit. Maroon Peak is only 0.4 mile away, but the traverse can be time-consuming. Descend southwest from the summit for 100 yards to a small, 13,820-foot saddle (Exposed Class 3). Scramble south along the ridge for 200 yards to a 30-foot drop-off. Either rappel over the pitch, downclimb the pitch (Class 4) or avoid the pitch on the ridge's west side via a series of horribly rotten gullies.

Continue south along the ridge to the 13,780-foot saddle at the top of Maroon Peak's Bell Cord Couloir. Climb a Class 4 cleft above the saddle, then zigzag up a series of north-facing, Class 3 ledges to Maroon Peak's summit. Descend Maroon Peak's South Ridge Route.

24.11 The Triple Feat III, Class 4
From Maroon Lake Trailhead: 11.5 miles, 8,600 feet

This climb collects both of the Maroon Bells and Pyramid. It requires excellent conditioning, and aficionados of the all-day workout lust after this challenge. Follow Combination 24.10 from North Maroon to Maroon Peak and descend Maroon Peak's South Ridge Route to 10,300 feet in West Maroon Creek. Ascend Pyramid's West Couloir Route and descend Pyramid's Northeast Ridge Route. The Triple Feat works equally well in the opposite direction.

25. Castle Group

Castle Peak   14,265 feet
Conundrum Peak   14,060 feet

See Map 25 on page 210

These peaks are 12 miles south of Aspen and are usually climbed together. Castle is the monarch of the Elk Range, and Conundrum is really just a false summit of Castle. Conundrum receives its status on lists of fourteeners because it is named on the Hayden Peak Quadrangle. Both peaks offer a choice of routes.

Maps

Required: Hayden Peak, White River National Forest
Optional: Maroon Bells

Trailheads

Castle Creek Trailhead

This trailhead is at 9,800 feet and provides access to Castle's east and north sides. From Aspen's north side, leave Colorado 82 and turn west onto the Maroon Lake Road. After 30 yards, turn south (left) onto the Castle Creek Road (paved) and measure from this point. Pass Ashcroft after 11.0 miles and turn west (right) onto a dirt road (National Forest 102) at 13.0 miles before the main road crosses to Castle Creek's east side. Go south on the dirt road as it parallels Castle Creek. There are some informal campsites along this stretch of road. Park at 13.5 miles before the road steepens and becomes dramatically rougher. Four-wheel-drive vehicles can continue up Castle Creek and North Castle Creek to an astonishing 12,800 feet. In winter the road is open to Ashcroft.

Conundrum Creek Trailhead

This trailhead is at 8,800 feet and provides access to Castle's west side. From Aspen's north side, leave Colorado 82 and turn west onto the Maroon Lake Road. After 30 yards, turn south (left) onto the Castle Creek Road (paved) and measure from this point. Go south for 4.9 miles and turn southwest (right) onto a paved road. Descend, cross Castle Creek at mile 5.1 and turn south (left) onto a dirt road. Follow this road south past many private driveways to the public parking area of the trailhead at mile 6.0. In winter the road is open to within 0.5 mile of the trailhead, but parking is limited. Respect private property and its owners here and park on the Castle Creek Road.

Middle Brush Creek Trailhead

This trailhead is at 9,180 feet and provides access to Castle's southwest side. From the town of Crested Butte, go southeast for 2.1 miles on Colorado 135. Turn north (left) onto the Brush Creek Road, marked with a sign for the Country Club, and measure from this point. Follow the Brush Creek Road past the Country Club golf course, stay east (right) after 0.5 mile and turn east then north into the East River drainage. Cross the East River at 2.8 miles and cross Brush Creek at 4.6 miles. Turn northeast (right) at 4.7 miles into the Brush Creek drainage on a rougher road. Turn east (right) at 5.7 miles onto the Pearl Pass Road (FS 738) and park at 6.0 miles.

Beyond this point, the road narrows and fords West Brush Creek. This ford stops most two-wheel-drive vehicles. Four-wheel-drive vehicles can continue 6.9 miles on the Pearl Pass Road to unmarked parking at 10,820 feet. The Pearl Pass Road is well known as one of Colorado's roughest, and it can stop four-wheel-drive vehicles when it is wet. In winter the road is closed at the Cold Springs Ranch, 3.1 miles from Colorado 135.

25. Castle Peak   14,265 feet

See Map 25 on page 210

Castle is the highest peak in both Gunnison and Pitkin Counties. Castle is the Elk Range's highest peak and southernmost fourteener. After neighboring Conundrum, Castle is also the Elks' easiest fourteener. If you are climbing in the Elk Range for the first time and are uncertain about these dangerous peaks, climb Castle as a warm-up before trying the Maroon Bells or Capitol.

Routes

25.1 Northwest Ridge II, Class 2, Moderate Snow

From Castle Creek Trailhead: 10.0 miles, 4,500 feet

Depending on conditions, this is the easiest route up Castle and the easiest route on an Elk Range fourteener. There is a four-wheel-drive road all the way to 12,800 feet. If you drive that high, this climb becomes a lark. Start at the Castle Creek Trailhead and go southwest up the popular four-wheel-drive road for 2.3 miles to a road junction. In this 2.3 miles, you cross Castle Creek twice, at 10,180 feet and at 11,000 feet. From the junction, continue on the main (right) road northwest into Montezuma Basin. Pass under the ruins of the old Montezuma Mine at 12,400 feet and continue west on the relentless road to its end at 12,800 feet.

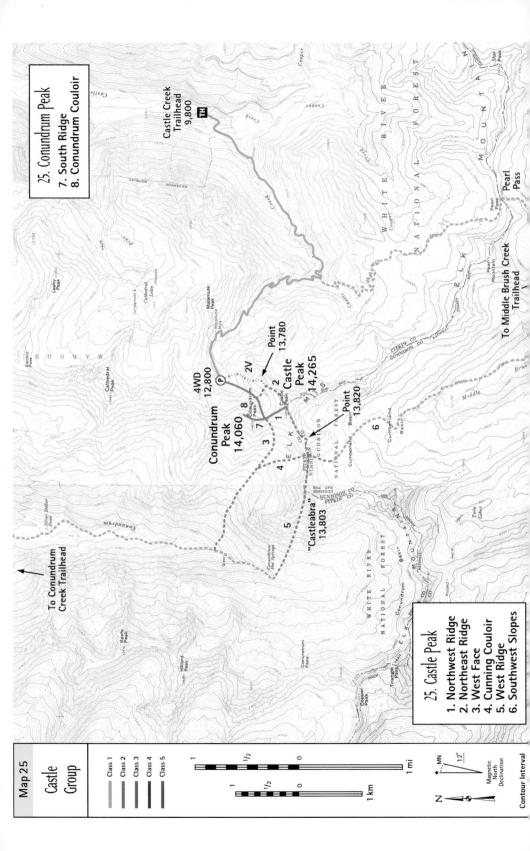

Map 25

Castle
Group

25. Conundrum Peak

7. South Ridge
8. Conundrum Couloir

25. Castle Peak

1. Northwest Ridge
2. Northeast Ridge
3. West Face
4. Cunning Couloir
5. West Ridge
6. Southwest Slopes

Castle Creek
Trailhead
9,800

Point
13,780

4WD
12,800

2V

Castle
Peak
14,265

Point
13,820

Conundrum
Peak
14,060

"Castleabra"
13,803

To Conundrum
Creek Trailhead

To Middle Brush Creek
Trailhead

Pearl
Pass

Class 1
Class 2
Class 3
Class 4
Class 5

1 mi
1/2
0

1 km
1/2
0

Magnetic
North
Declination

12°

MN

N

Contour Interval

Castle Peak from the west.

Hike southwest into upper Montezuma Basin on rocks and snow slopes. The basin under Castle's north face is an exciting place. There are several unavoidable, permanent snow slopes in this basin, and an ice ax is useful on this route year-round. Climb west up a large, moderate snow slope to the 13,820-foot saddle between Castle and 14,060-foot Conundrum Peak, which is 0.4 mile north of Castle. In late summer, the top of the snow slope melts out, revealing 200 feet of steep dirt just below the saddle. When this is the case, the Northeast Ridge Route is easier. From the saddle, turn south (left) and follow a climber's trail up the rocky but easy ridge for 0.25 mile to the summit. You can easily pass several ridge steps on the west.

25.2 Northeast Ridge II, Class 2+, Easy Snow
From Castle Creek Trailhead: 10.0 miles, 4,500 feet

This ridge is slightly harder than the northwest ridge, but this route avoids the moderate snow climb to the Castle–Conundrum Saddle. However, after the snow below that saddle has melted, this is Castle's easiest route. Start at the Castle Creek Trailhead and follow the Northwest Ridge Route beyond the end of the four-wheel-drive road to 13,400 feet in Montezuma Basin. Instead of continuing up the basin, climb south up a good trail through an otherwise loose shale slope to a small, 13,740-foot saddle just west of Point 13,780 on Castle's northeast ridge. From the saddle, follow a climber's trail southwest along the rocky ridge for 0.4 mile to the summit. The steeper parts of this ridge require some Class 2+ scrambling.

Variation 25.2V

This variation avoids all the snow climbing and some of the crowds. From the end of the four-wheel-drive road at 12,800 feet, climb southwest on the south side of a northern buttress below Castle's northeast ridge. You can find reasonable footing between the shale slope south of this buttress and the rocks of the buttress itself. Climb to the summit of Point 13,780 and soak up a marvelous view. Descend slightly to the 13,740-foot saddle and rejoin the Northeast Ridge Route.

25.3 West Face II, Class 3

From Conundrum Creek Trailhead: 19.0 miles, 5,500 feet

This long, seldom climbed route offers a wilderness backpacking alternative to Castle's more pedestrian east side. Start at the Conundrum Creek Trailhead and walk south up the scenic Conundrum Creek Trail for 8.0 miles to Conundrum Hot Springs at 11,200 feet. There are marked campsites below and above the springs, and two pools at the hot springs offer unsophisticated soaking under Castle's western ramparts.

For the ascent, backtrack 0.5 mile north down the trail to 10,800 feet, leave the trail, cross Conundrum Creek and climb steeply east into an unnamed basin west of Castle and Conundrum. This basin is full of obnoxious talus, and this route is best done when the rocks are completely snow-covered. The broad west face between Castle and Conundrum has several scruffy cliffs below Conundrum and below the Castle–Conundrum Saddle. The easiest route stays south of these cliffs. Choose a route up these steep slopes, reach Castle's northwest ridge at 13,900 feet and follow that ridge to the summit.

25.4 Cunning Couloir II, Class 3, Steep Snow (Seasonal)

From Conundrum Creek Trailhead: 19.0 miles, 5,500 feet

This hidden couloir may excite your spirit of adventure. Follow the West Face Route to 12,200 feet, then climb southeast to 13,000 feet and spy the crafty couloir to the south. This north-facing couloir retains snow longer than other routes on Castle and is often a better escape from the basin than the West Face Route. Climb south through embracing cliffs to the 13,380-foot saddle between Point 13,803 to the west and Castle to the east. Continue on Castle's West Ridge Route to Castle's summit.

25.5 West Ridge III, Class 3

From Conundrum Creek Trailhead: 21.0 miles, 6,700 feet

This arduous ascent is best done from a camp at Conundrum Hot Springs. Start at the Conundrum Creek Trailhead and walk south up the scenic Conundrum Creek Trail for 8.0 miles to Conundrum Hot Springs at

11,200 feet. From the hot springs, cross to the creek's east side and go south on a trail for 100 yards to the snout of a large rock glacier. Leave the trail, climb east along the rock glacier's northern edge, then climb steeply east into a tiny basin west of Point 13,803. Persevere up this tiny basin all the way to a 13,620-foot saddle just south of Point 13,803. Early season snow can make this ascent easier. From the 13,620-foot saddle, climb north up scree for 100 yards to the summit of Point 13,803, alias "Castle-abra." This summit is a "Bi," one of Colorado's 200 highest peaks, and provides a suspended view of all the Elk Range fourteeners.

From Castleabra, descend east to the 13,380-foot saddle between Castleabra and the unranked Point 13,820 (Class 2). This saddle is at the top of the Cunning Couloir to the north and the Southwest Slopes Route from Cumberland Basin to the south. Climb east through two small cliff bands (Class 3) and continue up the ridge to Point 13,820. You can see the rest of the route from here. Descend to a 13,580-foot saddle and climb Castle's upper west ridge to Castle's summit. This traverse has several scruffy cliff bands on it that require Class 3 scrambling, but they are not sustained.

25.6 Southwest Slopes II, Class 3
From Middle Brush Creek Trailhead: 22.2 miles, 5,650 feet

This route has a long approach but takes you through Cumberland Basin, one of Colorado's private places. A four-wheel-drive vehicle can shorten the distance considerably, but even that aid can be problematic in wet conditions. The four-wheel-drive road over Pearl Pass is well known as one of Colorado's worst. Consider using a bicycle.

Start at the Middle Brush Creek Trailhead and go 2.5 miles up the four-wheel-drive road in the Middle Brush Creek drainage to a junction at 9,480 feet. Continue north (left) on the Pearl Pass Road in the Middle Brush Creek drainage for an additional 3.2 miles to a junction with the Twin Lakes Trail. Continue on the Pearl Pass Road, ford Middle Brush Creek twice and reach a meadow at 10,820 feet. Four-wheel-drive vehicles can park here. This point is 6.9 miles from the Middle Brush Creek Trailhead.

The old trail up Cumberland Basin is now badly overgrown. The sparse trail will speed you on your way, then desert you when you need it most. It is still worth finding and will reduce your bushwhacking adventure. Walk up the road to a switchback where the road climbs southeast toward Pearl Pass. Leave the road and hike west down to the trail that is visible from here. Hike north on the trail into the Maroon Bells–Snowmass Wilderness. Your wilderness adventure begins shortly beyond the small sign marking the boundary.

The trail leads you down to Middle Brush Creek, where the trail appears to cross and continue on the creek's west side. The astute hiker will stop, check their map and observe that the old trail stays on the creek's east side. You will wonder where as you backtrack along a wall of bushes, but the old trail *does* stay on the creek's east side. It is buried in the bushes near the creek. Depending on your disposition, either find the trail in the bushes or hike east then north around the initial bushes and find the trail farther up the valley. Continue north and make several similar route choices as the bushes persist for 1.5 miles.

Break free from the bushes at 11,700 feet and behold Cumberland Basin. In addition to the basin, you are be treated to an uninterrupted view of Castle's south ridge with its namesake turrets. Hike up through the basin on grass benches, dodging any little cliffs that intervene. Climb north to the 13,380-foot saddle between Point 13,803, alias "Castleabra," and Point 13,820 on Castle's west ridge. The slope up to the saddle is best climbed when snow-covered but provides reasonable passage on scree after the snow melts. Once on the ridge, continue on the West Ridge Route to Castle's summit (Class 3).

25. Conundrum Peak   14,060 feet

See Map 25 on page 210

Because of Conundrum's proximity to Castle, and because Conundrum rises less than 300 feet above its connecting saddle with Castle, it has not qualified as an official fourteener on most peak lists. Nevertheless, the peak is named, it is above 14,000 feet and it provides a worthwhile trip. Conundrum has the distinction of being the easiest fourteener in the Elk Range.

25.7 South Ridge II, Class 2, Moderate Snow

From Castle Creek Trailhead: 10.0 miles, 4,360 feet

This is the easiest route on Conundrum. Follow Castle's Northwest Ridge Route to the 13,820-foot saddle between Castle and Conundrum. When the snow melts below this saddle, the final climb to the saddle becomes an insulting effort tantamount to ascending a slope of ball bearings. Even the Elks' easiest fourteener can provide the uninitiated with a taste of the range's woeful rock!

From the saddle, climb north for 0.15 mile to Conundrum's southern summit. Conundrum has two summits above 14,000 feet. They are 200 yards apart. The southernmost is shown as 14,022 feet on the Hayden Peak Quadrangle. Hike north over this summit, descend into a notch and climb to the slightly higher 14,060-foot summit.

Conundrum Peak from the southeast.

25.8 Conundrum Couloir II, Class 3, Steep Snow (Seasonal)

From Castle Creek Trailhead: 9.6 miles, 4,260 feet

This is the northeast-facing couloir that reaches the notch between Conundrum's two summits. Try it in early summer when it still has continuous snow. Follow Castle's Northwest Ridge Route to 13,400 feet in the bowl between Castle and Conundrum. The deeply inset Conundrum Couloir is easily seen from here as it splits Conundrum's northeast face. There may be some scree below the couloir.

Ascend the arrow-straight defile for 600 feet to the notch. The steepness reaches 47 degrees. There is usually a cornice at the top, and climbing around it is the route's crux. In the notch, Conundrum's highest point waits for you 150 feet to the north. Ascending the Conundrum Couloir and descending the South Ridge Route is a smart Tour de Conundrum. Altitude aficionados may want to continue to Castle.

Leave No Trace!

Pack It in, Pack It Out

- Protect wildlife and your food by storing rations securely.
- Pick up all spilled foods.
- Inspect your campsite for trash and pack it out.

Chapter Six

San Juan Range

Introduction

The San Juan Range is Colorado's finest range. Other Colorado ranges are linear, long and narrow. From their summits, you can almost always see civilization. The San Juans are a vast mountain area in Colorado's southwest corner covering more than 4,000 square miles!

The San Juans contain 11 county summits and 13 fourteeners. Only the Sawatch Range has more fourteeners. Not only are San Juan peaks numerous, they are rugged. Many of Colorado's hardest fourteeners are in the San Juans. The San Juans contain six wilderness areas, including Colorado's largest—the Weminuche Wilderness. The San Juans are less crowded than other ranges closer to the eastern slope's metropolitan areas. It is not reasonable to climb in the San Juans on a two-day weekend from Denver, and this reduces the number of visitors. Even if you live in Durango, there are many San Juan areas that still require a multi-day backpack. The San Juans are full of jagged wilderness!

One unpleasant San Juan reality is rotten rock. If you climb a dozen San Juan peaks, you are bound to find a chip-rock slope to curse. If you climb in the San Juans long enough, you will eventually find yourself on a hard-packed dirt slope covered with ball-bearing debris at the angle of repose. If you are unlucky, there will be a cliff below you. If you keep looking, you will find diseased, knife-edge ridges with no logical means of support. Hardened San Juan veterans will run across exposed junk that can strike terror into the heart of a San Juan novice. If you stick to the standard routes on the fourteeners, you will not encounter these extremes, but approach San Juan peaks with caution.

The large, high area of the San Juans collects a lot of winter snow. The avalanche danger is often extreme in these steep mountains. The deep snow mantle takes a long time to melt, and some areas are not easily accessible until July. Many San Juan peaks carry a lot of snow into August. You should consider carrying an ice ax.

26. San Luis Peak   14,014 feet

See Map 26 on page 218

San Luis is perhaps the least climbed of Colorado's fourteeners. The shy peak is far from everywhere and offers little technical excitement. San Luis, the San Juans' easternmost fourteener, is located in the heart of the La Garita Wilderness, 9 miles north of Creede, 20 miles east of Lake City and 40 miles south of Gunnison. It is precisely San Luis' reclusive nature that makes the peak well worth climbing. Many elk live here, and your chances of seeing a large elk herd on San Luis are good. Also, moose have been reintroduced to Stewart Creek.

Maps

Required: San Luis Peak, Stewart Peak, Elk Park,
Gunnison National Forest
Optional: Halfmoon Pass, Rio Grande National Forest

Trailheads

Stewart Creek Trailhead

This trailhead is at 10,460 feet and provides access to San Luis' east side. There are multiple routes to this trailhead and they are all complicated. The Forest Service maps are a big help in finding this trailhead. Winter road closures are far from this trailhead. Two summer routes are described.

1. Turn south onto Colorado 114 from U.S. 50. This junction is 33.0 miles west of Monarch Pass and 7.5 miles east of Gunnison. Go south on Colorado 114 for 20.0 miles, turn right onto the Old Agency Road (Forest Service 3083) along Cochetopa Creek and measure from this point. Go south along Cochetopa Creek for 3.5 miles and turn west (right) onto Forest Service 3084, which continues as Forest Service 788. Go straight (left) at 12.3 miles and continue on Forest Service 790. Pass Blue Park and, at 22.5 miles, turn left onto Forest Service 794.28 (Perfecto Creek Road). Go south on Forest Service 794.28, cross Pauline and Perfecto Creeks, then turn right at 26.3 miles onto Forest Service 794. Cross Chavez and Nutras Creeks, then descend to the Stewart Creek Trailhead at mile 30.9.

2. From the Colorado 50–Colorado 149 junction west of Gunnison, go south on Colorado 149 for 45.3 miles to Lake City. Continue through Lake City on Colorado 149, then go an additional 8.0 miles to Slumgullion Pass. At Slumgullion Pass, turn north (left) onto Forest Service 788 and

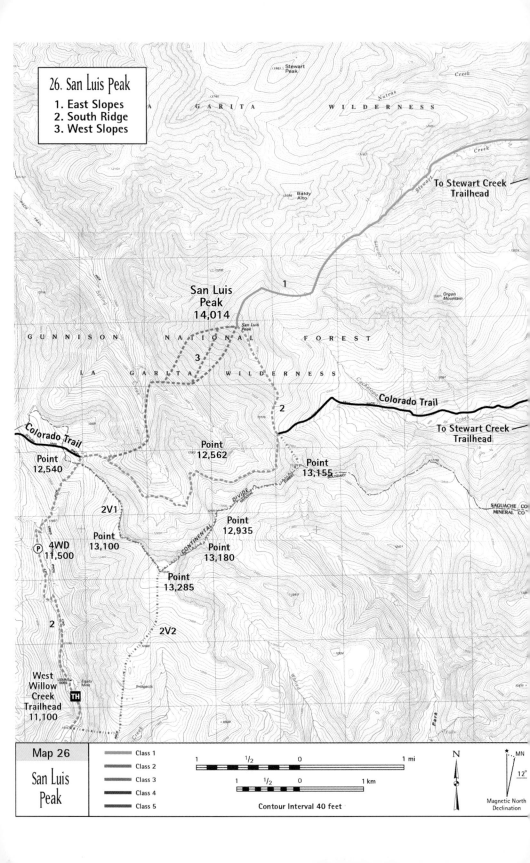

26. San Luis Peak
1. East Slopes
2. South Ridge
3. West Slopes

Stewart Peak

GARITA   WILDERNESS

Natras Creek

Creek

To Stewart Creek
Trailhead

Baldy
Alto

San Luis
Peak
14,014

San Luis
Peak

Organ
Mountain

GUNNISON   NATIONAL   FOREST

3

LA   GARITA   WILDERNESS

2

Colorado Trail

1

To Stewart Creek
Trailhead

Colorado Trail

Point
12,540

Point
12,562

Point
13,155

SAGUACHE CO
MINERAL CO

2V1

DIVIDE

Point
13,100

Point
12,935

CONTINENTAL

Point
13,180

4WD
11,500

Point
13,285

2

2V2

West
Willow
Creek
Trailhead
11,100

TH

Prospects

Map 26		Class 1
		Class 2
San Luis		Class 3
Peak		Class 4
		Class 5

1   1/2   0   1 mi

1   1/2   0   1 km

Contour Interval 40 feet

N

MN

12°

Magnetic North
Declination

San Luis Peak
14,014

2

San Luis Peak from the southwest.

measure from this point. Go 15.0 miles to Cathedral, cross Cebolla Creek, turn right and continue on Forest Service 788. Climb east, cross Los Pinos Pass at mile 20.6 and turn right onto Forest Service 790 at mile 21.7. Go south then east on Forest Service 790, then turn right onto Forest Service 794.28 (Perfecto Creek Road) at mile 31.5. Go south on Forest Service 794.28, cross Pauline and Perfecto Creeks, then turn right at mile 35.3 onto Forest Service 394. Cross Chavez and Nutras Creeks, then descend to the Stewart Creek Trailhead at mile 39.9.

West Willow Creek Trailhead

This trailhead is at 11,100 feet and provides access to San Luis' south side. From the U.S. 160–Colorado 149 junction, go 21.4 miles north to the Willow Creek bridge just south of Creede. You also can reach Creede by driving south on Colorado 149 from Lake City via Slumgullion Pass. From Creede, two approaches to the trailhead are possible. Winter road closure varies but is not far above Creede.

1. This approach is longer and gentler than the second approach. From the Willow Creek bridge just south of Creede, go south on Colorado 149 on the west side of Willow Creek for 0.3 mile to three dirt roads leading west (right). Turn west onto the northernmost (rightmost) of the three dirt roads and measure from this point. Climb the hill southwest of Creede, pass the Creede cemetery turnoff at 0.5 mile, turn west (left) at a T-junction at 1.2 miles, pass the southern turnoff for the Rat Creek–

West Willow Creek 4x4 Loop Road at 3.3 miles and continue on the main road to Allens Crossing over West Willow Creek at mile 6.3. Turn north (left) at a T-junction just east of Allens Crossing and go north to a parking area below the Equity Mine at mile 8.6. The road is excellent to this point, and this is the trailhead.

2. This scenic approach is steep. Measure from the Willow Creek bridge just south of Creede. Go north through Creede and continue north on the dirt road out of town. Pass the Phoenix Park Road at 1.2 miles and continue north up the spectacular West Willow Creek Gorge. Pass the East Willow Creek 4x4 Loop Road at 3.2 miles, pass the Nelson Mountain Road at 4.9 miles and continue north to Allens Crossing, where the first approach joins this route at mile 5.3. From Allens Crossing, go north to the trailhead parking area below the Equity Mine at mile 7.6.

The trailhead parking area is 100 yards north of the northern junction with the Rat Creek–West Willow Creek 4x4 Loop Road. Four-wheel-drive vehicles can continue north on this road for an additional 1.6 miles, crossing West Willow Creek twice, to a parking spot at 11,500 feet, just before the road leaves the valley and climbs steeply up the hill to the west.

Routes

26.1 East Slopes II, Class 1
From Stewart Creek Trailhead: 12.0 miles, 3,600 feet

This is the easiest route on San Luis. From the Stewart Creek Trailhead, hike west up Stewart Creek on a trail for 4.0 miles through a wonderful wilderness to tree line at 12,000 feet. Climb southwest on a climber's trail to the 13,107-foot saddle between San Luis and 13,801-foot Organ Mountain, which is 2.0 miles east of San Luis. From the saddle, climb west on a good climber's trail through the scree below a rounded ridge to San Luis' 13,700-foot northeast shoulder and follow the ridge southwest for 0.5 mile to the summit.

26.2 South Ridge II, Class 1
From West Willow Creek Trailhead: 13.8 miles, 3,900 feet
From 4WD parking: 10.6 miles, 3,500 feet

This interesting alternative route is only slightly longer than the East Slopes Route. The route is almost entirely above tree line. Start at the West Willow Creek Trailhead, go south for 100 yards and go north on the Rat Creek–West Willow Creek 4x4 Loop Road for 1.6 miles, crossing West Willow Creek twice en route, until the road turns steeply up the hill to the west (left) at 11,500 feet.

Leave the Rat Creek–West Willow Creek 4x4 Loop Road here and continue north on an old four-wheel-drive road that soon crosses back to the creek's east side. Follow the old road as it climbs northeast up a shoulder to the broad, 12,300-foot saddle just southeast of Point 12,540. You can see the old road and the rocky Point 12,540 from below. You will first see San Luis when you reach the saddle, and this is a postcard view.

Cross the saddle southeast of Point 12,540 and descend north for 100 yards to the excellent Colorado Trail. Follow this trail east as it descends to a low point of 11,900 feet in the trees, then contours and climbs around a basin to a 12,380-foot saddle in the upper Spring Creek drainage. Continue east on the excellent trail as it contours around a second basin, then climbs north to the 12,620-foot saddle between San Luis and Point 13,155, which is 1.5 miles south of San Luis. The approach is over. From this saddle, walk north up San Luis' gentle, easy south ridge for 1.1 miles to the summit.

Variations
26.2V1

This major variation allows you to stay even higher and climb three thirteeners on your way to San Luis. From the 12,300-foot saddle just southeast of Point 12,540, climb southeast up the gentle ridge for 0.8 mile to Point 13,100. This is a false summit, but it provides a good view of the terrain ahead. Continue southeast for an additional 0.5 mile to Point 13,285—a ranked thirteener. Curiously, the highest point is 200 yards northeast of the rounded summit that the map marks as 13,285. The true high point is at least 5 feet higher. The map does not record this fact.

The next stretch of ridge requires some Class 3 scrambling and is out of character with the rest of this gentle hike. Descend steeply on the south side of the rough ridge leading northeast from Point 13,285 (some Class 3). Pick your way to a point near the 12,900-foot saddle between Point 13,285 and Point 13,180, then ascend Point 13,180 via some nifty Class 3 scrambling. Point 13,180 has a soft rank (see "Peak List" in the Appendix for a definition of *soft rank*) and only appears on peak lists that record such minutia.

Follow the now gentle ridge northeast over or around Point 12,935 and on toward Point 13,155, another ranked thirteener. Another rough stretch of ridge southwest of this summit requires some Class 3 scrambling. Climb the spectacular summit block of Point 13,155 on its north side via a solid, 40-foot, Class 3 scramble. Descend north from Point 13,155 to the 12,620-foot saddle between Point 13,155 and San Luis and continue up San Luis' south ridge.

26.2V2

Start your climb 0.5 mile south of (below) the West Willow Creek Trailhead where another road crosses to the creek's east side. Climb east up the steep, grassy slope above this point to yet another road on the broad ridge above. Follow this road north up the gentle ridge to the summit of Point 13,285 and join Variation 26.2V1 here.

26.3 West Slopes II, Class 2, Easy Snow (Seasonal)
From West Willow Creek Trailhead: 11.2 miles, 5,140 feet

This used to be the standard route on San Luis, but access problems in Spring Creek have relegated it to an alternate route. Still accessible from the West Willow Creek Trailhead, this route offers an interesting approach and a seasonal snow climb. People usually do this route to experience good snow in the Yawner Gullies on San Luis' southwest face.

Start at the West Willow Creek Trailhead and follow the South Ridge Route to the Colorado Trail below the 12,300-foot saddle southeast of Point 12,540. Descend east on the Colorado Trail for 0.35 mile to a switchback at 11,940 feet. Leave the Colorado Trail and boldly descend into the upper Spring Creek drainage. Descend to 11,200 feet and contour around the north end of Point 12,562 to the base of San Luis' southwest face.

If you are here for a snow climb, choose one of the three Yawner Gullies. The northern and central gullies reach the upper part of San Luis' rounded west shoulder, while the southern Yawner follows a classic line directly to the summit. The central gully's steepness does not exceed 30 degrees. If you are here after the snow is gone, climb steeply up San Luis' rounded west shoulder north of the Yawner Gullies directly to the summit. Ascending this route and descending the South Ridge Route makes a fine Tour de San Luis.

27. Uncompahgre Group
Uncompahgre Peak   14,309 feet
Wetterhorn Peak   14,015 feet

See Map 27 on page 223

These dramatic peaks guard the San Juans' northern edge about 10 miles west of Lake City. Uncompahgre's great height and Wetterhorn's classic shape make them siren sentinels. They can be seen from many vantage points. Together, they provide an excellent outing.

Maps
Required: Uncompahgre Peak, Wetterhorn Peak, Uncompahgre National Forest
Optional: Lake City, Courthouse Mountain

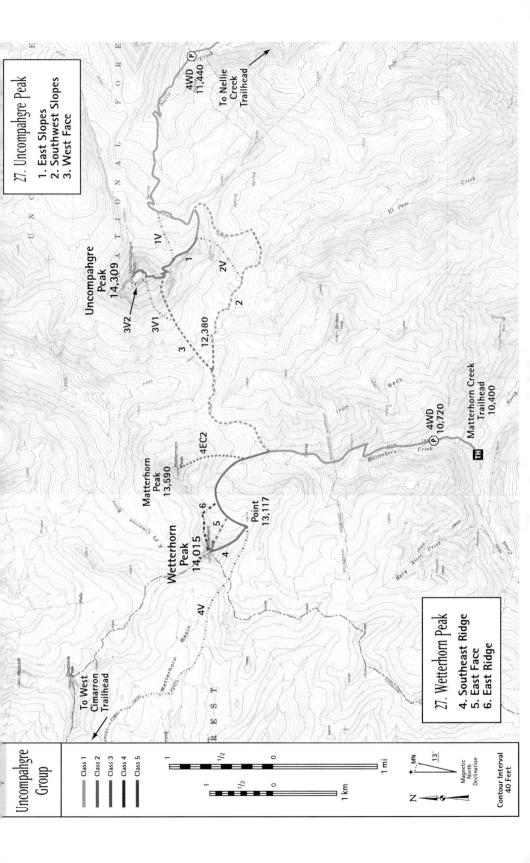

27. Uncompahgre Peak
1. East Slopes
2. Southwest Slopes
3. West Face

Uncompahgre Peak
14,309

Matterhorn Peak
13,590

Wetterhorn Peak
14,015

Point 13,117

Matterhorn Creek Trailhead
10,400

4WD
10,720

4WD
11,440

To Nellie Creek Trailhead

To West Cimarron Trailhead

27. Wetterhorn Peak
4. Southeast Ridge
5. East Face
6. East Ridge

Uncompahgre Group

Class 1
Class 2
Class 3
Class 4
Class 5

1 mi
1 km

MN
13°
Magnetic North Declination

N

Contour Interval
40 Feet

Trailheads

Nellie Creek Trailhead

This trailhead is at 9,300 feet and provides access to Uncompahgre's east side. From the Colorado 50–Colorado 149 junction west of Gunnison, go south on Colorado 149 for 45.3 miles to Lake City. Measure from the junction of Second Street and Gunnison Avenue (Colorado 149) in downtown Lake City. There is a sign here for Engineer Pass. Leave Colorado 149 and go west on Second Avenue for two blocks to a T-junction at Bluff Street. Turn south (left) and follow the dirt Henson Creek Road (Hinsdale County Road 20) west up Henson Creek. Pass the old Henson townsite at 3.9 miles and reach the signed Nellie Creek Road at 5.2 miles. Passenger cars should park here, at 9,300 feet. There is a legal campsite at Nellie Creek, but camping is not permitted elsewhere along this portion of the Henson Creek Road. In winter the Henson Creek Road is plowed to Nellie Creek.

The road up Nellie Creek requires a four-wheel-drive vehicle. From the Henson Creek Road, turn north and follow the Nellie Creek Road as it climbs along Nellie Creek's east side. The road crosses to Nellie Creek's west side at 7.1 miles. Turn west (sharp left) at 7.4 miles and continue northwest into upper Nellie Creek to the end of the road at 9.1 miles. The road ends at 11,440 feet at the boundary of the Big Blue Wilderness, and Uncompahgre's great mass dominates the view to the west.

Matterhorn Creek Trailhead

This trailhead is at 10,400 feet and provides access to Wetterhorn's south side and Uncompahgre's west side. From the Colorado 50–Colorado 149 junction west of Gunnison, go south on Colorado 149 for 45.3 miles to Lake City. Measure from the junction of Second Street and Gunnison Avenue (Colorado 149) in downtown Lake City. There is a sign here for Engineer Pass. Leave Colorado 149 and go west on Second Avenue for two blocks to a T-junction at Bluff Street. Turn south (left) and follow the dirt Henson Creek Road (Hinsdale County Road 20) west up Henson Creek. Pass the old Henson townsite at 3.9 miles, pass the signed Nellie Creek Road at 5.2 miles, pass El Paso Creek at 7.4 miles and reach the North Henson Creek Road in the old Capitol City townsite after 9.2 miles. This point is at 9,700 feet and is easily reached with passenger cars. Other than the campsite at Nellie Creek, camping is not permitted along the Henson Creek Road between Lake City and Capitol City. The road to Capitol City is often open in late April.

Leave the main Henson Creek Road and continue northwest on the North Henson Creek Road (Forest Service Road 870), which is steep and rough but still passable for most passenger cars. Reach Matterhorn Creek at 11.2 miles. This point is at 10,400 feet. This is the trailhead, and most parties park here. There are some pleasant campsites between Capitol City and Matterhorn Creek. From 10,400 feet, a four-wheel-drive road goes up Matterhorn Creek's east side for 0.6 mile to 10,720 feet, where there is a parking area below a Forest Service gate.

West Cimarron Trailhead

This trailhead is at 10,750 feet and provides access to Wetterhorn Basin on Wetterhorn's west side. The trailhead can be reached from either the Cimarron Creek Road or the Owl Creek Pass Road.

For the Cimarron approach: On U.S. 50, go 2.7 miles east of Cimarron. Cimarron is 45 miles west of Gunnison and 20 miles east of Montrose. Turn south onto the well-maintained Cimarron Creek Road and measure from this point. Go around Silver Jack Reservoir's east side at 18.0 miles, turn right at 20.3 miles, turn right at 20.5 miles, pass the Owl Creek Pass turnoff at 27.1 miles, cross a stream at 30.0 miles and reach the trailhead after 30.6 miles.

For the Owl Creek approach: On U.S. 550, go 1.8 miles north of Ridgway. Ridgway is 26 miles south of Montrose and 11 miles north of Ouray. Drive east for 13.0 miles over Owl Creek Pass to the Cimarron Creek Road, turn south (right) and reach the trailhead after 16.5 miles. The last 2.0 miles are rough, and you may choose to park before you reach the trailhead.

Middle Cimarron Trailhead

This little-used trailhead is at 10,000 feet and provides access to Wetterhorn's north side. On U.S. 50, go 2.7 miles east of Cimarron. Cimarron is 45 miles west of Gunnison and 20 miles east of Montrose. Turn south onto the well-maintained Cimarron Creek Road and measure from this point. Go around Silver Jack Reservoir's east side at 18.0 miles, turn right at 20.3 miles, then turn left at 20.5 miles onto the rougher Middle Fork Road and follow it to the trailhead at 25.2 miles.

27. Uncompahgre Peak   14,309 feet

See Map 27 on page 223

This *uncompahrable* peak claims many titles. It is Colorado's sixth highest peak, the highest peak in the San Juans and the highest peak in Hinsdale County. *Uncompahgre* is a Native American word from the Ute Nation meaning "hot-water spring." You can easily recognize its shapely size from many viewpoints. Uncompahgre is a peak of contrasts. A trail reaches the summit from the south, but the peak has a fearsome, vertical, 700-foot-high north face. Courtly cliffs grace this compelling peak's lower ramparts, and clever routes winding past them will draw you upward.

Routes

27.1 East Slopes I, Class 2

From Nellie Creek Trailhead: 15.4 miles, 5,000 feet

From 4WD parking at wilderness boundary: 7.6 miles, 2,870 feet

This is the easiest route on Uncompahgre, but without a four-wheel-drive vehicle, it is long. From the Nellie Creek Trailhead at 9,300 feet, follow the four-wheel-drive Nellie Creek Road as it climbs along Nellie Creek's east side. The road crosses to Nellie Creek's west side after 1.9 miles. Turn west (sharp left) after 2.2 miles and continue northwest into upper Nellie Creek to the end of the road at the wilderness boundary, 3.9 miles above the trailhead.

From the wilderness boundary at 11,440 feet, follow the well-worn trail west as it climbs steadily toward the peak. At 12,700 feet, the trail swings south to reach the south ridge at 13,300 feet. The trail follows this ridge north, dodges cliffs between 13,800 feet and 14,000 feet and finishes on the gentle, upper south slopes.

Variation 27.1V

Leave the trail at 12,700 feet and climb straight west up the slope to rejoin the trail at 13,400 feet.

27.2 Southwest Slopes II, Class 2

From Matterhorn Creek Trailhead: 14.0 miles, 4,300 feet

From 4WD parking at 10,720 feet: 12.8 miles, 3,980 feet

This easy route is longer than the East Slopes Route but allows you to climb Uncompahgre and Wetterhorn together. This route dodges all the cliffs on Uncompahgre's west side and is little more than a long trail hike.

Start at the Matterhorn Creek Trailhead and follow the four-wheel-drive road up Matterhorn Creek's east side to the Forest Service gate at 10,720 feet. Continue on the old road beyond the gate. At 11,200 feet, 0.7 mile above the gate, do not follow the trail that continues up Matterhorn Creek. Instead, switchback up the steep hill east of Matterhorn Creek and enter the Big Blue Wilderness at 10,580 feet.

You will see Matterhorn Peak (13,590 feet) first, then Wetterhorn. Matterhorn is the stately peak between Uncompahgre and Wetterhorn. From the wilderness boundary, continue north on the trail to the 12,458-foot pass southeast of Matterhorn. Uncompahgre is not visible until you reach this pass, but the view from the pass will knock your socks off.

Cross the pass, contour east and descend slightly to a broad, 12,380-foot saddle southwest of Uncompahgre. Cross this saddle and contour southeast under all the lower cliffs on Uncompahgre's west side. When

Uncompahgre Peak from the southwest.

clear of the cliffs, climb east to join a spur of the East Slopes Trail. Follow this trail to the East Slopes Trail, then follow that trail north to the summit. This is the same finish as the East Slopes Route.

Variation 27.2V

This shortcut is especially useful when the slopes are snow-covered. From 12,200 feet, climb east then north to rejoin the route at 13,260 feet.

27.3 West Face II, Class 2, Moderate Snow (Seasonal)

From Matterhorn Creek Trailhead: 10.0 miles, 4,300 feet

From 4WD parking at 10,720 feet: 8.8 miles, 3,980 feet

This route provides a direct, sporting alternative to the Southwest Slopes Route. Uncompahgre's west face provides a good snow climb in May and June of a normal snow year. Later in the summer, the scree on the west face is unpleasant, and climbing it is environmentally incorrect.

Start at the Matterhorn Creek Trailhead and follow the four-wheel-drive road up Matterhorn Creek's east side to the Forest Service gate at 10,720 feet. Continue on the old road beyond the gate. At 11,200 feet, 0.7 mile above the gate, do not follow the trail that continues up Matterhorn Creek. Instead, switchback up the steep hill east of Matterhorn Creek and enter the Big Blue Wilderness at 10,580 feet. Continue north on the trail to the 12,458-foot pass southeast of Matterhorn Peak.

From the pass, you can see three shallow gully systems on Uncompahgre's west face. Cross the pass, contour east and descend to 12,240 feet. Continue east and ascend the southernmost of the three gullies to reach a broad shoulder on the south ridge at 13,800 feet. Follow the trail north to the summit.

Variations

27.3V1 II, Class 2, Moderate Snow (Seasonal)

Ascend the central gully on the west face instead of the southernmost gully. The central gully's difficulty is the same as the southernmost gully, but the central gully is longer. The central gully ends under the final summit cliff. Angle south (right) to avoid the cliff and reach the easy, upper south slopes at 14,100 feet. Stroll north to the highest point. The central gully is a test piece for skiers.

27.3V2 II, Class 4, Moderate Snow (Seasonal)

This dangerous variation allows a direct approach to the summit from the west. Follow Variation 27.3V1 to the final summit cliff. Angle north (left) under the cliff for 200 yards. A series of debris-covered ledges hide on the summit cliff's north end. Zigzag up these ledges, climbing short sections of rock between them, and arrive on the summit plateau 100 feet west of the highest point.

27. Wetterhorn Peak   14,015 feet

See Map 27 on page 223

Colorado's Wetterhorn is named after the extant Wetterhorn rising above Grindelwald in Switzerland's Bernese Alps. The Swiss Wetterhorn is the more famous of the two, and its ornamental shape dignifies many postcards. Nevertheless, Colorado's Wetterhorn has several advantages. It is higher—the Swiss Wetterhorn rises to a paltry 12,142 feet, while Colorado's Wetterhorn exceeds the magic 14,000-foot height. Also, if you live in the western United States, Colorado's Wetterhorn is more accessible. It is good to remember a peak's roots, however. *Wetterhorn* means "weather peak" in German.

Colorado's Wetterhorn is an elegant peak with four ridges and four faces. The near-vertical, 800-foot-high north face gives the peak its distinctive shape, and the southeast ridge offers a more moderate approach to the summit. Even by its easiest route, Wetterhorn is a challenging peak. It has more to offer the technical mountaineer than many of Colorado's easy fourteeners.

Routes

27.4 Southeast Ridge II, Class 3 *Classic*

From Matterhorn Creek Trailhead: 8.0 miles, 3,600 feet

From 4WD parking at 10,720 feet: 6.8 miles, 3,280 feet

This is the easiest route up Wetterhorn. It is an engaging climb with a spectacular finish to a tiny summit. This route is a good introduction to the harder fourteeners for hikers who have climbed several easy fourteeners and are ready to advance.

Start at the Matterhorn Creek Trailhead and follow the four-wheel-drive road up Matterhorn Creek's east side to the Forest Service gate at 10,720 feet. Continue on the old road beyond the gate. At 11,200 feet, 0.7 mile above the gate, do not follow the trail that continues up Matterhorn Creek. Instead, switchback up the steep hill east of Matterhorn Creek and enter the Big Blue Wilderness at 10,580 feet. You will see Matterhorn Peak first, then Wetterhorn. Matterhorn (13,590 feet) is the stately peak between Uncompahgre and Wetterhorn.

Leave the trail at 12,040 feet and climb into the south-facing basin between Matterhorn and Wetterhorn. Climb into the basin, turning west then southwest under Wetterhorn's sweeping east face. The southeast ridge soars above and looks impressive. Take heart, because it is easier to climb than it appears. Climb to the 13,060-foot saddle on the southeast ridge between Point 13,117 and Wetterhorn. The introduction is over.

Turn northwest (right) and ascend the southeast ridge. The ridge is easy at first, but the difficulties increase as you approach the summit. Pass some gnarly-looking towers between 13,400 feet and 13,700 feet on the west (left) side of the ridge. The climbing in this section is mostly Class 2, with an occasional Class 3 spot. Above the initial towers is a prominent tower called the "Ship's Prow" just below the final summit cliff. Pass easily by the Ship's Prow on the ridge's east (right) side. Climb into the easternmost of two notches between the Ship's Prow and Wetterhorn's summit. You can now see the west-facing summit pitch for the first time.

The summit pitch is Class 3. From the notch, traverse north for 15 feet, then ascend a shallow gully for 150 feet to the summit. The easiest climbing is occasionally in the gully, but is more often on the gully's north (left) side. The pitch ends abruptly a few feet from the highest point. Although the difficulty of the summit pitch is only Class 3, it is exposed and somewhat loose. Some parties choose to use a rope on it and some do not. Use your judgment.

Variation 27.4V

You can approach this climb from Wetterhorn Basin on Wetterhorn's west side. This much longer approach is suitable for a backpacking trip.

Start at the West Cimarron Trailhead and follow the West Fork Trail south for 3.5 miles to the 12,500-foot pass west of Coxcomb Peak (13,656 feet). Cross the pass, descend on the trail into Wetterhorn Basin and cross Wetterhorn Creek at 11,720 feet. Continue southeast on the trail for an additional 0.6 mile to 12,060 feet. Leave the trail and climb southeast for 0.7 mile to a 12,860-foot pass west of Wetterhorn. The view of Wetterhorn from here is neck-bending.

Cross the 12,860-foot pass and continue southeast for an additional 0.5 mile to the 13,060-foot saddle on Wetterhorn's southeast ridge between Point 13,117 and Wetterhorn. Continue up the Southeast Ridge Route.

Extra Credit
27.4EC1 Class 3

Climb the Ship's Prow. From the westernmost notch between the summit cliff and the Ship's Prow, you can reach the tower's summit with 40 feet of exposed, north-facing, Class 3 scrambling.

27.4EC2 Class 3

Climb Matterhorn Peak (13,590 feet). Colorado's Matterhorn is only a faint echo of *the* Matterhorn. Colorado's Matterhorn is between Wetterhorn and Uncompahgre, and people often climb it with the fourteeners. Matterhorn can provide a good warm-up climb. The easiest route on Matterhorn is up the broad south slopes that narrow to a ridge, which requires some minor Class 3 scrambling near the summit. From Matterhorn's summit, there are great views of both Wetterhorn and Uncompahgre.

27.5 East Face II, Class 3, Steep Snow (Seasonal)
From Matterhorn Creek Trailhead: 8.0 miles, 3,600 feet
From 4WD parking at 10,720 feet: 6.8 miles, 3,280 feet

Wetterhorn's sweeping east face lies between the east ridge and the southeast ridge. It provides a direct snow climb when snow conditions permit in May and June. After the snow melts, avoid this face. Follow the Southeast Ridge Route into the basin between Matterhorn and Wetterhorn. Climb directly up the east face, dodging any rock outcroppings, to the base of the summit cliff. Skirt west (left) under the summit cliff and finish the climb with the Southeast Ridge Route's summit pitch.

27.6 East Ridge II, Class 4
From Matterhorn Creek Trailhead: 8.0 miles, 3,600 feet
From 4WD parking at 10,720 feet: 6.8 miles, 3,280 feet

This ridge connects Wetterhorn with Matterhorn. It is harder and more complicated than the southeast ridge. It provides an interesting alpine

Wetterhorn Peak from the east.

challenge, especially with the addition of snow. The complete traverse from Matterhorn to Wetterhorn is arduous.

Follow the Southeast Ridge Route into the basin between Matterhorn and Wetterhorn. Gain the east ridge near its low point on the west side of a cone-shaped tower. Follow the rocky ridge west to the base of the summit tower. Skirt the summit tower on its south side and finish the climb with the Southeast Ridge Route's summit pitch.

27. Uncompahgre and Wetterhorn Combination

See Map 27 on page 223

27.7 II, Class 3, Moderate Snow (Seasonal and Optional)
From Matterhorn Creek Trailhead: 11.6 to 16.5 miles, 5,550 to 5,850 feet
With Matterhorn Peak: 13.0 to 17.9 miles, 6,680 to 6,980 feet

People often climb Uncompahgre and Wetterhorn together, but it is not a slam dunk. The two peaks are 3 miles apart, and Matterhorn Peak is between them. The length of the combination depends on whether you use Uncompahgre's Southwest Slopes or West Face Route.

You can do the peaks in either order, but it makes more sense to do Uncompahgre first. Start at the Matterhorn Creek Trailhead and follow either the Southwest Slopes or West Face Route up Uncompahgre. Return to the 12,458-foot pass below Matterhorn, contour west into the basin between Matterhorn and Wetterhorn, then continue up Wetterhorn's Southeast Ridge Route.

28. Handies Group

Redcloud Peak	14,034 feet
Sunshine Peak	14,001 feet
Handies Peak	14,048 feet

See Map 28 on page 234

These engaging peaks rise in moderate, complicated terrain 10 miles southwest of Lake City. They offer a variety of modest routes in a beautiful setting. These peaks are in the San Juans! This alone recommends them.

Maps

Required: Redcloud Peak, Handies Peak, Uncompahgre National Forest
Optional: Lake San Cristobal, Lake City

Trailheads

Mill Creek Trailhead

This trailhead is at 9,440 feet and provides access to Sunshine Peak's south side. From the junction of Colorado 50 and Colorado 149 west of Gunnison, go south on Colorado 149 for 45.3 miles to Lake City. Measuring from the bridge over Henson Creek in downtown Lake City, go south on Colorado 149 for 2.2 miles and turn right onto the Lake San Cristobal Road. Go around Lake San Cristobal's west side and continue up the beautiful Lake Fork of the Gunnison River. Pass the Williams Creek Campground at 9.1 miles, pass the Wager Gulch–Carson Road at 11.3 miles and reach the Mill Creek Campground after 13.1 miles. Park in or near the campground. This trailhead is often accessible in winter.

Silver Creek–Grizzly Gulch Trailhead

This trailhead is at 10,400 feet and provides access to the Silver Creek and Grizzly Gulch Trails. The Silver Creek Trail leads to Redcloud's north side, and the Grizzly Gulch Trail leads to Handies' east side.

From the Mill Creek Campground (mile 13.1), continue west on the main road and turn northwest (right) onto Cinnamon Pass Road at 14.3 miles. Follow the Cinnamon Pass shelf road as it climbs northwest and reach the trailhead after 18.3 miles. Park on the east side of the road. The road is passable for passenger cars to this point, and there are camping spots at or near the parking area. The Silver Creek Trail heads east from the parking area. The Grizzly Gulch Trail starts on the west side of the road and heads west across the Lake Fork of the Gunnison River.

The other approach to this trailhead requires a four-wheel-drive vehicle. From Durango, go north on U.S. 550 to Silverton. Measuring from Silverton's north end, follow the Animas River Road (Colorado 110) for 12.3 miles to Animas Forks, climb steeply east to reach Cinnamon Pass at 15.3 miles, cross the pass and descend on its east side to reach the Silver Creek–Grizzly Gulch Trailhead after 21.1 miles.

American Basin Trailhead

This summer trailhead is at 11,300 feet and provides access to American Basin and Handies' northwest side. From the Silver Creek–Grizzly Gulch Trailhead (mile 18.3 from Lake City), continue on the Cinnamon Pass Road, pass the Cooper Creek Road at 19.1 miles and reach the American Basin Trailhead after 21.9 miles. The trailhead is just before a steep switchback on the Cinnamon Pass Road, and parking here is limited. The last mile to the trailhead is steep but passable for most passenger cars. From the trailhead, a four-wheel-drive road continues south into American Basin under Handies' west side.

The other approach to this trailhead requires a four-wheel-drive vehicle. From Durango, go north on U.S. 550 to Silverton. Measuring from Silverton's north end, follow the Animas River Road (Colorado 110) for 12.3 miles to Animas Forks, climb steeply east to reach Cinnamon Pass at 15.3 miles, cross the pass and descend on its east side to reach the American Basin Trailhead after 17.5 miles.

Grouse Gulch Trailhead

This trailhead is at 10,760 feet and provides access to the Grouse Creek Trail, American Basin and Handies' west side. This trailhead is a much shorter drive when approaching from the Durango area, and you do not need a four-wheel-drive vehicle.

From Durango, go north on U.S. 550 to Silverton. Measuring from Silverton's north end, go east on Colorado 110 for 4.2 miles to Howardsville, continue northeast up the Animas River Valley and reach the Eureka townsite at 8.0 miles. Cross to the Animas River's west side, continue up the steep shelf road, pass the Burns Gulch turnoff at 11.0 miles and reach the Grouse Gulch Trailhead after 11.2 miles. The Grouse Gulch Trail (initially a road) heads east from the Animas River Road just after the road crosses back to the river's east side.

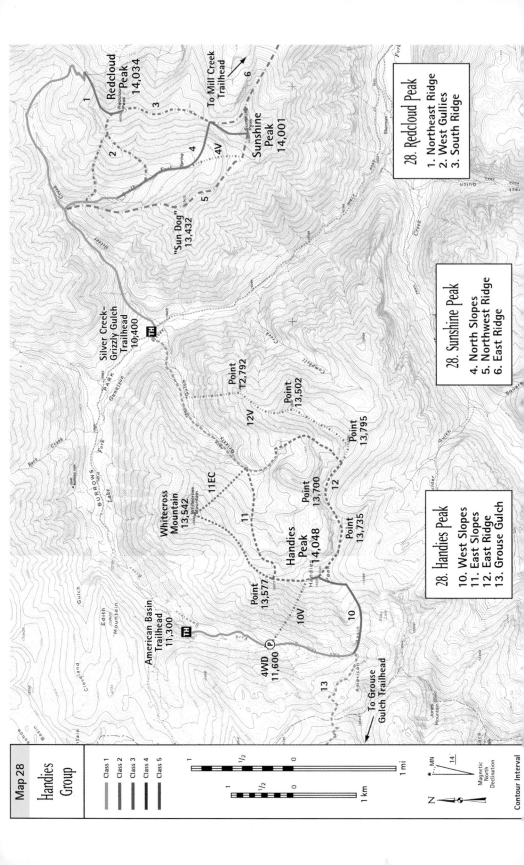

Map 28

Handies Group

Class 1
Class 2
Class 3
Class 4
Class 5

1 mi
1 km

MN
14°

Magnetic
North
Declination

N

Contour Interval

28. Redcloud Peak
1. Northeast Ridge
2. West Gullies
3. South Ridge

28. Sunshine Peak
4. North Slopes
5. Northwest Ridge
6. East Ridge

28. Handies Peak
10. West Slopes
11. East Slopes
12. East Ridge
13. Grouse Gulch

Redcloud
Peak
14,034

To Mill Creek
Trailhead

Sunshine
Peak
14,001

"Sun Dog"
13,432

Silver Creek-
Grizzly Gulch
Trailhead
10,400

Point
12,792

Point
13,502

Point
13,795

Whitecross
Mountain
13,542

Point
13,700

Handies
Peak
14,048

Point
13,735

Point
13,577

American Basin
Trailhead
11,300

4WD
11,600

To Grouse
Gulch Trailhead

BURROWS

12V

11EC

11

10V

10

13

Redcloud Peak from the east.

28. Redcloud Peak 14,034 feet

See Map 28 on page 234

You cannot easily see this well-named peak from surrounding valleys. Only by climbing out of the valleys and spying on it from afar, or by approaching it directly, will you come to know it. People usually climb Redcloud together with its southern neighbor, Sunshine.

Routes

28.1 Northeast Ridge II, Class 2

From Silver Creek–Grizzly Gulch Trailhead: 8.6 miles, 3,650 feet

This is the easiest route up Redcloud. The route climbs steadily as it circles the peak to reach the summit. Start at the Silver Creek–Grizzly Gulch Trailhead and hike northeast up the Silver Creek Trail. After 1.5 miles, pass the junction with the south fork of Silver Creek, which drains the basin northwest of Redcloud and Sunshine. Continue east on the main Silver Creek Trail into the basin north of Redcloud, then gradually turn south and switchback up to the 13,020-foot pass northeast of Redcloud. The trail is good to this point.

From the pass, ascend a strong climber's trail up Redcloud's northeast ridge for 0.4 mile. The trail is surprisingly steep for several hundred feet, but the angle relents at 13,800 feet. Follow the now gentle ridge for 0.2 mile as it curves south to the summit.

28.2 West Gullies II, Class 2, Moderate Snow (Seasonal)

From Silver Creek–Grizzly Gulch Trailhead: 7.0 miles, 3,650 feet

Redcloud's west side sports several gullies that provide shorter routes than the Northeast Ridge Route. When snow conditions are good, these gullies can provide a direct ascent route or a speedy descent. Avoid the gullies when they are snow-free, because the scree on this side of Redcloud is steep and unpleasant.

Start at the Silver Creek–Grizzly Gulch Trailhead and hike northeast up the Silver Creek Trail for 1.5 miles to the junction with the south fork of Silver Creek at 11,300 feet. Leave the Silver Creek Trail, cross Silver Creek and find a good trail in the bushes south of Silver Creek and east of the south-fork creek. Follow the south-fork trail on the east side of the creek into the rugged gulch under Redcloud's west face.

There are two main gullies to choose from on Redcloud's west face. The northern gully is the steepest and most direct, while the southern gully provides a slightly longer, gentler route. The bottom of the northern gully is only 0.25 mile up the south fork from Silver Creek, and the bottom of the southern gully is 0.9 mile up the south fork. There is a comfortable camping spot in the south fork between the two gullies at 11,950 feet.

Choose your gully and climb it. The gullies end below the summit, and the routes rejoin at 13,400 feet. The scree from here to the summit can be unpleasant after the snow melts.

28.3 South Ridge II, Class 2

From Silver Creek–Grizzly Gulch Trailhead: 7.8 to 8.6 miles, 3,650 feet

Use this ridge when climbing Redcloud and Sunshine together. Follow Sunshine's North Slopes Route to the 13,500-foot saddle between Redcloud and Sunshine. From this saddle, it is an easy mile north to Redcloud's summit. There is a trail on the ridge that skirts several minor false summits on the ridge's west side.

28. Sunshine Peak   14,001 feet

See Map 28 on page 234

Sunshine is 1.3 miles south of Redcloud; people often climb these two peaks together. The ridge between Sunshine and Redcloud is gentle and easy. Sunshine has one distinction its higher neighbor lacks: It is the lowest fourteener in North America. But even the lowest fourteener needs to be climbed!

Routes

28.4 North Slopes II, Class 2, Moderate Snow (Seasonal)
From Silver Creek–Grizzly Gulch Trailhead: 7.6 miles, 3,600 feet

This route has a lot to recommend it when snow conditions are good. It provides a trail approach through an enchanted forest, a picturesque cirque and a snow climb leading to a distinctive summit.

Start at the Silver Creek–Grizzly Gulch Trailhead and hike northeast up the Silver Creek Trail for 1.5 miles to the junction with the south fork of Silver Creek at 11,300 feet. Leave the Silver Creek Trail, cross Silver Creek and find a good trail in the bushes south of Silver Creek and east of the south-fork creek. Follow the south-fork trail on the east side of the creek into the rugged gulch under Redcloud's west face. There is a comfortable camping spot in the south fork at 11,950 feet just below tree line.

Pass tree line and continue south to 12,600 feet in the basin under Sunshine's north slopes. The south-fork trail is good to this point. Climb a steep slope onto a rock glacier and continue on the climber's trail as it curves southeast. At 12,800 feet, the route steepens dramatically and ascends the scruffy slope to the 13,500-foot Sunshine–Redcloud Saddle. This west-facing slope provides a nice snow climb when snow-covered, but the snow melts early on this slope. When snow-free, the trail dodges some small rock outcrops as it winds upward. Loose rocks can be a hazard on this slope. From the 13,500-foot Sunshine–Redcloud Saddle, climb southwest for 0.4 mile up Sunshine's northeast ridge to the summit.

Variation 28.4V

This is a more sporting finish. From 12,600 feet in the basin, climb southwest up a moderate snow slope to a small plateau at 13,300 feet, 0.4 mile northwest of the summit. The easiest route from the plateau to the summit follows an old trail that angles up east to join Sunshine's northeast ridge 250 feet below the summit.

28.5 Northwest Ridge II, Class 2+
From Silver Creek–Grizzly Gulch Trailhead: 7.6 miles, 3,950 feet

This is an interesting route up Sunshine that allows you to bag a thirteener en route. Start at the Silver Creek–Grizzly Gulch Trailhead and hike northeast up the Silver Creek Trail for 1.5 miles to the junction with the south fork of Silver Creek at 11,300 feet. Leave the Silver Creek Trail, cross Silver Creek and hike south up onto the ridge west of the south fork. Do not hike up the bottom of the south-fork gulch. The hike up onto the ridge is steep, rugged and short.

Once on the ridge, follow it up to Point 13,432, alias "Sundog." This is a ranked thirteener that rises at least 312 feet above its connecting saddle with Sunshine. Sundog is a "Tri," one of Colorado's 300 highest peaks. Descend southeast from Sundog to the plateau at 13,300 feet, north of Sunshine (Class 2+). Cross the plateau and follow an old trail angling up east to join Sunshine's northeast ridge 250 feet below the summit.

28.6 East Ridge II, Class 2
From Mill Creek Trailhead: 6.0 miles, 4,560 feet

This rugged route has more elevation gain than others on Sunshine, but it is accessible when the road up to the Silver Creek–Grizzly Gulch Trailhead is impassable. Start at the Mill Creek Trailhead and hike north into the woods at the base of Sunshine's vast south slopes. Hike northwest up to tree line, then continue northwest up to Sunshine's east ridge and follow this ridge up to the summit. When descending this route, be sure to head east from the summit. Descending south or even southeast from the summit will lead you into cliffs.

28. Redcloud and Sunshine Combinations
See Map 28 on page 234

28.7 II, Class 2, Moderate Snow (Seasonal)
From Silver Creek–Grizzly Gulch Trailhead: 9.8 to 11.4 miles, 4,700 feet

This is the standard way to climb Redcloud and Sunshine together. Start at the Silver Creek–Grizzly Gulch Trailhead and ascend Redcloud's Northeast Ridge Route. Descend Redcloud's south ridge to the 13,500-foot Redcloud–Sunshine Saddle, then ascend Sunshine's northeast ridge to Sunshine's summit. Descend Sunshine's North Slopes Route. Some people choose to avoid the steep descent west from the Redcloud–Sunshine Saddle and return over Redcloud's summit to descend Redcloud's Northeast Ridge Route.

28.8 II, Class 2, Moderate Snow (Seasonal)
From Silver Creek–Grizzly Gulch Trailhead: 8.7 to 9.5 miles,
4,150 to 4,500 feet

This traverse can be done in either direction, but doing Sunshine first allows you to start with the more difficult terrain and glissade down one of Redcloud's west gullies. Start at the Silver Creek–Grizzly Gulch Trailhead and ascend either Sunshine's North Slopes or Northwest Ridge Route. Descend Sunshine's northeast ridge to the 13,500-foot Redcloud–Sunshine Saddle, then ascend Redcloud's south ridge to Redcloud's summit. Descend Redcloud's West Gullies or Northeast Ridge Route.

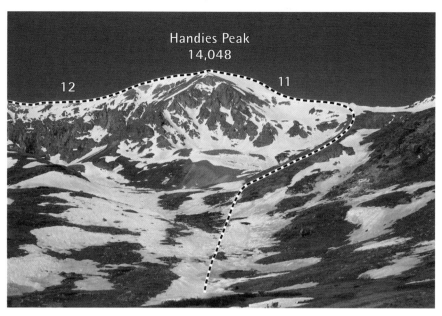

Handies Peak from the east.

28.9 II, Class 2

From Mill Creek Trailhead: 8.5 miles, 5,100 feet

This combination provides a good way to climb both peaks when the Cinnamon Pass Road is in bad shape. Start at the Mill Creek Trailhead and ascend Sunshine's East Ridge Route. Descend Sunshine's northeast ridge to the 13,500-foot Redcloud–Sunshine Saddle, ascend Redcloud's south ridge to Redcloud's summit, then return to the 13,500-foot saddle. Instead of climbing Sunshine again, contour across Sunshine's northeast face to rejoin and descend Sunshine's East Ridge Route.

28. Handies Peak   14,048 feet

See Map 28 on page 234

This winsome peak stands by itself 5 miles west of Redcloud and Sunshine. The upper end of the Lake Fork of the Gunnison River embraces Handies in a wide horseshoe, and the peak lies deep in the heart of the eastern San Juans. The view from Handies' summit is famous and spectacular. On the summit, you are surrounded by mountains as far as the eye can see, in all directions. If civilization is pressing in on you, climb Handies and spend a long hour or two on the summit.

Routes

28.10 West Slopes I, Class 2

From American Basin Trailhead: 5.6 miles, 2,750 feet

Beautiful in its brevity, this is the shortest, easiest route up Handies. Start at the American Basin Trailhead and go south into American Basin on the four-wheel-drive road under Handies' west face for an additional 0.9 mile to an old mine at 11,600 feet. Continue south on a trail for 0.9 mile to 12,400 feet in upper American Basin. When the main trail climbs west, leave it and climb east on a climber's trail for 0.7 mile to the 13,460-foot saddle between Handies and Point 13,588, which is on Handies' south ridge 0.5 mile south of Handies. From the saddle, climb north up Handies' south ridge for 0.3 mile to the summit.

Variation 28.10V

From American Basin Trailhead: 3.4 miles, 2,750 feet

For a shorter, steeper route, follow the four-wheel-drive road 0.9 mile to the old mine at 11,600 feet in American Basin. Leave the trail and climb southeast up a large talus slope directly to the summit.

28.11 East Slopes II, Class 2 *Classic*

From Silver Creek–Grizzly Gulch Trailhead: 7.6 miles, 3,650 feet

This is the most scenic route on Handies. From the Silver Creek–Grizzly Gulch Trailhead, go north up the road for 100 yards and find the start of the Grizzly Gulch Trail west of an abandoned cabin. Leave the road, cross the Lake Fork of the Gunnison River and climb west on the Grizzly Gulch Trail. The trail stays on the creek's north side as it climbs for 2.0 miles to tree line at 11,800 feet. Handies' picturesque east face will lure you on.

Leave the trail, continue west into the upper basin and ascend northeast-facing slopes to a 13,460-foot saddle on Handies' north ridge between Handies and Point 13,577. Climb south for 0.4 mile up Handies' north ridge to the summit. If you reach Handies' north ridge north of Point 13,577, you will have to do some Class 2+ scrambling to reach Point 13,577.

Extra Credit 28.11EC

Adding Whitecross Mountain to this route works best on the descent from Handies. From Handies' summit, descend Handies' north ridge, cross Point 13,577 and descend northeast to the 12,980-foot saddle between Handies and 13,542-foot Whitecross Mountain. The ridge between Point 13,577 and the 12,980-foot saddle is rough and requires some Class 2+ scrambling. From the 12,980-foot saddle, climb northeast to Whitecross' summit. Descend Whitecross' south slopes and regain the Grizzly Gulch Trail near tree line at 11,800 feet.

28.12 East Ridge II, Class 2 *Classic*

From Silver Creek–Grizzly Gulch Trailhead: 9.3 miles, 4,450 feet

With descent of East Slopes: 8.5 miles, 4,050 feet

This interesting route allows you to climb Point 13,795 en route to Handies. Follow the Grizzly Gulch Trail to tree line at 11,800 feet. Continue south up the trail to a small unnamed lake at 12,323 feet. From here, climb south up a steep, rocky slope into a miniature basin under the north slopes of Point 13,795. Ascend southwest up this basin to the 13,580-foot saddle just west of Point 13,795, then walk east up the gentle ridge to the summit of Point 13,795. This is a significant summit that rises at least 475 feet above its connecting saddle with Handies Peak, and it is a "Bi," one of Colorado's 200 highest peaks.

From Point 13,795, descend west, climb over or around the south side of Point 13,700 and descend west to a 13,300-foot saddle. Continue west over Point 13,735 and finally reach Handies' summit from the southeast. Ascending the East Ridge Route and descending the East Slopes Route makes a classic, circular Tour de Handies.

Variation 28.12V
II, Class 2, Moderate/Steep Snow (Seasonal)

From Silver Creek–Grizzly Gulch Trailhead: 8.8 miles, 4,675 feet

With descent of East Slopes: 8.2 miles, 4,160 feet

This variation adds a mountaineering flavor to your ascent. Follow the Grizzly Gulch Trail for 1.0 mile to a small clearing at 11,100 feet. Leave the trail, cross Grizzly Gulch and ascend the westernmost of three north-facing avalanche gullies to Point 12,792. When snow conditions are favorable, this gully provides more than 1,000 feet of moderate snow climbing with one steep crux. In a normal snow year, this gully is dangerous before June, in good condition in June and snow-free later in the summer. In June an ice ax is recommended, and the steep crux may require crampons.

From Point 12,792, ascend the ridge south to Point 13,502 and continue south to Point 13,795 on the East Ridge Route. Continue on that route to the summit. Either descend the East Slopes Route or continue over Whitecross Mountain via 28.11EC for a complete tour of the Grizzly Gulch Basin.

28.13 Grouse Gulch II, Class 2

From Grouse Gulch Trailhead: 8.0 miles, 4,100 feet

This route provides access to Handies from the south and west. When approaching from the Durango area, you do not need a four-wheel-drive vehicle, and you can avoid the long drive to Lake City.

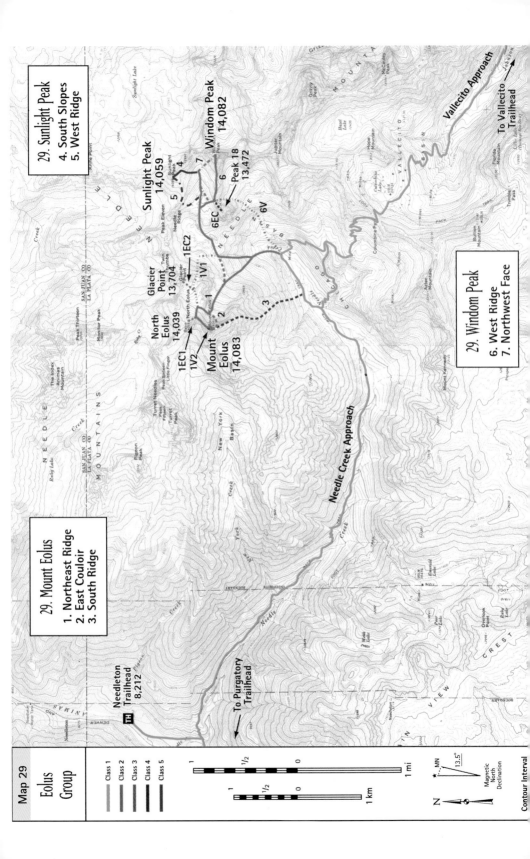

Map 29

Eolus Group

29. Mount Eolus
1. Northeast Ridge
2. East Couloir
3. South Ridge

29. Sunlight Peak
4. South Slopes
5. West Ridge

29. Windom Peak
6. West Ridge
7. Northwest Face

Sunlight Peak
14,059

Windom Peak
14,082

Peak 18
13,472

Glacier Point
13,704

North Eolus
14,039

Mount Eolus
14,083

Needleton Trailhead
8,212

To Purgatory Trailhead

Needle Creek Approach

Vallecito Approach

To Vallecito Trailhead

Class 1
Class 2
Class 3
Class 4
Class 5

Magnetic North Declination

Contour Interval

Start at the Grouse Gulch Trailhead and climb east for 2.0 miles up the Grouse Gulch Trail to the 13,020-foot pass at Grouse Gulch's east end. From the pass, you can see Handies' west side across American Basin. Descend east into American Basin on the trail to 12,400 feet and join the West Slopes Route.

From 12,400 feet in American Basin, climb east on a climber's trail for 0.7 mile to the 13,460-foot saddle between Handies and Point 13,588, which is on Handies' south ridge 0.5 mile south of Handies. From the saddle, climb north up Handies' south ridge for 0.3 mile to the summit.

29. Eolus Group

Mount Eolus   14,083 feet
Sunlight Peak   14,059 feet
Windom Peak   14,082 feet

See Map 29 on page 242

These wild, rugged peaks are the most remote of Colorado's fourteeners. They lie buried in the heart of Colorado's greatest range—the San Juans. Eolus, Sunlight and Windom harbor the zenith of the Colorado fourteener experience.

Eolus, Sunlight and Windom are the highest peaks in the Needle Mountains and in the Weminuche Wilderness. The peaks are 15 miles southeast of Silverton, far from roads and difficult to see. They are most often seen from other high San Juan peaks, and they always seem to be far away.

The remote sanctity of such peaks is what wilderness is all about. These peaks are popular—a testimony that we need wilderness now more than ever. Knowledge of wilderness is a prerequisite for its preservation. Tread lightly on this special place as you learn about it.

Maps

Required: Columbine Pass, Storm King Peak, Mountain View Crest, San Juan National Forest
Optional: Snowdon Peak, Electra Lake, Engineer Mountain, Vallecito Reservoir

Trailheads

Needleton Trailhead

This trailhead is at 8,212 feet and provides access to Chicago Basin from the west. Chicago Basin is the popular approach for the standard routes up all three peaks. Needleton is deep in the Animas River Canyon 13 miles south of Silverton. You reach Needleton by rail or foot, not by road. The Durango and Silverton Narrow Gauge Railroad runs through the canyon, but the gorge is too narrow to accommodate both tracks and a road. The nearest road, U.S. 550, is many miles to the west and separated from the Animas River Canyon by the West Needle Mountains. Approaching these peaks behind a 100-year-old steam locomotive puffing through a wild canyon is one of the trip's charms. The greatest hazard of the approach is hanging your head out the window and getting a cinder in your eye!

The privately owned Durango and Silverton Narrow Gauge Railroad starts operation on May 9, runs three trains a day between Durango and Silverton in the summer and continues with a reduced schedule until October 31. All the trains stop at Needleton. Backpackers can board trains in Durango or Silverton. The Durango train depot is at 479 Main Avenue, Durango, CO 81301, and you can make reservations by calling (970) 247-2733. Make reservations early. Backpackers without a ticket can board in Needleton on a space-available basis and must have the exact fare.

A complete schedule and a table of fares follow. This information is current as of 1999.

Schedule

Durango to Silverton	Silverton to Durango	Operating Dates
8:15 A.M.–11:45 A.M.	2:00 P.M.–5:30 P.M.	May 9–Oct. 31
9:00 A.M.–12:30 P.M.	2:45 P.M.–6:15 P.M.	May 19–Oct. 11
9:45 A.M.–1:15 P.M.	3:30 P.M.–7:00 P.M.	June 8–Aug. 20 and Sept. 14–Sept. 27

Fares

Route	Adult (ages 12+)	Child (ages 5–11)
Durango–Needleton	$44.90 (RT)/$29.95 (OW)	$22.45 (RT)/$14.30 (OW)
Durango–Silverton	$49.10 (RT)/$32.70 (OW)	$24.65 (RT)/$16.45 (OW)
Silverton–Needleton	$29.10 (RT)/$19.40 (OW)	$17.70 (RT)/$11.85 (OW)

RT = round trip; OW = one way. There is no charge for children under 5 if they do not occupy a seat.

Purgatory Trailhead

This trailhead is at 8,800 feet. The Purgatory Creek Trail and Animas River Trail provide a long trail-access to Needle Creek and Chicago Basin. For those who find the train to Needleton Trailhead too expensive, this is the best alternative. The start of the Purgatory Creek Trail is at the entrance to the Forest Service Purgatory Campground on the east side of U.S. 550

across from the Purgatory Ski Area, 27 miles north of Durango. This trailhead is accessible in winter.

Vallecito Trailhead

This trailhead is at 7,900 feet and provides access to Chicago Basin from the east via a long trail-hike over 12,700-foot Columbine Pass. This trailhead is seldom used to approach the fourteeners, but it does provide a refreshing alternative for a long backpacking vacation. Go to Vallecito Reservoir, which is 13.0 miles north of Bayfield on U.S. 160, or 20.0 miles east of Durango on Florida Road. Go around the west side of Vallecito Reservoir for 5.0 miles to a well-marked junction, stay left and continue for 3.0 miles to the Vallecito Campground and the trailhead.

Approaches

29.A1 Needle Creek Approach

From Needleton Trailhead: 13.6 to 15.6 miles, 3,000 to 4,300 feet
From Purgatory Trailhead: 30.0 to 32.0 miles, 4,600 to 5,900 feet

This is the standard approach to Eolus, Sunlight and Windom. If you take the train, get off at Needleton, cross the good bridge to the Animas River's east side, turn south (right) and walk 0.8 mile south along the Animas River to the start of the Needle Creek Trail. The Needle Creek Trail is on Needle Creek's north side.

If you start at the Purgatory Trailhead, follow the Purgatory Creek Trail east then south down Cascade Creek for 3.7 miles to the Animas River at 7,700 feet. Cross to the Animas River's southeast (far) side on a footbridge just east (upstream) of the confluence of Cascade Creek and the Animas River. Follow the good Animas River Trail east along the Animas River's south side for an additional 5.1 miles to Needle Creek and the Needle Creek Trail. The railroad is on the river's north side.

From the junction of the Animas River Trail and the Needle Creek Trail, turn east and follow the Needle Creek Trail for 5.3 miles to the start of the Columbine Pass Trail at 11,000 feet in lower Chicago Basin. You do *not* want to go to Columbine Pass. Continue straight for an additional 0.7 mile to some campsites near tree line at 11,200 feet. There is a steep but serviceable climber's trail on the creek's west side that climbs north to Twin Lakes at 12,500 feet. Camping is not permitted around Twin Lakes.

29.A2 Vallecito Approach

From Vallecito Trailhead: 33.4 to 35.4 miles, 5,000 to 6,300 feet

This seldom used approach requires a long backpack trip, but it avoids the train's cost and crowds. This approach is suitable for an extended trip. Consider doing a traverse and only using the train one way.

Start at the Vallecito Trailhead and follow the Vallecito Creek Trail north for 8.3 miles to its junction with the Johnson Creek Trail at 9,120 feet. There are many good campsites near here. Cross to Vallecito Creek's west side on a good bridge and follow the Johnson Creek Trail west for 6.4 miles as it climbs steadily up Johnson Creek to Columbine Pass at 12,700 feet. Johnson Creek is beautiful and rugged, and you are deep in the wilderness here. Cross Columbine Pass and descend 2.0 miles into Chicago Basin. Camp in the trees at 11,200 feet. Camping is not permitted at Twin Lakes at 12,500 feet.

29. Mount Eolus   14,083 feet

See Map 29 on page 242

Eolus is the highest peak in La Plata County and the monarch of the San Juans' rugged heartland. This reclusive mountain carefully guards its secrets. Eolus' singular splendor forms Chicago Basin's northwest rampart. Eolus is named after a Greek god of the winds, and the name fits this massive monarch. The peak attracts its own winds, and the weather here can be violent. In summer, warm air from the Utah desert rises into the San Juans and creates intense thunderstorms. The storms seem to reach a climax near Eolus. In winter, moisture-laden air wraps Eolus in a deep mantle of snow.

Routes

29.1 Northeast Ridge II, Class 3

From Chicago Basin: 2.6 to 4.6 miles, 1,600 to 2,900 feet
From Needleton Trailhead: 18.2 miles, 5,900 feet

This is the standard route on Eolus. From camp at 11,200 feet in Chicago Basin, climb north on a good climber's trail on the west side of the creek to Twin Lakes at 12,500 feet. It is not necessary to go all the way to Twin Lakes. Before reaching the lakes, angle northwest into the small basin under Eolus' steep east face.

Climb west up the basin under Eolus' east face past a large, sweeping slab to the north (right). Pass an initial ledge leading northeast across the slab, then do an ascending traverse northeast (right) onto a higher, broader ledge. Reach the upper, western end of a flat area between Eolus and Glacier Point (13,704 feet). This flat area has a small lake at its lower, eastern end. This temporal paradise is suspended high and wild. Turn west (left) and scramble up to the northernmost saddle between Eolus and North Eolus (Easy Class 3). North Eolus (14,039 feet) is a spur summit 0.25 mile north of Eolus.

From the saddle, walk or crawl southwest along a famous stretch of ridge called the "Catwalk" (Class 2). The ridge narrows to a width of 2 feet,

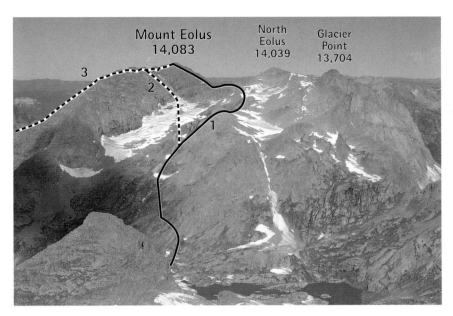

Mount Eolus from the summit of Windom Peak.

and there is exposure on both sides of the ridge. Beyond the Catwalk, Eolus' northeast ridge rears up above you. Do *not* climb directly up the steep part of the ridge, but traverse south on the ridge's *east* side. Scramble up a series of exposed steps and ledges on the upper east face to reach the summit (Class 3). The easiest route can be difficult to follow. Take your time and look before launching. If you find yourself attempting a significantly harder move than those you have been making, you are probably off-route. From the summit, you have a commanding view of a vast sea of San Juan peaks. You also can see Shiprock—and you may feel the desert's pull.

Variations
29.1V1 Class 4

Climb directly up the upper northeast ridge instead of traversing onto the upper east face. This is a harder, more spectacular finish on highly fractured blocks.

29.1V2 Class 3

From Twin Lakes, climb straight west up a steep, Class 3 couloir to reach the small lake at the eastern end of the flat area between Eolus and Glacier Point (13,704 feet). This couloir retains snow through June and can provide a refreshing, moderate snow climb. Continue west across the flat area and rejoin the Northeast Ridge Route below the Eolus–North Eolus Saddle.

Extra Credit
29.1EC1 Class 3

From the Eolus–North Eolus Saddle, scramble north for 200 yards to the summit of North Eolus (14,039 feet). This easy, Class 3 scramble is fun, and it is easier than the final scramble on Eolus. You can do it before you summit Eolus to tune up your technique and survey the route on Eolus. You can do it after you summit Eolus to take a photo and feel good about what you have just done. North Eolus does not have a lot of power, but it is a named summit above 14,000 feet.

29.1EC2 Class 2

From the flat area below the Eolus–North Eolus Saddle, hike northeast and ascend steep talus to Glacier Point's 13,704-foot summit. This perch gives you a spectacular view north into the Noname Creek drainage. You can easily climb Glacier Point with Eolus when you use the Variation 29.1V2 couloir above Twin Lakes.

29.2 East Couloir II, Class 3, Steep Snow (Seasonal)
From Chicago Basin: 2.0 to 4.0 miles, 1,600 to 2,900 feet
From Needleton Trailhead: 17.6 miles, 5,900 feet

When it is in good condition, this hidden couloir offers a nifty way to avoid the crowds on the Northeast Ridge Route. Don't climb this couloir after the snow melts. The couloir angles to the south as it splits the east face and reaches the south ridge near the summit.

Follow the Northeast Ridge Route to 13,400 feet in the basin under the east face. You can see the couloir from here. Leave the Northeast Ridge Route before it traverses northeast to reach the shelf under North Eolus. Climb south, enter the narrow couloir and ascend it for 600 exciting feet to a deep, spectacular notch on the south ridge. From the notch, traverse on the west face until you are under the summit then climb directly to the summit.

29.3 South Ridge II, Class 4
From Chicago Basin: 3.0 miles, 3,000 feet
From Needleton Trailhead: 15.2 miles, 5,900 feet

This challenging mountaineering route is seldom climbed. The complicated ridge hides a wilderness adventure. Perhaps the ridge should be named "Discovery Ridge."

If you want to discover your adventure, leave the Needle Creek Trail at 11,080 feet in lower Chicago Basin, 0.15 mile east of the Columbine Pass Trail junction. Climb north up a long approach slope and angle slightly west toward the ridge crest above you. The ridge steepens and narrows between 12,200 feet and 13,400 feet. Stay close to the ridge crest when you can, and leave the ridge to avoid difficulties when you need to. "Discover" your route all the way to the summit. This ridge provides spectacular positions, but it is not a good ridge to be on when electric storms roll in from the desert.

29. Sunlight Peak   14,059 feet

See Map 29 on page 242

This luminescent peak rests in secretive splendor at Chicago Basin's extreme northeast corner. Sunlight is 1.6 miles east of Eolus and even more difficult to see than Eolus. Sunlight supports three craggy ridges, and from certain vantage points, the view of Sunlight is startling. Sunlight is perhaps best known for its exposed summit block. The final move onto this block is the hardest move required to reach the summit of a Colorado fourteener by its easiest route. If the term *hardest* hinges on the difficulty of a single move, then Sunlight can be called Colorado's hardest fourteener.

Routes

29.4 South Slopes II, Class 4

From Chicago Basin: 2.0 to 4.0 miles, 1,560 to 2,860 feet

From Needleton Trailhead: 17.6 miles, 5,860 feet

This is the easiest route on Sunlight. From 11,200 feet in Chicago Basin, hike steeply north for 1.0 mile to Twin Lakes at 12,500 feet. From Twin Lakes, climb east for 0.7 mile to 13,300 feet in the high basin between Sunlight and Windom. Sunlight is north of you. The spectacular Sunlight Spire (13,995 feet) is above you on the connecting ridge between Sunlight and Windom. If Sunlight Spire were 5 feet higher, it would be Colorado's hardest fourteener!

Turn north (left) toward Sunlight Peak and climb scrawny open slopes flanked by small cliffs. The difficulties increase as you approach the summit. The south slopes narrow to a ridge before you reach the summit. A clever, Class 3 traverse avoids the pinnacles on this ridge, but there is more than one route in this area. Reach an alcove just south of the famous, 30-foot-high summit block. Many souls have elected to stop here, but this is not the summit.

Scramble up to the summit block's east end (Class 3). The final, committing, Class 4 move onto the summit block requires you to step across an exposed gap, then pull yourself up onto the rounded, smooth block. As you straddle the gap, you can peer down the north face between your legs. A less exposed but harder alternative is to climb the summit block's south

Sunlight Peak from the west.

face (Class 5). Many people enjoy the protection of a rope on this summit block. Sunlight's exciting summit can only accommodate two or three people at a time!

Extra Credit 29.4EC

Most summit shots show people sitting on the summit. Center yourself and *stand* on the summit. For triple points, do a headstand on the summit.

29.5 West Ridge II, Class 4 *Classic*
From Chicago Basin: 2.0 to 4.0 miles, 1,560 to 2,860 feet
From Needleton Trailhead: 17.6 miles, 5,860 feet

This is a more difficult route than the South Slopes Route. It is recommended because the rock is solid (for the San Juans!), and because the positions encountered are spectacular. Ascending this route and descending the South Slopes Route makes a scintillating Tour de Sunlight.

From 11,200 feet in Chicago Basin, hike steeply north for 1.0 mile to Twin Lakes at 12,500 feet. From Twin Lakes, you can see the jagged Needle Ridge that forms the lower end of Sunlight's west ridge. The complete traverse of Needle Ridge is a difficult undertaking and is not part of the route described here.

Windom Peak from the north.

From Twin Lakes, climb east for 0.4 mile to 13,000 feet in the lower end of the basin between Sunlight and Windom. Turn north (left) and climb a rubble-filled gully to a 13,300-foot saddle between Needle Ridge and Sunlight. Make sure you climb to the saddle *east* of Needle Ridge. The rubble-filled gully is unpleasant, but such are the dues you must pay to reach the exciting upper climbing.

From the 13,300-foot saddle, the west ridge looks formidable. Overcome it one step at a time. Meet the challenge immediately with the ascent of a steep, Class 4 wall. The climbing above this initial wall alternates between the broken ridge and more short walls. One lower-angled, solid wall is positively primal. The climbing remains interesting, but the difficulties ease as you approach the summit. Join the South Slopes Route south of the final, Class 3 traverse to the alcove below the summit block. Continue on the South Slopes Route to the tippy top.

29. Windom Peak   14,082 feet

See Map 29 on page 242

Windom is 1.7 miles east of Eolus and 0.5 mile south of Sunlight. Windom is the first fourteener you see when hiking up Needle Creek, and it appears friendly. Windom is easier to climb than Eolus and Sunlight. If you are looking for a fourteener in the heart of San Juan wilderness with views and charm, but not much commitment, climb Windom.

Routes

29.6 West Ridge II, Class 2+ *Classic*

From Chicago Basin: 2.0 to 4.0 miles, 1,600 to 2,900 feet
From Needleton Trailhead: 17.6 miles, 5,900 feet

This is the easiest route on Windom. You can see the upper part of the west ridge from tree line in Chicago Basin. This is a surrealistic tour in the heart of Colorado's wilderness. I have done this route many times, and it always reminds me of why I started climbing.

From 11,200 feet in Chicago Basin, hike steeply north for 1.0 mile to Twin Lakes at 12,500 feet. From Twin Lakes, climb east for 0.4 mile to 13,000 feet in the lower end of the basin between Sunlight and Windom. Stay south of a waterfall on this ascent. Turn south (right) and ascend snow or talus to the 13,260-foot saddle between Windom and Peak 18 (13,472 feet). Peak 18 is the small, prominent peak at the west end of Windom's west ridge. It has a dramatic west face that you can easily see from Chicago Basin. Peak 18 is not named on the Columbine Pass Quadrangle.

From the saddle between Windom and Peak 18, turn east (left) and ascend Windom's west ridge for 0.5 mile to the summit. Wilderness views rise above the surrounding peaks as you climb. The ridge is Class 2 talus hiking at first, then the ridge steepens as you approach the summit. The Class 2+ scrambling over the boulders near the summit is not as hard as the Class 3 climbing on Eolus. From the summit, you have expansive views in all directions.

Variation 29.6V

You can reach the saddle between Windom and Peak 18 from the south. From 11,200 feet in Chicago Basin, climb east through some cliff bands to reach the lower end of the high basin between Windom and Jupiter Mountain (13,830 feet), which is 0.6 mile south of Windom. Turn north (left) and climb a couloir to the saddle. This route is more difficult than the northern approach to the saddle.

Extra Credit 29.6EC

From the 13,260-foot saddle between Windom and Peak 18, climb west to the summit of Peak 18 (13,472 feet). The easiest route is Class 4 on the ridge's south side.

29.7 Northwest Face II, Class 3, Moderate Snow (Seasonal)

From Chicago Basin: 2.0 to 4.0 miles, 1,600 to 2,900 feet
From Needleton Trailhead: 17.6 miles, 5,900 feet

This face is almost always climbed or descended when climbing Windom together with Sunlight. From 11,200 feet in Chicago Basin, hike steeply north for 1.0 mile to Twin Lakes at 12,500 feet. From Twin Lakes, climb east for 0.7 mile to 13,300 feet in the high basin between Sunlight and Windom. Turn south (right) and ascend Windom's northwest face to the summit. Your exact line is a matter of choice. This face retains some snow until late in the summer, and the exposed rock slabs are often wet. Choose your line carefully.

29. Eolus, Sunlight and Windom Combinations

See Map 29 on page 242

Note: These combinations are Grade III only if you climb them in one day from Needleton.

29.8 II or III, Class 4

From Chicago Basin: 3.0 to 5.0 miles, 2,600 to 3,900 feet
From Needleton Trailhead: 18.6 miles, 6,900 feet

This is the easiest way to climb Sunlight and Windom together. Climb Sunlight's South Slopes Route and descend that route to 13,100 feet in the basin between Sunlight and Windom. Climb to the saddle between Windom and Peak 18 and continue on Windom's West Ridge Route to Windom's summit. Descend Windom's West Ridge Route. By giving up some elevation to reach Windom's west ridge, you avoid the vagaries of Windom's northwest face.

29.9 II or III, Class 4, Moderate Snow (Seasonal)

From Chicago Basin: 2.6 to 4.6 miles, 2,400 to 3,700 feet
From Needleton Trailhead: 18.2 miles, 6,700 feet

This is a more exciting way to climb Sunlight and Windom together. Climb Sunlight's West Ridge Route and descend Sunlight's South Slopes Route to 13,300 feet in the basin between Sunlight and Windom. Continue up Windom's Northwest Face Route and descend Windom's West Ridge Route.

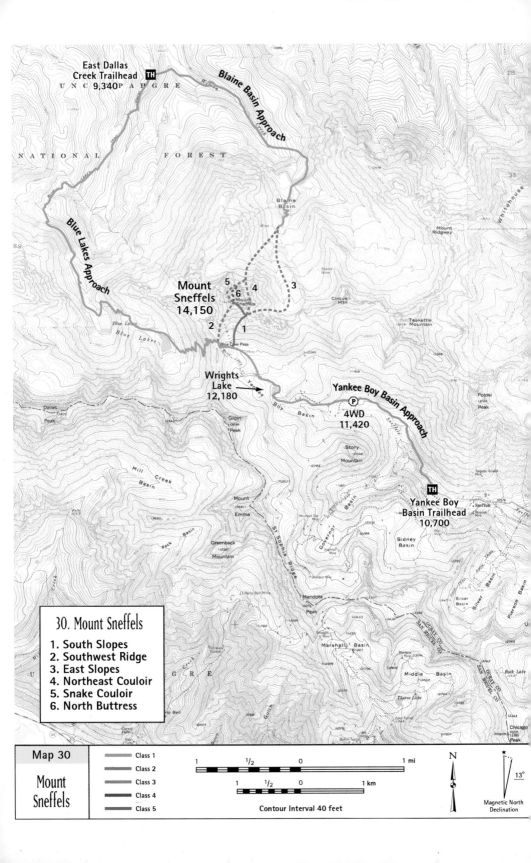

East Dallas
Creek Trailhead **TH**
U N C 9,340 P A H G R E

Blaine Basin Approach

N A T I O N A L   F O R E S T

Blue Lakes Approach

Blaine
Basin

Mount
Sneffels
14,150

5
6
4
3

2
1

Wrights
Lake
12,180

Yankee Boy Basin Approach

P
4WD
11,420

TH
Yankee Boy
Basin Trailhead
10,700

30. Mount Sneffels
1. South Slopes
2. Southwest Ridge
3. East Slopes
4. Northeast Couloir
5. Snake Couloir
6. North Buttress

Map 30		Class 1
		Class 2
Mount		Class 3
Sneffels		Class 4
		Class 5

1   1/2   0   1 mi

1   1/2   0   1 km

Contour Interval 40 feet

N

13°

Magnetic North
Declination

29.10 II or III, Class 4
From Chicago Basin: 5.6 to 7.6 miles, 4,200 to 5,500 feet
From Needleton Trailhead: 21.2 miles, 8,500 feet

This is the easiest way to climb all three peaks in one day. Climb Eolus' Northeast Ridge Route and return to Twin Lakes. Continue with Combination 29.8. These peaks can be done in any order, but doing Eolus first puts the difficulties of Eolus behind you early. Doing Windom last allows you to descend Windom's easy west ridge at the end of the day.

30. Mount Sneffels   14,150 feet
See Map 30 on page 254

This stunning peak is 7 miles west of Ouray and 5 miles north of Telluride. Mount Sneffels is the highest peak in Ouray County. Sneffels rules an abrupt escarpment on the San Juans' northwest edge that is visible for great distances to the north. As you approach the range, Sneffels' distinctive shape predominates, and it becomes clear that Sneffels is the monarch of this area. As you come even closer, Sneffels' great north face looms over your head in a neck-bending view. The views of Sneffels from the highway between Ridgway and Dallas Divide are renowned, and when the aspens change colors in the fall, this panorama represents Colorado.

Maps
Required: Mount Sneffels, Telluride, Uncompahgre National Forest
Optional: Ironton

Trailheads
Yankee Boy Basin Trailhead
This trailhead is at 10,700 feet and provides access to Sneffels' south side. On U.S. 550, go 0.4 mile south past Ouray's south edge. Turn south onto Ouray County 361 (dirt) and measure from this point. Follow Ouray County 361 as it turns and climbs steeply west up Canyon Creek. Stay right at 4.7 miles, continue west on a spectacular shelf road, go straight at 6.0 miles and reach a short side road on the left after 6.7 miles. Ample parking is available on the side road; it is best to park passenger cars here. The road beyond this point becomes rougher rapidly , but four-wheel-drive vehicles can continue for an additional 1.3 miles to 11,420 feet. Amazingly, this trailhead is often accessible in winter.

East Dallas Creek Trailhead

This trailhead is at 9,340 feet and provides access to Sneffels' north side. If approaching from the north or south, go west on Colorado 62 for 4.8 miles from the U.S. 550–Colorado 62 junction in Ridgway. Ridgway is 26 miles south of Montrose and 11 miles north of Ouray. If approaching from the west, go east on Colorado 62 for 18.5 miles from the junction of Colorado 145 and Colorado 62.

Turn south onto Ouray County 7 (East Dallas Creek Road) and measure from this point. Go south on Ouray County 7 (dirt), stay left at 0.3 mile, stay right at 2.0 miles and enter the Uncompahgre National Forest at 7.2 miles. The views of Sneffels from here are remarkable. Stay right and cross East Dallas Creek at 8.2 miles. Take the middle of three forks at 8.8 miles and reach the trailhead after 9.0 miles. Two trails start at this trailhead. Make sure you follow the trail you want. The road to this trailhead is not plowed in winter.

Approaches

30.A1 Yankee Boy Basin Approach

From Yankee Boy Basin Trailhead: 4.2 miles, 1,700 feet

This is the approach for Sneffels' standard South Slopes Route. Start at the Yankee Boy Basin Trailhead and go west up the Yankee Boy Basin Road. Stay right after 0.2 mile. A spectacular view of Potosi Peak emerges behind you as you climb. Continue up the rough, four-wheel-drive road as it switchbacks up to a level area at 12,200 feet, north of tiny Wrights Lake. Hike north to just below the road's highest point. The Blue Lake Trail starts here at 12,300 feet and heads west through the scree.

30.A2 Blaine Basin Approach

From East Dallas Creek Trailhead: 6.0 miles, 1,500 feet

This approach gives access to all the routes on Sneffels' north and east sides. Start at the East Dallas Creek Trailhead, cross to East Dallas Creek's east side and proceed onto the Blaine Basin Trail. Climb steeply to a ridge, then contour east to Wilson Creek. The lower part of this trail is not marked on the Mount Sneffels Quadrangle. Climb southeast up Wilson Creek and reach Blaine Basin at 10,800 feet after 3.0 miles. The trail crosses Wilson Creek four times, and these bridgeless crossings can be tricky in June. Blaine Basin's open camping spots have impressive views of Sneffels' north face.

Routes

30.1 South Slopes II, Class 2+ *Classic*

From Yankee Boy Basin Trailhead: 7.0 miles, 3,450 feet

This is the shortest and easiest route on Sneffels. It is harder than Colorado's Class 1 and Class 2 walk-up routes but not as hard as the Class 3 routes found on the Crestones, Maroon Bells and Wilsons. This is a good route for someone who has climbed all the easy fourteeners and wants a taste of what the harder ones are like.

Use the Yankee Boy Basin Approach. From just below the road's upper end, walk west on the Blue Lakes Trail for 0.5 mile. Although this trail is not accurately marked on the Telluride Quadrangle, it is worth finding, because it provides easy passage through the scree. You cannot see the route up Sneffels until you reach 12,600 feet, so avoid any temptation to leave the trail too soon. The peak above you before you reach 12,600 feet is "Kismet" (13,694 feet).

Leave the trail at 12,700 feet just before it starts switchbacking up to Blue Lake Pass. You can see the next portion of the route from here. Climb north up a wide slope to 13,500-foot Scree Col, southeast of Sneffels' summit. Scree Col, also called "Lavender Col," is the saddle between Sneffels and Kismet. The slope leading to Scree Col is covered with talus and laced with dirt alleys. Stay on the large talus, because the dirt alleys are eroding rapidly under too many boots.

You can see the rest of the route from Scree Col. Climb northwest and ascend the obvious, deep couloir leading toward the summit. This couloir retains some snow in early summer, when an ice ax is recommended. Ascend the couloir to within 20 feet of the 14,020-foot notch at its top. Climbing all the way into the notch is slightly off-route but worthwhile for the chance to peer down Sneffels' steep north side.

From 20 feet below the notch, climb west out of the couloir via a 30-foot exit crack (Class 2+). This crack is the route's key passage. From the top of the crack, scramble west for 200 feet up broken ledges to the summit (Class 2+). This is an exciting finish leading to a wonderful summit. From the summit, you can peek down the north face, and the view reminds you that you are on a monarch.

Variation 30.1V

Instead of climbing to within 20 feet of the notch at the top of the couloir, exit the couloir 300 feet below the notch. This Class 2+ exit is one-third of the way up the couloir. Once out of the couloir, climb broken ledges on the couloir's west side (Class 2+). Rejoin the regular route near the summit. This variation is snow-free much earlier in the year than the couloir is. If snow conditions in the couloir are not to your liking and the ledges are dry, this alternative can be safer.

Mount Sneffels from the south.

30.2 Southwest Ridge II, Class 3 *Classic*

From Yankee Boy Basin Trailhead: 7.0 miles, 3,450 feet

This is a more exciting route than the standard South Slopes Route. The southwest ridge is on the west (left) edge of Sneffels' south face, and you can easily see it from upper Yankee Boy Basin. The ridge looks ferocious, but the climb is not as hard as it looks.

Use the Yankee Boy Basin Approach. From just below the upper end of the road in Yankee Boy Basin, follow the Blue Lakes Trail west to Blue Lakes Pass at 12,980 feet. You can also reach Blue Lakes Pass by following the Blue Lakes Trail for 4.8 miles from the East Dallas Creek Trailhead.

Leave the trail in the pass, turn north and climb the ridge toward Sneffels. Easily bypass some jagged pinnacles low on the ridge on the ridge's west (left) side. Once you are past the pinnacles, climb into a prominent, 13,500-foot notch on the ridge crest north of the pinnacles. From the notch, climb a south-facing gully leading to the upper ridge (Class 3). Ascend the upper ridge directly on or slightly east (right) of the ridge crest. There is often considerable exposure on the ridge's west side, making this a dramatic approach to Sneffels' summit.

Variation 30.2V

When snow conditions permit, climb snow on the ridge's east side to reach the prominent, 13,500-foot notch north of the pinnacles.

30.3 East Slopes II, Class 2+

From Blaine Basin: 4.0 miles, 3,350 feet
From East Dallas Creek Trailhead: 10.0 miles, 4,810 feet

This is the easiest route on Sneffels from Blaine Basin, north of the peak. This route provides an opportunity to experience Sneffels' wild north side without climbing it. This is also a good descent route after an ascent of a more difficult north-face route.

Use the Blaine Basin Approach. From Blaine Basin, climb south for 1.0 mile under Sneffels' east face. You will not see the route until you reach 12,400 feet. At 12,500 feet, turn west (right) and ascend a wide trough to 13,500-foot Scree Col, southeast of Sneffels' summit. This trough provides a moderate snow climb early in the summer, and reasonable passage later in the summer. From Scree Col, continue on the South Slopes Route to the summit.

30.4 Northeast Couloir II, Class 3, Steep Snow

From Blaine Basin: 3.4 miles, 3,450 feet
From East Dallas Creek Trailhead: 9.4 miles, 4,900 feet

This improbable route provides an amicable snow climb in early summer. You can see the route from Colorado 62 west of Ridgway, and you can preview snow conditions from a distance. Ascending this route and descending the East Slopes Route makes a northern Tour de Sneffels.

Use the Blaine Basin Approach. The broad, northeast couloir is the easternmost of three major couloirs on Sneffels' north face, and you can see it from Blaine Basin. Do not mistake the northeast couloir for two other narrower couloirs in the center of the north face. Climb up under the north face's eastern edge and enter the couloir at 13,000 feet. The couloir is quite wide at the bottom, then narrows and steepens near its top. Ascend the couloir and climb into the eastern of two 13,480-foot notches at the top of the couloir. The snow melts from the upper part of the couloir first, and some Class 3 scrambling may be required to reach the notch. Descend on the notch's south side and contour south to reach Scree Col, southeast of Sneffels' summit. From Scree Col, continue on the South Slopes Route to the summit.

30.5 Snake Couloir III, Class 3, Steep Snow/Ice *Classic*

From Blaine Basin: 2.6 miles, 3,350 feet

From East Dallas Creek Trailhead: 8.6 miles, 4,810 feet

When snow conditions are good, this is one of the best mountaineering routes on Colorado's fourteeners. When snow conditions are bad, or after the snow melts, avoid this couloir. The Snake Couloir is the westernmost of the three major couloirs on Sneffels' north face. The deeply inset Snake Couloir is well named, because it snakes up through the heart of the complex north face.

The bottom of the Snake Couloir faces northeast, and the upper part faces northwest. Because of the turn in the couloir, there is no single vantage point that allows you to see the entire couloir. You can see the upper part of the couloir from Colorado 62 west of Ridgway, but the lower part is hidden. You can see the lower part of the couloir from Blaine Basin, but the upper part is hidden. The snow in this natural avalanche chute gradually turns to ice as summer progresses.

Use the Blaine Basin Approach. Climb southwest for 1.0 mile to the base of the north face and enter the couloir at 13,000 feet. The average angle of the couloir is 40 degrees, but the angle is not consistent. The steepest portion of the couloir is the 200 feet below the turn in the couloir at 13,550 feet. The angle here reaches 50 degrees.

After the turn, the couloir gradually becomes less inset until it ends below a cliff leading directly to the summit. The easiest finish does not climb this cliff but angles east to the top of the north ridge. From here, do an ascending traverse east to reach a small notch 150 feet east of the summit. This notch is just west of and above the 14,020-foot notch at the top of the couloir on the South Slopes Route. Scramble west to the summit.

Variation 30.5V

You can do a more difficult finish by climbing directly to the summit from the top of the couloir (Class 5.6).

30.6 North Buttress III, Class 5.6 *Classic*

From Blaine Basin: 2.6 miles, 3,350 feet

From East Dallas Creek Trailhead: 8.6 miles, 4,810 feet

The north buttress is the large buttress forming the eastern edge of the Snake Couloir. The North Buttress and the Snake Couloir Routes provide a matched pair of great climbs. The soaring north buttress is between the Snake Couloir and the seldom climbed central couloir on Sneffels' complex north face. The north buttress was a test piece for early mountaineers and remains a test piece today.

Use the Blaine Basin Approach. Climb southwest for 1.0 mile to the base of the north face and proceed onto the buttress near the bottom of the Snake Couloir. You can also start by climbing 100 feet up the central couloir and proceeding onto the rock. The climb's greatest difficulties are on the bottom half of the buttress. Stay on the eastern side of the buttress. Above the turn in the Snake Couloir, follow the crest of the buttress. Either finish the climb by climbing the summit cliff directly (Class 5.6), or traverse east as described with the Snake Couloir Route.

31. Wilson Group

Wilson Peak   14,017 feet
Mount Wilson   14,246 feet
El Diente Peak   14,159 feet

See Map 31 on page 262

These peaks are remote and rugged. They are 13 miles southwest of Telluride, and they are the sentinels of the San Miguel Mountains in the western San Juans. These are some of Colorado's most difficult fourteeners. They all require at least Class 3 scrambling by their easiest route, and rotten rock adds to the challenge. The traverse between Mount Wilson and El Diente (see Combination 31.10) is one of Colorado's four great fourteener traverses. Approach these peaks with care.

Maps
Required: Mount Wilson, Dolores Peak, San Juan National Forest, Uncompahgre National Forest
Optional: Little Cone, Gray Head

Trailheads
Silver Pick Trailhead
This trailhead is at 10,420 feet and provides access to the north side of all three peaks. If approaching from the north or west, go 6.7 miles east on Colorado 145 from the junction of Colorado 145 and Colorado 62. If approaching from the south, go 6.0 miles west on Colorado 145 from the Telluride spur junction on Colorado 145.

Turn south onto the Silver Pick Road (dirt) and measure from this point. Cross the San Miguel River, stay left at 3.3 miles, take the middle of three roads at 4.0 miles, enter the Uncompahgre National Forest at 6.3 miles, stay left at 6.4 miles and reach the trailhead near some good campsites after 7.2

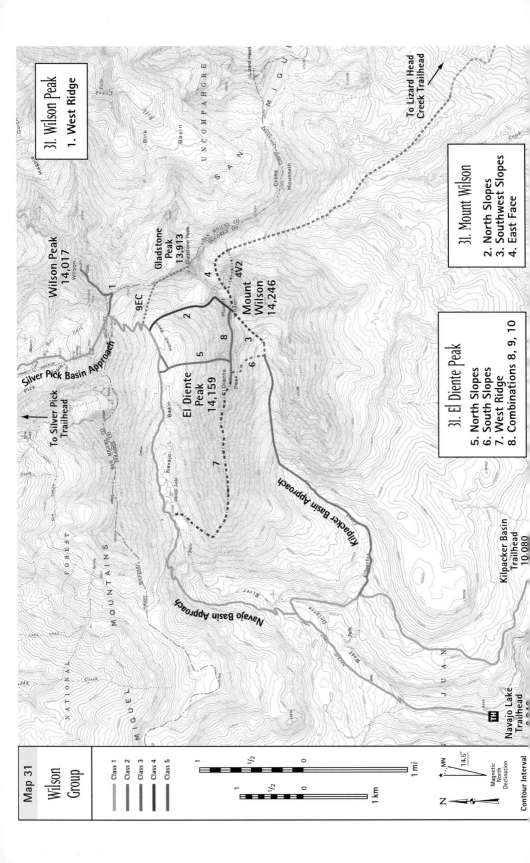

Map 31

Wilson Group

Class 1
Class 2
Class 3
Class 4
Class 5

1 mi
1/2
0
1 mi

1 km
1/2
0
1 km

N

★ MN
14.5°
Magnetic North
Declination

Contour Interval

31. Wilson Peak
1. West Ridge

Wilson Peak
14,017

Gladstone
Peak
13,913

9EC

Silver Pick Basin Approach

To Silver Pick
Trailhead

31. Mount Wilson

2. North Slopes
3. Southwest Slopes
4. East Face

Mount
Wilson
14,246

4V2

El Diente
Peak
14,159

31. El Diente Peak

5. North Slopes
6. South Slopes
7. West Ridge
8. Combinations 8, 9, 10

Navajo Basin Approach

Kilpacker Basin Approach

Kilpacker Basin
Trailhead
10,080

Navajo Lake
Trailhead

To Lizard Head
Creek Trailhead

SAN MIGUEL

UNCOMPAHGRE

SAN MIGUEL CO.
DOLORES CO.

MIGUEL

MOUNTAINS

NATIONAL

FOREST

JUAN

The Wilson Group from the northwest.

miles at a gate that is usually locked. The Silver Pick Road is steep and rough but passable for most passenger cars. If the gate at the trailhead is unlocked, vehicles can continue to the privately owned Silver Pick Mine.

Navajo Lake Trailhead

This trailhead is at 9,340 feet and provides access to Navajo Basin on the north side of Mount Wilson and El Diente. If approaching from the north, go south on Colorado 145 for 5.4 miles from the summit of Lizard Head Pass (10,250 feet). If approaching from the south, go north on Colorado 145 for 9.5 miles from the Rico Post Office.

Turn west onto the Dunton Road (Forest Service 535) and measure from this point. Go west on the Dunton Road (dirt) as it climbs to the meadows near Coal Creek. Go straight at 4.2 miles, pass Morgan Camp (private) at 5.0 miles, descend to the West Dolores River, turn hard south (left) at 7.2 miles and reach the trailhead after 7.3 miles. The Dunton Road is passable for passenger cars, and there is ample parking at the well-marked trailhead. The Dunton Road is not plowed in winter.

Kilpacker Basin Trailhead

This trailhead is at 10,080 feet and provides access to Kilpacker Basin on the south side of Mount Wilson and El Diente. If approaching from the north, go south on Colorado 145 for 5.4 miles from the summit of Lizard Head Pass (10,250 feet). If approaching from the south, go north on Colorado 145 for 9.5 miles from the Rico Post Office.

Turn west onto the Dunton Road (Forest Service 535) and measure from this point. Go west on the Dunton Road (dirt) as it climbs to the meadows near Coal Creek. Go straight at 4.2 miles, pass Morgan Camp (private) at 5.0 miles, turn north (right) onto Forest Service 207 at 5.1 miles and reach the trailhead after 5.3 miles. There are pastoral camping spots in the trees near the trailhead. The Dunton Road is not plowed in winter.

Lizard Head Creek Trailhead

This trailhead is at 10,050 feet and provides access to Mount Wilson's east side. This trailhead is 0.1 mile northwest of Colorado 145, 2.0 miles south of the summit of Lizard Head Pass (10,250 feet). There is a small parking area here, and trail signs near the trees to the north. This trailhead is accessible in winter.

Approaches

31.A1 Silver Pick Basin Approach

From Silver Pick Trailhead: 5.6 miles, 2,620 feet

You can approach Wilson Peak's West Ridge Route, Mount Wilson's North Slopes Route and El Diente's North Slopes Route from Silver Pick Basin. Start at the Silver Pick Trailhead and go south up the road to the Silver Pick Mine at 10,960 feet.

There are two routes leading from the Silver Pick Mine to upper Silver Pick Basin. The longer, easier route follows the four-wheel-drive road above the mine, turns left at 11,200 feet and continues up a four-wheel-drive road through the rocks on the basin's west side to the remains of an old mine building at 12,140 feet. A shorter, more scenic route follows an old trail that leaves the four-wheel-drive road 300 yards above the mine. The trail climbs around rocky outcrops on the basin's east side before rejoining the road at the mine building at 12,140 feet.

From 12,140 feet, switchback up a trail to the 13,020-foot saddle, called the "Rock of Ages Saddle," between Wilson Peak and Point 13,540, which is 1.0 mile west of Wilson Peak. The trail does not climb directly to the pass but switchbacks up the scree west of the pass. You cannot easily see this trail from below, and it is not marked on the Mount Wilson Quadrangle. The trail is well worth finding, because the scree below the pass is very loose. When you reach the pass, you will see a startling view of Mount Wilson and El Diente across Navajo Basin.

31.A2 Navajo Basin Approach

From Navajo Lake Trailhead: 12.2 to 15.2 miles, 3,100 to 4,000 feet

You can approach Wilson Peak's West Ridge Route, Mount Wilson's North Slopes Route and El Diente's North Slopes and West Ridge Routes from Navajo Basin. Start at the Navajo Lake Trailhead and follow the Navajo Lake Trail north and east for 5.0 miles to Navajo Lake at 11,154 feet. There are campsites here in the trees. Hike around Navajo Lake's north side and follow a trail east up a long scree slope to reach the grassy benches in upper Navajo Basin. There are many open camping sites on these benches.

For El Diente's North Slopes Route, hike east to 12,100 feet in upper Navajo Basin. For Mount Wilson's North Slopes Route, hike east to 12,300 feet in upper Navajo Basin. For Wilson Peak's West Ridge Route, hike east to the upper end of Navajo Basin, then follow a good trail switchbacking north to the 13,020-foot saddle between Wilson Peak and Point 13,540, which is 1.0 mile west of Wilson Peak. There is a shack just below the saddle at the Rock of Ages Mine.

31.A3 Kilpacker Basin Approach
From Kilpacker Basin Trailhead: 11.0 miles, 2,400 feet

You can approach Mount Wilson's Southwest Slopes Route and El Diente's South Slopes Route from Kilpacker Basin. Start at the Kilpacker Basin Trailhead and follow the Kilpacker Trail northwest for 1.0 mile, then north for an additional 1.6 miles into the Lizard Head Wilderness. This trail rolls through several captivating aspen groves and reminds you that you are in the San Juans.

Leave the Kilpacker Trail 200 yards south of (before) Kilpacker Creek and follow a good spur trail east into Kilpacker Basin. This trail starts on Kilpacker Creek's south side, crosses to Kilpacker Creek's north side after 0.5 mile, then rapidly fades into a series of large, grassy meadows. Stroll northeast up the meadows as El Diente watches your progress.

Kilpacker Basin has two waterfalls near tree line. The upper one can be seen from a distance and ornaments the already impressive view of El Diente. Trees hide the lower falls, and there is good camping below the lower falls. This is an enchanting place.

The enchantment rapidly fades as you engage upper Kilpacker Basin's scree. The rock is wretched, sharp and unpleasant to walk on. This is another reminder that you are in the San Juans. Stay on the creek's north side, engage the scree and find a faint climber's trail going straight up the west side of a patch of nasty bushes north of the upper waterfall. The trail then climbs east above the bushes and upper falls. The trail soon dies into immense scree slopes, and the challenge of this untamed place becomes obvious.

Wilson Peak
14,017

Wilson Peak from the north.

31. Wilson Peak   14,017 feet

See Map 31 on page 262

Wilson Peak has the distinction of being the highest peak in San Miguel County. Wilson Peak is 1.5 miles north of Mount Wilson, and people often confuse the two peaks. Wilson Peak is easier to climb than Mount Wilson and El Diente. Many people ascend Wilson Peak as a tune-up for the other two. People often photograph Wilson Peak from Colorado 145 north of Lizard Head Pass, especially in the fall when the charming aspen groves surrounding Wilson Peak change color.

Route

31.1 West Ridge II, Class 3

From Silver Pick Trailhead: 7.0 miles, 3,650 feet

From Navajo Lake Trailhead: 16.0 miles, 5,000 feet

This is the easiest route up Wilson Peak. You can approach the west ridge from either Silver Pick Basin or Navajo Basin. The Silver Pick Basin Approach is shorter if reaching Wilson Peak is your only objective. A high camp in Navajo Basin provides good access to all three peaks. Use either approach to reach the 13,020-foot saddle between Wilson Peak and Point 13,540, which is 1.0 mile west of Wilson Peak.

From the 13,020-foot Rock of Ages Saddle, hike east along the crest of the ridge for 150 yards, then do an ascending traverse below the cliffs on the ridge's south (right) side to a small saddle on the ridge between Wilson Peak and Gladstone Peak (13,913 feet). Do not climb too high on this ascending traverse. From the small saddle, the view opens and you can see the San Juans' vast expanse to the east. Lizard Head's spire will attract your attention.

You can see the rest of the route from the small saddle. Cross to the east side of the Wilson Peak–Gladstone Peak Ridge and contour north across some broken cliffs (Class 3), or descend on the east side of the small saddle to avoid the cliffs (Class 2). Beyond the cliffs, stay below the ridge crest and scramble northeast up broken rock to regain the ridge at 13,500 feet (Class 2). Follow the ridge up to a false summit at 13,900 feet. You can easily see the remaining challenge and the route's crux from here.

Descend 50 feet on the ridge's north (left) side, contour east for 50 feet under the ridge crest then scramble back to the ridge crest (Class 3). Scramble east for 150 feet to the summit (Class 3). From the summit, you have a free view of Mount Wilson, El Diente and beyond.

31. Mount Wilson 14,246 feet

See Map 31 on page 262

Mount Wilson is the monarch of the San Miguel Mountains and the highest peak in Dolores County. The peak is in the center of the massif between Wilson Peak and El Diente. Mount Wilson is a rugged alpine peak with several permanent snowfields, but because of its many neighbors, you seldom see it to good advantage. Mount Wilson remains a reclusive test piece for mountaineers.

Routes

31.2 North Slopes II, Class 4

From Silver Pick Trailhead: 9.0 miles, 5,300 feet

From Navajo Lake Trailhead: 16.0 miles, 5,200 feet

This is the easiest route on Mount Wilson. You can approach the route from either Silver Pick Basin or Navajo Basin. Use either approach to reach 12,300 feet in upper Navajo Basin. From here, climb south up a rounded shoulder just west of a large, permanent snowfield between Mount Wilson and Gladstone Peak. This snowfield is sometimes called the "Navajo Glacier." By ascending the shoulder, it is not necessary to get on the glacier;

however, snow persists through the summer on Mount Wilson's north side, so an ice ax is recommended for this route.

Ascend the shoulder to 13,800 feet, just below Mount Wilson's northeast ridge. Do not climb all the way to the ridge. From 13,800 feet, climb southwest up steep talus below the ridge crest, cross a gully (possibly snow-filled) and continue southwest to a notch just north of Mount Wilson's summit. If you follow the easiest route, the climbing to this point is Class 2+. From the notch, you can look west down into Kilpacker Basin and east down a long snow slope above Slate Creek.

From the notch, climb south for 150 feet on or near the ridge crest to the summit (Class 4). This final ridge is the route's crux, and the hardest move is immediately below the summit. There is considerable exposure on both sides of the ridge, and some parties choose to use a rope here. From the summit, you command a view from Shiprock to Uncompahgre.

31.3 Southwest Slopes II, Class 4, Moderate Snow
From Kilpacker Basin Trailhead: 13.2 miles, 4,200 feet

When snow conditions are good, this route is a refreshing alternative to the North Slopes Route. After the snow melts, the route becomes a scree-and-rubble challenge that is best avoided. Follow the Kilpacker Basin Approach, climb east into Kilpacker Basin past El Diente's summit and continue east toward Mount Wilson. You cannot see the route up Mount Wilson until you reach 13,000 feet, and your escape from this confining basin may seem improbable.

Above 13,000 feet, stay on the basin's north side and climb northeast up a hidden trough. When snow-filled, this trough provides a straightforward snow climb. As the snow melts, rubble and dirt are exposed. Some snow and ice remain in this trough all summer. Climb the narrow couloir leading to the notch just north of the summit. This is the high notch on the North Slopes Route. Climb south for 150 feet to the summit (Class 4).

31.4 East Face II, Class 4, Moderate Snow
From Lizard Head Creek Trailhead: 10.0 miles, 4,600 feet

When snow conditions are good, which for once is most of the summer, this route is one of the best moderate snow climbs on Colorado's fourteeners. Unfortunately, this exceptional climb requires a heinous approach. If you have a passion for solitude and wilderness, the joys of climbing in the upper Slate Creek Basin will compensate for the bushwhack approach.

Start at the Lizard Head Creek Trailhead and follow the Lizard Head Creek Trail north for 0.25 mile. Continue northwest for 1.0 mile on an old closed road to 11,000 feet. The bushwhack begins here. Leave the trail and contour northwest for 1.0 mile at 11,000 feet. Drop into Slate Creek at 10,800 feet. This high traverse keeps you from enduring the even greater misery of climbing through the dreaded Slate Mounds that abound in lower Slate Creek.

Bushwhack north-northwest up the Slate Creek Drainage for 1.0 mile to tree line. Continue north and climb toward the basin you have worked so hard to reach. At 12,400 feet, you enter the sheltered sanctuary under Mount Wilson's east face and Gladstone Peak's south face. Climb into the center of the basin and turn west. You are in a privileged position here. Enjoy your passage.

The unbroken sweep of snow on Mount Wilson's east face steepens at 13,000 feet. Climb the clean sweep directly toward the summit. As you approach the summit rocks, stay to the south (left) and climb to the end of the snow just south of the summit. Climb north up Class 4 rock to the summit. Your solitude may be broken if you meet other climbers on the summit, but if you share the joy of your ascent, you will feel even better.

Variations
31.4V1 II, Class 4, Steep Snow

For another elegant finish, stay to the north of the summit rocks and climb a short, steep couloir to reach the notch just north of Mount Wilson's summit. Join the North Slopes Route here and climb south on that route's final, Class 4 pitch to reach the summit.

31.4V2 Boxcar Couloir II, Class 4, Steep Snow

For even more excitement, leave the East Face Route at 12,400 feet and climb straight west up the S-shaped Boxcar Couloir. This steep, sinuous passage splits Mount Wilson's east buttress. Exit the Boxcar Couloir at 13,600 feet and rejoin the East Face Route. Reclusive and remote, this ascent may make you feel like an explorer from an ancient age.

31. El Diente Peak   14,159 feet

See Map 31 on page 262

El Diente means "the tooth" in Spanish, and the name fits this feral peak. El Diente is the Colorado fourteener farthest from Denver and is also Colorado's westernmost fourteener. El Diente is 0.8 mile west of Mount Wilson; a jagged ridge that drops to 13,900 feet connects the two peaks. El Diente rises only 259 feet above the low point of the ridge and, by more than one criterion, does not qualify as an official fourteener. However, El Diente remains on most peak lists because it is named and it has stature as

El Diente Peak from the east (photo by Steve Hoffmeyer).

a sentimental favorite. Most people who traverse the ridge from Mount Wilson to El Diente feel like they have climbed a peak!

Routes

31.5 North Slopes II, Class 3, Steep Snow
From Silver Pick Trailhead: 9.5 miles, 5,600 feet
From Navajo Lake Trailhead: 14.8 miles, 5,100 feet

This is the most often climbed route on El Diente, but depending on conditions, it may not be the easiest route. El Diente's north side retains some snow through most of the summer and this may aid or hinder progress depending on the climber. People climb the route because it is above Navajo Basin, and Mount Wilson and Wilson Peak can be climbed from there as well. You can approach the route from either Silver Pick Basin or Navajo Basin. Use either approach to reach 12,100 feet in upper Navajo Basin.

From 12,100 feet in upper Navajo Basin, climb south up a prominent couloir leading toward the El Diente–Mount Wilson Ridge, 0.25 mile east of El Diente's summit. The couloir retains some snow through the summer, so an ice ax is recommended for this route. The couloir ends in a rock face below the ridge crest. To avoid this obstacle, angle west (right) and reach the ridge crest at 13,900 feet. Cross to the ridge's south side and traverse west below the ridge crest to avoid some towers called the "Organ Pipes" (some Class 3). Climb back to the ridge crest via a gully, cross the ridge and finish the climb on the ridge's north side (some Class 3). The summit appears abruptly.

31.6 South Slopes II, Class 3

From Kilpacker Basin Trailhead: 12.0 miles, 4,100 feet

When it is snow-free, this route is probably the safest and easiest route on El Diente. Unpleasant scree replaces the steep snow on the North Slopes Route. Follow the Kilpacker Basin Approach and climb east into Kilpacker Basin past El Diente's summit to 12,800 feet. Avoid the temptation to leave the basin and climb up toward the summit too soon.

From 12,800 feet, climb north up steep talus toward the low point in the El Diente–Mount Wilson Ridge. The route to the ridge is not a straight line. Climb up under a cliff at 13,500 feet, do an ascending traverse west (left) to avoid it and proceed onto an easier slope west of the cliff. Ascend this slope on steep scree (Class 2) or the nearby rock ribs (Class 3). Some Class 3 scrambling is required as you approach the ridge. Depending on your disposition, the scrambling may come as a welcome relief from the scree.

It is not necessary to go all the way to the ridge. The South Slopes Route joins the North Slopes Route below the Organ Pipes on the ridge's south side. Traverse west below the Organ Pipes (some Class 3). Climb to the ridge crest via a gully, cross the ridge and finish the climb on the ridge's north side (some Class 3). The summit appears abruptly.

31.7 West Ridge II, Class 4

From Navajo Lake Trailhead: 14.6 miles, 5,100 feet

This is the westernmost route in this book. Solitude comes with that geographic distinction. Use the Navajo Basin Approach to reach Navajo Lake at 11,154 feet. From the west end of the lake, do an ascending traverse southwest for 0.5 mile to 11,600 feet at the bottom of the west ridge. Climb east and stay on the increasingly well defined ridge for 1.7 miles to the summit. That's a long distance to be on a ridge of this stature, and there are several surprises along the way, including a nasty notch near the summit. Be prepared for exacting route finding. This ridge is in a magnificent position and provides expansive views to the west.

31. Wilson Peak, Mount Wilson and El Diente Combinations

See Map 31 on page 262

31.8 III, Class 4, Steep Snow *Classic*

From Silver Pick Trailhead: 11.0 miles, 7,175 feet

This is the most expedient way to climb all three peaks in one day from a trailhead. Start at the Silver Pick Trailhead and follow Wilson

Peak's West Ridge Route to Wilson Peak's summit. Return to the 13,020-foot saddle, descend south into Navajo Basin and continue on Mount Wilson's North Slopes Route to Mount Wilson's summit.

The traverse from Mount Wilson to El Diente is one of Colorado's four great fourteener traverses. It is long and time-consuming. Time spent to complete this traverse will range from two to four hours. Escape from the ridge is difficult, and this is a bad ridge to be trapped on during an electrical storm. Consider the weather carefully before launching.

From Mount Wilson's summit, descend north for 150 feet to the high saddle described with Mount Wilson's North Slopes Route (Class 4). From the high saddle, descend west down a couloir, then traverse west under the ridge crest on the south side of the Mount Wilson–El Diente Ridge. Reach the ridge crest at a 14,060-foot saddle.

From the 14,060-foot saddle, climb west on the ridge crest and traverse a narrow, exposed coxcomb (Class 3). The exposure on both sides of the coxcomb is sensational, and this is a particularly bad place to be during an electrical storm. As you approach the coxcomb's west end, the ridge drops down to a 13,980-foot saddle. If you stay on the ridge crest, you will discover that the drop becomes abrupt. A 60-foot rappel will overcome the problem.

You also can overcome the problem by doing a Class 3 downclimb on the ridge's south side. Because of its sinuous nature, the exact line of this devious downclimb is difficult to describe. Start the downclimb before you reach the end of the coxcomb. End the downclimb 100 feet southeast of and slightly below the 13,980-foot saddle. This downclimb has the traverse's most difficult climbing.

At the 13,980-foot saddle, you are one-quarter of the way along the traverse, and the enormity of your endeavor will be apparent. Take heart, because the ridge is easier for a while. Traverse west on a broader section of ridge over a 14,100-foot summit (Class 2). The next obstacle is a series of towers near the west end of the 14,100-foot summit. These towers are *not* the Organ Pipes.

The easiest way around the towers is to descend 250 feet down the ridge's south side, traverse below the towers, then climb back to the ridge west of the towers. Shorter routes traverse below the towers on the ridge's south side without losing so much elevation, but these routes are harder and difficult to find.

From the west side of the towers, traverse another easy stretch of ridge and reach the 13,900-foot saddle where El Diente's North Slopes Route reaches the ridge. Traverse west below the ridge crest on the ridge's south side to avoid the Organ Pipes (some Class 3). Climb back to the ridge crest via a gully, cross the ridge and climb to El Diente's summit on the ridge's north side (some Class 3). Descend El Diente's North Slopes Route and return to Silver Pick Basin over the 13,020-foot saddle west of Wilson Peak.

Consider doing El Diente first and completing the tour in the opposite direction. This will put you on the Mount Wilson–El Diente Ridge sooner rather than later, which can help you beat thunderstorms. It is easier to ascend El Diente's North Slopes Route than to descend it. Doing the traverse from El Diente to Mount Wilson has trade-offs at the steep pitch just east of the 13,980-foot saddle. It is easier to climb up this Class 3 pitch than downclimb it, but you lose the option of rappelling over the pitch.

31.9 III, Class 4, Steep Snow

From Navajo Lake: 8.4 miles, 5,600 feet

From Navajo Lake Trailhead: 18.4 miles, 7,600 feet

From the Navajo Lake Trailhead, this combination is longer than Combination 31.8, but from a camp at Navajo Lake, it is shorter. Start at the Navajo Lake Trailhead and hike to Navajo Lake. Hike into Navajo Basin and climb all three peaks as described in Combination 31.8. Return to Navajo Lake at the end of the day instead of climbing back over the 13,020-foot saddle to Silver Pick Basin.

Extra Credit 31.9EC

From Navajo Lake: 9.4 miles, 6,600 feet

From Navajo Lake Trailhead: 19.4 miles, 8,600 feet

Climb Gladstone Peak (13,913 feet) in addition to the fourteeners. Gladstone is the dramatic peak between Wilson Peak and Mount Wilson, and people usually climb it via its north ridge. This ridge requires some Class 3 scrambling on questionable blocks. Including Gladstone makes this tour a grand slam.

31.10 III, Class 4 *Classic*

From camp in Kilpacker Basin: 12.0 miles, 4,900 feet

From Kilpacker Basin Trailhead: 19.5 miles, 5,500 feet

Now for something completely different. This combination may provide the easiest means of doing Mount Wilson and El Diente together. You can see two valleys for the price of one! Start at the Kilpacker Basin Trailhead and hike to the lower waterfall in Kilpacker Basin, where you can make camp. Climb El Diente's South Slopes Route, traverse to Mount Wilson and descend Mount Wilson's North Slopes Route to Navajo Lake. Follow the Navajo Lake Trail west then south for 2.3 miles, then turn east onto the Kilpacker Trail's upper end. Follow the Kilpacker Trail south for 1.0 mile and hike back up Kilpacker Creek to your camp. The trail miles are much easier than upper Kilpacker Basin's scree.

Leave No Trace!

Properly Dispose of What You Can't Pack Out

- Deposit human waste in catholes dug 6 to 8 inches deep.
- Use toilet paper or wipes sparingly. Pack them out.
- Scatter wash water 200 feet away from streams or lakes.

Leave What You Find

- Treat our national heritage with respect.
- Leave plants, rocks and historical artifacts as you find them.
- Good campsites are found, not made.
- Altering a campsite should not be necessary.
- Let nature's sounds prevail.
- Keep loud voices and noises to a minimum.
- Control pets at all times. Remove dog feces.
- Do not build structures or furniture or dig trenches.

Minimize Use and Impact of Fires

- Campfires cause lasting impacts to the backcountry.
- Always carry a lightweight stove for cooking.
- Enjoy a candle lantern instead of a fire.
- When fires are permitted, use established fire rings, fire pans or mound fires.
- Do not snap branches off live, dead or downed trees.
- Put out campfires completely.

Appendix

In Defense of Mountaineering Guidebooks

I am always amazed when I see stumps of once large trees near tree line. They are not going to grow back, at least not until a comet hits the earth and changes the balance of nature. I am equally amazed that nothing grows on mine tailings. Even a comet may not make them fertile. We are the future generation and we have stumps and tailings to look at. Yet the mountains are not dead. We can climb them then loll about in fields of flowers.

Ironically, we now drive up the miners' old roads in four-wheel-drive vehicles made of mined metals, hike uphill for a few hours to a summit and claim a personal victory or conquest. Miners and loggers make physical extractions from the mountains. Climbers make mental extractions from the mountains. For now, we have driven mining and logging offshore. We no longer rush to the mountains to get the gold, we go to get their good tidings.

The debate today swirls around the opinion that even climber's mental extractions are causing unacceptable environmental damage. We leave too many footprints. Those who choose to make an effort are being cast as pseudo-criminals who are loving the mountains to death. Eh? I take a longer view. Death to a mountain is when it is mined into oblivion like Bartlett Mountain. Death to a mountain is when it commits suicide like Mount St. Helens. As violent as those actions were, we can still climb the stumps of those peaks. There are still good tidings there.

Any long view must compare the damage done by climber's boots with that of monster trucks. Obviously, boots pale in comparison. Still, are boots too much? Sometimes, yes. What do we do? Rather than lament the lost age when we could walk unfettered by such concerns, we should strap in and solve the problem. For a government agency to shut the door and refuse entry is not a solution. Excess footprints are easily dealt with. We need sustainable trails through the fragile alpine zone. The Colorado Fourteener Initiative is creating these trails. Their efforts are a grand example of the public's ability to strap in and solve the problem. There is no environmental problem created by climbers that cannot be solved by climbers.

Our mental extractions from the mountains are going to continue to increase. So is the positive social value of these gifts. As society creaks and groans in other arenas, we need the mountain's good tidings more than ever. The gift mountains offer society is immense. Mountains give us an arena where we can lift not just our bodies, but our spirits. Without uplifted spirits, we devolve. Mountaineering is a great metaphor for life. It is worth fighting for. I view guidebooks as part of the solution, not part of the problem.

I started climbing in 1956. For nearly 20 years I could not conceive of writing a guidebook. I reasoned, like a miner, that the good tidings were hidden and, once found, should be protected by some sort of claim. I felt a proprietary ownership of the secrets I found with my efforts. I felt that sharing the secret would diminish it as a microscope can change the microbe. I dashed across the globe to discover it before it was diminished. While I had many unique climbs and experiences, this effort left me frustrated and exhausted. I could not dash fast enough. Too many people were ahead of me. After an ascent of the Matterhorn in 1973 that I shared with a hundred other people, I pointed to the heavens and started pontificating about the lost age. Then I realized no one was listening. They were just climbing the Matterhorn. Society had jumped my claim. I pondered this for many years.

Still, I did not write a guidebook. I reasoned that sharing would attract still more people and hasten the demise. I clung to this view as the population quietly doubled and mountain use increased tenfold. My pontifical finger withered. I was alone with my memories of the lost age. Then, early one morning in 1981, I sat upright in bed and started writing a guidebook. It was done in a week. At the time, I could not explain it but I knew that not sharing would hasten the demise. Finally, I just set the demise aside. I knew that what the mountains needed was love.

Approached with love, the mountains can endure our mental extractions forever. Approached with malice, greed or ignorance, the mountains will indeed suffer. Worse, even with love, climbers may lose their access because of other interests and opinions. The government agencies and monster trucks stand ready. The best we can do is love the mountains and share this love. Climbers as a group need to evolve. We must spread our arms wide and embrace not just the mountains, but other user groups as well. The mountains need loving user groups intimate with their secrets to be their ambassadors. I offer my guidebooks from a deep love for the mountains so that future ambassadors can also share the mountain's good tidings.

In Defense of Feet

The world is in a big rush to abandon feet and replace feet with meters. Why? Let's see ... my dictionary defines a meter as 39.37 inches, and an inch is one-twelfth of a foot. Aren't we trying to define meters in terms of feet here? Ah! My dictionary goes on to say that a meter was meant to be one ten-millionth of the distance along a meridian from the equator to the pole. Yeah, I can really identify with that.

But a meter isn't actually what it was meant to be. When I looked deep into my inviolable handbook of chemistry and physics, I learned that a meter is 1,553,164.13 times the wavelength of the red cadmium line in air under 760 millimeters of pressure at 15 degrees Centigrade. Now, I *positively* have an intrinsic feeling for that! And aren't we using millimeters in the definition of a meter?

The whole point of meters seems to be that we can divide them by 10 because we have 10 fingers. Dividing by 10 is something that scientists and engineers do all the time, but they usually have computers to help them do it. Now, sports-minded people don't usually carry computers around, nor do they need to divide by 10, so they need something they can understand—like a foot. Now, a foot was the length of some old king's foot. I can identify with that because my foot is just about the same length as his foot. The best part is that I can see my foot. It is 4 feet away when I am sitting down and 6 feet away when I am standing up. I have a foot. I do not have a meter.

A foot is a good measure to use when I am throwing, jumping, running or climbing. In 1955 the national track and field championships were held in my hometown of Boulder, Colorado. All the kids went because it was the biggest meet ever to hit town. Back in 1955, Parry O'Brien was the only man who could shotput more than 60 feet. He came to the meet, and the officials drew a big line out at 60 feet. Parry whirled and let out a huge grunt that was heard across the stadium. The shotput flew and flew. It landed with a thud and kicked up the dust on the 60-foot line. The crowd went wild. For the next week, kids all over town were whirling and grunting. The rocks sailed. We all learned from Parry O'Brien exactly how far 60 feet is. At that time, 60 feet was over in the middle of the neighbor's yard. You need feet if you are going to have a 60-foot shotput.

Back in 1955, no one had high-jumped 7 feet. It seemed impossibly high. It was higher than me and higher than anybody I knew. Imagine jumping higher than your head! John Thomas wanted to be the first person to high-jump 7 feet, so he painted a big red line around his room at 7 feet to get used to the idea. My room was 8 feet high, and I lay in bed visualizing jumping up and over my imaginary line. You need feet if you are going to have a 7-foot high-jump.

The four-minute mile is the perfect event. Four laps, four minutes, one mile. The first four-minute mile by Roger Bannister is as well known as the first ascent of Everest. Most of today's metric track meets still cling to the mile. Why? Because it's the perfect event. You need feet if you are going to have a four-minute mile.

I grew up with all these magic events, and they taught me how long a foot is. The essence of a foot is deeply imbedded in my soul. My trusty Scout pace measures 5 feet for two steps. I can pace off 60 feet to within a few inches, and that is good enough for anything I want to do outdoors. I still don't know how long a meter is.

When I started climbing, I quickly learned what it meant to climb a vertical foot. You had to climb 1,000 vertical feet per hour or you couldn't go on the trip. I was young and strong and could easily climb 3,000 feet per hour. If I pushed myself, I could climb 5,000 feet per hour for a while. I learned to eyeball a slope and tell just how high it was—in feet.

I learned what it felt like at 14,000 feet. I grew up in Colorado, and fourteeners were magic. I idolized people who had climbed them all. I climbed them too, trying to be one of the elite. I knew all the fourteener elevations by heart and could recite them on demand. Better yet, given an elevation, I would recite the peak name. The imaginary line in the sky at 14,000 feet separated the chosen few from the rank and file. The name of the game was to get as high as possible and stay there for as long as possible. You need feet if you are going to have a fourteener. You need feet if you are going to climb it.

The scientists and engineers are hard at work trying to impose their fingers over my feet. The USGS maps of the Sierra are already appearing in meters. Gack! In time, the memories will fade and the magic will be lost. There will be no more 70-foot shotputs, 8-foot high-jumps or four-minute miles. When they replace feet with meters, there will be no more fourteeners. Feet—and this book—will be obsolete.

I intend to go out kicking and screaming. I hope this book will preserve the magic for a little longer. If the Colorado maps become metric, I will go into the mountains without them. I will rely on my eye and trusty Scout pace. From the high summits, the fourteeners will still be visible.

Map Lists

I have written this book to be used with good maps. I recommend the USGS topographic quadrangles. They are available in many shops and also at the Map Sales Office in the Denver Federal Center; call (303) 236-7477 for information. You can mail-order maps from the Federal Center, but they will not accept phone orders. All the quadrangles referred to in this book are 7.5-minute quadrangles, and they all use feet, not meters. The non-topographic National Forest maps are also useful. The National Forest maps give you the big picture and they often have more current road information than the USGS quadrangles. I have listed the required and optional USGS quadrangles and National Forest maps with each peak or group of peaks, both in the text and in the following lists.

Front Range Maps

Longs
Required: *Longs Peak, Roosevelt National Forest*
Optional: *McHenrys Peak, Isolation Peak, Allens Park*

Grays, Torreys
Required: *Grays Peak, Arapaho National Forest*
Optional: *Montezuma*

Evans, Bierstadt
Required: *Mount Evans, Arapaho National Forest*
Optional: *Georgetown, Harris Park, Idaho Springs, Pike National Forest*

Pikes
Required: *Pikes Peak, Pike National Forest*
Optional: *Manitou Springs*

Tenmile–Mosquito Range Maps

Quandary
Required: *Breckenridge, Arapaho National Forest*
Optional: *Copper Mountain*

Lincoln, Cameron, Bross, Democrat
Required: *Alma, Climax, Pike National Forest*

Sherman
Required: *Mount Sherman, Pike National Forest*
Optional: *San Isabel National Forest*

Sawatch Range Maps

Holy Cross
Required: *Mount of the Holy Cross, White River National Forest*
Optional: *Minturn, Mount Jackson*

Massive
Required: *Mount Massive, San Isabel National Forest*

Elbert
Required: *Mount Elbert, Mount Massive, San Isabel National Forest*
Optional: *Granite*

La Plata
Required: *Mount Elbert, San Isabel National Forest*
Optional: *Winfield, Independence Pass*

Huron
Required: *Winfield, San Isabel National Forest*

Belford, Oxford, Missouri
Required: *Mount Harvard, Winfield, San Isabel National Forest*
Optional: *Harvard Lakes*

Harvard, Columbia
Required: *Mount Harvard, Mount Yale, San Isabel National Forest*
Optional: *Harvard Lakes, Buena Vista West*

Yale
Required: *Mount Yale, San Isabel National Forest*
Optional: *Buena Vista West*

Princeton
Required: *Mount Antero, San Isabel National Forest*
Optional: *St. Elmo, Buena Vista West, Mount Yale*

Antero
Required: *Mount Antero, St. Elmo, San Isabel National Forest*

Shavano, Tabeguache
Required: *Maysville, Garfield, St. Elmo, Mount Antero, San Isabel National Forest*

Sangre de Cristo Range Maps

Crestone Peak, Crestone Needle, Humboldt, Challenger, Kit Carson

Required: *Crestone Peak, San Isabel National Forest*
Optional: *Crestone, Beck Mountain, Rio Grande National Forest*

Blanca, Little Bear, Ellingwood, Lindsey

Required: *Blanca Peak, Twin Peaks, Rio Grande National Forest*
Optional: *Mosca Pass, San Isabel National Forest*

Culebra

Required: *Culebra Peak, El Valle Creek*
Optional: *Taylor Ranch*

Elk Range Maps

Capitol

Required: *Capitol Peak, White River National Forest*

Snowmass

Required: *Snowmass Mountain, White River National Forest*
Optional: *Capitol Peak, Maroon Bells*

Maroon Peak, North Maroon Peak, Pyramid

Required: *Maroon Bells, White River National Forest*

Castle, Conundrum

Required: *Hayden Peak, White River National Forest*
Optional: *Maroon Bells*

San Juan Range Maps

San Luis

Required: *San Luis Peak, Stewart Peak, Elk Park, Gunnison National Forest*
Optional: *Halfmoon Pass, Rio Grande National Forest*

Uncompahgre, Wetterhorn

Required: *Uncompahgre Peak, Wetterhorn Peak, Uncompahgre National Forest*
Optional: *Lake City, Courthouse Mountain*

Redcloud, Sunshine, Handies
Required: *Redcloud Peak, Handies Peak, Uncompahgre National Forest*
Optional: *Lake San Cristobal, Lake City*

Eolus, Sunlight, Windom
Required: *Columbine Pass, Storm King Peak, Mountain View Crest,*
            San Juan National Forest
Optional: *Snowdon Peak, Electra Lake, Engineer Mountain, Vallecito*
            Reservoir

Sneffels
Required: *Mount Sneffels, Telluride, Uncompahgre National Forest*
Optional: *Ironton*

Wilson Peak, Mount Wilson, El Diente
Required: *Mount Wilson, Dolores Peak, San Juan National Forest,*
            Uncompahgre National Forest
Optional: *Little Cone, Gray Head*

Shopping List for All USGS Quadrangles

Allens Park
Alma
Beck Mountain
Blanca Peak
Breckenridge
Buena Vista West
Capitol Peak
Climax
Columbine Pass
Copper Mountain
Courthouse Mountain
Crestone
Crestone Peak
Culebra Peak
Dolores Peak
El Valle Creek
Electra Lake
Elk Park
Engineer Mountain
Garfield

Georgetown
Granite
Gray Head
Grays Peak
Halfmoon Pass
Handies Peak
Harris Park
Harvard Lakes
Hayden Peak
Idaho Springs
Ironton
Isolation Peak
Lake City
Lake San Cristobal
Little Cone
Longs Peak
Manitou Springs
Maroon Bells
Maysville
McHenrys Peak

Minturn
Montezuma
Mosca Pass
Mount Antero
Mount Elbert
Mount Evans
Mount Harvard
Mount of the Holy Cross
Mount Jackson
Mount Massive
Mount Sherman
Mount Sneffels
Mount Wilson
Mount Yale
Mountain View Crest

Pikes Peak
Redcloud Peak
St. Elmo
San Luis Peak
Snowdon Peak
Snowmass Mountain
Stewart Peak
Storm King Peak
Taylor Ranch
Telluride
Twin Peaks
Uncompahgre Peak
Vallecito Reservoir
Wetterhorn Peak
Winfield

Shopping List for National Forest Maps

Arapaho National Forest
Gunnison National Forest
Pike National Forest
Rio Grande National Forest
Roosevelt National Forest

San Isabel National Forest
San Juan National Forest
Uncompahgre National Forest
White River National Forest

Difficulty of Easiest Routes

This list sorts the Colorado fourteeners by difficulty of easiest route. The easiest route is determined by the Class, not the Grade. The standard route is not always the easiest route. When the standard route and easiest route differ, I list the easiest route here if I also describe it in the text. Because they are on private property, I have not described Lindsey's or Little Bear's easiest routes in the text. These routes do not appear on these lists either. The routes are listed in the order they appear in the text.

Class 1

Grays–North Slopes
Pikes–East Slopes
Quandary–East Slopes
Lincoln–East Shoulder

Bross–East Slopes
Elbert–Northeast Ridge
San Luis–East Slopes

Class 2

Torreys—South Slopes
Evans—Chicago Creek
    and Northeast Face
Bierstadt—West Slopes
Democrat—East Ridge
Sherman—Fourmile Creek
Holy Cross—North Ridge
Massive—East Slopes
La Plata—Northwest Ridge
Huron—Northwest Slopes
Belford—West Slopes
Oxford—West Ridge
Missouri—Northwest Ridge
Harvard—South Slopes
Columbia—West Slopes

Yale—South Slopes
Princeton—East Slopes
Antero—West Slopes
Shavano—East Slopes
Tabeguache—Southwest Ridge
Humboldt—West Ridge
Blanca—Northwest Face
Ellingwood—Southwest Face
Culebra—Northwest Ridge
Castle—Northwest Ridge
Uncompahgre—East Slopes
Redcloud—Northeast Ridge
Sunshine—North Slopes
Handies—West Slopes

Class 2+

Challenger—North Slopes
Lindsey—North Face

Windom—West Ridge
Sneffels—South Slopes

Class 3

Longs—Keyhole
Crestone Peak—South Face
Crestone Needle—South Face
Kit Carson—West Ridge
Snowmass—East Slopes

Maroon Peak—South Ridge
Wetterhorn—Southeast Ridge
Eolus—Northeast Ridge
Wilson Peak—West Ridge
El Diente—South Slopes

Class 4

Little Bear—West Ridge
Capitol—Northeast Ridge
North Maroon—Northeast Ridge

Pyramid—Northeast Ridge
Sunlight—South Slopes
Mount Wilson—North Slopes

Classic Routes

The routes are listed in the order they appear in the text.

Front Range *Classic* Routes

Keyhole of Longs	II, Class 3, Moderate Snow (Seasonal)
Kieners of Longs	III, Class 5.3–5.4, Moderate Snow/Ice
Stettner's Ledges of Longs	III, Class 5.7+
Notch Couloir of Longs	III, Class 5.0–5.2, Steep Snow/Ice
Loft of Longs	II, Class 3, Moderate Snow (Seasonal)
The Grand Slam of Longs	III, Class 3, Moderate Snow (Seasonal)
Kelso Ridge of Torreys	II, Class 3
East Ridge of Bierstadt	II, Class 3
The Sawtooth of Evans and Bierstadt	II, Class 3
Evans and Bierstadt Combination 3.19	I, Class 3
East Slopes of Pikes	III, Class 1
Y Couloir of Pikes	II, Class 3, Steep Snow/Ice (Seasonal)

Tenmile–Mosquito Range *Classic* Routes

East Slopes of Quandary	II, Class 1
West Ridge of Quandary	I, Class 3
North Ridge of Democrat	II, Class 3

Sawatch Range *Classic* Routes

Holy Cross Couloir of Holy Cross	III, Class 3, Steep Snow (Seasonal)
East Ridge of Elbert	II, Class 1
Ellingwood Ridge of La Plata	III, Class 3
West Slopes of Belford	II, Class 2
East Ridge of Yale	II, Class 2
Angel of Shavano	II, Class 2, Easy Snow (Seasonal)

Sangre de Cristo Range *Classic* Routes

South Face of Crestone Peak	II, Class 3, Moderate Snow (Seasonal)
North Pillar of Crestone Peak	III, Class 5.8
South Face of Crestone Needle	II, Class 3, Moderate Snow (Seasonal)
Ellingwood Arête of Crestone Needle	III, Class 5.7

Crestone Traverse
    Combination 19.12   II, Class 4
Crestone Traverse
    Combination 19.13   II, Class 4
North Ridge of Kit Carson   II, Class 4
The Prow of Kit Carson   III, Class 5.8
Ormes Buttress of Blanca   III, Class 5.6
Northwest Face of Little Bear III, Class 4
Southwest Ridge of Ellingwood III, Class 3
Little Bear–Blanca
    Traverse 20.10   III, Class 5.0–5.2

Elk Range *Classic* Routes

Northeast Ridge of Capitol   II, Class 4
Northwest Ridge of Capitol III, Class 5.7, Steep Snow/Ice
East Slopes of Snowmass   II, Class 3, Moderate Snow
Bell Cord Couloir
    of Maroon Peak   III, Class 4, Steep Snow/Ice
North Face of
    North Maroon Peak   III, Class 4, Steep Snow/Ice
Maroon Bells Traverse 24.10 II, Class 4

San Juan Range *Classic* Routes

Southeast Ridge of Wetterhorn II, Class 3
East Slopes of Handies   II, Class 2
East Ridge of Handies   II, Class 2
West Ridge of Sunlight   II, Class 4
West Ridge of Windom   II, Class 2+
South Slopes of Sneffels   II, Class 2+
Southwest Ridge of Sneffels II, Class 3
Snake Couloir of Sneffels   III, Class 3, Steep Snow/Ice
North Buttress of Sneffels   III, Class 5.6
Wilson–El Diente
    Traverse 31.8   III, Class 4, Steep Snow
Wilson–El Diente
    Traverse 31.10   III, Class 4

What Is a Peak?

The question about what constitutes an official peak and what is just a false summit has plagued mountaineers for decades. Most mountaineers know all about false summits. When you reach what you think is the summit and discover that the peak you are trying to climb is still farther and higher, you are on a false summit. For many mountaineers, this is all they need to know, and the following discussion will seem banal.

The traditional list of Colorado fourteeners has varied from 52 to 55 peaks over the years and has always been based on a healthy degree of emotionalism. Peaks have come and gone for sentimental reasons. In this high-tech peak-bagging age, however, many climbers are interested in peak lists based on a rational system. These climbers are interested in the discussion about what constitutes a peak because the answer determines a list's contents and, hence, their climbs.

For some time in Colorado, a single, simple criterion has been used to determine if a summit is a peak or a false summit: For a summit to be a peak, it must rise at least 300 vertical feet above the saddle connecting it to its neighbor. If just one criterion is to be used, this is a good one. There is nothing sacred about 300 feet. It is just a round number that seems to make sense in Colorado. It is a criterion that serves most people most of the time, and the peak list that follows uses it.

When Is a Peak Climbed?

After grappling with the question of what is a peak, we need to think about another question: When is a peak climbed? Stated differently: What constitutes an ascent? Most people would wince if you drove a vehicle to just a few feet from the summit and then walked to the top, and most people would wince if you didn't reach the highest point at all. So, two necessary conditions seem to be that you must reach the highest point under your own power and that you must gain a certain amount of elevation. But how much? That question seems to be the crux.

An obvious answer is that, to climb a mountain, you must climb from the bottom to the top. Although the top of most mountains is well defined, the bottom is not. One definition is that the bottom of all mountains is sea level. This flip definition makes little topographic sense, however, and it means that almost nobody has ever climbed anything.

In Colorado there has been a long-standing informal agreement that one should gain 3,000 feet for a "legal" ascent of a fourteener. Of course, there is nothing sacred about the number 3,000. It is approximately equal to the vertical distance between tree line and summit, and it represents a nice workout, but other than that, it's just a one-number estimate for defining the bottom of a Colorado mountain. Even people who are careful to gain 3,000 feet on the first fourteener of the day often hike the connecting ridge to the next fourteener and claim a legal ascent of the second peak after an ascent of only a few hundred feet. Most people who climb fourteeners do this.

A good minimum criterion for climbing a peak is that you should gain a vertical height under your own power equal to your peak's rise from its highest connecting saddle with a neighbor peak. If you do less than that, you are just visiting summits, not climbing mountains. Beyond this minimum gain, you are free to gain as much altitude as your peak-bagging conscience requires. The greater your elevation gain, the greater your karmic gain. Except for ridge traverses, 3,000 feet seems to satisfy most people.

There are other interesting questions. If someone rides a bicycle up the Mount Evans Road, then walks up to the highest point, have they climbed Evans? They ascended under their own power and even hauled up the bicycle's weight. Suppose someone else runs on a treadmill all winter and charges up a bank of batteries. When summer comes, they load the batteries into a battery-powered car and drive to the top of Evans in comfort. Has this person climbed Evans? This may be an "ascent," but it isn't a climb. The cyclist ascended Evans under their own power, but with considerable aid from mechanical advantage. The motorist used stored energy for propulsion. Both these activities seem to be outside the sport of mountaineering. Climbers should carry their equipment, not let their equipment carry them.

Peak List

The following list covers not just Colorado's fourteeners, but all Colorado peaks 13,800 feet or above. By my 300-foot criterion, this covers Colorado's 100 highest peaks. I present this extended list in the hope that you will be inspired by Colorado's fourteeners and return to the high country again and again for more adventures. The list covers 118 peaks, 9 of which have unofficial names but are ranked, and 9 of which have official names but are unranked.

A peak qualifies for this list if it is named or ranked. Named summits are on the list if they are ranked or unranked. The officially named summits include peaks, mounts, mountains, named ridges, named benchmarks if they do not have a peak name, named rocks and named hills. Unofficial names are enclosed in quotation marks. If a summit has both a peak name and a named benchmark, the peak name takes precedence.

I list ranked summits whether they are named or not. I rank a summit if it rises at least 300 feet from the highest connecting saddle to a higher ranked summit. The closest, higher ranked summit is the "parent." A fine point is that this may be a different peak from the higher ranked summit above the highest connecting saddle. In the rare case where there are two or more connecting saddles of the same elevation leading to different higher-ranked summits, the closer summit is the parent. My list differs from other lists in that I search for a higher, ranked parent, not just another peak on the list that may be lower and unranked. That would be a "neighbor." It is interesting to be on a summit and know where the nearest higher peak is.

I give interpolated elevations to summits and saddles that are only shown with contour lines. Most USGS quadrangles covering Colorado have 40-foot contour intervals. Thus, I add 20 feet to the elevation of the highest closed contour for a summit without a given elevation. I give unmarked saddles an elevation halfway between the highest contour that does not go through the saddle and the lowest contour that does go through the saddle.

If, using either given or interpolated elevations, a summit rises at least 300 feet from its highest connecting saddle to a higher ranked summit, it has a "hard rank." Summits that do not have a hard rank but could rank if interpolated elevations were *not* used for either the summit or connecting saddle have a "soft rank." There are three soft-ranked summits on this list: Point 14,340, alias "North Massive"; Point 13,900; and 13,831-foot Iowa Peak. These summits have an *S* in the Rank column. Lack of an *S* means the peak has a hard rank.

The Range column shows the peak's range as follows: *FR* for Front, *TM* for Tenmile–Mosquito, *SW* for Sawatch, *SC* for Sangre de Cristo, *EL* for Elk and *SJ* for San Juan. The Mile column shows the straight-line map distance in miles between the peak and its parent. The Quadrangle column gives the USGS 7.5-minute quadrangle that shows the summit of the peak. The parent may be on a different quadrangle. Use the Ascent column to track your climbs. The following abbreviations are used: *Pk* for Peak, *Mt* for Mount, *Mtn* for Mountain, *BM* for Benchmark, *NE* for Northeast, *NW* for Northwest and *SE* for Southeast.

Two named and famous fourteeners, El Diente and North Maroon, do not rank under the 300-foot criterion. The topography speaks without emotion. In compensation, a new fourteener with a soft rank, "North Massive," appears on the list. The list of the 100 highest peaks is sorted twice—by elevation and by quadrangle. I have also noted several other unnamed, unranked 14,000-foot summits on a separate list. If you are a real fourteener aficionado, you will climb every fourteener on both lists.

Colorado's 100 Highest Peaks 13,800 Feet and Above

Sorted by Elevation

Ascent	Rank	Range	Elev.	Peak Name	Parent	Rise	Mile	Quadrangle
☐	1	SW	14,433	Elbert, Mt	Whitney, Mt	1,961	667.0	Mt Elbert
☐	2	SW	14,421	Massive, Mt	Elbert, Mt	2,360	5.1	Mt Massive
☐	3	SW	14,420	Harvard, Mt	Elbert, Mt	5,326	15.0	Mt Harvard
☐	4	SC	14,345	Blanca Pk	Harvard, Mt	280	103.0	Blanca Pk
☐	5	S/SW	14,340	"North Massive"	Massive, Mt	2,276	0.9	Mt Massive
☐	6	SW	14,336	La Plata Pk	Elbert, Mt	4,249	6.3	Mt Elbert
☐	7	SJ	14,309	Uncompahgre Pk	La Plata Pk	4,554	84.0	Uncompahgre Pk
☐	8	SC	14,294	Crestone Pk	Blanca Pk	3,866	27.5	Crestone Pk
☐	9	TM	14,286	Lincoln, Mt	Massive, Mt	2,770	22.3	Alma
☐	10	FR	14,270	Grays Pk	Lincoln, Mt	2,503	25.2	Grays Pk
☐	11	SW	14,269	Antero, Mt	Harvard, Mt	560	17.7	Mt Antero
☐	12	FR	14,267	Torreys Pk	Grays Pk	2,337	0.6	Grays Pk
☐	13	EL	14,265	Castle Pk	La Plata Pk	1,125	20.8	Hayden Pk
☐	14	TM	14,265	Quandary Pk	Lincoln, Mt	2,764	3.2	Breckenridge
☐	15	FR	14,264	Evans, Mt	Grays Pk	2,940	9.8	Mt Evans
☐	16	FR	14,255	Longs Pk	Torreys Pk	4,026	43.5	Longs Pk
☐	17	SJ	14,246	Wilson, Mt	Uncompahgre Pk	138	33.1	Mt Wilson
☐		TM	14,238	Cameron, Mt	Lincoln, Mt	1,619	0.5	Alma
☐	18	SW	14,229	Shavano, Mt	Antero, Mt	1,337	3.8	Maysville
☐	19	SW	14,197	Belford, Mt	Harvard, Mt	457	3.3	Mt Harvard
☐	20	SC	14,197	Crestone Needle	Crestone Pk	2,431	0.5	Crestone Pk
☐	21	SW	14,197	Princeton, Mt	Antero, Mt	1,896	5.2	Mt Antero
☐	22	SW	14,196	Yale, Mt	Harvard, Mt	312	5.6	Mt Yale
☐	23	TM	14,172	Bross, Mt	Lincoln, Mt	1,025	1.1	Alma
☐	24	SC	14,165	Kit Carson Mtn	Crestone Pk		1.3	Crestone Pk

Ascent	Rank	Range	Elev.	Peak Name	Parent	Rise	Mile	Quadrangle
		SJ	14,159	El Diente	Wilson, Mt	259	0.8	Delores Pk
	25	EL	14,156	Maroon Pk	Castle Pk	2,336	8.1	Maroon Bells
	26	SW	14,155	Tabeguache Pk	Shavano, Mt	455	0.7	Saint Elmo
	27	SW	14,153	Oxford, Mt	Belford, Mt	653	1.2	Mt Harvard
	28	SJ	14,150	Sneffels, Mt	Wilson, Mt	3,930	15.8	Mt Sneffels
	29	TM	14,148	Democrat, Mt	Lincoln, Mt	768	1.7	Climax
	30	EL	14,130	Capitol Pk	Maroon Pk	1,750	7.5	Capitol Pk
	31	FR	14,110	Pikes Pk	Evans, Mt	5,530	60.3	Pikes Pk
	32	EL	14,092	Snowmass Mtn	Capitol Pk	1,152	2.3	Snowmass Mtn
	33	SJ	14,083	Eolus, Mt	Wilson, Mt	3,863	25.5	Columbine Pass
	34	SJ	14,082	Windom Pk	Eolus, Mt	1,022	1.7	Columbine Pass
	35	SC	14,081	Challenger Point	Kit Carson Mtn	301	0.2	Crestone Pk
	36	SW	14,073	Columbia, Mt	Harvard, Mt	893	1.9	Mt Harvard
	37	SW	14,067	Missouri Mtn	Belford, Mt	847	1.3	Winfield
	38	SC	14,064	Humboldt Pk	Crestone Needle	1,204	1.4	Crestone Pk
	39	FR	14,060	Bierstadt, Mt	Evans, Mt	720	1.4	Mt Evans
		EL	14,060	Conundrum Pk	Castle Pk	240	0.4	Hayden Pk
	40	SJ	14,059	Sunlight Pk	Windom Pk	399	0.5	Storm King Pk
	41	SJ	14,048	Handies Pk	Uncompahgre Pk	2,148	11.2	Handies Pk
	42	SC	14,047	Culebra Pk	Blanca Pk	4,667	25.0	Culebra Pk
	43	SC	14,042	Ellingwood Point	Blanca Pk	342	0.5	Blanca Pk
	44	SC	14,042	Lindsey, Mt	Blanca Pk	1,542	2.3	Blanca Pk
		SJ	14,039	North Eolus	Eolus, Mt	179	0.2	Storm King Pk
	45	SC	14,037	Little Bear Pk	Blanca Pk	377	1.0	Blanca Pk
	46	TM	14,036	Sherman, Mt	Democrat, Mt	896	8.1	Mt Sherman
	47	SJ	14,034	Redcloud Pk	Handies Pk	1,454	4.9	Redcloud Pk
	48	EL	14,018	Pyramid Pk	Maroon Pk	1,518	2.1	Maroon Bells
	49	SJ	14,017	Wilson Pk	Wilson, Mt	877	1.5	Mt Wilson
	50	SJ	14,015	Wetterhorn Pk	Uncompahgre Pk	1,635	2.8	Wetterhorn Pk
		EL	14,014	North Maroon Pk	Maroon Pk	234	0.4	Maroon Bells
	51	SJ	14,014	San Luis Pk	Redcloud Pk	3,116	27.1	San Luis Pk

Ascent	Rank	Range	Elev.	Peak Name	Parent	Rise	Mile	Quadrangle
☐	52	SW	14,005	Mt of the Holy Cross	Massive, Mt	2,105	18.9	Mt of the Holy Cross
☑	53	SW	14,003	Huron Pk	Missouri Mtn	1,503	3.2	Winfield
☑	54	SJ	14,001	Sunshine Pk	Redcloud Pk	501	1.3	Redcloud Pk
☐	55	SW	13,988	Grizzly Pk	La Plata Pk	1,928	6.7	Independence Pass
☐	56	SJ	13,983	Stewart Pk	San Luis Pk	883	2.5	Stewart Pk
☐	57	SC	13,980	"Kat Carson"	Kit Carson Mtn	360	0.2	Crestone Pk
☐	58	SJ	13,972	Pigeon Pk	Eolus, Mt	1,152	1.5	Snowdon Pk
☐	59	SW	13,971	Ouray, Mt	Shavano, Mt	2,671	13.5	Mt Ouray
☐	60	TM	13,951	Fletcher Mtn	Quandary Pk	611	1.2	Copper Mtn
☐		TM	13,951	Gemini Pk	Sherman, Mt	171	0.7	Mt Sherman
☐	61	SW	13,951	Ice Mtn	Huron Pk	1,011	2.1	Winfield
☐	62	TM	13,950	Pacific Pk	Fletcher Mtn	570	1.4	Breckenridge
☐	63	EL	13,943	Cathedral Pk	Castle Pk	523	1.7	Hayden Pk
☐	64	SW	13,940	French Mtn	Elbert, Mt	1,080	2.1	Mt Massive
☐	65	SW	13,933	Hope Mtn	La Plata Pk	873	2.9	Mt Elbert
☐	66	EL	13,932	"Thunder Pyramid"	Pyramid Pk	312	0.6	Maroon Bells
☑	67	SC	13,931	Adams, Mt	Kit Carson Mtn	871	1.9	Horn Pk
☐	68	SJ	13,913	Gladstone Pk	Wilson, Mt	733	0.6	Mt Wilson
☐	69	FR	13,911	Meeker, Mt	Longs Pk	451	0.7	Allens Park
☐	70	SW	13,908	Casco, Mt	French Mtn	648	1.2	Mt Elbert
☐	71	SC	13,908	Red Mtn	Culebra Pk	448	0.7	Culebra Pk
☐	72	SW	13,904	Emerald Pk	Missouri Mtn	564	1.3	Winfield
☐	73	S/TM	13,900	Point 13,900	Fletcher Mtn	280	0.6	Copper Mtn
☐	74	TM	13,898	Horseshoe Mtn	Sherman, Mt	758	2.8	Mt Sherman
☑	75	SJ	13,895	"Phoenix Pk"	San Luis Pk	1,515	5.0	Halfmoon Pass
☐	76	SJ	13,894	Vermillion Pk	Gladstone Pk	3,674	9.2	Ophir
☐	77	SW	13,876	Frasco BM	French Mtn	256	0.5	Mt Massive
☐	78	SW	13,870	"North Carbonate"	Antero, Mt	1,050	2.4	St. Elmo
☐	79	TM	13,865	Buckskin, Mt	Democrat, Mt	725	1.5	Climax
☐	80	SJ	13,864	Vestal Pk	Sunlight Pk	1,124	4.3	Storm King Pk
☐		SW	13,860	Apostle North	Ice Mtn	400	0.4	Winfield

Ascent	Rank	Range	Elev.	Peak Name	Parent	Rise	Mile	Quadrangle
☐	81	SJ	13,860	Jones Mtn	Handies Pk	520	1.7	Handies Pk
☐	82	TM	13,857	Clinton Pk	Democrat, Mt	517	2.0	Climax
☐	83	TM	13,855	Dyer Mtn	Sherman, Mt	475	1.2	Mt Sherman
☐	84	TM	13,852	Crystal Pk	Pacific Pk	632	0.9	Breckenridge
☐		TM	13,852	Traver Pk	Clinton Pk	232	0.7	Climax
☐	85	FR	13,850	Edwards, Mt	Grays Pk	470	1.3	Grays Pk
☐	86	SC	13,849	California Pk	Ellingwood Point	629	2.2	Blanca Pk
☐	87	SW	13,845	Oklahoma, Mt	Massive, Mt	745	1.8	Mt Champion
☐		FR	13,842	Spalding, Mt	Evans, Mt	262	1.1	Mt Evans
☐	88	EL	13,841	Hagerman Pk	Snowmass Mtn	341	0.6	Snowmass Mtn
☐	89	SJ	13,841	Half Pk	Handies Pk	1,501	3.9	Pole Creek Mtn
☑	90	TM	13,841	"Atlantic Pk"	Fletcher Mtn	421	0.7	Copper Mtn
☐	91	SJ	13,835	Turret Pk	Pigeon Pk	735	0.5	Snowdon Pk
☐	92	SJ	13,832	Point 13,832	Redcloud Pk	812	1.4	Redcloud Pk
☐	93	SW	13,831	Holy Cross Ridge	Holy Cross, Mt of	331	0.6	Mt of the Holy Cross
☐	94 S	SW	13,831	Iowa Pk	Missouri Mtn	291	0.6	Winfield
☐	95	SJ	13,830	Jupiter Mtn	Windom Pk	370	0.6	Columbine Pass
☐	96	SC	13,828	Point 13,828	Lindsey, Mt	688	1.2	Blanca Pk
☐	97	SJ	13,824	Jagged Mtn	Sunlight Pk	964	1.4	Storm King Pk
☐	98	SW	13,823	"Lackawanna Pk"	Casco Pk	883	1.8	Independence Pass
☐	99	TM	13,822	Silverheels, Mt	Bross, Mt	2,283	5.5	Alma
☐	100	SJ	13,821	Rio Grande Pyramid	Jagged Mtn	1,881	10.8	Rio Grande Pyramid
☐	101	SJ	13,819	Teakettle Mtn	Sneffels, Mt	759	1.7	Mt Sneffels
☐	102	SJ	13,811	Point 13,811	Point 13,832	551	1.2	Redcloud Pk
☐	103	SJ	13,809	Dallas Pk	Sneffels, Mt	869	2.0	Telluride
☐	104	SJ	13,807	Niagara Pk	Jones Mtn	587	0.6	Handies Pk
☐	105	SJ	13,806	"American Pk"	Jones Mtn	466	0.8	Handies Pk
☐	106	SJ	13,805	Trinity Pk	Vestal Pk	945	1.2	Storm King Pk
☐	107	SJ	13,803	Arrow Pk	Vestal Pk	943	0.5	Storm King Pk
☐	108	EL	13,803	"Castleabra"	Castle Pk	423	0.9	Maroon Bells
☐	109	SJ	13,801	Organ Mtn	San Luis Pk	694	2.0	San Luis Pk

Other 14,000-foot Summits

Ascent	Range	Elev.	Peak Name	Parent	Rise	Mile	Quadrangle
☐	SW	14,300	"Massive Green"	Massive, Mt	120	0.4	Mt Massive
☐	SC	14,260	"East Crestone Pk"	Crestone Pk	80	0.1	Crestone Pk
☐	SC	14,260	"NE Crestone Pk"	Crestone Pk	120	0.1	Crestone Pk
☐	FR	14,256	"West Evans"	Evans, Mt	116	0.3	Mt Evans
☐	SW	14,180	"East La Plata"	La Plata Pk	80	0.2	Mt Elbert
☐	SW	14,169	Point 14,169	"North Massive"	29	0.4	Mt Massive
☐	SW	14,134	"South Elbert"	Elbert, Mt	234	1.0	Mt Elbert
☐	SW	14,132	"South Massive"	Massive, Mt	232	0.7	Mt Massive
☐	SJ	14,110	"South Mt Wilson"	Wilson, Mt	170	0.3	Mt Wilson
☐	SJ	14,100	"West Mt Wilson"	Wilson, Mt	120	0.3	Mt Wilson
☐	FR	14,060	"SE Longs"	Longs Pk	240	0.2	Longs Pk
☐	TM	14,020	"South Bross"	Bross, Mt	80	0.6	Alma
☐	SC	14,020	"South Little Bear"	Little Bear Pk	80	0.2	Blanca Pk
☐	SW	14,020	Point 14,020	"North Massive"	40	0.5	Mt Massive
☐	SC	14,020	"NW Lindsey"	Lindsey, Mt	40	0.2	Blanca Pk
☐	EL	14,020	"North Snowmass"	Snowmass Mtn	40	0.2	Snowmass Mtn

Index

Photo by Clyde Soles.

About the Author

Gerry Roach is a world-class mountaineer. After climbing Mount Everest in 1983, he went on to become the second person to climb the highest peak on each of the seven continents in 1985. In more than 40 years of mountaineering, Gerry has climbed in dozens of states and countries. He has been on 12 Alaskan expeditions, 10 Andean expeditions and 7 Himalayan expeditions, including first ascents in the kingdom of Bhutan. In 1997, he summited Gasherbrum II in the Karakorum. He is a member of the American Alpine Club.

Closer to home, Gerry has climbed more than 1,200 named peaks in Colorado, including all the fourteeners, which he completed for the first time in 1975. He finished climbing every named peak in the Indian Peaks Wilderness and Rocky Mountain National Park in 1978. He has also climbed every named peak in the Colorado counties of Boulder, Gilpin, Clear Creek and Jefferson.

Gerry is also an accomplished rock climber. His first book, *Flatiron Classics,* is a guide to the trails and easier rock climbs in the Flatirons above Boulder. His second book, *Rocky Mountain National Park,* is a guide to the classic hikes and climbs in the park. His guide *Colorado's Indian Peaks,* now in its second edition, remains the definitive mountaineering guide to that special area.

In *Colorado's Fourteeners* Gerry continues to convey his intimate knowledge of and love for Colorado's high peaks. He climbed his first Colorado peak in 1956 and continues to climb there actively today. Gerry returns to Colorado's mountains time and time again to hone his skills. Mountaineering in this rugged and beautiful state forms the foundation for his successful expeditions to earth's great peaks. Gerry lives in Boulder, Colorado, with his wife and climbing partner, Jennifer Roach.

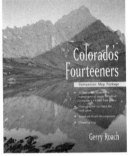
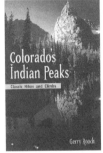

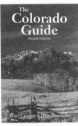
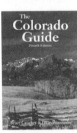
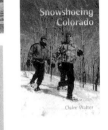